AF608053

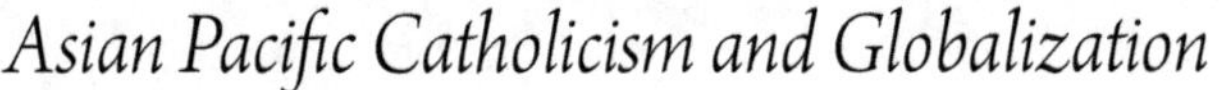
Asian Pacific Catholicism and Globalization

Asian Pacific Catholicism and Globalization

HISTORICAL PERSPECTIVES AND CONTEMPORARY CHALLENGES

JOSÉ CASANOVA and PETER C. PHAN, editors

GEORGETOWN UNIVERSITY PRESS / WASHINGTON, DC

Library of Congress Cataloging-in-Publication Data

Names: Casanova, José, editor. | Phan, Peter C., 1943– editor.
Title: Asian Pacific Catholicism and globalization : historical perspectives and contemporary challenges / editors, José Casanova and Peter C. Phan.
Description: Washington, DC : Georgetown University Press, 2023. | Includes bibliographical references and index.
Identifiers: LCCN 2023020182 (print) | LCCN 2023020183 (ebook) | ISBN 9781647123789 (hardcover) | ISBN 9781647123796 (paperback) | ISBN 9781647123802 (ebook)
Subjects: LCSH: Catholic Church—Asia—History. | Catholic Church—Australia—History. | Globalization—Religious aspects—Catholic Church.
Classification: LCC BX1615 .A85 2023 (print) | LCC BX1615 (ebook) | DDC 282/.5—dc23/eng/20230627
LC record available at https://lccn.loc.gov/2023020182
LC ebook record available at https://lccn.loc.gov/2023020183

24 23 9 8 7 6 5 4 3 2 First printing

Cover design by Nathan Putens
Interior design by BookComp, Inc.

Contents

Illustrations

FIGURES

TABLES

Introduction

JOSÉ CASANOVA AND PETER C. PHAN

The main premise guiding this volume is that the development of Catholicism in Asia, and later in the Oceania-Pacific region, was closely connected with three phases of globalization. Studying the spread and development of Catholicism in Asia and the Pacific through the lens of the processes of globalization and, conversely, viewing globalization in Asia and the Pacific through the prism of Catholicism illuminates the interconnections between globalization and the Catholic Church in these two regions.

This volume adopts a very broad conception of globalization: we mean, in general terms, the increasing connectivity of all the peoples and cultures of the earth and the accompanying growth in the planetary consciousness of globalized humanity. Any discussion of globalization must pay equal attention to its objective structural dimensions ("global connectivity") and its subjective reflexive ones ("global consciousness"). In addition, following Göran Therborn, we hold that "the concept should be abstract, not containing any a priori statements of concrete content" precisely to leave open its plural, multidimensional, and diverse forms at different times and in various places.[1] We approach the historical processes of globalization not as explanatory causes, independent variables, structural agencies, or causal forces, but rather as historical contexts that condition all possibilities for human action and reaction in the world.

Another central assumption of this work is that Catholicism, as a world religion and religious regime in all its institutional, ideational, and agential complexity, has served as an important carrier of the processes of globalization while itself being continuously transformed by these same global processes. Through its missionary expansion and rootedness in peoples and cultures throughout the globe, the Catholic Church has contributed significantly, at least since the sixteenth century, to global connectivity, while at the same time having also transformed and expanded significantly the Church's own "catholic" global consciousness.

Before the early modern Age of Discovery there existed many "archaic" or "proto" globalization events, that is, many processes of increasing regional, continental, and transcontinental connectivity between and among different parts of the world. But those connections were not yet of a "global" nature, nor was there yet present some subjective dimension of global planetary consciousness.

The Iberian colonial expansion of the fifteenth and sixteenth centuries made possible the connection of the "Old World" of Afro-Eurasia to the "discovered" "New World," linking the East and West "Indies" to form for the first time one truly global world in novel transatlantic and transpacific exchanges. The globe became, for the first time, a reality that could be circumnavigated and represented in maps. In this respect, the early modern phase of globalization constitutes the "first globalization," when proto-globalization could rightly be distinguished from earlier "archaic" and later "modern" and "contemporary" forms of globalization.

Catholicism in Asia and Oceania has gone through three distinct phases of development corresponding to the three phases of globalization: *early modern*, from the sixteenth to the eighteenth century, before Western hegemony; *modern* Western hegemonic, from the 1780s to the 1960s; and *contemporary*, after Western hegemony.

1. The *early modern* phase of globalization, initiated by Iberian colonial expansion, was also the golden age of global Catholic missions. Catholic missionaries, most preeminently the Jesuits, served as pioneer globalizers and primary cultural brokers between East and West and between North and South, making in the process significant contributions to the growth in global connectivity and global consciousness. It was also the first era of the broad expansion of Catholicism in Asia and of sustained intercultural and interreligious exchanges between European and Asian civilizations. This era preceded Western hegemony, a time period that also saw the growth and expansion of prominent Muslim "gunpowder empires" (Ottoman, Safavid, Mughal) and long-standing Asian kingdoms and empires (in China, Japan, Korea, Vietnam, Siam, Burma, among others), which Western colonial powers could not subjugate. One cannot speak of a global "world system" or even of a single "world history." Rather, following Sanjay Subrahmanyam, one can speak only of globally "connected histories."[2]
2. The *modern* Western hegemonic phase of globalization, initiated by the Enlightenment and the democratic movements and the Industrial Revolution at the end of the eighteenth century, ushered in what has been appropriately called the "birth of the modern world."[3] The time period was marked by a new wave of Western hegemonic colonial expansion over the entire globe, this time including for the first time Oceania and many of the Pacific Islands as well as most of Africa. Despite a surge of global decolonization following World War II, Western hegemony lasted well into the 1960s. Only in this modern phase can one recognize a global "world system," that is, "systemic" processes of economic, political, and cultural forces shaped hegemonically by the Western colonial "centers" affecting the entire world of "peripheries," albeit in different ways. This phase of globalization also witnessed the golden age of Protestant Christian missions, accompanying first the British, then the American global imperial expansions.

   Throughout the nineteenth century there was also a renewed expansion of Catholic missions throughout Asia and the Pacific, carried out by the restored Society of

Jesus as well as by new male and female missionary and teaching religious orders and congregations. Many of them, such as the Société des Missions étrangères de Paris (MEP), the Marianists, and the Spiritans, were primarily French orders that accompanied the French colonial empire in its *mission civilisatrice* and establishing what could be called French colonial religious protectorates throughout Asia and the Pacific. It coincided with the global expansion of Anglo-Saxon (Irish and American) Catholicism and also accompanied British and American global imperial expansion.

In the 1920s, following Pope Benedict XV's encyclical *Maximum Illud* (1919), which called for a renewal of Catholic missions by fostering local inculturation instead of exporting European cultures, there began the formation of Native postmissionary national Catholic churches throughout the region. These national churches played various roles in independence movements and postcolonial activities. In the case of the Philippines, the prominent Catholic-majority country in Asia, the process had already begun a few decades earlier, after its independence from Spain, with the consecration of Jorge Barlin as the first Native Filipino bishop in 1906.

3. The *contemporary* phase of globalization can be properly denominated "the age of globalization." It is no longer constituted by a Western center with multiple non-Western radiating peripheries but by multiple centers and peripheries, North and South and East and West, with increasing geopolitical and economic prominence of Asian countries in global developments. We have entered a new phase of globalization *after* Western hegemony, where the globe is assuming the shape of a polyhedron, an image frequently used by Pope Francis. In terms of the global transformation of Catholicism, this phase was initiated with the Second Vatican Council in the 1960s, the first truly global ecumenical council of any Christian denomination. The process of Catholic *aggiornamento* connected with Vatican II had tremendous repercussions in the transformation of Catholicism around the world. In Asia and the Pacific it inaugurated a new pan-Asian phase of Catholicism connected with the formation of the Federation of Asian Bishops' Conferences (FABC) in 1972 and the Federation of Catholic Bishops Conferences of Oceania (FCBCO) in 1992. Those processes led to the development of new pan-Asian and Pacific Catholic networks, new theological discourses, and new global, regional, and local identities.

Except in the Philippines and Timor-Leste, Catholicism in Asia is and is likely to remain a minority religion for the foreseeable future. For this reason it can serve as a unique prism through which to look at the processes of globalization in Asia, precisely because the historical processes through which Catholicism took root in the entire region and became enculturated as an Asian religion are so intimately connected with the processes of globalization.

Under European hegemony the processes of globalization became irremediably connected with geopolitical imperialism, colonial capitalist exchanges, and cultural orientalism. Consequently, the expansion of Catholicism into Asia and the Pacific also became inextricably intertwined with imperialism, colonialism, and orientalism. But the processes of global connectivity and the formation of a global consciousness always have the potential of transcending the dynamics of hierarchical power relations, unequal capitalist exchanges, and discriminatory cultural encounters. In particular, the inculturation of Asian Catholicism is evidence of the possibility of transcending the unequal processes of globalization despite their embeddedness in structures of unequal relations. Religious inculturation entails complex dynamics of intercultural encounters, communicative practices, and personal conversions that call into question any kind of cultural, nativist, or territorial essentialism. This is perhaps one of the most important insights gained from the study of globalization through the complex prism of religious inculturation.

Catholic inculturation in Asia or elsewhere is only one of the paradigmatic forms through which the development of global human connectivity and global human consciousness may emerge. In the meantime, this new global human connectivity and new global consciousness have led Asian Catholicism to a deeper awareness of its relationship with other Asian religions and a humble and sincere interreligious dialogue. Furthermore, since globalization in Asia has exacerbated economic and political inequality, Asian Catholicism has entered into solidarity with the Asian poor and marginalized to achieve their integral human development. We hope that this volume will make a contribution to the understanding of the processes of globalization by highlighting its neglected aspects.

The volume is divided into two parts. Part 1, "Historical Perspectives," contains José Casanova's chapter, which presents in detail the three phases of globalization and connects them to the three periods of the development of Catholicism in Asia and the Pacific. Casanova provides a new paradigm for the study of the history and development of Catholicism in Asia and the Pacific, revealing that both external factors, secular and ecclesiastical, and local agency have contributed to the rise and flourishing of Catholicism in these two parts of the world. The following chapters test the applicability and usefulness of Casanova's thesis by exploring whether it sheds new light on the history of Catholicism in Asia (East Asia, Southeast Asia, and South Asia) and Oceania and, if it does, how. Kevin M. Doak opens the discussion of globalization and Catholicism in East Asia with his characterization of Catholicism in Japan as a "globalist culture." He argues that the introduction of Catholicism to Japan in 1549 by St. Francis Xavier and the Jesuits who followed him transformed Japanese culture in profound and lasting ways. The history of Catholicism in Japan has ever since been one of both minority religious faith, severely persecuted at times but never extinguished, and deep and broad cultural influence. Consequently, when modern missionaries, including Protestant Christians, arrived after 1854, Catholicism had already established a centuries-old relationship with the Japanese people and their culture. This unique history has given today's Catholics in Japan a particular perspective on their modern society, one that contrasts with the Protestant position and complicates the narrative of the Church's globalism after Vatican II.

Richard Madsen argues that the three historical globalizations of Catholicism in China differed from each other in what was globalized and how it was localized. The first globalization, in the seventeenth and eighteenth centuries, occurred before the rise of modern nation-states. Counter-Reformation Catholicism that came to China was not tightly implicated with European national cultures, but in its various versions it was intimately connected with the organizational ethos of different religious orders. The second globalization took place in the nineteenth and early twentieth centuries, which Madsen suggests could be called the age of nation-state-driven imperialism. The spread of Catholicism was deeply intertwined with the national, imperial aspirations of European (and American) nation-states. The third globalization took place after the founding of the People's Republic of China in 1949. The Chinese Catholic Church developed along different paths within communities under the control of the Communist regime and within communities of the "free world." All of the areas of the Chinese world in this latest phase of globalization share the same basic Chinese traditional culture, but differences in their political, social, and economic circumstances led the same Catholic theology to be heard, practiced, and institutionalized in different ways.

Denis Woo-seon Kim examines the globalization of the Korean Catholic Church (KCC). Despite its short history, the KCC has been transformed from a church that received missionaries and economic support from abroad to a missionaries-sending one. Not only has it sent missionaries to foreign countries; it also has engaged in international development by providing financial support and running developmental international nongovernmental organizations. Kim examines the ecclesial and social factors that have brought about this transformation and elaborates its implications for Korean and global Catholicism. Among ecclesial factors, Kim highlights not only the KCC's growth but also the decline of religious and priestly vocations in traditionally Catholic countries of the West. He also stresses Korea's globalization as a social factor. The KCC's globalization approach challenges the conventional stereotypes of both "Christian West" and "Confucian Korea." Contemporary Korea is influenced by Christianity, both Protestantism and Catholicism, no less than by Confucianism. Kim notes that Korean Catholicism has been enriched by Western Christianity, but also that Western Christianity has been enriched by Korean Catholicism.

The discussion of globalization and Catholicism in Southeast Asia begins with Jose Mario C. Francisco's study of Philippine Catholicism. Francisco argues that the Philippine Catholic Church owes its vibrant and continuing presence to its long engagement with global historical currents and platforms of exchange. During the Spanish colonial era this presence emerged through the dynamic translation of sixteenth-century Catholicism into the Native ethos. Local languages and social practices provided the platform by which Catholicism "became Native." Beginning with the late-nineteenth-century rise of nationalism and the nation-state, Catholics navigated through contentious relations between the Church and the body politic. While taking socially progressive positions on certain issues but often finding itself on both sides of the political divide, the Catholic Church remains an important presence in the social landscape. Given today's extensive mobility of persons and peoples across geographical and digital spaces, Philippine Catholicism has had to learn how to use constantly evolving platforms to proclaim its faith in a culturally diverse and religiously pluralistic world.

Peter C. Phan proposes a new reading of the history of the Catholic Church in Vietnam, where the perspective of globalization is understood as a historical process of global communications that produces both structures of global connectivity and a new global consciousness. This globalizing process occurred in three phases. The first began with the arrival of Jesuit missionaries in the early seventeenth century, in Cochinchina in 1615, and in Tonkin in 1627, who later were joined by Dominicans, Franciscans, Augustinians, and Carmelites, all under the authority of the Portuguese *padroado.* The second phase began in the latter half of the nineteenth century, with the French colonization of Vietnam, and lasted until the middle of the twentieth century, when French occupying forces were defeated and Vietnam declared independence. The third phase began with the First Indochina War (1946–54) and especially the Second Indochina (Vietnam) War (1965–75).

John Mansford Prior's chapter assesses globalization and Catholicism in the Indo-Malayan Archipelago. He begins by looking back over the past five hundred years, when the religious geography of the Indo-Malayan Archipelago was transformed when more than half of the population encountered Islam or Christianity. The upheavals of these centuries still determine how Catholicism and Islam relate to each other today. While in the mid-nineteenth century Christians accounted for only 0.7 percent of the population, 85 percent were Muslim, a percentage that has been maintained. The percentage of Christians increased after independence in 1949, so that by the end of the twentieth century almost 10 percent of Indonesians were Christian, including 4 percent who were Catholic. Today, the Malaysian and Indonesian churches are no longer simply subsidiaries of Rome; they have developed into local churches in Asia. Prior concludes by looking at five key transformations of the Church brought about by the impact of globalization and four major challenges the Church faces today.

The study of globalization within Catholicism in South Asia opens Chandra Mallampalli's chapter on the Catholic Church in India. Since the early 1500s Catholics have maintained dual participation in global networks and local societies of India. From era to era, changing social and political influences refashioned this dual participation. Under Portuguese rule, imperial ties to Lisbon and Jesuit missionary endeavors brought global Catholicism into a dynamic encounter with the Mughal rule in India. Jesuit-Mughal interactions during the reign of the emperor Akbar (1556–1605) illustrate both imperial and interreligious encounters. With the rise of British power in India, Catholics had to reorient themselves to a new global framework, this time mediated through a Protestant imperial power. The emergence of Catholic printing presses and newspapers nurtured in Indian Catholics a growing sense of their place in India and their ties to a wider Catholic world. In independent India, rising Hindu nationalism led to the vilification of Christians and Muslims as members of so-called foreign religions. The current campaign to Hinduize India has sparked a surge in anti-minority sentiments and violence.

Evelyn Monteiro examines some major features of Indian theology that originated from Vatican II and are relevant for today's ecclesial public life and the upcoming Synod on Collegiality and Synodality (2021–23). India's heritage of perplexing diversity and appalling disparity call for a gospel-like transformation of the Catholic Church. This has led to the emergence of several theologies that have contributed significantly to the self-understanding of Indian Catholicism. The post–Vatican II theological trajectory in India has followed two main streams: theologizing with a religiocultural perspective and theologizing with a sociopolitical perspective. Monteiro surveys some key trends in current Indian theology, such as religious pluralism, inculturation, and liberation, and contextualized theologies such as Dalit, Tribal, and feminist theologies. She also addresses the Catholic Church *ad intra* in the light of the impetus provided by the insightful and historic All India Seminar on the Church in India Today held in 1969. The Indian Catholic Church is deeply committed to promoting justice for and liberation and humanization of oppressed groups, dialogue for reconciliation, and evangelization of cultures.

The investigation of globalization and Catholicism in Oceania begins with Robert Dixon's study of the Catholic Church in Australia, which concentrates on the third phase of globalization by examining the huge demographic shifts in Australia's Catholic population around 1960. Dixon begins with a summary of four distinctive features of the origins of Catholicism in Australia: there was no Catholicism in Australia before the second stage of globalization; there was no initial attempt to evangelize the Indigenous peoples; the first Catholics and first priests were primarily Irish rather than French, Spanish, or Portuguese; and the early Australian Church was largely built through the efforts of laypeople and secular clergy rather than the work of religious order priests. The comfortable and insular position that Australian Catholicism had reached by around 1960 was transformed during the 1960s and beyond. As the twentieth century ended, Catholicism in Australia came to be plagued by declining church attendance and the terrible scourge of the clergy sexual abuse crisis.

Philip Gibbs examines the global influences on the growth of the Catholic Church in the Pacific region. Catholicism entered the Pacific in the early modern phase of globalization with the first exploratory visits of Portuguese seafarers in the early sixteenth century and with evangelization by Spanish Jesuits in the seventeenth century. Beginning in the mid-1700s, for two centuries—during a time of Western hegemonic colonial expansion—missionaries from Europe, mostly from France but later from Germany, journeyed to the Pacific on a civilizing mission that included conversion to Christianity. Political rivalries, economic instability, and religious tensions originating in Europe and the Americas had severe repercussions for the founding of the Church in far-off Oceania. The years following the Second World War and the Second Vatican Council have seen major changes in the Catholic Church in the Pacific, with the establishment of an Indigenous hierarchy and a federation of four episcopal conferences in the region. The rise of tensions was inevitable, as people sought a change from being objects of colonial power to becoming subjects of their own history. The challenge now for the Church in the Pacific region is to foster visionary leadership that will provide a realistic alternate narrative to modern global trends and promote a credible moral discourse about what kind of societies people seek to collectively create.

Part 2, "Contemporary Challenges," examines some of the critical issues that have emerged in our contemporary phase of globalization. Turning to the Catholic Church in Asia and Oceania, Mary John Mananzan examines the impact of the three phases of globalization on women in relation to the Catholic Church. In the first phase of globalization, with the spread of Western culture and mores and the patriarchal values of Spanish society, a negative impact was made on the *mujer indigena*, who lost her status of equality and was forced into domestic work by these values. But she has retained the subversive memory of her equality, which inspires the struggle of modern-day Filipino feminists. The second stage of globalization was no longer confined to Spain: it widened the spread of Western culture to include those of Europe and the Americas and saw the growth of religious congregations of women who have played an invaluable role in the life of the Catholic Church of the Philippines and elsewhere. The third phase of globalization included a giant leap in information and communication technology, which has literally brought all countries into a global world, facilitating the spread of culture, ideas, and news at an unbelievable speed. The Second Vatican Council, which occurred in this period, brought out a turning point in the life of the Church, most especially in the life of the laity, who experienced an unprecedented involvement in the life and activities of the Church. Nevertheless, the virtual inequality of women in the Catholic Church persists despite the theoretical acceptance of her equality. The practice in the Church has not kept up with the progress of women's empowerment in the larger society.

Gemma Tulud Cruz examines another challenge facing the Catholic Church, namely, human migration. Asia has a long history of permanent, temporary, and cyclical migration that dates back to precolonial times. In contemporary times Asian migration has been marked by the search not only for a better life but also for a *bare life,* as political and economic crises, wars, and religiocultural conflicts fuel the migration of millions of Asians within and outside the continent. Cruz's chapter explores the experience of migration among Asians, notably Filipinos, and the religious and pastoral response in the context of globalization, on the part of migrants themselves and by the Catholic Church. The chapter begins with a snapshot of the roots and routes, faces and facets of migration, then is followed by a discussion of the plight of migrant workers in low-skilled occupations, particularly the experience of overseas Filipino workers, including reflections on the public role that Catholicism assumes in such a landscape. Cruz contends that the complex and problematic character of contemporary Asian labor migration in the context of globalization necessitates a church that becomes a sacrament of faith and solidarity in order to foster a pan-Asian Catholic Church.

Edmund Kee-Fook Chia assesses the origins and achievement of the Federation of Asian Bishops' Conferences (FABC), arguably the most influential organization of the Catholic Church in Asia. The FABC was founded around the same time that the colonial empire in Asia was disintegrating. Social and cultural enhancements, especially in the fields of communication, technology, and travel, and threats and opportunities presented by extra-national interests contributed to the need for transnational relationships and cooperation and an evolution of unified bodies that could speak on behalf of individual entities. The FABC has played such a role and can be regarded as the only entity that can credibly claim to speak for pan-Asian Catholicism, especially in providing leadership to local churches in Asia as they try to negotiate their way through the variety of challenges posed by the increasingly globalized world. Chia explores the significance of the FABC and the extent to which it is both shaped by the advances brought about by global forces and shaping Asian Catholicism in its attempts to deal with the onslaught of globalization. The chapter focuses on how the FABC has served as a forum for the evolution of pan-Asian theologies and pastoral strategies that have enabled members of local churches in Asia to be less reliant on colonial expressions of Christianity in favor of contextualized forms of Christian thinking and living.

Bringing the book to a close, Peter C. Phan presents the main trends and developments of Catholic theology in South, Northeast, and Southeast Asia under three rubrics of inculturation, liberation, and interreligious dialogue. Inculturation, corresponding to the first phase of globalization, begins with the first entrance of the Catholic Church into Mongolia with two missions of Friars Minor in 1245 and 1253. Real missions, however, began only with the arrival of the Jesuits at the end of the sixteenth century under the Ming dynasty, among whom the most famous was Matteo Ricci, whose writings marked the beginnings of Asian Catholic theology. Unfortunately, Ricci's method was not followed during the Chinese Rites Controversy and its continuation was stymied during the second phase of globalization by the Taiping Rebellion and the French protectorate's influence on the Chinese Catholic Church. It was reprised briefly during the republican era (1912–49), but was eventually wiped out during the third phase of globalization after the victory of the Communist Party in 1949. In India the successful inculturation of St. Thomas Christians was demolished by the Padroado Latin Catholics during the Synod of Diamper (1599). Inculturation in India was practiced again by the Jesuit Roberto de Nobili, but his method was ultimately condemned by Rome in the so-called Indian Rites Controversy. In the third phase of globalization, Vatican II gave rebirth to Indian inculturation theology. Inculturation theologies in Sri Lanka, the Philippines, and Vietnam are also considered. The second trend of Asian Catholic theologies is to conceive salvation as an integral liberation from all forms of oppression. Phan pays attention to feminist theologies and the liberation theologies developed in India, Korea, the Philippines, and Vietnam. Lastly, Phan considers the third trend, namely, interreligious dialogue, which is arguably the most difficult challenge presented to the Church by religious pluralism.

This volume is the outcome of a three-year research project (2016–18) that was co-directed by José Casanova and Peter C. Phan and co-sponsored by the Berkley Center for Religion, Peace, and World Affairs at Georgetown University and the Institute for Religion, Politics and Society at Australian Catholic University. The project brought together an interdisciplinary group of fourteen scholars (five social scientists, six theologians, and three historians), all of whom are experts on various aspects of Catholicism in Asia and the Pacific region. Three workshops were held: one in Melbourne, Australia (May 2016), one in Washington, DC (November 2016), and one in Manila, Philippines (February 2017). A final public conference was held at Australian Catholic University in Melbourne in (June–July 2017).

The project was based on the premise that the study of complex processes of globalization requires collective interdisciplinary collaboration to illuminate diverse processes of "glocalization," that is, the intertwining and mutual interrelation of the global, the regional, the national, and the local. We are convinced that the insightful work that emerged out of this project forms a coherent unit that will be of interest to diverse groups of readers and publics, most especially scholars and students of globalization and global history, of Catholicism and religious studies, of regional Asian and Pacific studies, and of the histories of specific Asian and Pacific countries. It is also our hope that the critical self-reflection provided by this historical study of Asian and Pacific Catholicism and globalization will help the Asian Pacific church continue in its dedication to the promise of accompanying and serving all the peoples and cultures of Asia and Oceania.

To the memory of
John Mansford Prior, SVD (1946–2022)
Priest, Missionary, Pastor, Theologian

NOTES

1. Göran Therborn, "Globalizations: Dimensions, Historical Waves, Regional Effects, Normative Governance," *International Sociology* 15, no. 2 (June 2000): 151–79.
2. Sanjay Subrahmanyam, "Connected Histories: Notes Toward a Reconfiguration of Early Modern Eurasia," *Modern Asian Studies* 31, no. 3 (1977): 735–62.
3. C. A. Bayly, *The Birth of the Modern World, 1780–1914: Global Connections and Comparisons* (Malden, MA: Blackwell, 2004).

PART 1

Historical Perspectives

1

The Three Phases of Globalization and the Long Formation of Asian Pacific Catholicism

JOSÉ CASANOVA

The spread and development of Catholicism in Asia and later in the Oceania Pacific region was closely connected with processes of globalization. This is the guiding premise of the work presented in this collection. If this assumption is correct, then viewing the spread and development of Catholicism in Asia and the Pacific through the lens of globalization and, conversely, viewing globalization in Asia and the Pacific through the lens of Catholicism, will illuminate the interconnections between both processes.[1]

In the last decades the term "globalization" has become both a ubiquitous buzzword and a fuzzy, analytically imprecise, and highly charged and controversial concept. The term is constantly used and evaluated by politicians, journalists, various publics, and ordinary people in the most contradictory ways. Even among social science experts there is no consensus about the concept's origins, its dynamics, its structural characteristics, or its consequences and effects.

Not only are there raging debates concerning each of these issues among the various disciplines that study globalization, there is no consensus *within* any of the disciplines. For instance, within sociology, the discipline that first embraced the term and perhaps has contributed the most to globalization research, one finds profound divergences—theoretical, analytical, and empirical—among the various competing schools.[2]

For the purposes of this project, globalization means, in very general terms, the increasing connectivity of all the peoples and cultures of the earth and the accompanying growth in the planetary consciousness of global humanity. Global connectivity and global consciousness are, therefore, the two main dimensions of globalization. Both, moreover, are matters of degree, that is, they are not uniformly distributed around the globe and they vary significantly across history, indeed, across the three phases of globalization, among and within all societies, peoples, and cultures of the world.

Any discussion of globalization needs to pay equal attention to its objective structural dimensions ("global connectivity") and its subjective reflexive ones ("global consciousness"). Beyond that, however, following Göran Therborn, we assume that "the concept should be abstract, not containing any a priori statements of concrete content," precisely to leave open an understanding of its plural, multidimensional, and diverse forms in different historical times and places.[3] In other words, we approach historical processes of globalization not as explanatory causes, not as independent variables, nor as structural agencies or causal forces. Rather, they are the historical contexts that condition the possibilities for human action and reaction in the world.

Most discussions of globalization take for granted that processes of globalization are carried by two main dynamics, namely, the formation of a single world capitalist system encompassing the entire globe and the formation of an international system of territorial nation-states encompassing the entire globe. Our goal is to contribute to the understanding of a neglected third dynamic of globalization which, in our view, is as intrinsic and relevant to understanding the processes of globalization as the other two, namely, the formation of a plural and pluralist global system of religions.

The world capitalist system is a single global economy with its own internal divisions between capital and labor, between centers and peripheries, between markets and distributors, and so forth. It is a single internally constituted and differentiated system, intrinsically characterized by unequal exchanges. The world system of nation-states, by contrast, is a system of plural yet isomorphic units. It is constituted by the formation of a plurality of entities, all assuming a similar form that is formally equal yet grounded in the hierarchical and hegemonic world of superpower geopolitics. This system became globalized through the expansion of the European Westphalian system of territorial nation-states to the entire globe through Western colonialism and anti-Western anticolonial independence movements.

By contrast, the global world system of religions is not only plural, but pluralist. Each religion is and claims to be unique and different yet equal to the others. It is, therefore, a system based on the principle of equal pluralist diversity. In this respect the pluralist system is a radical departure from the old nomenclatura of "true" and "false" religions, themselves differentiated into "schismatic," "heretic," "infidel," and "pagan" or "idolatrous" religions. The global pluralist system of religions is still being formed through a dual process of differentiation: through the modern differentiation of religion from nonreligion (that is, the secular) and through the differentiation of each and all religions from one another.

Of course, many of the world religions are much older than any modern world system. But all religions have been transformed by these global transformations in the same way that the old economies were transformed by the emergence of the world capitalist system and the old polities were transformed by the emergence of the world system of nation-states. Like the formation of a world capitalist system and the formation of a global system of nation-states, the formation of a global system of religions is intrinsically connected with the global expansion of European colonialism that was initiated by Iberian colonial expansion into the East and West Indies in the sixteenth century, opening the way for what has been called the "first globalization."

One of the central assumptions guiding this project is that Catholicism, as a world religion and religious regime, in all its institutional, ideational, and agential complexity, has served as an important carrier of the processes of globalization while being continuously transformed by those same global processes. In other words, the Catholic Church, through its missionary expansion and its rootedness in peoples and cultures throughout the globe, has contributed significantly, at least since the sixteenth century, to global connectivity and at the same time this global expansion and rootedness has transformed and expanded significantly the Church's own "Catholic" global consciousness.

If one takes the qualifier "global" literally, one can only talk of globalization proper as the time following the "discovery" of "the New World," when circumnavigations around the globe created for the first time the conditions of possibility for real "global" connectivity and real "global" consciousness. Prior to the early modern age of discoveries, there had been many "archaic" or "proto" globalizations, that is, processes of increasing regional, continental, and transcontinental connectivity among and between different parts of the world. But those connections were not yet of a global nature, nor was there yet present some subjective dimension of global planetary consciousness.

One can certainly reconstruct the concurrent emergence of projects of "universal" kingdoms and empires alongside "universal" ethical and religious visions in various parts of Eurasia during the so-called axial age, around the middle of the first millennium BCE.[4] Those projects contributed to the development of the subjective dimension of imagining a single humanity sharing one earth. They also contributed to the universalist missionary impetus of "world religions" such as Buddhism, Christianity, and Islam. Between the eighth and the fifteenth centuries the world of Islam and the Mongol Empire were catalysts and carriers of powerful transcontinental dynamics throughout much of Afro-Eurasia, entailing increasing interconnectivity and parallel political, economic, and cultural transformations and affecting, no doubt, the many different forms of human "imagined communities."[5] But, given the limitations of maritime technology, this incipient move toward globalization was limited to the "Old World."

The Iberian colonial expansion of the fifteenth to sixteenth centuries made possible the connection of the Old World and the "discovered" New World, linking the East and West "Indies" and forming for the first time one truly global world in novel transatlantic and transpacific exchanges. In this respect the early modern phase of globalization constitutes literally the "first globalization," a form of proto-globalization that can rightly be distinguished from earlier "archaic" and later "modern" and "contemporary" forms of globalization.[6]

Looking at Catholicism in Asia, one can see that it has gone through three distinct phases of development that correspond to three different phases of globalization: *early modern*, from the sixteenth to the eighteenth centuries, before Western hegemony; *modern* Western hegemonic, from the 1780s to the 1960s; and our *contemporary* phase following Western hegemony. The remainder of this chapter aims to offer a schematic view of the development of Asian Catholicism across these three historical phases of globalization.

THE FIRST PHASE OF GLOBALIZATION: THE GOLDEN AGE OF CATHOLIC MISSIONS

Non-Latin "Eastern" forms of Christianity had a presence and had taken deep roots in different parts of Asia at least a millennium before "the first globalization." Greek-Byzantine Christianity had been the religion of large parts of Asia Minor (the eastern part of the Roman

Empire) until it was supplanted by the expansion of Islam. Similarly, Syriac-Aramaic Christianity, "the Church of the East," had a strong presence throughout the Sassanid Empire.[7] Furthermore, throughout the first millennium, Syriac-speaking monks and bishops brought the new faith as far away as India, China, and islands in the Indian Ocean, including Ceylon, so that, for Robert Louis Wilken, "more than any other ancient Christian community the Church of the East made Christianity into a global religion."[8]

Nestorian Christianity also was present and became rooted for several centuries along the Asian Silk Road.[9] Franciscan friars had traveled as papal legates along the same road to the Mongol court in Cathay decades before the famous travels of Marco Polo. Most significantly, Saint Thomas Christian churches were first founded probably by Greek-speaking Christians sailing from Roman Egypt in the first century AD. Later, in the third and fourth centuries, these churches came under the jurisdiction of the Syriac *Catholicos* of the Church of the East in Persia. They were still flourishing on the Malabar Coast when Cabral's Portuguese fleet arrived in Calicut in 1500. Traveling with Cabral were "a vicar, eight secular priests, and eight Franciscans," a clear indication that the purpose of the Portuguese colonial enterprise was not only the spice trade but also the evangelization or "the spiritual conquest" of the East.[10]

Cabral's expedition marked the beginning of the expansion of Latin Catholicism into South Asia, East Asia, and Southeast Asia. Certainly, the Christian missionary enterprise was intrinsic to the establishment of the Portuguese Estado da Índia, under the administrative jurisdiction of the *padroado,* the system whereby the Portuguese Catholic monarchy gained papal legitimacy for its imperial expansion in exchange for its obligation to "Christianize" the colonized populations. Yet, one could also argue that the missionary enterprise had a dynamic motivation of its own, which explains why it penetrated further and had a greater and more lasting impact upon Asian societies than the Portuguese colonial enterprise.

The Iberian colonial expansion into the East and West Indies was undertaken in many respects as a continuation of the Christian "reconquest" of the Iberian Peninsula from Islam and was informed by the same crusading expansionist ideology.[11] Beginning with the conquest, colonization, and evangelization of the Canary Islands at the beginning of the fifteenth century, a series of papal bulls provided the kingdoms of Portugal and Castile with theological and "juridical" legitimation for their colonial expansion.[12] On the basis of the theological construct of papal jurisdiction over non-Christian lands and peoples, the 1494 Treaty of Tordesillas drew an imaginary meridian line of demarcation, whereby all the lands newly "discovered" or to be discovered west of the line would belong to the Kingdom of Castile, while all the lands east of the line would belong to the Kingdom of Portugal. In 1529, the Treaty of Zaragoza between Spain and Portugal drew a similar imaginary anti-meridian line, this time dividing the colonial rights and the duties of evangelization of "the East Indies." On those same grounds and well before the start of their colonization, Brazil in the West Indies was claimed by Portugal, while the Philippines in the East Indies was claimed by Spain. Despite some tensions, both Catholic kingdoms upheld the treaties and recognized reciprocally their exclusive imperial claims to the colonization and evangelization of their respective hemispheres. Naturally, neither the other European powers (France, England, and the Dutch Republic) nor the non-Christian powers that existed at the time recognized papal jurisdiction over these lands, much less the exclusive colonial claims of the Iberian empires.

Yet it was on the basis of such a juridical theological fiction that the expansion of Catholicism in Asia first took place under the control and sponsorship of the Portuguese *padroado régio* and the Spanish *patronato real*. The Estado da Índia, with its capital in Goa, was a grandiose imperial territory that in principle extended from the Cape of Good Hope all the way to Melaka and Macao. It also was, however, a primarily trading "seaborne empire," having minimum territorial control of any land beyond the chain of strategic *entrepôts*, which the Portuguese took over mainly from Muslim traders.[13] Its impact on Asia was negligible overall. In the words of Felipe Fernández-Armesto, "Western imperialism in the Indian Ocean in Vasco's wake is now seen as a feeble affair and the 'Vasco da Gama era' is regarded as not much different, in that part of the world, from the period that preceded it. Indigenous empires and trading states remained dominant and largely intact, with European sovereignty confined—at least until well into the seventeenth century—to spots which hardly modified the overall picture."[14]

The Philippines is a different case altogether, insofar as the Spanish Empire reproduced the model of colonization of the Americas there. As in Mexico and Peru, the politico-military territorial conquest of the islands and "the "spiritual conquest" of the Indigenous populations by the mendicant orders went hand in hand.[15] Until the independence of Mexico from Spain at the beginning of the nineteenth century, the colonial as well as the ecclesiastical administration of the Philippines was under the jurisdiction of the Vice-Royalty of New Spain in Mexico. Precisely because the eastern sea route from Europe to the East Indies, circumnavigating Africa, was closely controlled by the Portuguese Estado da Índia, all the connections between Spain and its colony in the East Indies took place via New Spain. In this respect the Philippines, and particularly Manila, played a crucial nodal role in connecting East Asia and Southeast Asia with Spain and the rest of Europe via "the "New World." Once or twice a year the Manila galleons made their annual route from Manila to Acapulco. They left Manila loaded with silk, porcelain, and other Chinese and East Asian wares, Indian cotton, and Indian and Southeast Asian spices and returned from Acapulco loaded with American silver and all the procurements as well as the personnel (military, civil, and religious) needed to keep the colony running.

The Asian wares were transported farther down the Pacific coast to Panama and Lima and overland to Veracruz, Portobello, and Cartagena to join the galleons of the West Indies' fleet that twice a year sailed across the Atlantic to and from Havana and Seville. It is not surprising to find that at the beginning of the seventeenth century, the inhabitants of Mexico City had acquired already a consciousness of their city being a central node of global commerce crisscrossing the Atlantic and the Pacific and bringing news and products from the four quadrants of the globe.[16]

Among the popular products reaching Catholic New Spain and Peru were ivory crosses and statues of the Child Jesus and the Virgin Mary made by Chinese craftsmen (*sangleyes*) in Manila's Binondo, the world oldest Chinatown outside of China.[17] Among the news first reaching New Spain on its way to Spain and Rome were reports celebrating the fate of Japanese martyrs who died in defense of their Catholic faith at the end of Japan's "Christian Century."[18]

By the middle of the eighteenth century, as the first phase of globalization was coming to an end and other Western powers were beginning to trade directly with China, Spanish Manila and Portuguese Macao ceased to play the nodal global role between China and Europe they had played for two centuries. The independence of the Spanish American colonies also brought to an end the transpacific connections between the Philippines and the New World. The Philippines remained still for some time a Spanish colony, and Filipino Catholicism remained intimately connected to Spanish Catholicism and to Spanish religious orders until the Spanish-American War in 1892.[19] The Philippines is today the single largest Asian Catholic country, with the third largest Catholic population in the world after Brazil and Mexico.[20]

The historian Stanley Payne expresses received wisdom concerning the fusion of the Iberian colonial expansion and the global expansion of Catholicism into the New World and into Asia when he writes: "The expansion of the faith was inextricably intertwined with military glory and economic profit. Because of this it is idle to ask, as is frequently done, whether the Portuguese pioneers and Castilian conquistadores were motivated by greed or by religious zeal."[21]

Yet it may not be so idle to ask whether the religious zeal of Catholic missionaries had a dynamic of its own that transcended the colonial motivation and purpose. Even though they traveled in and through the Estado da Índia to reach their missions, and even though they were sponsored by the padroado and remained under its jurisdictional control, nevertheless they managed to go beyond the frontiers of the Estado da Índia to initiate encounters with all the main Asian peoples, cultures, and religions in a way that contributed to global connectivity and global consciousness. Moreover, the patterns of those European-Asian encounters of the first globalization were different from ones more characteristic during the second phase of Western hegemonic globalization that began to unfold in the nineteenth century.

The global Catholic missionary expansion of the early modern age has to be understood not only within the context of Iberian colonial expansion but also within the broader context of the early modern Catholic renewal that flourished in Italy and the Iberian Peninsula before the Protestant Reformation of the sixteenth century. New historiography has challenged the older characterization of the Catholic renewal as a "Counter-Reformation," most importantly because of the narrow Eurocentrism that the old term implies.[22]

Irrespective of the name one prefers to use, relevant is the fact that this was the era when Catholicism attained global reach from East Asia to North America, from the Philippines to South America, and, as Simon Ditchfield has shown, when it became a "world religion."[23] R. Po-Chia Hsia has argued that "the centuries of Catholic renewal formed the first period of global history," in that the early modern era was shaped by "the encounter between Catholic Europe and the non-Christian world."[24]

The discovery of the New World revived old millenarian expectations about "the end of times."[25] But the encounter with so many yet-unknown non-Christian cultures and peoples, particularly in Asia, also led to a more sober recognition of the immense task of evangelization ahead. Old religious orders (Augustinians, Franciscans, Dominicans), newly reformed orders (Capuchins, Discalced Carmelites) and newly founded ones (Jesuits) all participated enthusiastically and competitively in the global missionary effort.

Of the many new orders established during the religious ferment of the sixteenth century, none was to prove as dynamic, successful, influential, or controversial as the Society of Jesus, founded by Ignatius of Loyola and his companions in 1540.[26] The order's initial sponsorship by King John III of Portugal as well as by the padroado was crucial for its rapid and successful expansion into Asia, first into Goa and Macao and then into Japan and China. No other Catholic religious order played such a crucial role in the early modern Christian encounter with the peoples and cultures of Asia.[27]

Some unique characteristics gave the Society of Jesus clear competitive advantages in becoming pioneer globalizers. Among those characteristics were its uniquely centralized and hierarchical administrative structure, minutely written down in the lengthy *constitutions;* its particular ethos, derived from the *spiritual exercises;* its transnational and global mobility, signified by the oath of obedience to the universal Bishop of Rome; and the unique combination of being simultaneously a professional missionary and a professional teaching order.[28] Those same characteristics, however, also became the source of unending controversy.[29]

What makes Jesuit global missionary practices particularly relevant is the fact that, under certain "circumstances," their controversial method of "accommodation" took a form we would call today "nativist inculturation" or Christian "glocalization." One should avoid, of course, anachronistic interpretations of early modern Jesuit practices from our contemporary global perspective of cultural and religious pluralism. Nevertheless, the famous instruction of Alessandro Valignano, the influential administrator of the Jesuit missions in India, Japan, and China—that the priest's task was not to "Portugalize" the Chinese converts, but to make Christianity Chinese through their own "sinicizing"—points to a formula of globalization that rejects unidirectional Westernization and opens itself to multicultural encounters and reciprocal learning processes.[30]

In fact, as Antoni Ucerler has pointed out, this method of accommodation was not invented by European Jesuits as a missionary strategy, but rather was an accommodation that was forced upon them by their Japanese and Chinese interlocutors, particularly Christian converts.[31] The method emerged, therefore, in the very practice of intercultural encounters in early modernity before European political, economic, scientific, and cultural hegemony was taken for granted on both sides.[32]

The differentiation of a truly universal *religion* and particular *culture,* as well as the differentiation between *civilization* and *idolatry* first introduced by the Jesuits, allowed the various accommodating syntheses of supposedly Christian universalism and cultural particularism.[33] The fact that the method was so vehemently attacked by the other missionary orders and even by other Jesuits in India and China, before it exploded into the Chinese and Malabar rites controversies, indicates the extent to which it challenged Eurocentric notions of a uniform Roman Catholic globalization.[34]

The most insightful paradigm to use in understanding the construction of the early modern globe is not that of a structured "world system" but rather of "connected histories."[35] In this respect, the ultimate dramatic and sudden failure of the most successful and celebrated Jesuit global missions opens highly instructive insights for an understanding of the complexities of early modern patterns of globalization and how they differed from later modern patterns once Western hegemony was achieved.

Perhaps no other Eurasian encounter appeared as promising as the encounter in Japan during "the Christian Century" that lasted from the mid-sixteenth to the mid-seventeenth century.[36] Striking, in comparison with the encounter with other Asian cultures, was not only the high level of conversions to Christianity among Japanese from all social strata, but even more important, the evident openness manifested by Japanese culture to this encounter with "the southern barbarians" at a time when East and West were not yet defined as radically "other" and as essentially incompatible civilizations.[37]

The sharp boundaries on both sides were actually drawn first as a result of the sudden expulsion of the Christian padres and the subsequent violent persecution and enforced reconversion of Japanese Christians to "orthodox" Japanese ways. Yet, Japanese "orthodoxy," if one may use such an expression to describe the assertion of a nativist essence to be protected from foreign intrusion, did not precede this Christian century in Japan. Rather, the construction of a nativist Japanese essentialist identity took place after the encounter with Christianity and to a large extent against Christianity, in a kind of fundamentalist rejection of the first wave of globalization.[38] Moreover, this fundamentalist rejection emerged in the process of constructing an absolutist Japanese state, which in paradoxical ways resembled the Westphalian absolutist leviathan being constructed across Continental Western Europe. Anti-Christian ideology played a central role in the construction of the Japanese state, as the Tokugawa regime adopted a principle analogous to the Westphalian *cuius regio eius religio*, forcing all its Japanese subjects to be territorially registered in Buddhist monasteries, the equivalent to the European confessional (Catholic or Protestant) territorial parish.[39]

Equally instructive is the proscription of Catholic missions in China after a promising foundation. In 1692, a century after the arrival of Mateo Ricci in Beijing, the Jesuits were able to obtain from the Kangxi emperor an edict of toleration of Christianity in China. Thirty years later, in 1721, that same Kangxi emperor banned all Catholic missions from China after Rome prohibited the use of "Chinese rites," such as the veneration of Chinese ancestors. Once again the failure was not due to some inherent incompatibility between "Eastern" Chinese civilization and "Western" Christianity, as argued by some older influential interpretations.[40] The collapse of the Catholic mission in China was due to the opposition in Rome and in Paris to the Jesuit attempt to find an accommodation between Christianity and Chinese culture.

The Chinese rites controversy was simultaneously fought in the Kangxi imperial court in Beijing, in the papal court of the Roman Curia, and in the theological debates of the Sorbonne in Paris. As Paul Rule has pointed out,

> the forces allied against the "permissive" policies of the missionaries of the Society of Jesus were in some ways a strange coalition: Roman curial centralizers, Gallican supporters of national autonomy in religion, Europeanizers who wished to impose Western style of Christianity everywhere, and those who, for want of a better term, we may call "Augustinians" with a deep pessimism about the possibility of salvation outside of the Catholic Church. Added to this potent mixture were old jealousies and rivalries among religious orders and between "regular and "secular" clergy, and especially between colonizing powers.[41]

The Chinese Rites Controversy also revealed the fundamental tensions between three parallel projects of global Catholicism during the first early modern globalization. These were, first, the competing projects of royal colonial evangelization sponsored first by the Portuguese padroado and the Spanish patronato, and later by French *patronage*. Each Catholic monarch served as the patron of the Catholic missions in their colonies, while both advancing their particular imperial project of a universal Christian monarchy and trying to control the religious orders and the national ecclesiastical institutions for their own imperial goals.

Second was the semiautonomous system of global missions developed most clearly by the Jesuits throughout Asia and the Americas. Those missions were sponsored in each case by different Catholic monarchs. But the Jesuit missions often went beyond the frontiers of the given Catholic colonial empires, claiming to be under the jurisdiction of the universal Bishop of Rome, from whom they sought papal apostolic legitimation and patronage. For over a century this unique interstitial position between royal and papal patronage served as the basis of the autonomy of the global Jesuit missions.

There was, finally, the project of Romanization that had begun to take place with the foundation of the Sacra Congregatio de Propaganda Fide in 1622.[42] Thereafter, the Roman Curia began the slow process of assuming greater control of global evangelization, taking over the Catholic missions in Asia first from the Portuguese padroado and eventually from the Jesuits. As Portuguese and Spanish colonial power began to decline in confrontation with the emerging Dutch and English sea-trading empires, Rome began to rely more greatly on the emerging power of Catholic France.

In 1658–63 the Society of Foreign Missions of Paris (Société des Missions étrangères de Paris, or MEP) was established in close collaboration with the Propaganda Fide. Its founders were soon ordained bishops and named vicar apostolics, independent of the padroado and with jurisdiction over Asian missions. François Pallu was named vicar apostolic of Tonkin, with jurisdiction over Laos and five adjacent provinces of southern China. Lambert de la Motte was named vicar apostolic of Cochinchina, with jurisdiction over five provinces of southeastern China. Ignace Cotolendi was named vicar apostolic of Nanjing, with jurisdiction over five provinces of northern China, including Korea and Tartary.[43] In 1664, the same year that the Séminaire des Missions Étrangères was established in Paris, the French East India Company was chartered by King Luis XIV to compete with the Dutch and English East India Companies in the booming Asian trade and to begin the French colonization of Asian territories.

After the expulsion of the Jesuits from Portugal and from the Estado da Índia in 1759 and their final suppression by Pope Clement XIV in 1773, MEP priests and Capuchin missionaries, who worked closely with Propaganda Fide, took over most of the Jesuit missions in India and Southeast Asia.[44] With the exception of the Philippines, where the Jesuit missions and pastoral centers were taken over by the other Spanish mendicant orders without much disruption, the expulsion of the Jesuits from other Asian countries marks a profound disruption, in some cases a full-fledged cleavage, in the development of Catholicism from the first to the second phase of globalization.[45]

THE SECOND PHASE OF GLOBALIZATION: WESTERN HEGEMONY AND CATHOLIC MISSIONS

The suppression of the Jesuits in 1773 symbolically marks the end of the first phase of globalization and coincides with what historian C. A. Bayly has appropriately called "the birth of the modern world."[46] For the first time, there existed one single world in which events happening in one place reverberated in other places. In 1776, three years after the suppression of the Society of Jesus, the American Revolution and the Declaration of Independence constituted such an event. The declaration stated, for the benefit of all future humanity, that not just Americans but "all men are created equal and are endowed by their creator with certain unalienable rights." The French Revolution, with its own "universal" Declaration of the Rights of Man and of the Citizen, followed a decade later in 1789. It found its immediate reverberation in the Haitian Revolution (1791–1804), with its own declaration of liberation from slavery and from French colonialism, the first of many postcolonial liberation movements of nonwhite peoples to take place over the next two centuries.

The subsequent Napoleonic wars spread both cosmopolitan revolutionary fever and nationalist anti-French, anti-imperial fever from Spain to Germany and from Egypt to Russia. From then on, cosmopolitan globalization and anti-cosmopolitan nationalism would be intertwined with aspects of the same global historical dynamics and reactive counter-dynamics which in many ways have lasted until today. The anti-Napoleonic wars of independence on the Iberian Peninsula (1808–14) in turn reverberated in the New World in the form of national liberation movements and wars of independence, creating nearly twenty new postcolonial Latin American nation-states. Paradoxically, at the same time that the New World was freeing itself from European colonialism, European colonization was spreading in earnest across the old continents of Asia and Africa and throughout the new world of Australia and Oceania. The seemingly antithetical dynamics of decolonization in the Americas and colonization in Asia and the Pacific were happening synchronically, as related processes during the second phase of Western hegemonic globalization.

The British East India Company and the Dutch East India Company had been established in 1600 and 1602 as officially chartered private capitalist corporations, to wage war with the Iberian colonial powers and to compete for the profitable trade in East Indies spices and East Asian silks, porcelains, and other commodities. Soon thereafter, the Dutch established their first permanent trading post in Banten, West Java, marking the beginning of the colonization of the Dutch East Indies. By the mid-seventeenth century the Dutch had taken control of most of the trading posts and the sea routes previously occupied by the Portuguese Estado da Índia. By the end of the century, however, the British had begun to displace the Dutch and to gain hegemony over the whole region.[47]

As private capitalist corporations, the Dutch and British East India Companies had been primarily interested in trade and profits, less in territorial colonization. Moreover, unlike the Catholic colonial powers that were equally interested in territorial colonization and in evangelization, the Protestant colonial powers during the first phase of globalization initially showed very little interest in the missionary evangelization or any "civilizing mission" of the Native Asian population.

In general, religion, and particularly Catholicism, played a diminished role in the second phase of globalization, which extended into the twentieth century. The Enlightenment critique of religion had been directed mostly at the Catholic Church. The French Revolution not only weakened further the Catholic Church in France and its Catholic missions in Asia; it also threatened the papacy and the Papal States. When the Society of Jesus was restored in 1814 at the end of the Napoleonic Wars, the world-historical conjuncture had changed dramatically. The Iberian Catholic powers and their colonial empires were in tatters, being supplanted on the global stage by the expansionist North Atlantic Protestant powers carrying a different dynamic of "modern" globalization fueled by industrial capitalism and liberalism.

There were still some signs of Catholic revival manifested in the proliferation of new male and female religious orders, such as the Assumptionists, the Sisters of Jesus and Mary, the Missionaries of Africa (White Fathers), and the Society of the Divine Word (SVD). Besides caring for the poor and disprivileged, most of them were dedicated to education and to global missions, the two ministries first pioneered by the Jesuits. But the papacy and the world of "traditional" Catholicism appeared to be on the defensive, shaken by the accumulative shocks of the modern secular forces of the Enlightenment, democratic revolution, and liberal nationalism.

Britain came out of the Napoleonic Wars as the undisputed world power. For the century from 1814 to 1914, Britain ruled the world, imposing its Pax Britannica and free trade all over the globe through the undisputed power of its Royal Navy, its industrial supremacy, and its control of global finances and colonial markets. India, ruled first by the East India Company from 1757 to 1858 and then directly by the Crown as the British Raj until 1947, became the most important and the most profitable of its colonies.

Following the nationalization of the Dutch East India Company in 1800, the Dutch government assumed the direct colonial rule over the Dutch Batavia Republic. Throughout the nineteenth century the Dutch expanded their colonial rule over the entire Indonesian Archipelago.[48] The French colonial expansion in Asia, particularly in India, was halted by the British expansion in the middle of the eighteenth century, but resumed in the second half of the nineteenth century into what became French Indochina. On the eve of World War I, the world's colonial population, a large majority of which was in Asia, totaled about 560 million, of whom 70 percent were under British rule, 10 percent under French rule, and 8.6 percent under Dutch rule.

While the sixteenth century had been the golden age of global Catholic missions, the nineteenth century became the golden age of Protestant missionary expansion, particularly in Asia and the Pacific. In the early eighteenth century, German Pietists from Halle had pioneered Protestant Christian missions in India, sponsored by the Protestant Kingdom of Denmark.[49] By contrast, at the beginning of its colonial rule in India, the East India Company had shown no interest in promoting or supporting Christian missions. Eventually, however, under pressure from evangelical groups in Britain, the protection and promotion of Christian missionaries became part and parcel of the civilizing mission of the British Empire.[50] The formation of the London Missionary Society in 1795 marks a turning point. By 1807 the society had opened its first mission in China, in Guangzhou.[51] By the middle of the nineteenth century the European colonial powers were using the right to Christian evangelization and the protection of European missionaries as a pretext for military colonial interventions, opening borders and battering walls from Vietnam to Korea and from China to Japan. As I have written elsewhere, "the second phase of Western hegemonic globalization begins in global East Asia with the unequal treaties, unilaterally enforced, all of them demanding free trade, Western colonial access through foreign protectorates or outright colonization as in French Indochina, and freedom of religion for competing Protestant and Catholic missionaries."[52]

Once again, as in the first globalization, free trade, freedom of religion, and colonial military interventions became closely entangled.[53] Yet, while Western colonial powers had been unable to impose their rule upon Asia in the first globalization, the alleged superiority of Protestant Christianity could now dress itself up in the obvious superiority of Western civilization. For Max Weber, the great theorist of Western modernity, "modern" Western capitalism, "modern" Western science, "modern" Western military and industrial might, and "modern" Western religion, represented by "the Protestant ethic," appeared imbued with the same "rational" spirit.[54]

In the second half of the nineteenth century, during the imperial rule of Napoléon III (1852–70), France became the Catholic colonial power in Asia. Persecution of Catholic missionaries in Vietnam, China, and Korea became the pretext for French colonial interventions in all three countries. Colonial France assumed the role of protector of Catholicism in Asia and the Pacific.[55] Even during the Third Republic (1870–1914), when in the French metropolis monarchist Catholicism and anti-clerical laic republicanism were often at loggerheads, in the colonies, in French Indochina, and in French Polynesia the French Catholic Church and the French Republic collaborated closely in their *mission civilisatrice*.[56]

Irish Catholic convicts were the first to bring Catholicism to Australia.[57] Throughout the nineteenth century, global migrations of Irish Catholics into North America and different parts of the British Empire became an additional carrier of the globalization of Catholicism. Irish secular priests followed every Irish migration. Moreover, the Industrial Revolution that had begun in Britain advanced into Continental Europe, followed by massive rural migrations into the growing industrial cities as well as overseas into North America and the Southern Hemisphere (South America, Southern Africa, and Oceania). At the start of World War I, over sixty million Europeans, a majority of them Catholic, had migrated to other continents. Catholic secular priests and older religious orders accompanied these Catholic migrants and established new Catholic communities wherever they went. Some religious orders, such as the Missionaries of St. Charles Borromeo and the Scalabrinians, founded in 1877 by John Baptist Scalabrini, Bishop of Piacenza, were established for the specific purpose of serving the pastoral needs of Italian immigrants all over the world.[58]

At the same time, the United States became a receiving country for migrants as well as for missionaries accompanying them. Moreover, Protestant America, with its constitutional protection of the free exercise of religion, became a refuge for many Catholic religious orders expelled repeatedly from European and Latin American Catholic countries in the context of liberal revolutions and anti-clerical secularization laws. As the paradigmatic transnational and papal religious order, no other Catholic order was forced into exile as frequently or as repeatedly by the globalizing dynamics of nationalism as the Society of Jesus. For that very reason, perhaps no other Catholic religious order took as much advantage of the institutional freedoms offered by the United States. For the nineteenth-century Jesuits, the United States became a safe haven from exile, a frontier missionary society in its own right, a place where they could build new educational institutions more freely than anywhere else in the world, and a platform from which to start anew the building of global Catholic missions.[59]

The Jesuits of that time could hardly be viewed as a pioneering avant-garde of globalization. Rather, they saw themselves and were viewed by others as a reactionary rear guard countering the global spread of nationalism and liberalism. Nonetheless, they emerged once again as a truly global order, enabled by ongoing revolutions in communications and transportation technology. Paradoxically, as John McGreevy points out, even in the high age of capitalist and Western imperial globalization, "some of the most global citizens of the nineteenth century were not cotton exporters developing global markets or physicians tracking the spread of disease. Instead, they were Jesuits."[60]

Ironically, global capitalism created for the first time the material and ideal conditions for the emergence of the kind of global civil society in which the kind of global autonomous missions that the Jesuits had sought in early modernity could function relatively freely. However, when the Jesuits returned to Asia as missionaries during the nineteenth century, they no longer displayed the openness for intercultural encounters and Native inculturation, which had been a hallmark of their way of proceeding in the early globalization. Now they had truly become the papal order and the carriers of global romanization. Moreover, with few exceptions, they also aligned themselves with the status quo Western subjugation of colonial peoples.

Only after the publication of Benedict XV's encyclical *Maximum Illud* (1919) did the process of formation of an Indigenous Asian Catholic Episcopate begin in earnest. The Belgian missionary to China, Lazarist Frédéric-Vincent Lebbe, who had campaigned for the appointment of Indigenous bishops to replace French missionary bishops, served as an important advisor in the writing of *Maximum Illud*.[61] After the May Fourth Movement in China in 1919 there was a significant turn toward the principle of "Indigenous" inculturation within both Catholic and Protestant missiology in China.[62] This trend, at first still resisted by some Western missionaries, was reinforced by the process of global decolonization after World War II. It created the conditions for the renewal of a self-reflexive Christian inculturation in Asia, which came to fruition fully after Vatican II and after the formation of the Federation of Asian Bishops' Conferences (FABC).[63]

One of the novel dynamics of the second phase of globalization was the crucial role played by female missionary religious orders in the expansion of Catholicism in Asia and Oceania, particularly in the expansion of Catholic education to girls, Catholic hospitals, and Catholic welfare services of all kinds. Equally important was the role women played in the indigenization of female religious orders throughout the region. Asian female religious orders from Korea, India, and the Philippines are today at the forefront of global Christian evangelization. Today we know of some local histories and institutional histories of particular female religious orders.[64] But a comprehensive history of the role of religious sisters in the expansion of Catholicism in Asia and elsewhere during the second phase of globalization remains to be written.

THE THIRD PHASE OF GLOBALIZATION: CONTEMPORARY TRANSFORMATION OF CATHOLICISM

The roots of the contemporary phase of globalization can be traced to the emergence of the United Nations system and the breakup of the remaining Western colonial empires in the post–World War II decades. Paradoxically, the process of decolonization served as the vehicle through which the Westphalian system of states, which had emerged in Continental Europe during the first phase of globalization, became fully globalized through processes of postcolonial nation-state formation encompassing the entire globe. To a certain extent the globalization of the nation form opened the way for the third phase of globalization marked by the decline of Western hegemony.[65]

However, its distinctive characteristics—deeper technological connectivity, the relative decline of the United States and Europe, and greater political, cultural, and ideological pluralism—did not begin to emerge until the 1980s. Since then, an ongoing communications and transportation revolution has spurred the deeper integration of the global economy and brought more people across more regions into contact than at any point in history. Thanks to the global expansion of the internet in particular and new social media in general, the subjective dimension of globalization and the awareness of living within a single global frame is much more pronounced and generalized today than it had been in the first two phases of globalization.

Well before the term globalization was invented, however, the Catholic bishops who gathered in Rome at the Second Vatican Council, from October 1962 to December 1965, saw and experienced the phenomenon of globalization as a "sign of the times." This is evident when one reads the last three and arguably the most important documents of Vatican II.

The Declaration on the Relation of the Church to Non-Christian Religions (*Nostra aetate*), begins with the words, "In our time . . . day by day mankind is being drawn closer together, and the ties between different peoples are becoming stronger" (no. 1). The Declaration on Religious Freedom (*Dignitatis Humanae*), reiterates the same idea in its concluding paragraph, where it recognizes "among the signs of the times . . . the fact that men of the present day want to be able to freely profess their religion in private and public" and that therefore "religious freedom is greatly necessary especially in the present condition of the human family. . . . All nations are coming into even closer unity. Men of different cultures and religions are being brought together in closer relationship" (no. 15).

The entire text of *Gaudium et Spes* (Pastoral Constitution on the Church in the Modern World) can be read as a critical and prophetic discernment of both the positive dynamics and the negative consequences brought by contemporary globalization:

> Today the human race is involved in a new stage of history. . . . Never has the human race enjoyed such an abundance of wealth, resources and economic power, and yet a huge proportion of the world citizens are still tormented by hunger and poverty. Although the world of today has a very vivid awareness of its unity and of how one man depends on another in needful solidarity, it is most grievously torn into opposing camps by conflicting forces. . . . True, there is a growing exchange of ideas, but the very words by which key concepts are expressed take on quite different meanings in diverse ideological systems (no. 4).

All three documents went through lengthy and heated debates through various sessions of the council and were passed in the council's final days by consistent overwhelming majorities (97 percent), while being opposed by the same traditionalist minority (3 percent).

The council could adopt such a prescient global perspective because, as stressed by the German theologian Karl Rahner, this was the first truly global ecumenical council of the Catholic Church, a gathering of church fathers from all over the globe into a "world church."[66] One can understand the creative effervescence that this global encounter of bishops produced as it was accompanied by the Pentecostal certainty of the experience of the Holy Spirit in their midst.[67] But such a gathering of Catholic bishops from practically every country in the world was itself made possible only by the previous processes of missionary expansion during the previous historical phases of globalization.

This was not a self-referential church, nor one obsessed with its conflict with liberalism and Western secular modernity. It was, rather, a global church open to the entire world, in dialogue with global humanity, that was scrutinizing prophetically global trends well before they became platitudes in global media or in social scientific jargon.[68] Sociologically there are solid reasons to assert that perhaps no other institution in the world is simultaneously as "global" and as "local" as the Catholic Church.

For most Asian bishops, Vatican II offered the first opportunity to encounter and develop personal relations with other bishops from within an entire region. The impact was similar to the one experienced by the six hundred Latin American bishops who first encountered one another in Rome during the council. The 1968 CELAM II (Latin American Episcopal Conference) meeting in Medellín has been interpreted as the actualization of a pan–Latin American Catholic Church with a continental consciousness, identity, and vocation in a new global context as first revealed by Vatican II.[69] As the analysis of Edmund Chia makes clear, the collective experience of the council had a similar effect upon Asian bishops, leading to the formation of the FABC.[70]

The contemporary global secular age and secular world present the Catholic Church with very serious challenges, to which the Church will need to find some creative responses if it is to realize its global potential and its global responsibility.

Other chapters in this volume examine in detail some of the ways in which the Catholic Church of Asia and Oceania is responding to the challenges of globalization. One could argue that in the last decades Asia, at least large swaths of the immense continent, have profited more than any other region of the world from some of the economic and technological benefits brought by contemporary globalization. It is true, however, that the abundance of wealth, resources, and power newly attained by the rising upper-middle classes in Asia is accompanied by extreme forms of ecological degradation and by the socioeconomic and cultural deprivation suffered by large masses of the population. Nowhere is this more evident than in China and India, the two emerging global superpowers, which had been the centers of great civilizations well before "the rise of the West."

Clearly, the Catholic Church is a minority religion in Asia and Oceania, accounting for only 1–2 percent of the population. Yet one can also argue that remarkably no other Asian religion, nor any other secular organization, for that matter, has assumed such a clear and persistent general pan-Asian or pan-Pacific voice for all the peoples and cultures of Asia and Oceania, especially the poor, immigrants, refugees, and those who are the greatest victims of the contemporary phase of globalization. Pope Francis has characterized this as a "globalization of indifference."

The global response to the Covid-19 pandemic has made evident the dysfunctional character of our global system of governance and its inability to respond in a globally responsible and solidaristic manner to a global public health crisis. It comes on top of an inability to offer credible responses to the growing global environmental crisis, to the growing global challenge of immigration and refugees, and to the global challenge of ever-increasing inequality between and within nations around the world. Global challenges demand global responses which neither the world capitalist system nor the world system of nation-states seems able to provide on its own.

In his encyclical *Fratelli tutti,* Pope Francis expressed this idea in stark prophetic terms: "For all of our hyper-connectivity, we witnessed a fragmentation that made it more difficult to resolve problems that affect us all. Anyone who thinks that the only lesson to be learned was the need to improve what we were already doing, or to refine existing systems and regulations, is denying reality" (no. 7).

As the most global and local institution in the world, the Catholic Church has an unparalleled network of transnational religious orders, religious movements, and religious organizations running educational, health, and charitable institutions dedicated to serving the integral human development of the most needy, dedicated to peace-making and the advancement of social justice, and dedicated to serving and accompanying immigrants and refugees. But these unparalleled networks and transnational resources need to develop much greater coordination so that they can serve not only to ameliorate existing problems at the local level but also respond creatively in the formation of new transnational structures that address the global challenges. In *Fratelli tutti* Francis cites the encyclical *Caritas in veritate,* by his predecessor Pope Benedict XVI, to express most succinctly the global role of the Catholic Church: "The Church 'has a public role over and above her charitable and educational activities.' She works for 'the advancement of humanity and of universal fraternity'" (no. 276).

I have tried to show the complex ways in which the global expansion of Catholic missions since the early modern era has contributed to the globalization and indigenization of Catholicism in Asia and Oceania, opening up structures of increasing global connectivity. General processes of globalization in turn have contributed to the formation of a global Catholic Church evermore conscious of its own "catholicity" and ever more aware of the challenges, opportunities, and responsibilities presented by *Nostra aetate.* At a time when the peoples of Asia and the Oceania-Pacific region constitute over 60 percent of the global population, the churches of Asia and the Pacific are called to play an ever-greater role within the world church as well as in ongoing dynamics of globalization.

NOTES

1. In this respect, this project was conceived as a sequel to the recently completed project, "The Jesuits and Globalization." See Thomas Banchoff and José Casanova, eds., *The Jesuits and Globalization: Historical Perspectives and Contemporary Challenges* (Washington, DC: Georgetown University Press, 2016).

2. The disarray within the discipline of sociology concerning "the nebulous phenomena" of globalization is well-captured in Janet Abu-Lughod, "Globalization in Search of a Paradigm," in Ino Rossi, ed., *Frontiers of Globalization Research: Theoretical and Methodological Approaches* (New York: Springer, 2007), 353–60. For a representative collection, see Frank J. Lechner and John Boli, eds., *The Globalization Reader*, 4th ed. (Malden, MA: Wiley-Blackwell, 2012); and Mauro F. Guillén, "Is Globalization Civilizing, Destructive or Feeble? A Critique of Five Key Debates in the Social Science Literature," *Annual Review of Sociology* 27 (2001): 235–60.
3. Göran Therborn, "Globalizations: Dimensions, Historical Waves, Regional Effects, Normative Governance," *International Sociology* 15, no. 2 (June 2000): 151–79.
4. See Shmuel N. Eisenstadt, ed., *The Origins and Diversity of Axial Age Civilizations* (Albany: SUNY Press, 1986); Johann P. Arnason, Shmuel N. Eisenstadt, and Björn Wittrock, eds., *Axial Civilizations and World History* (Leiden: Brill, 2005); Robert N. Bellah, *Religion in Human Evolution: From the Paleolithic to the Axial Age* (Cambridge: Harvard University Press, 2011); and Robert N. Bellah and Hans Joas, eds., *The Axial Age and Its Consequences* (Cambridge: Harvard University Press, 2012).
5. Johann P. Arnason and Björn Wittrock, eds., *Eurasian Transformations, Tenth to Thirteenth Centuries: Crystallizations, Divergences, Renaissances* (Leiden: Brill, 2011); Marshall G. S. Hodgson, *Rethinking World History: Essays on Europe, Islam, and World History* (Cambridge University Press, 1993); Janet L. Abu-Lughod, *Before European Hegemony: The World System A.D. 1250–1350* (New York: Oxford University Press, 1989); K. N. Chaudhuri, *Asia Before Europe: Economy and Civilisation in the Indian Ocean from the Rise of Islam to 1750* (Cambridge: Cambridge University Press, 1990); John O. Voll, "Islam as a Special World-System," *Journal of World History* 5, no. 2 (Fall 1994): 213–26.
6. See Geoffrey C. Gunn, *First Globalization: The Eurasian Exchange, 1550–1800* (Lanham, MD: Rowman & Littlefield, 2003); and C. A. Bayly, "'Archaic' and 'Modern' Globalization in the Eurasian and African Arena, ca. 1750–1850," in A. G. Hopkins, ed., *Globalization in World History*, (New York: Norton, 2002), 45–73.
7. Robert Louis Wilken, *The First Thousand Years: A Global History of Christianity* (New Haven, CT: Yale University Press, 2012), 228.
8. Wilken, 245.
9. Richard Foltz, *Religions of the Silk Road: Premodern Patterns of Globalization*, 2nd ed. (New York: Palgrave, 2010).
10. Donald F. Lach, *Asia in the Making of Europe, Vol 1, The Century of Discovery* (Chicago: University of Chicago Press, 1965), 231.
11. Charles R. Boxer, *The Church Militant and Iberian Expansion, 1440–1770* (Baltimore: Johns Hopkins University Press, 1978).
12. Eduardo Aznar Vallejo, "The Conquests of the Canary Islands," in Stuart B. Schwartz, ed., *Implicit Understandings: Observing, Reporting, and Reflecting on the Encounters Between Europeans and Other Peoples in the Early Modern Era* (New York: Cambridge University Press, 1994), 134–56.
13. Charles R. Boxer, *The Portuguese Seaborne Empire, 1415–1825* (London: Hutchinson, 1969).
14. Felipe Fernández-Armesto, "The Indian Ocean in World History," in Anthony Disney and Emily Booth, eds., *Vasco da Gama and the Linking of Europe and Asia* (New Delhi: Oxford University Press, 2000), 11–12. For a brief analysis of the changing character of European colonialism in the region, which in a certain sense concurs with our model of three different phases of globalization, see in the same volume: Anthony Reid, "Five Centuries: Five Modalities: European Interaction with Southeast Asia, 1497–1997," 167–77.
15. See the classic work on the spiritual conquest of the Americas: Robert Ricard, *The Spiritual Conquest of Mexico: An Essay on the Apostolate and the Evangelizing Methods of the Mendicant Orders in New Spain, 1523–1572* (Berkeley: University of California Press, 1966).

16. See the 1604 poem by Bernardo de Balbuena, *La Grandeza Mexicana* (Mexico: Editorial Porrúa, 1971), 77–79; and a fascinating analysis in Serge Gruzinski, *Les quatre parties du monde: Histoire d'une mondialisation* (Paris: Éditions de la Martinière, 2004), particularly part 1, "La mondialisation ibérique," and chap. 5, "En toi se rejoignent l'Espagne et la Chine," 13–75, 103–28.
17. Simon Ditchfield, "Catholic Reformation and Renewal," in Peter Marshall, ed., *The Oxford Illustrated History of the Reformation* (New York: Oxford University Press, 2015).
18. Charles R. Boxer, *The Christian Century in Japan, 1594–1650* (Berkeley: University of California Press, 1951).
19. On Filipino Catholicism, see the chapters by José Mario Francisco, SJ, and Sr. Mary John Mananzan in this volume.
20. Ironically, the former Portuguese colony of East Timor became a majoritarian Catholic country only after annexation by Indonesia in 1975 and the introduction of the Indonesian *pancasila* system's enforcement of five recognized forms of "monotheistic" religion. While not yet a majority in 1975, after independence in 2002 over 96 percent of the East Timorese population claimed Catholic affiliation. On East Timor and its links to global Portuguese Catholicism, see Alynna Lyon, "The Activist Catholic Church in Post-Portuguese East Timor: 'The Church Is Not a Political Institution,'" in Paul Christopher Manuel, Alynna Lyon and Clyde Wilcox, eds., *Religion and Politics in a Global Society: Comparative Perspectives from the Portuguese-Speaking World* (Lanham, MA: Rowman & Littlefield, 2013), 75–92.
21. Stanley G. Payne, *A History of Spain and Portugal in Two Volumes* (Madison: University of Wisconsin Press, 1973), 218.
22. New historiography in the last two decades has challenged traditional interpretations. Compare John O'Malley, *Trent and All That: Renaming Catholicism in the Early Modern Era* (Cambridge, MA: Harvard University Press, 2000); and Robert Bireley, *The Refashioning of Catholicism, 1450–1700: A Reassessment of the Counter Reformation* (Washington, DC: Catholic University of America Press, 1999).
23. Ditchfield, "Catholic Reformation and Renewal."
24. R. Po-Chia Hsia, *The World of Catholic Renewal, 1540–1770* (Cambridge: Cambridge University Press, 2005), 7.
25. John Leddy Phelan, *The Millennial Kingdom of the Franciscans of the New World* (Berkeley: University of California Press, 1956). Columbus himself shared in the messianic millenarianism of his age. See Alain Milhou, *Colón y su mentalidad mesiánica en el ambiente franciscanista español* (Valladolid, Spain: Casa-Museo Colon, 1983); and Pauline Moffit Watts, "Prophecy and Discovery: On the Spiritual Origins of Christopher Columbus's 'Enterprise of the Indies,'" *American Historical Review* 90, no. 1 (1985): 73–102.
26. John O'Malley, *The First Jesuits* (Cambridge, MA: Harvard University Press, 1993).
27. Dauril Alden, *The Making of an Enterprise: The Society of Jesus in Portugal, Its Empire and Beyond, 1540–1750* (Stanford, CA: Stanford University Press, 1996).
28. José Casanova, "The Jesuits through the Prism of Globalization, Globalization through a Jesuit Prism," in Thomas Banchoff and José Casanova, eds., *The Jesuits and Globalization: Historical Perspectives and Contemporary Challenges* (Washington, DC: Georgetown University Press, 2016), 261–85.
29. Sabina Pavone, "The History of Anti-Jesuitism: National and Global Dimensions," in Thomas Banchoff and José Casanova, eds., *The Jesuits and Globalization: Historical Perspectives and Contemporary Challenges* (Washington, DC: Georgetown University Press, 2016), 111–30.
30. The literature on Valignano and the Jesuit method of *accommodation* is immense. See Josef Franz Schütte, SJ, *Valignano's Mission Principles for Japan*, 2 vols. (St Louis: Institute of Jesuit Sources, 1980); Adolfo Tamburello, M. Antoni J. Üçerler, SJ, and Marisa Di Russo, eds., *Alessandro Valignano S.I. Uomo del Rinascimento: Ponte tra Oriente e Occidente* (Rome: IHSI, 2008); M. Antoni J. Üçerler, SJ, *Christianity and Cultures: Japan and China in Comparison, 1543–1644* (Rome: IHSI,

2009); Liam Matthew Brockey, *Journey to the East: The Jesuit Mission to China, 1579–1724* (Cambridge, MA: Harvard University Press, 2007); Bonnie B. C. Oh and Charles E. Ronan, eds., *East Meets West: The Jesuits in China, 1582–1773* (Chicago: Loyola University Press, 1988); Jacques Gernet, *China and the Christian Impact: A Conflict of Cultures* (Cambridge: Cambridge University Press, 1985); Jonathan D. Spence, *The Memory Palace of Matteo Ricci* (New York: Penguin, 1984); and Nicolas Standaert, *"L'autre" dans la mission: Leçons à partir de la Chine* (Brussels: Lexius, 2003).

31. Antoni Ucerler, SJ, "The Jesuits in East Asia in the Early Modern Age: A New 'Aeropagus' and the '*Re*-Invention' of Christianity," in Thomas Banchoff and José Casanova, eds., *The Jesuits and Globalization: Historical Perspectives and Contemporary Challenges* (Washington, DC: Georgetown University Press, 2016), 27–48.
32. For an insightful analysis of the mode of intercultural communication before European hegemony, see Nicolas Standaert, "Methodology in View of Contact Between Cultures: The China Case in the 17th Century," *CSRCS Occasional Paper No. 11* (Hong Kong: Chinese University of Hong Kong, 2002), 1–64.
33. Joan Pau Rubiés, "The Concept of Cultural Dialogue and the Jesuit Method of Accommodation: Between Idolatry and Civilization," *Archivum Historicum Societati Iesu LXXIV* 147 (2005): 237–80.
34. On the internal Jesuit disputes concerning missionary methods in India, see Ines G. Županov, *Disputed Mission: Jesuit Experiments and Brahmanical Knowledge in Seventeenth-Century India* (New Delhi: Oxford University Press, 1999).
35. Sanjay Subrahmanyam, "Connected Histories: Notes Toward a Reconfiguration of Early Modern Eurasia," in Victor Lieberman, ed., *Beyond Binary Histories: Re-Imagining Eurasia to c. 1830* (Ann Arbor: University of Michigan Press, 2002), 289–316; and Sanjay Subrahmanyam, "Holding the World in Balance: The Connected Histories of the Iberian Overseas Empires, 1500–1640," *American Historical Review* 112, no. 5 (December 2007): 1359–85.
36. Boxer, *The Christian Century in Japan.*
37. See Kevin Doak's chapter in this volume.
38. George Elison (J. A. S. Elisonas), *Deus Destroyed: The Image of Christianity in Early Modern Japan* (Cambridge, MA: Harvard University Press, 1973).
39. Kiri Paramore, *Ideology and Christianity in Japan* (London: Routledge, 2010).
40. Jacques Gernet, *China and the Christian Impact: A Conflict of Cultures* (New York: Cambridge University Press, 1985).
41. Paul A. Rule, "The Chinese Rites Controversy: A Long-Lasting Controversy in Sino-Western Cultural History," *Pacific Rim Report* 32 (February 2004): 3, http://www.ricci.usfca.edu/assets/prr32.pdf.
42. See more on Propaganda Fide at www.archiviohistoricopropaganda.va.
43. Georges Goyau, *Les prêtres des missions étrangères* (Paris: B. Grasset, 1932); and Jean Guennou, *Missions étrangères de Paris* (Paris: Le Sarment, 1986).
44. Concerning MEP missionaries taking over Jesuit missions in India, see Jean-Félix-Onésime Luquet, *Lettres à Mgr. l'évêque de Longres sur la Congrégation des Missions-Etrangéres* (Paris: Gaume frères, libraires-éditeurs, 1842).
45. After the expulsion of the Jesuits and other Catholic missionary orders from China and other Asian societies, female "virgins" often took over the religious leadership role in many local Catholic communities left without priests. See Eugenio Menegon, *Ancestors, Virgins and Friars: Christianity as a Local Religion in Late Imperial China* (Cambridge, MA: Harvard University Press, 2010).
46. C. A. Bayly, *Birth of the Modern World* (Oxford: Blackwell, 2004).
47. The old city of Melaka on the Strait of Malacca reveals clearly the sedimented strata of Chinese, Indian, Arab, and Javanese trading settlements, which were later superseded by the successive

colonizations by the Portuguese, Dutch, and British. Francis Xavier, the patron saint of Catholic missions throughout Asia and the Pacific, was first buried in Melaka, before his "incorruptible body" was transferred to Goa.

48. On Indonesia, see the chapter by John Mansford Prior in this volume.
49. On the pioneering mission of the German Pietist Bartholomoeus Ziegenbalg in the Danish colonial trade establishment of Tranquebar see, https://www.bu.edu/missiology/missionary-biography/w-x-y-z/ziegenbalg-bartholomaus-1682–1719/, accessed October 3, 2021. See also: Daniel Jeyaraj, *Der Beitrag der Dänisch-Halleschen Mission zum Werden einer indisch-ein-heimischen Kirche, 1706–1730* (Erlangen: Verlag der Ev.-Luth. Mission, 1996).
50. Peter van der Veer, *Imperial Encounters: Religion and Modernity in India and Britain* (Princeton, NJ: Princeton University Press, 2001).
51. Richard Lovett, *History of the London Missionary Society, 1795–1895* (London: Henry Frowde, 1899).
52. José Casanova, "Locating Religion and Secularity in East Asia Through Global Processes: Early Modern Jesuit Religious Encounters," *Religions* 9 (2018): 338.
53. Ivan Strenski, "The Religion in Globalization," *Journal of the American Academy of Religion* 72, no. 3 (2004): 631–52.
54. See Max Weber's "Prefatory Remarks to the Collected Essays in the Sociology of Religion," in his *The Protestant Ethic and the Spirit of Capitalism*, rev. ed., trans. and intro. by Stephen Kalberg (New York: Oxford University Press, 2011), 233–50.
55. H. M. Cole, "Origins of the French Protectorate Over Catholic Missions in China," *American Journal of International La,* 34, no. 3 (1940): 473–91; and Ernest R. Young, *Ecclesiastical Colony: China's Catholic Church and the French Religious Protectorate* (New York: Oxford University Press, 2013).
56. J. P. Daughton, *An Empire Divided: Religion, Republicanism and the Making of French Colonialism, 1880–1914* (New York: Oxford University Press, 2006). On Indochina and French Polynesia, see the chapters by Peter C. Phan and Philip Gibbs in this volume.
57. On Australian Catholicism, see the chapter by Robert Dixon in this volume.
58. The Scalabrinians have become a prominent Catholic religious order specializing in serving the needs of migrants and refugees all over the world, through pastoral care, their pioneering Centers for Migration Studies, and their advocacy network, the Scalabrinian International Migration Institute (SIMI). The Asian Province of St. Francis Xavier Cabrini has centers in Australia, Philippines, Indonesia, Taiwan, Japan, and Vietnam. http://www.scalabrini.org.
59. John McGreevy, *American Jesuits and the World: How an Embattled Religious Order Made Modern Catholicism Global* (Princeton, NJ: Princeton University Press, 2016).
60. John McGreevy, "Restored Jesuits: Notes Towards a Global History," in Thomas Banchoff and José Casanova, eds., *The Jesuits and Globalization: Historical Perspectives and Contemporary Challenges* (Washington, DC: Georgetown University Press, 2016), 132.
61. See Stephanie Marie Wong, *National Witness: Chinese Catholicism After the Age of Empires* (New York: Oxford University Press, forthcoming). See also: Pasquale M. de Elia, *Catholic Native Episcopacy in China: Being and Outline of the Formation and Growth of the Chinese Catholic Clergy, 1300–1926* (Shanghai: Tusewei, 1927).
62. Albert Monshan Wu, *From Christ to Confucius: German Missionaries, Chinese Christians, and the Globalization of Christianity, 1860–1950* (New Haven, CT: Yale University Press, 2016). The missionary-turned-historian Kenneth Scott Latourette confirms that the term "Indigenous," which had had a negative and "divisive" connotation, "became a slogan" in the decade after World War I. See Kenneth Scott Latourette, *A History of Christian Missions in China* (London: Society for Promoting Christian Knowledge, 1929), 801.
63. On the FABC, see the chapter by Edmund Kee-Fook Chia in this volume.

64. Ji Li, *God's Little Daughters: Catholic Women in Nineteenth-Century Manchuria* (Seattle: University of Washington Press, 2015); and Beatrice Leung and Patricia Wittberg, "Catholic Religious Orders of Women in China: Adaptation and Power," *Journal for the Scientific Study of Religion* 43, no. 1 (2004): 67–82.
65. Irfan Ahmad and Jie Kang, eds., *The Nation Form in the Global Age: Ethnographic Perspectives; Essays in Honour of Peter van der Veer* (New York: Palgrave Macmillan, 2022).
66. Karl Rahner, "Basic Theological Interpretation of the Second Vatican Council," *Theological Investigations* 20 (1981): 77–89; and Colleen Frances O'Reilly, "The Emergence of a World Church: Karl Rahner's Basic Theological Interpretation of the Second Vatican Council," Ph.D. diss., University of Toronto, 1998.
67. For a Durkheimian interpretation of Vatican II as a formative global event, see Melissa J. Wilde, *Vatican II: A Sociological Analysis of Religious Change* (Princeton, NJ: Princeton University Press, 2007).
68. José Casanova, "Foreword," in Karl Gabriel, Christian Spiess, and Katja Winkler, eds., *Catholicism and Religious Freedom: Renewing the Church in the Second Vatican Council* (Munich: Ferdinand Schöningh, 2019), 7–11.
69. José Casanova, "Bedeutung und Auswirkung Medellíns in globaler Perspektive," in Margit Eckholt, ed., *Religion als Ressource befreiender Entwicklung: 50 Jahre nach der Konferenz des Lateinamerikanischen Episkopats in Medellín: Kontinuitäten und Brüche* (Meaning and impact of Medellín from a global perspective) in Margit Eckholt, ed., *Religion as a Source of Liberating Development* (Ostfildern: Matthias Grünewald Verlag, 2019), 245–54.
70. On Vatican II, see the chapter by Edmund Chia in this volume.

2

Catholicism in Japan as Globalist Culture

KEVIN M. DOAK

GLOBALIZATION PHASE ONE: SIXTEENTH TO EIGHTEENTH CENTURIES

When Francis Xavier, SJ, landed at Kagoshima, Japan, on August 15, 1549, he brought not only the Catholic faith to Japan (and subsequently to northeast Asia), but he simultaneously introduced a powerful globalist culture that has played a tremendous, if often unacknowledged, role in the history of the region. Francis Xavier was not the first westerner to arrive in the country: a Portuguese ship had washed up on the remote Tanegashima Island in 1543, introducing the firearm (arquebus) to the Japanese, who subsequently named the guns *tanegashima.* Subsequent interactions in the next few years between Portuguese and Japanese were sporadic and superficial: in those early years the Portuguese traders did not penetrate beyond a few miles of the coasts of the western islands and their interactions were limited to material exchange. The most notable achievement of the time was a report by the Portuguese captain Jorge Alvares to Francis Xavier when they met in Malacca in late December 1547—and Alvares's introducing the saint to the Japanese refugee Yajiro (also known as Anjiro). It was Yajiro, having converted to Catholicism, who guided Francis Xavier back to his hometown of Kagoshima, thus setting the stage for the sustained introduction of Catholicism, Western culture, and globalist thought to Japan.[1]

Thus the Feast of the Assumption in 1549 marked the beginning of what C. R. Boxer famously called "the Christian century in Japan." In truth, this era of globalism was the *Catholic* century in Japan, as Protestant influence was all but nonexistent and limited mainly to the political influence of Will Adams, following his arrival in 1600. Adams successfully advocated to the Tokugawa *bakufu* that Japan continue Europe's religious wars—of course, on the Protestant side. By then, the "Catholic century" was half over. While the first half of the Catholic century was an exclusively Catholic period with a broad and deep globalist influence on Japanese culture, the second half of that "century" was a period of persecution, martyrdom, and futile efforts to withdraw from the currents of globalism that had come with Catholicism. Even so, Catholic missionaries continued to work in the country under extremely dangerous circumstances.

Historians working from a modernist bias have seen Japan after 1650 as a "closed" country in relation to Catholic and globalist influences. They have portrayed this period as one of insularity and withdrawal *tout court* from the West until the Protestants arrived in force in the mid-nineteenth century, bringing the light of modernity and freedom—and, perhaps, "true internationalism." More recent approaches, however, have adopted a globalist cultural perspective that emphasizes the transformation of Japanese culture beginning with the mid-sixteenth century arrival of Jesuit missionaries. In any event, the closed country edicts from 1633–39 did not close Japan to the West nor even to all knowledge of world affairs: throughout the entire closed country period, the little window of Dejima was left open to Dutch traders and to "practical" (secular) information from the West. What was rigorously enforced, however, was a prohibition on Christianity. But the door was closed too late. Globalist Catholic values had permeated the society and continued to simmer throughout the subsequent two centuries of "closed" Japan. In this sense we may best understand the closed country policies as a failed experiment in modernization through secularization. They failed because the Pandora's box of globalism, once opened, could never again be "unopened."

Even Boxer has noted the explosion of global forces that transformed Japanese culture beginning in the Catholic century: thanks to the Jesuit press, Western works ranging from *Aesop's Fables* to Cicero's *Speeches* (not to mention Scripture, Catholic prayers, the Creed, etc.) were translated and published in Japan.[2] This new European culture (which was largely interchangeable with Catholic culture) fascinated the Japanese people to the extent that many adopted Western names, clothing styles, architecture, even foods. The eyewitness account of Francisco Paiso, SJ, in 1594 of this new globalist culture in Japan is striking:

> [Hideyoshi] has a great liking for Portuguese clothing, and the members of his retinue, in emulation, are often attired in the Portuguese style. The same is true even of those daimyos who are not Christian. They wear rosaries of driftwood on their breasts, hang a crucifix from the shoulder or waist, and sometimes even hold a handkerchief. . . . This is not done in ridicule of the Christians, but simply to show off their familiarity with the latest fashion, or because they think it good and effective in bringing success in daily life.[3]

Although Hideyoshi had many Catholic *daimyō* among his closest retainers and was himself quite inclined toward the Catholic faith, he held back from formal conversion due to the Church's strong stand on monogamy.[4] Religious faith aside, the new globalist culture swept across Japan from the highest social echelon to the lowest. Ironically, the widely successful influence of this new culture makes it nearly impossible to get an accurate estimate of how many Japanese were converts to the Catholic faith (rather than merely converts to the new globalist culture). However, recent research suggests that the accepted estimate of 300,000 Catholics is too low and that there may well have been 750,000 Catholic Japanese converts by 1605, with 5,000 to 6,000 additional converts added every year.[5] Shifting the focus from the largely fruitless debate over numbers of the baptized to the impact of the global culture allows us to see the tremendous cultural and social influence on Japan of this encounter with the Iberian missionaries. Unfortunately, much of the material evidence of this global impact was destroyed in the persecutions that followed.

Some evidence remains. The most vivid are the Nanban ("Southern barbarian" or Iberian) screens of the Kano, Tosa, and Sumiyoshi art schools of the time.[6] Deeper cultural influences resulting from the introduction of Catholicism have been felt in the tea ceremony, castle architecture, diet, language, and literature.[7] Looking at this history through the lens of globalization provides an important new way of appreciating the cultural impact of the mid-sixteenth century Japanese encounter with Europeans, a cultural transformation that continued even during and after the centuries of persecution that followed the close of the Catholic century.

Haruko Nawata Ward has traced the transformations Catholicism brought to traditional Japanese gender roles, revealing the Jesuit mission in Japan "as a catalyst that encouraged women to exert a powerful social, cultural, and political influence on their own people and government."[8] Fundamentally, this globalist or "transcendental" value was rooted in what Derek Massarella calls the sixteenth-century Thomist revival in which both Francis Xavier, SJ, and Alessandro Valignano, SJ (1533–1606), participated and which rested on a shared concept of the "natural law [that] enabled one to envisage a world community, a common humanity among rational beings, regardless of cultural or confessional differences.... The norms of natural law were not exclusively European ones."[9] From this new vantage point, the traditional interpretation that contrasts Xavier's culturally intolerant approach with Valignano's accommodationist one gives way to a uniform approach in which both Jesuits recognized the universality of right reason among all people and the legitimacy of Japan's own particular cultural forms.[10] This new sixteenth-century globalism meant that "in order to become Christian, a society such as Japan did not have to adopt European manners, to 'Europeanise' itself, either at the collective or individual level."[11] Of course, globalism cut the other way too: in order to adopt elements of European culture, Japanese people did not have to become Christian, either at the collective or individual level. In Japan, globalism was not inextricably tied to the Catholic faith in all respects, but neither was it historically independent of it.

Perhaps the best way to grasp this globalism as both a cultural and religious force in Japanese history is to consider two missions that were sent from Japan to Europe during the Catholic century: the Tenshō Youth Mission to Rome (1582–90) and the Keichō Mission to Rome (1613–20).[12] These missions illustrate how cultural exchange within the context of late sixteenth- and early seventeenth-century globalism was not a one-way street from the West to the East, but rather bore remarkable similarities to the model of "interculturality" that Joseph Cardinal Ratzinger outlines as lying at the heart of all interreligious encounters.[13] They may also be seen as bookends that frame the cultural possibilities Japan experienced during the period of high globalism.

The Tenshō Youth Mission to Rome (1582–90)

The Tenshō Youth Mission to Rome was sponsored by three Catholic *daimyō*: Ōtomo Francesco Sōrin (1530–87), Ōmura Bartolomé Sumitada (1533–87), and Arima Juan

FIGURE 2.1. *Newe Zeyttung aus der Insel Japonien.* Portrait of the Tenshō Youth Mission (Augsberg, AD 1586). Clockwise from top right: Itō, Chijiwa, Hara, Nakaura, and Father Mesquita, SJ. Photograph courtesy of the Main Library, Kyoto University. https://rmda.kulib.kyoto-u.ac.jp/en/item/rb00007683.

Harunobu (1567–1612).[14] The original idea for such a mission came from Valignano. Valignano's hope was that the mission would achieve two goals: economic and spiritual assistance for the Japanese missions from the pope and the kings of Spain and Portugal; and exposure of young Japanese to a firsthand experience of European Christendom so that on their return to Japan they could explain Christian culture to their compatriots.[15] Valignano accompanied the mission at the start, along with translator Diego de Mesquita, SJ (1553–1614), and Lourenço Mexia, SJ (1540–99). The four Japanese emissaries were Itō Mancio (1569–1612), delegate and representative of Lord Ōtomo; Chijiwa Miguel (1569–1633), nephew of Lord Ōmura; Blessed Nakaura Julian (1568–1633); and Hara Martinão (1569–1629).

The mission left Nagasaki on February 20, 1582, and sailed to Macao, where it arrived on March 9. On December 20, 1583, the emissaries reached Goa, having passed through Malacca and Cochin (Kochi). There Valignano left them, as he had been ordered by the superior general to remain in Goa. He turned the group over to the rector of the Jesuit college in Goa, Nuno Rodrigues, SJ, for the remainder of the journey.[16] They sailed on to Europe, arriving in Lisbon on August 11, 1584. The group lodged at the Igreja de São Roque and visited Archduke (and Cardinal) Albrecht von Österreich in his palace on the outskirts of

Lisbon. On November 25 they were received by Felipe II, King of Spain, in Madrid. On March 1, 1585, they arrived in Pisa, where they had an audience with Francesco I de' Medici, the Grand Duke of Tuscany. And on March 6, Ash Wednesday, they received the ashes on their foreheads along with the grand duke in the church of Santo Stefano dei Cavalieri. The following day they traveled to Florence, where they lodged in the Palazzo Vecchio. After spending ten days at the Villa Demidoff they entered Rome, where, on March 23, they had an audience with Pope Gregory XIII and were given Roman citizenship. They were in Rome for the coronation of Gregory's successor, Sixtus V, on May 1, 1585. After a month in Rome, they left the Eternal City, visiting Venice, Verona, and Milan on their way back to Lisbon. On April 13, 1586, they departed Europe, sailing out of Lisbon for the return trip. On May 29, 1587, they arrived back in Goa and were reunited with Father Valignano. At the seminary in Goa, Hara Martinão gave a speech (we know not on what, but we may presume on his impressions of Europe and especially of Rome).

When they finally returned to Nagasaki on July 21, 1590, there was a new, colder atmosphere awaiting them. The year 1587 had been a bad one for Catholics in Japan. Two of the mission's sponsors (Lord Ōmura and Lord Ōtomo) had died and Hideyoshi had issued his unevenly enforced Bateren Tsuihō edict, banishing all Catholic priests from Japan. Nonetheless, a sign of how erratic the persecution was (and how strong an interest there remained in globalist culture), the group of Japanese Catholic young men accompanied Valignano on March 3, 1591, for an audience with Hideyoshi at his newly completed Shurakutei Palace in Kyoto. There, dressed in European clothes, they described their travels to Hideyoshi, bringing with them Abraham Ortelis's *Theatrum Orbis Terrarum* and other souvenirs from Europe, including an astrolabe and a globe.[17] They even performed a concert of the music of Josquin des Prez using European musical instruments.

All four emissaries were admitted to the Society of Jesus on July 25, 1591. As persecutions intensified, Chijiwa left the society around 1603 and at some later point apostatized. Itō, Nakaura, and Hara, however, were ordained by Bishop Luis Cerqueira, SJ (1552–1614), in September 1608. Itō was subsequently executed in Nagasaki in 1612, Hara was exiled to Macao in 1614 and died there in 1639, and in 1633 Nakaura was tortured to death by being hung in the "pit." Nakaura's death was depicted in a sketch included in Antonio Cardim's *Fasciculus e Iapponicis Floribus,* which was published in Rome in 1646. We are reminded how globalism was a two-way street, with new ideas about the world and non-Western cultures reaching back to the West even as Catholicism brought globalist values into Japanese culture.

The Keichō Mission to Europe (1613–20)

The Keichō Mission to Europe contrasts with the earlier Tenshō Mission in several respects. First, it was not led by Jesuits but by a Franciscan. In 1608, Pope Paul V had authorized other religious orders, such as the Dominicans and Franciscans, to proselytize in Japan along with the Jesuits. The leader of the Keichō Mission was Blessed Luis Caballero de Sotelo, OFM (1574–1624), who had been in the Philippines by 1600.[18] After studying the Japanese language for four years in Manila, he entered Japan and tried to establish a Franciscan church in Edo (present-day Tokyo). Things in Edo did not go well for him. His church was destroyed, as

FIGURE 2.2. Portrait of the leader of the Keichō Mission, Hasekura Philip Francis Rokuemon Tsunenaga. https://commons.wikimedia.org/wiki/File:HasekuraPrayer.jpg.

Christianity had been outlawed in the territory of the Tokugawa clan in 1612. Sotelo was invited north to the fiefdom of Lord Date Masamune (1567–1636), where Christianity was still permitted. Lord Date had a global vision: he wanted to establish trade routes with Nueva España (Mexico), a plan that had the approval of the retired shogun, Tokugawa Ieyasu. This global vision underlay the Keichō Mission, which would leave Japan, not from Nagasaki (the historical center of Catholic activities) but from the more remote northern part of the country, where Christianity recently had reached, albeit with none of the strength it had experienced in southern Kyushu. This was also a Spanish mission, in contrast to the earlier Portuguese-flavored one. And it would take the Japanese to Europe by traversing the New World for the first time.

Lord Date appointed his retainer, Hasekura Rokuemon Tsunenaga (1571–1622), as head of the official mission of the more than 180 people traveling to Spain. These included Sotelo, as translator; Sabastian Vizcaino (1548–1628); and the Kyoto merchant Tanaka Francisco Shōsuke, who had traveled to Mexico in August 1610 with Rodrigo de Vivero y Velasco (1564–1636) aboard the first Western ship built in Japan.[19] The main objective of the mission was to establish a trade treaty with Nueva España. The group left Tsukinoura Bay in 1613 aboard the Japanese-built galleon *San Juan Bautista*, then crossed the Pacific and arrived safely at Acapulco. From there they continued overland across Mexico, sailed across the Atlantic and on to Seville and Madrid, eventually making their way to Rome. The mission had an audience with King Felipe III of Spain and Pope Paul V. In 1615 Hasekura and some other members of the mission converted to Catholicism while still in Spain (and after his return to Japan, Hasekura apparently converted his family and servants to Catholicism as well).

News of the Tokugawa bakufu's Decree Forbidding Christianity (Kinkyō Rei) in 1612 finally caught up with them and undermined the mission's ability to achieve its goals. The news of harsh persecution of Christians back in Japan also led many of the samurai on the mission who had converted to Catholicism to decide not to return home to near certain death but instead to remain in Spain. (One perhaps unintended consequence of this early seventeenth-century globalism is the approximately seven hundred descendants of the Japanese emissaries in the Coria del Río area near Seville who bear the surname "Japón.") Father Sotelo was ordered to return to Asia separately in 1622, and when he slipped into Japan from the Philippines he was imprisoned and burned at the stake in 1624. History is unclear as to whether Hasekura, who died in 1622, was executed or died of natural causes, but the fact that Hasekura's son, Tsuneyori, was executed in 1640 along with several Catholic servants suggests that Hasekura also may have been executed or died in prison, the usual penalty for conversion to Catholicism.[20] Statues of Hasekura near Acapulco Mexico, at Havana Bay in Cuba, in Coria del Río in Spain, and at the Viale Guglielmo Marconi near Port Livorno, Italy, testify to the global impact of this early seventeenth-century Catholic samurai.

By 1650 the Christian century was over, and some historians have maintained that all surviving Catholics in Japan had been extinguished or exiled. Others maintain that the "Christians" who survived in Japan either never understood what the Western missionaries were teaching in the first place or had begun to indigenize the faith almost immediately, rendering it into something other than Catholicism over the ensuing decades. Miyazaki Kentarō, the leader of this school, argues that those underground Catholics eventually developed their own Japanese version of Christianity called *kakure kirishitan* ("hidden Christianity").[21] Implicit in this argument is the idea that globalism had failed and that Japanese cultural particularism had triumphed over the universal values introduced by the sixteenth-century globalists. Miyazaki's thesis has been quite influential, in part because he himself stems from an underground Catholic family and in part because his views have been published widely in English. Certainly his ethnological emphasis on cultural particularism resonates with many academics today, both inside and outside Japan. But Miyazaki's thesis has received blistering criticism from another descendent of the underground Catholics, Nakazono Shigeo, who is curator of the Hirado City Ikitsuki Museum on Underground Catholics. Nakazono argues that Miyazaki's thesis reflects his poor grasp of the local dialect, among other problems, and that in fact there were no more variances in dogma or practice among the underground Japanese Catholics than among rural Catholics in medieval Europe. Japanese culture was no unique barrier to the faith. Most persuasively, Nakazono shows through a careful comparison of the Creed that the hidden Catholics intoned with copies of the Creed from 1878 and 1948 that the latter versions display more changes when there were bishops to approve the changes in contrast to the underground period, when there were no clerics to authorize changes and the faithful clung to the literal text with ferocious tenacity.[22]

Nakazono's argument on the staying power of authentic Catholic Japanese during the seventeenth and eighteenth centuries is really an affirmation of the underground globalist values that survived the "closed country" edicts. And his thesis enjoys independent confirmation in a discovery by William J. Farge, SJ. Farge has discovered that the publicist and political satirist Baba Bunkō (1718–59) was a hidden Catholic samurai active in Edo as late as 1759 (when Baba was executed). Farge's evidence is strong, including Baba's reference to a picture of the Eucharist as "a person," his execution for crimes that did not fit the punishment (in the context of a widespread judicial coverup of resurfaced Catholic Japanese when they were supposed to have been wiped out), and, most profoundly, his public advocacy of globalist values that were not consistent with the Japanese moral order based on Confucian, Buddhist, and Shinto values. Baba's globalist values were particularly expressed in terms of a partiality for the outcast and lowly and included strong denunciations of sexual behavior that was not considered immoral by the dominant traditional moral codes in Japan.[23]

Even if Japanese officials thought they could erase from history this Catholic samurai by executing him, they could not extricate "submerged globalism" from Japan.[24] In 1708, Fr. Giovanni Baptista Sidotti (1668–1714) entered Japan, was immediately arrested, and engaged in an important dialogue with the noted Confucian official Arai Hakuseki before dying in prison in 1715. Did tales of Sidotti's arrival and death encourage Baba in his political criticisms? We may never know. But Baba was not the last of the Catholics to emerge during the supposedly post-Catholic closed country period. In 1790, nineteen villagers in the Nagasaki area were accused of being Catholic, with evidence presented of the possession of statues of Mary and "a crucified Buddha." The local magistrate simply wished to bury the incident and discouraged further investigation. As Farge has written, "The Japanese government, in fact, had long known of the existence of communities of Christians because they had emerged from time to time throughout the Tokugawa period."[25] But the official position was that there were no Catholics in Japan, so every effort was made to ensure that reality matched theory.

GLOBALIZATION, PHASE TWO: 1850s TO 1960s

The consequences of the 1853 arrival of Comm. Matthew C. Perry's "black ships" (as they are known in Japan) doomed the theory that there were no Catholics in Japan and that Japan could remain a country closed to the gathering forces of globalization. Indeed, this second phase of globalization in Japan eventually became a time of open and even legal expression of Catholicism from which Japan has never retreated. Two important points must be borne in mind when assessing this time period. First, that after 1859, Protestantism was the "new kid on the block" and Catholicism in Japan was forced into competing with Protestant Christianity for the first time; second, that Protestantism, although culturally new to Japan, had significant advantages over Catholicism, especially its affiliation with the dominant world powers, England and the United States (and, to a certain degree, Germany, which was under Bismarck's Kulturkampf against Catholics for much of this time).

While Protestant Christianity was largely an English-language affair, Catholicism in Japan began as an exclusively French one, with the French Société des Missions étrangères de Paris (MEP) holding a monopoly over Catholic work in Japan until the twentieth century and maintaining a dominance long after the turn of the century. After Isabella Sugimoto presented herself and her circle of Japanese Hidden Catholics to Father Bernard Petitjean, MEP, in the newly built Church of the Twenty-Six Martyrs in Ōura, Nagasaki, on March 17, 1865, eventually 50,000 surviving Japanese Catholics began to surface from the underground, just as the West was forcing Japan's ancien régime to open its country to trade with the West. The collapse of the French-allied Tokugawa *bafuku* in 1867 at the hands of Shinto revolutionaries supported by England proved to be greatly beneficial to Protestant missionaries. Japan's "modernization" seemed an unambiguously good thing to the Protestants, who now had access to the Japanese people for conversion (legally, beginning in 1873). But things were different for the Japanese Catholic population.

We must not forget the Fourth Urakami Kuzure. Beginning in 1867, on the eve of the "modern" Meiji Restoration then intensifying under the new Meiji government, 3,414 Japanese Catholics were arrested and incarcerated in various concentration camps around the country. Those who survived were not released until 1873, when Christianity was finally legally permitted. Fully aware that their liberation came due to pressure by western powers, Catholics in modern Japan retained and augmented the values of the critical globalism that was linked to the culture of mid-sixteenth-century Japan. In that sense we may contrast it to the nationalism of Shintoism, Buddhism, and Confucianism (all of which were largely revised and modernized to fit the modern Japanese nation-state) as well as to the more sanguine modern "internationalism" of the Protestants. The initial baptism of fire with which modernity greeted Japanese Catholics provided them with a critical globalist perspective regarding Japan's modernization, whether based on Shinto, Buddhist, Confucian, or even Protestant narratives, and thus provided them with greater sympathy for other nations for whom modernity and internationalism often were aligned more with colonial exploitation and oppression than with freedom and empowerment.[26] Baba Bunkō's critical legacy, not to mention that of St. Francis Xavier, remained alive and strong.

However, it took nearly half a century for that critical legacy of globalist values to receive a powerful public form of expression in modern Japan. For most of the first fifty years of the resurrected faith, the French MEP had its hands full building the institutional structure of a religious faith throughout Japan that could provide for the sacramental and spiritual needs of the tens of thousands of Japanese Catholics who had emerged, as well as those who were converting to the faith after religious freedom was achieved in 1873.[27] But it should not be overlooked that, along with the French vernacular language that replaced the Spanish and Portuguese used in the earlier moment of globalism in Japan, the sacraments, including the Mass, were still conducted in the same Latin tongue that for centuries Japanese Catholics had been using for their baptisms and prayers. Even in everyday prayers, such as the Pater Noster and the Ave Maria, the use of Latin reinforced lines of continuity with the Catholic ancestors of nineteenth-century Japanese Catholics, linking them with St. Francis Xavier and the globalist transformation of the mid-sixteenth century in contrast to the English-dominated cultural changes of the modernist, Protestant nineteenth century.

Interestingly, it was neither the Jesuits nor the MEP who played the most important role in the reemergence of Catholic globalism in the early twentieth century. Rather, the seedbed was the Society of Mary ("the Marianists") and even Protestants, or at least Catholic converts from Protestantism.[28] The beginnings of this neoglobalist thought can be traced to Japan's most promising philosopher, Iwashita Sōichi (1889–1940). Iwashita came from an Anglican family but attended the Marianist Morning Star School from 1899 to 1905. He was baptized into the Catholic Church in 1901, while a student at Morning Star, taking the baptismal name of Francis Xavier, explicitly gesturing toward continuity with the earliest introduction of globalism in Japan. From there he pursued the most elite educational course in Japan, including studying European philosophy at Tokyo Imperial University. While pursuing advanced study in philosophy in Europe from 1919 to 1925, he expressed a desire to be ordained a priest, and Cardinal Pietro La Fontaine, the Patriarch of Venice, ordained him as a priest of his patriarchate on June 6, 1925. Iwashita then returned home to Tokyo as a missionary priest of the archdiocese of Venice, not incardinated in any Japanese diocese.[29] So, with his personal funds he opened a men's boarding house for Catholic students in Tokyo, the St. Philip Dormitory. St. Philip Dormitory became the center of Japanese Catholic intellectual activity during the next twenty years; it was the matrix of globalist Catholic culture in twentieth-century Japan.

Father Iwashita's successor as headmaster of St. Philip Dormitory was the theologian Yoshimitsu Yoshihiko (1904–45), who had converted in 1927 from Protestantism, specifically the nondenominational and American-influenced Protestantism of the important intellectual Uchimura Kanzō (1861–1930). At Father Iwashita's strong recommendation, Yoshimitsu worked with Jacques Maritain during his study in Europe from 1928 to 1930. Iwashita believed that Maritain's ideas held the key to Japan being able to "raise up men capable of thinking and arguing alongside the best in the world."[30] And Iwashita, Yoshimitsu, and several others in their circle contributed greatly to the spread of globalist ideas through their translations of leading Catholic thinkers, especially but not exclusively from the French tradition, which were often overlooked in modern Japan, where English and American ideas enjoyed pride of place.

Yoshimitsu's theology is enjoying something of a renaissance in Japan today.[31] The same is true for the ideas of Yoshimitsu's close friend and colleague Tanaka Kōtarō (1890–1974), a law professor and judge and, by any reckoning, one of the most globalist intellectuals of modern Japan. Like Yoshimitsu, Tanaka also left Uchimura's nondenominational Christian group in 1924 (a few years before Yoshimitsu), prior to joining the Catholic Church in 1926. A little over a decade later, Tanaka wrote a compelling account of his conversion from Uchimura's nondenominational Christianity to Catholicism in a short piece titled "Cured of Relativism." In it he credited the globalist tradition of the natural law as embraced by St. Francis Xavier, SJ and Alessandro Valignano, SJ for leading him to the Catholic Church. As he wrote,

> Catholic philosophy, and in particular its teaching of natural law, which has been passed down to us from Aristotle and the times of Scholasticism, aided me immensely to free myself from the subjectivism and formalism of Neo-Kantianism. At the same time I overcame my

> prejudice against inherent natural law, with its fixed standards of right and wrong. . . . We Catholics of the whole world, the past and future generations not excepted, are one in our voluntary subjection under a legitimate authority, and in working for the realization of the Kingdom of God on earth. The Catholic concept of society alone, with its spirit of helpfulness, can cure the ills of family and state, and of the world.[32]

Tanaka had already written an important book in 1927, just after his conversion, called *Law, Religion and Social Life,* that warned against a movement in Japan to restrict religious freedom through the passage of a religions act inspired by the 1926 Calles Law in Mexico, which had just sparked the Cristero War there.[33] Tanaka was successful in delaying the passage of such an act until 1940, when nationalism was strong enough to pass the Religious Organizations Bill.

In *Law, Religion and Social Life*, Tanaka outlined his theory of world law (sometimes called global law, and in Japanese *sekai hō*) as an integral part of his argument on the limitations of positive and municipal law and for the legitimacy of the natural law as a worldwide law that recognizes innate human rights. Tanaka's theory of world law became his signature contribution to jurisprudence, especially after publication of his prizewinning three-volume magnum opus, *A Theory of World Law*, in 1934. In essence, Tanaka refutes John Austin's theory that law is merely whatever the sovereign wills it to be and, drawing on the German sociological school of law (e.g., of Eugen Ehrlich, Rudolf Stammler, and Josef Kohler), argues that law has its foundations in society rather than in the state. From there Tanaka argues that it is only a small but important move to recognize the existence of a global society, given the tremendous increase in cultural intercourse, commodity exchange, and mobility of peoples around the world. Finally, drawing on the maxim often attributed to Aristotle, *Ubi societas ibi ius* (Wherever there is society, there is law), Tanaka concludes that the reality of a global society implies the existence of a global (or "world") law.[34] In the absence of a fully codified written world law, Tanaka notes that the underpinnings of this global jurisprudence are found in the natural law.

While much of Tanaka's legal writings were, by necessity, abstract and quite technical, his globalism was not limited to abstract statements or academic theory. He was one of the most widely traveled Japanese people of his generation. He first left Japan in 1919, traversing the United States and England on his way to Europe, where he intended to study law (but mostly studied art, literature, music, and philosophy) until 1922. His next overseas trip was as an exchange professor to Italy from 1935 to 1936 (also visiting the United States, France, Belgium, and Spain), followed by time as a "people's diplomat" to Brazil, Argentina, Chile, Peru, Panama, and Mexico for five months in 1939; as an observer of American legal institutions for three months in 1950; for two months as a guest of the American Bar Association to attend its meeting in Boston in 1953; as a state guest visitor to India, the Dominican Republic, Italy, and France for three months in 1956, stopping in Switzerland, West Germany, England, and the United States along the way; and all of December 1957 in Brazil at the invitation of the chief justice of the Brazilian Supreme Court, stopping off in Venezuela and Mexico on the way home. His next flurry of international travels came in August and September of 1960, when he traveled to Argentina, the United States, Tunisia, Italy, Austria,

Portugal, Spain, and France as a candidate for a position on the International Court. Tanaka won that appointment and served as a justice at The Hague from November 1960 to February 1970, the same year he was appointed an honorary councilor of the Vatican. Tanaka was conversant in English and French, with a strong reading ability in German, and he seems to have had some facility in Italian, Spanish, and Portuguese. English was a necessity of international life, but his love was for Italian and Latino cultures in particular. As Shibasaki Atsushi has noted, "one of the motives, which drove Tanaka into such assiduous activity, was that Latin American countries were the true example of his particular-universal formulation of international culture. Each country is independent and has its particular culture and they share Catholicism as a commonality."[35]

Throughout the 1950s, while serving as chief justice of the Japanese Supreme Court, Tanaka was also the best known and most influential Japanese Catholic.[36] Given that influence, we might heed his opinion on key aspects of culture and religion in modern Japan. First, Tanaka (who was also former minister of education) held that postwar education in Japan needed to reflect the globalist culture that Japanese Catholics had embraced for centuries:

> For the purpose of overcoming this crisis in education in Japan today, I consider that the emphasis should be put upon the importance of moral principles and the recognition of the existence of ethical natural laws which are universal to all human beings. The concrete expressions of our ideals have been clearly set forth in the new Constitution, on the one hand, and on the other in such articles of the UNESCO Charter as the rule of law, peace, security, and the prevention of war—all of which can be realized by converting the mind of the people.[37]

But Tanaka, ever the global law jurist, also argued that within law one can find the bridge between peoples and cultures and that Christianity is the best foundation for that bridge. Less than ten years before he died, and in the closing days of the Second Vatican Council, Tanaka offered the following reflections that succinctly summarize his life's work—and the four-hundred-year globalist Catholic tradition in Japan:

> Because Christian morality is that of the Natural Law, in no way does it contradict the morality of Japan or the Orient. As the Japanese or Oriental morality is lifted up to the supernatural position of Christianity and internalized, it is perfected. Thereupon will arise a true spiritual understanding and love and respect between East and West, indeed among all the peoples of the world, and we will be able then to build a foundation for world peace.[38]

These are stirring words. But they must be contextualized in Takeda Tomoju's sobering assessment of Tanaka's weak influence on later Catholic Japanese faithful. Takeda, a Catholic intellectual himself, noted in 1963 that already Tanaka, whose books had been widely read as recently as ten years prior, was now largely unknown in the "recent Church."[39] Whether this was due to Tanaka's relocation to The Hague in 1960, or to more profound changes in the culture of the Japanese Catholic Church, will have to await further research.

Certainly we must not overlook the effect on Japanese Catholicism of the global struggle against communism ("the Cold War"), which had reached its height during the 1950s but began to decline during the years of the Vietnam War, especially after the Tet Offensive of 1968. This earlier period was the very time when Tanaka and other Japanese Catholics held great prominence in Japanese society. Indeed, Japan's first postwar Catholic prime minister, Yoshida Shigeru, was inextricably linked to the American effort to roll back communism in East Asia. Yoshida, a kind of Japanese Konrad Adenauer, served as prime minister briefly from 1946 to 1947 (when he appointed Tanaka Kōtarō his minister of education) and then returned as prime minister from 1948 to 1954, when he established the foundations of the postwar Japanese political structure that continues today. While Yoshida himself held off his own formal baptism until his deathbed (claiming he would "steal heaven"), he made sure his wife and family were all baptized and practicing Catholics. His descendants include the Catholic Nobuko, Princess Tomohito of Mikasa, and her brother Asō Tarō, postwar Japan's second Catholic prime minister (2008–9). In retrospect, the globalist Catholic tradition in Japan that began in 1549, went underground around 1630, and flourished again in the first half of the twentieth century, especially during the Cold War, started to experience a fundamental retreat by the late 1960s and early 1970s.

GLOBALIZATION, PHASE THREE: 1960s TO THE PRESENT

The Second Vatican Council marks a flash point in the globalism of the Catholic Church in Japan. Fifteen Japanese bishops represented Japan at the council. Bishop Nagae Satoshi, one of the Japanese Council Fathers, reported that the Japanese bishops at the first session were most interested in the issue of a "Japanese expression of Christianity" in recognition that the Greco-Latin clothing which the faith had adopted is not the only one to be used.[40] As Nagae's comment suggests, Vatican II did not spur a new globalist movement within the Japanese Church; if anything, its effects, such as they were, have pushed the Japanese Church away from globalism and instead toward regionalism and even nationalism. *Aggiornamento* (opening the windows of the Church) did not have the same impact in Japan that it experienced in the United States and Europe, as Japanese Catholics felt they had had their own *aggiornamento* in the late nineteenth century when, at the end of the closed country period, the faith was allowed open expression in the context of universalism and globalist culture.

It should be pointed out that if Vatican II was seen as the springboard for social changes that in the West had reached a high point in 1968, as early as the 1960s the Japanese were already exhausted from public battles over social change. The 1950s had seen major battles from Marxists in the Matsukawa and Sunakawa incidents, and both had become major issues for the Supreme Court, whose Catholic chief justice, Tanaka Kōtarō, played a prominent role in the legal resolution of those incidents. But the biggest political event of postwar Japan was the US-Japan Security Treaty protests of 1960, which essentially paralyzed Tokyo and resulted in the death of a young female student. All three events took place against the backdrop of the Cold War, and Catholics in Japan generally sided with Tanaka in resisting the Japanese Communist Party and its fellow travelers. By the early 1960s, the Japanese people in general (and Japanese Catholics in particular) were in no mood for further battles over social change and revolution and simply wanted to return to ordinary life. Vatican II was not the answer to their longings, but rather was something that threatened to reopen old wounds and bring conflict back into a world that was just starting to heal.

It is telling very little scholarship has been expended on the effects of Vatican II on the Japanese Church, particularly in contrast to the vast amount of literature on Vatican II in the American Church. One who has written on the issue is Adolfo Nicolás Pachón, SJ. Pachón was a student in Japan during the 1960s and did not attend the Second Vatican Council. But he was in an ideal position to observe the impact of the council on the Japanese church. In a 2003 retrospective, he drew on Joseph A. Komonchak to assess whether Vatican II in Japan was "an event" (*dekigoto*) or merely a historical process. Pachón summarizes the question by saying that determining whether it was an event or mere process for Japan rests on knowing how it was received and the impact and influence it had on the life of the faithful and the local church. His conclusion is that the Second Vatican Council was not an event for the Church in Japan. Indeed, he notes that there was almost no article on Vatican II in the Japanese Catholic newspapers between 1963 and 1969, and that in Japan, Protestants showed more interest in the council than Catholics did. He believes it was not until the 1986 Fourth FABC meeting was held in Tokyo that the reforms of Vatican II really began to be felt in Japan.[41] If we accept Pachón's assessment, we know that Vatican II was implemented in Japan in the context of a growing regionalist, if not outright nationalist, cultural movement. It is important to also note that by 1980 many of the key globalist Catholics had died: Japan's first cardinal, Doi Tatsuo, in 1969; Tanaka Kōtarō in 1974; Archbishop Yamaguchi Aijirō (formerly of Nagasaki) in 1976; and Cardinal Taguchi Yoshigorō in 1978. Cardinal Taguchi was replaced by Bishop Satowaki, who was elevated to cardinal on June 20, 1979. Six months prior, on Christmas Day 1978, a provisional Japanese language edition of the Liturgy of the Mass was published. But there was little embracing of the spirit of Vatican II until the 1980s.

Yet already in 1976 the leading Japanese Catholic novelist Sono Ayako was publishing (in serial form) a quasi-autobiographical work that was a stinging indictment of the effects of Vatican II on the Japanese Church. *Fuzai no heya* (The empty room) came out as a book in 1979 and was republished in a popular paperback version in 1983. It powerfully depicted the emptying out of many Church institutions, including the pews themselves, as the liturgical reforms implemented in the 1970s were emphasizing not globalist values but regional and even national indigenous ones.

More broadly, Sono's perspective reminds us that many of the Japanese Catholic laity remained firmly ensconced in the globalism of the earlier Church. This was particularly true of literature, a field that ironically in Japan is more often than not filled with the motifs of local and national culture. Catholic writers—of whom there were surprisingly many in the postwar period—stand out for their implicit and ofttimes explicit embrace of globalist values. Sono is one of the best. Her 1973 novel *Miracles* takes the reader from France to Poland to Rome and Sardinia, all in pursuit of the miracles attributed to St. Maximilian Kolbe (who, the reader is reminded, spent much of the 1930s in Japan and is considered a "Japanese" saint). Sono is not alone in this regard. Other Catholic novelists, like Ogawa Kunio (1927–2008) and Kaga Otohiko (1929–2023), draw on their time in Europe and the

Mideast and highlight those places and cultures in their prizewinning novels. Ogawa's *The Isles of Apollo* (1957) is a masterpiece of globalist fiction, as is Kaga's *Winter in Flanders* (1968). Even Endō Shūsaku was part of this globalist Catholic literature. Often only known in the West for his historical novel *Silence* (which is often misinterpreted as a rejection of globalism), Endō in fact wrote many globalist works, including *Foreign Studies* in 1965 (based on his experience as a foreign student in France) and *Samurai* in 1980 (about the Keichō Mission to Rome in the seventeenth century). Significantly, Endō's Japanese readers tend to consider *Samurai*, not *Silence*, his best work.

This globalist Catholic fiction seems to be in decline today. It is not clear why that is the case. If the Japanese church has withdrawn from its earlier globalist stance in favor of a national or regional cultural identity, then it is not surprising that Catholic writers might find it difficult to find a globalist voice or audience. Even if the Catholic hierarchy in Japan often seems less robustly globalist, Japanese culture more broadly still seems to draw globalism from Catholic institutions and projects those globalist values through Catholic themes in popular culture. In this sense there is a public Catholicism that remains global, whether or not the Catholic Church in Japan embraces globalism.

If we follow Hugh Heclo in understanding "public" to include "philosophy," Catholicism as a public religion in Japan has an important role as "the intersections of religion and policymaking that involve ideas and modes of thought bearing on the fundamental ordering of a society's public life."[42] As a public religion in Japan, Catholicism has contributed mainly in the educational sector, as several Catholic informants in Japan have emphasized.[43] Catholic education has reached into the lives of many Japanese, far more than the number of Catholics in the country. Japanese Catholics number only about 500,000. But today there are 855 institutions of Catholic education in the country: 21 universities, 17 junior colleges, 113 high schools, 101 middle schools, 53 elementary schools, and no fewer than 537 kindergartens. Clearly, Catholic students must be in the distinct minority in most of these Catholic schools. Or, another way of putting it, is that many non-Catholic, even non-Christian Japanese people are exposed to Catholicism and mostly through Catholic schools, especially kindergarten. Whether or not they convert to Catholicism (most do not), this early familiarity with Catholics and Catholicism helps break down any sense of distance or potential hostility they might feel toward this minority religion. In fact, Catholicism seems to enjoy a positive image among the general Japanese public.

The impact of Catholicism as a public religion is not merely a matter of access to students, however. Catholic schools in Japan have had a significant impact on society, one that is disproportionate to the relatively low numbers of students they teach. Consider two schools: Sacred Heart Academy for women in Tokyo and the all-male Jesuit Eikō Gakuen High School (Gloriam Academy) in Kamakura. Sacred Heart Academy graduates include: Ogata Sadako (1927–2019), a Georgetown University alumna who was deeply connected to the political power structure in Japan, particularly the ruling Liberal Democratic Party; Yamatani Eriko (b. 1950), an LDP dietmember and former minister for the abduction issue, for ocean policy and territorial issues, for building national resilience, and for disaster management; Sono Ayako (b. 1931), Japan's leading Catholic novelist and essayist, former president of the

Nippon Foundation, and member of the National Council on Educational Reform (with strong LDP connections); and Michiko, Empress Emerita of Japan. Gloriam Academy boasts that, on average, 30 percent of their graduates have been accepted into the most elite (and most difficult to enter) Tokyo University. Their graduates also lean heavily toward the governing party, the LDP. They include Ishiwata Kiyoharu (1940–2014), former LDP dietmember; Hamada Takujirō (1941–2022), former LDP dietmember; Miyake Kunihiko (b. 1953), special advisor to the cabinet; and Ogura Masanobu (b. 1981), LDP dietmember. Of course, there are a few Gloriam Academy alumni who are non-LDP parliamentarians, such as former prime minister Hosokawa Morihiro (b. 1938) of the Democratic Party of Japan, who graduated from Gloriam Academy's middle school and later the Jesuit Sophia University. Gloriam Academy also has many influential graduates in industry, education, and other sectors.

The current buzzword in Japanese culture is "globalization," a term close to the hearts of most Japanese Catholic laymen and Catholic Japanese educators. The increasing inclusion of many non-Japanese as teachers (e.g., the JET Program) and students in Japanese education creates a general educational culture that is not limited to Catholic education but that is striking for its globalist cultural content and form. Another significant site for globalization and Catholicism within contemporary Japanese culture is anime, the enormously influential global pop cultural product of Japan. Christian themes play a role in many anime productions (e.g., *Neon Genesis Evangelion*, which was broadcast on Japanese television October 1995 to March 1996). In some anime works, specifically Catholic images are front and center. Takahashi Rumiko's *One Pound Gospel* features a young nun in habit and a professional boxer to whom she teaches the virtue of temperance. It was published first as a manga (1987–2007), then as anime (1988), and after that as a television drama that aired on NTV (January–March 2008). Then there is Konno Oyuki's unforgettable *Maria Watches Over Us*, which is set in a fictional Catholic all-girls high school in Tokyo. It was published first in thirty-nine light novel volumes from 1998 to 2012, in nine manga volumes from 2003 to 2010, and in several anime and television series. Affectionately known as *marimite* ("Mary watches"), the now-subtitled-in-English series is available around the world. While few if any of these anime are produced by Catholic Japanese artists, the very fact that non-Catholic Japanese companies produce them and largely non-Catholic Japanese people consume them suggests that the globalist values of Catholicism have a cultural appeal for many Japanese people, even if they do not always embrace the faith or doctrines of the Church.

Nevertheless, tensions remain between globalization (which interests most Japanese, whether Catholic or not), "inculturation" (the ideal of a more national Japanese mode of Christianity, which is chiefly of interest to foreign missionaries in Japan, especially Protestants), and pan-Asianism (which is promoted in certain formal ways by the Catholic Bishops' Conference of Japan in the face of very little interest from rank-and-file Japanese lay Catholics). These tensions between the hierarchy and the people in the Japanese Church are not merely on cultural issues, but also on political issues. Historically, Japanese bishops have not been political activists (with the notable exception of Cardinal Taguchi, who was quite active politically during World War II). In recent years, the Catholic Bishops' Conference of Japan has issued a number of partisan statements against the ruling Liberal Democratic Party and especially against former prime minister Abe Shinzō. The bishops position themselves within a regional pan-Asianism, in contrast to many LDP members and Japanese Catholics who support the LDP and its globalist view of the world. All of this has undermined much of the effectiveness of the Catholic Bishops' Conference of Japan on public issues and in Church leadership. While officially the bishops conference promotes pan-Asian relations, especially with Korea, few Japanese Catholics in the pews are interested in pan-Asianism. They remain interested in a globalism that is not restricted to the Asian region. Even their images of Christ and the saints, as one sister who works in the leading Catholic bookstore in Tokyo told me, "all come from Rome." The Catholic Bishops' Conference regularly denounces politicians' visits to the Shinto Yasukuni Shrine as a "violation of religious freedom," an argument that few find persuasive, particularly since several prominent Catholics intellectuals (Sono Ayako, Miura Shumon, Watanabe Shōichi) have supported these visits and made visits themselves, as do several Catholic politicians aligned with the LDP (e.g., former prime minister Asō Tarō and Dietmember Yamatani Eriko).

Most active in recent years in terms of representing Catholicism in the public realm have been private citizens like Ogata Sadako, and especially Sono Ayako, both Catholic women who in their works have adopted a globalist perspective rather than an Asianist or Japanist lens. Sono may be today's face of Catholicism as a public religion in Japan. An energetic nonagenarian, she continues to write essays on social and political issues from an explicitly Catholic identity. While not at all neglecting Asia (her NGO charitable work in Southeast Asia is well-known), her activities are truly global in scope, both in her former capacity as head of the Nippon Foundation and in her leadership of the Japan Overseas Missionary Assistance Society (JOMAS), which supports medical relief in underprivileged regions of the world, notably corrective surgery for Madagascar children born with cleft palates.

If there is a resurgence of globalism among contemporary Japanese Catholics, it seems to be among the laity, not the hierarchy. This is particularly so among certain lay intellectuals who have sparked a renaissance in Japanese Catholic studies, drawing on the Second Vatican Council's openness to non-Western cultures and its emphasis on a greater participation of the laity. These intellectuals—Yamamoto Yoshihisa, Wakamatsu Eisuke, Yamane Michihiro, Yamanashi Atsushi, Uno Kei—are mostly laypeople who foreground the appeal of the philosophy, theology, and literature of Japanese Catholics writing prior to Vatican II, such as Iwashita Sōichi, Yoshimitsu Yoshihiko, and Tanaka Kōtarō.[44] If a vitality in the Japanese Catholic Church grows further, particularly a vitality that draws on the legacy of Vatican II without succumbing to nationalist or regionalist limitations, it may well take place among younger lay Japanese Catholic intellectuals and their globalist vision.

NOTES

1. C. R. Boxer, *The Christian Century in Japan, 1549–1650* (Berkeley: University of California Press and Cambridge University Press, 1951), 36.
2. Boxer, 188–98.
3. Francisco Paiso, SJ, "Letter of September 1594," quoted in Yoshitomo Okamoto, *The Namban Art of Japan* (New York: Weatherhill/Heibonsha, 1972); also cited in Jennifer L. Welsh, "Cultural

Trends and Cross-Cultural Interest: The 'Southern Barbarian Screens' and Early Modern Japan," *Japan Studies Association Journal* 10 (2012): 142.

4. Boxer, *The Christian Century in Japan*, 139–40.
5. Tanaka Hidemichi, *Geijutsu kokka nihon no kagayaki, III: Muromachi jidai kara gendai* (Tokyo: Bensei, 2017), 72. For a sampling of the estimations historians have made over the years on the number of Japanese converts to Catholicism in the early seventeenth century (ranging from 200,000 to 1 million), see Kevin Doak, ed., *Xavier's Legacies: Catholicism in Modern Japanese Culture* (Vancouver and Toronto: University of British Columbia Press, 2011), 25n6.
6. On Nanban art, see Welsh, "Cultural Trends and Cross-Cultural Interest."
7. For the globalist impact of Catholicism on Japanese culture during this period, see Tanaka, *Geijutsu kokka nihon no kagayaki*, 53–78.
8. William J. Farge, SJ, "Review of Haruko Nawata Ward's *Women Religious Leaders in Japan's Christian Century, 1549–1650*," *Catholic Historical Review* 97, no. 1 (January 2011): 192.
9. Derek Massarella, "Revisiting Japan's Christian Century," *Casahistoria* (January 2008): 7, http://www.casahistoria.net/japanchristaincentury.pdf, accessed October 4, 2016.
10. A recent groundbreaking work that emphasizes St. Francis Xavier's respect for Japanese culture and his Japanese language facility is Nanyan Guo, *Making Xavier's Dream Real: Vernacular Writings of Catholic Missionaries in Modern Japan* (Tokyo: JPIC, 2020), 39–46.
11. Massarella, "Revisiting Japan's Christian Century," 7.
12. The names of these missions come from the Japanese reign eras during which they took place: Tenshō (AD 1573–93) and Keichō (AD 1596–1615). Christian years are used, according to the Gregorian calendar.
13. See Joseph Cardinal Ratzinger, *Truth and Tolerance: Christian Belief and World Religions* (San Francisco: Ignatius, 2004), 64–71.
14. Japanese names are given in Japanese order (surname, given name), except for Japanese Americans or when a Japanese person is known mainly through his or her English publications, in which case the usual English order is followed.
15. Derek Massarella, "The Japanese Embassy to Europe (1582–1590)," *Journal of the Hakluyt Society* (February 2013): 1.
16. Massarella, 2.
17. Massarella, 6.
18. Luis Sotelo was beatified by Pope Pius IX on July 7, 1867. His feast day is August 25.
19. Vizcaino had come to Japan in 1611 to pay respects to the *bakufu* on behalf of Spain for the return of the shipwrecked Rodrigo de Vivero y Velasco (1564–1636). History remembers Tanaka Shōsuke as the first Japanese person to cross the Pacific. He had traveled to Mexico in August 1610 to take Vivero back home on the first Western ship built in Japan. He was baptized in Mexico and returned to Japan in 1611 with Vizcaino. What happened to him after his return home is unknown.
20. Endō Shūsaku's historical novel *Samurai* is a masterful narrative about the Keichō Mission.
21. See Miyazaki Kentarō, *Kakure kirishitan no jitsuzō: nihonjin no kirisuto-kyō rikai to juyō* (Tokyo: Yoshikawa Kōbunkan, 2014).
22. Nakazono Shigeo, "*Kakure kirishitan no jitsuzō* ni okeru shinkō ninshiki to mondai," *Shima no kan dayori* 18 (March 2014): 15–17.
23. William J. Farge, SJ, *A Christian Samurai: The Trials of Baba Bunkō* (Washington, DC: Catholic University of America Press, 2016).
24. My idea of "submerged globalism" follows, but is not equivalent with, Robert N. Bellah's notion of "submerged transcendence" in premodern Japanese culture. See Bellah, *Imagining Japan: The Japanese Tradition and Its Modern Interpretation* (Berkeley: University of California Press, 2003). But also see the powerful critique of Bellah by José Casanova, "Religion, the Axial Age, and Secular Modernity in Bellah's Theory of Religious Evolution," in Robert N. Bellah and Hans Joas, eds., *The Axial Age and Its Consequences* (Cambridge, MA: Harvard University Press, 2012), 191–221.

25. William J. Farge, SJ, "Review of Kiri Paramore's *Ideology and Christianity in Japan*," *Journal of Japanese Studies* 36, no. 1 (2010): 214.
26. For more on how French Catholicism in late nineteenth and early twentieth-century Japan provided an alternative way of being modern, see my "Introduction: Catholicism, Modernity and Japanese Culture" in Kevin Doak, ed., *Xavier's Legacies: Catholicism in Modern Japanese Culture* (Vancouver: University of British Columbia Press, 2011), 1–30.
27. Despite the barriers of the French and Latin languages, by the end of the century the MEP had increased the number of Catholics in Japan from about 25,000 (roughly half of the 50,000 who had emerged after 1865 refused to unite with the Catholic Church) to 138,624 (including forty-eight Japanese priests). See https://en.wikipedia.org/wiki/Paris_Foreign_Missions_Society#Japan, accessed October 11, 2016. A more modest number of 58,261 Catholics in early twentieth-century Japan is given in Doak, "Introduction," 4. The larger MEP number includes Japanese people in Korea, but by all accounts there were few Catholics in Korea at this time. The total probably also includes westerners in Japan and Korea who were Catholic.
28. On the role of the Society of Mary in shaping early twentieth-century Japanese Catholic intellectuals, see Kei Uno, "The Activities of the Marianists and Catholic Intellectuals in Japan Prior to the Second World War," *Logos: A Journal of Catholic Thought and Culture* 18, no. 4 (Fall 2015): 155–75.
29. Kosakai Sumi, *Ningen no bunzai: shimpu Iwashita Sōichi* (Nagasaki: Seibo no Kishi Sha, 1996), 344–48.
30. Wakamatsu Eisuke, "Yoshimitsu Yoshihiko," *Mita Bungaku* 90, no. 106 (Summer 2011): 155.
31. See Wakamatsu Eisuke, *Yoshimitsu Yoshihiko: shi to tenshi no keijijōgaku* (Tokyo: Iwanami Shoten, 2014); Kei Uno, *Newman and Modern Japan* (Chiba, Japan: Kyōyūsha, 2010); Yamane Michihiro's presentation, "Endō Shūsaku ni okeru katorishizumu no juyō to hasshin: Yoshimitsu Yoshihiko to Inoue Yōji no eikyō ni furete," Symposium on the Genealogy of Spirituality in Japanese Catholicism, Sophia University, Tokyo, June 20, 2015.
32. Tanaka Kōtarō, "Cured of Relativism," in Severin and Stephen Lamping, OFM, eds. and trans., *Through Hundred Gates By Noted Converts from Twenty-Two Lands* (Milwaukee, WI: Bruce, 1939), 264.
33. Tanaka Kōtarō, *Hō to shūkyō to shakai seikatsu* (Tokyo: Kaizōsha, 1927). For Tanaka's warning about the Calles Law, see 170–74.
34. Tanaka Kōtarō, *Sekai hō no riron*, vol. 1 (Tokyo: Iwanami Shoten, 1932), 295–96.
35. Atsushi Shibasaki, "Christianity and the Making of a Modern Worldview in Japan: International Thought of Tanaka Kotaro (1890–1974)," *Journal of Global Media Studies* 7 (August 2010): 35.
36. This is according to Takeda Tomoju, professor at Catholic Seisen University in Tokyo writing in 1963 and cited in Yamanashi Atsushi, "Sōvūru Kandō shinpu to kindai nihon no chishikijin," *Katorikku Kenkyu* 81 (August 2012): 116.
37. Tanaka Kōtarō, "The Present Crisis of Japanese Education," *Contemporary Japan* (January–March 1951): 14.
38. Tanaka Kōtarō, "Shinkō no ronri: katorishizumu josetsu," in Tanaka Kōtarō, ed., *Wakaki hi no shinkō* (Tokyo: Mikasa Shobō, 1965), 193 (revised version of lecture on Catholicism that Tanaka gave to Emperor Hirohito and family on April 30, 1946). Lines quoted here do not appear in the original lecture.
39. Takeda Tomoju, cited in Yamanashi, "Sōvūru Kandō shinpu to kindai nihon no chishikijin," 116.
40. Nagae Satoshi, "Kyōkai itchi e no michi," *Yomiuri Shimbun* (January 6, 1963): 9.
41. Adolfo Nicolas, SJ, "Dai-ni bachikan kōkaigi gō no nihon shakai to senkyō," in Mori Kazuhiro, ed., *Nihon no kyōkai no senkyō no hikari to kage: kirishitan jidai kara no senkyō no rekishi wo furikaeru* (Tokyo: San Pauro, 2003), 218–21.
42. Hugh Heclo, "An Introduction to Religion and Public Policy," in Hugh Heclo and Wilfred M. McClay, eds., *Religion Returns to the Public Square: Faith and Policy in America* (Washington,

DC: Woodrow Wilson Center Press, 2003) 5, quoted in José Casanova, "What Is a Public Religion?" in the same volume, p. 123.

43. These informants include clerics and laymen, all involved in higher education in Japan today.
44. See *Kirisutokyō bunka kenkyūjo kiyo* 34 (Sophia University, 2015).

3

Globalization of Catholicism in China

RICHARD MADSEN

The three historical globalizations of Catholicism in China differed in what was globalized and how they were localized. The first globalization, of the seventeenth and eighteenth centuries, occurred before the rise of the modern nation-state. The Counter-Reformation Catholicism that came to China was not tightly implicated with European national cultures but in its various versions it was tightly connected with the organizational ethos of different religious orders. These different versions of a globalizing Catholicism were then localized into the various cultures of different regions and social strata in the geographical area that we now call China.

The second globalization took place in the nineteenth and early twentieth centuries, a period that could be called the age of nation-state-driven imperialism. The spread of Catholicism then was deeply intertwined with the national, imperial aspirations of European (and American) nation-states. It was localized into the lower strata and poorer regions of a weak and disorganized Qing Dynasty empire, and when that empire collapsed helped to provoke modern forms of Chinese nationalism while taking on some of the elements of a nationalistic culture.

The third globalization is currently taking place, following the founding of the People's Republic of China in 1949. The Chinese Catholic Church developed along different paths: within the communities under the control of the Communist regime and within the "free world." These divisions took new forms in the ways that the reforms of Vatican II interacted with Asian anti-imperialism and the waning of the Cold War. Finally, the Church has had to contend with the rise of China within an economically globalized and multicultural world.

THE FIRST GLOBALIZATION

It is anachronistic to ask how the "Catholic Church entered China" during the first globalization of the long seventeenth century. First of all, "China" did not exist when Matteo Ricci and his Jesuit confreres left the Portuguese colony of Macao in 1583 to travel north, with the hope of eventually getting to the court of the Ming emperor in Beijing, which they reached in 1601. The emperor regarded himself the Son of Heaven, a political-religious office charged not only with maintaining order and stability within the empire but also with mediating between Heaven (seen as an ultimate deity) and Earth. Through this mediation the seasons would unfold in their regular order, producing abundant harvests and avoiding natural disasters, and the many people under Heaven would live in harmony, respecting their elders and adhering to a proper division of labor within loyal families. In principle the emperor's sway extended over the four corners of the earth (they did not yet know that it was round), but in practice during the Ming dynasty it extended west only as far as the Great Wall, built to ward off barbarians who did not (yet) accept the civilizing mission of the emperor. The Jesuits would later give the name "China" to this empire because they learned that their interlocutors understood the form of imperial order to have begun with Emperor Qin (Chin) about eighteen hundred years before. Later they would determine that this was the same place as the "Cathay" that Marco Polo had visited four centuries earlier. Having thus created China—or at least a Western image of it, conceived as a culturally unified society—they set out to convert it to Christianity.

Although the first waves of Jesuits accompanying Ricci sailed to China under the Portuguese *padronado*, they came from many different nationalities: Ricci, an Italian, Adam Schall von Bell a German, Ferdinand Verbiest, Flemish. Europe had not yet become consolidated into rival nation-states, and the disputes among Jesuits and their rivals were about religion, not national politics. It is perhaps more accurate to say that what first came to the territory governed by the Ming dynasty was not so much Catholicism as the Jesuit version of it.

The Christianity that missionaries of that era sought to propagate was no unitary culture or institution. It had been rent asunder by the Reformation and, although a semblance of doctrinal orthodoxy had been created by the Church of Rome in the Council of Trent, the ways of interpreting and practicing that orthodoxy differed widely among the various religious orders, which often engaged in bitter rivalry. The Jesuits offered only one version of this orthodoxy, although of course they tried to tell their Chinese interlocutors that it was the only version—a version that made possible, so they said (seemingly having been granted dispensation from the commandment against lying), the marvelous harmony and prosperity of the faraway culturally unified society called Europe.[1]

The Ming dynasty ruled over myriad local cultural communities. Most, but by no means all, were of Han Chinese ethnicity, but even the Hans were divided by language, local custom, and religious practice. Chinese popular religion was polytheistic and different communities fashioned their own particular mix of deities from among a large pantheon. What unity there was in the system was provided by an extensive bureaucratic apparatus, which extended as far as the practical reach of the emperor's power. Positions in the bureaucracy were allocated through exams based on a diverse philosophical system derived from the canonical works of Confucius and his disciples and synthesized with certain aspects of Buddhism in the thirteenth century. The Jesuits called this "Confucianism," but the Chinese just called it the teaching of the scholars, who themselves were actually divided into many schools of thought.

The most elite scholars tended to be rationalistic, showing distain for popular polytheism. The emperors for their part tolerated all manner of popular beliefs, not just the teaching of the scholars but also the teaching of the Dao and the Buddha, and many combinations in between. These were mostly called "orthodox teachings," in contrast to others that historically showed a propensity to foment rebellion. It was one of the jobs of administrative officials to keep followers of heterodox teachings under surveillance and control.[2]

In this system there was not a public sphere in the modern sense, or a sphere of life in which citizens could come together to discuss the direction of their society. The emperor made governing decisions with advice from some of his top scholar-officials, then the officials implemented the decisions and the people were supposed to follow. The strategy of Ricci and his associates was to gain acceptance by top scholar-officials and to invite them to accept the Christian God. The Jesuits saw the moral life of scholar-officials admirable—except for their customs like polygamy, which they required the officials to give up if they wanted to be Christians. Otherwise, the Jesuits required officials who wanted to become Christians to make minimal changes in their way of life. In particular they allowed them to carry out the customary rituals to honor their ancestors, which the Jesuits, on the testimony of (at least partially disingenuous) elite officials themselves, saw as purely moral gestures, not some form of worship. Their hope seemed to be that if they could convert leading scholar-officials and maybe even the emperor himself, then they could make China a Christian society. But the China they imagined did not really exist. Even had they succeeded in converting the emperor himself, it is probable that millions of ordinary Chinese would have still clung to their traditional gods within their traditional communities.

The Jesuits' rivals, the Franciscans and the Dominicans, brought different versions of Counter-Reformation orthodoxy to the empire of the Son of Heaven. (In style and substance these differences were much deeper than found among these same religious orders today.) They also focused on different parts of that empire, especially local communities far removed from the scholar-officials reached by some of the Jesuits. (Other Jesuits, however, did indeed, attempt to evangelize in rural communities.) These were villages whose community life was structured by worship of many different deities. The Franciscans and Dominicans saw this as irredeemable paganism that had to be utterly rejected. Usually approaching poor outgroups at odds with their local culture and working through the local leaders of such marginalized communities, the Franciscans and Dominicans got villages and lineages to destroy their idols and their temples and to replace them with churches. In doing so they constructed another image of China as a backward idolatrous pagan land. This was different from the China envisioned by the Jesuits, but in its own way just as one-dimensional and unrealistic.

This version of China actually did have an incipient public sphere or, more accurately, a universe of micro public spheres. Almost every village had an active public life centered especially on its local temple, which was a place for meetings, marketing, and all sorts of leisure activities. The common affairs of villages were usually managed by local elites, mainly economically successful elders. When entire communities became Catholic, the local church served as a community center in a way similar to the old temples, and public affairs were managed by local leaders, now partially subordinate to but sometimes in tension with the missionary priest. A potential problem, however, with the rejection of the gods and rituals that gave meaning and a sense of community to most Chinese was that the small public spheres of the Catholics could be set against the public spheres of neighboring communities.

The different theological and sociological visions of the Jesuits and their rival missionaries led to the infamous "rites controversy." The pope was presented with two visions of China as a unified social system, both inaccurate, and two versions of Counter-Reformation theology, both incomplete. Unable in that social context to accept ambiguity, he had to choose one over the other and make it the new missionary orthodoxy. In 1704, Pope Clement XI chose the version of the Jesuits' rivals. In the empire of the Son of Heaven, the consequences were severe.[3]

In 1644, the Ming dynasty had fallen to an invasion of Manchus from the northeast. The Jesuits promptly curried favor with the new dynasty, even helping forge weapons to use against remnants of the Ming. Jesuits entered the court of the ensuing Qing dynasty and one of them even became a tutor to the future emperor, Kangxi. In 1692, after Emperor Kangxi had ascended the throne, he declared Christianity an orthodox teaching, to be given protection and acceptance by the government. After the pope rendered his decision in the rites controversy, however, Christianity was declared a heterodox teaching. Most missionaries were expelled. Bereft of priests and treated with suspicion by local officials, Catholic communities were left to their own devices. Ironically, this facilitated a kind of "indigenization from below." The public affairs of the communities were carried on by an increasingly strong lay leadership. Catholic communities took on some of the forms of life common to other local "heterodox sects," such as those lumped under the name of White Lotus, which carried out a great rebellion in the late eighteenth century.[4]

Catholics therefore sometimes attracted the kind of hostile attention from government officials as heterodox groups like the White Lotus sectarians had earned, and they were persecuted along with the White Lotus. Like the White Lotus, they brought men and women together morning and evening for prayer, and some officials accused them of using this as a cover for licentious behavior. The Catholics may not have been guilty of licentious behavior, but they did give special leadership roles to women. They developed institutes of "Catholic virgins," who lived the celibate life of Catholic nuns but without belonging to an established religious order, which was not allowed by European Catholic Church authorities. Although missionaries had established these institutes, they had become concerned that the women were taking things too far, even presiding over common prayers in assemblies that included men. With the missionaries gone, the role of such women increased.[5]

Although these self-governing Catholic communities attracted suspicion and persecution from government officials tasked with controlling heterodoxy, there is little evidence that these communities attracted the hostility of neighboring grassroots communities. It appears that their local leaders knew how to mediate with neighboring communities to avoid disharmony.[6]

THE SECOND GLOBALIZATION

Missionaries returned to China in the mid-nineteenth century during the second globalization, the Age of Imperialism driven by European nation-states. Now the missionaries included Protestants as well as Catholics, and besides bringing the Gospel they also represented European-nation states. The British demanded that China accept its Protestant missionaries after it defeated China in the Opium War of 1839. This was part of the "unequal treaties" forced on China after military defeat. In the treaty signed after another defeat in 1858, the French followed suit, demanding equal access for its Catholic missionaries. The Christian missionaries were not only beneficiaries of their countries' expansion into China, but they were agents of national rivalries. After the 1850s, all European Catholic missionaries were under a French protectorate, although there were still rivalries between missionary societies connected with different nations. The French government was willing to defend them with military force when necessary, and French diplomats used their offices to press the Chinese government for special privileges for all Chinese Catholics, even those not served by French priests.

The French protectorate amounted to what historian Earnest Young calls an "ecclesiastical colony."[7] The French government demanded that missionary bishops be given the same privileges—such as being carried around on sedan chairs—as provincial government officials and that missionaries and Catholic believers were subject to French law and thus could not be prosecuted in Chinese courts. In return, missionaries were under the control of the French government. Communications to the Vatican had to go through Paris.

The Catholic missionaries worked mostly in the countryside among poor farmers and fishermen. After the rites controversy they had no credibility among the ruling elite of scholarly officials. Indeed, the special privileges wrested for them by the foreign powers incurred the animosity of the ruling elite. Although the missionaries evangelized in the countryside, their material support was channeled through their fellow countrymen in the foreign concessions—urban enclaves established through the unequal treaties that were controlled by the foreign powers under their national laws.

The local lay community leaders who had been leading their communities since the early missionaries had been expelled were not too happy to get the foreign missionaries back. There were some ugly skirmishes when the European priests tried to reestablish control. The Europeans tried to firm up Catholic orthodoxy. This time there were no disputes about the nature of that orthodoxy among Jesuits and other religious orders, although there were different styles of evangelization and pastoral care in churches controlled by French, Italians, Germans, and Belgians. The Europeans brought new money into Catholic communities but demanded new kinds of accounting. They now required annual "spiritual reports," listing how much money was spent to what effect—how many baptisms, how many Communion recipients (determined by counting the number of hosts given out at Masses), how many churches, schools, and clinics built. The pattern of building Catholic communities consisting of whole villages or at least whole lineages occupying a distinctive part of a village continued.[8] Missionaries called these *christianitas* or "little Christendoms," and Chinese Catholics sometimes referred to them as "worlds of God."[9]

These worlds contained their own public sphere, but it was different from the minipublic spheres that had existed before the missionaries returned. Before, under the leadership of laymen, communities fended for themselves. Now, under the direction of priests, they were connected to a larger ecclesiastical colony and, through that, to the European Church. Handsome churches sprung up in Catholic communities and, like Chinese temples, they served as local community centers. But village temples had been built up over generations by the local people. The new churches came down from above, courtesy of money raised in Europe through the Society for Propagation of the Faith, through the mediation of foreign priests. Catholics had special access to the Chinese government. Their bishops now were considered as equals to provincial officials, and they also had the power of the French diplomatic corps and the French military at their disposal. Catholics from disparate areas were pulled together into a hierarchically dominated public.

These new vertical connections helped to destroy the horizontal connections Catholic communities likely had with their non-Catholic neighbors. Their special access to the judicial system angered other Chinese. Even more provocative was the refusal of Catholics to pay to support the local temple fairs that brought village communities together for commerce, entertainment, and worship of the gods. These were public events to which all members of local communities were expected to contribute. Strict enforcement of rules of orthodoxy forced Catholics to withdraw their contributions. Catholic noncontribution diminished the quality of these celebrations, which were considered a public good. At the same time, Catholics were enjoying material and legal protections because of their status. Animosity generated by this situation led to a large number of attacks against Catholics. These "religion cases" (*jiao'an*) then provoked French intervention, sometimes with gunboats, and the intervention was sometimes used as a pretext to increase the amount of territory under French control. At the end of the nineteenth century these tensions culminated in the Boxer Uprising (1899–1901) during which thousands of Catholics and Protestants were killed.[10]

After the Boxer Uprising was crushed by an allied army of European powers and the Qing government was forced to pay huge indemnities, Chinese elites, especially those from new commercial sectors formed by incipient industrialization, began promoting a new national consciousness. As the Qing dynasty collapsed in 1911, reformers and revolutionaries gave their society a new name—the Middle Kingdom, or China. The aim was to make China a modern nation-state similar to the European powers, with clearly defined borders, a common culture, and a unified central government—all of which was more aspiration than reality until the Communist victory in 1949. Overall, Catholic Church missionaries were not supportive of this nationalistic movement.

There were exceptions that proved the rule, most notably the Belgian Lazarist (Vincentian) missionary Fr. Vincent Lebbe, who came to China in 1901, while the country was still reeling from the Boxer Uprising. Lebbe was forced out in 1920 for his active support of the nationalistic ferment of the 1910s, which became known as the May Fourth Movement. Unlike many of his fellow missionaries, he became fluent in Chinese and attracted reform-minded intellectuals through public lectures about issues of the day. He also founded in 1915 the *Yishi Bao* (Social welfare news), which would become one of China's major newspapers, conveying a strong anti-imperialist message. One of the first causes that this newspaper undertook was a protest against French plans to expand their concession in order to encompass a new cathedral built outside the boundaries of the concession. For his role Lebbe was denounced by the French embassy and censured by his French missionary bishop, after which he was expelled from the Tianjin Diocese and sent to Ningbo in southern China. He appealed, however, to Pope Benedict XV, who had his own reasons for reasserting control from the French and more of an ability to do so after France had been weakened by the First World War. The result was the 1919 papal apostolic letter, Maximum Illud, which called for missionaries to develop native clergies by educating them up to the same level as foreign clergies and to cultivate native bishops who could take over leadership of the local churches. Lebbe's vision was vindicated in the long run, but even after Maximum Illud the French missionary bishops had him expelled from China.[11]

In 1926, the pope personally ordained the first six Chinese bishops in St. Peter's Basilica. Although the door was now open for the creation of a Chinese church run by Chinese bishops, many missionary clergy resisted by delay and foot-dragging.

In 1927, the Nationalist Party (KMT) led by Chiang Kai-shek, having gained control over China's urban areas and purged Communists from its ranks, established the Republic of China. The new government purported to represent the Chinese nation as a whole, even though it had minimal control over many rural areas. One of its avowed aims was to eventually eliminate all foreign concessions, but this had to be postponed due to the pressing need to tackle a host of domestic problems, including a vigorous communist insurgency in the rural areas and Japanese aggression. The Catholic Church depended on the overall goodwill of the Nationalist government, although its leaders, especially the foreign missionaries, were not necessarily enthusiastic about the nationalist cause. Most Chinese bishops, however, did firmly support the Nationalists. In 1946, after the end of the war against Japan and the beginning of the civil war between Communists and Nationalists, the Vatican formally established the Chinese Church as a national church under a local hierarchy (although many foreign missionary bishops remained) and appointed as Vatican nuncio Msgr. Antonio Riberi. Riberi openly supported the Nationalist government and in 1947, under orders from Rome, forbade Catholics from joining any Communist-controlled organization. In 1948, Riberi helped establish the Legion of Mary and charged it with fighting communism. In July 1949, with a Communist victory imminent, Riberi forbade any Catholic, under pain of excommunication, to sympathize with the Communist Party or publish, read, or write any communist literature. In 1951, he extended the ban of excommunication even to parents and guardians of anyone who violated the prohibition.[12] The Communist victory initiated the third globalization.

THE THIRD GLOBALIZATION

The third globalization unfolded in three phases, the first of which was the global struggle for power that we call the Cold War.

Cold War Globalization

After the Communist victory in 1949, the Church in the People's Republic of China was rapidly cut off by a "bamboo curtain" from the rest of the global Church. Although the primary responsibility for this separation rested with the Chinese government, the Church, with its implacable opposition to communism, was not without responsibility. In important ways, the Church and the Communist Party were mirror images. Both were hierarchical institutions with power concentrated at the top. Both claimed a sacred mission. Especially under Mao Zedong, the Chinese Communist Party claimed not only to be an instrument of power but the founder of a new moral order linking China to the ultimate purposes of history. In the self-understandings of their hierarchical leadership at the time, the Church and the Communist Party were two implacable foes with no possibilities for compromise.

Although in the end the Chinese Communist Party proved to be strongly nationalistic, in the decade after its assumption of power it presented itself as an ally of the Soviet Union in the global communist movement. In its policies toward religion it followed the strategies developed by Vladimir Lenin and refined by Joseph Stalin in suppressing the Russian Orthodox Church. This strategy did not fit well with much of the Chinese religious landscape, where most religion was decentralized and embedded in local communal life, but it did fit well against the hierarchically organized Catholic Church—which may help explain the fierceness of its implementation. In its constitution the government proclaimed freedom of religious belief but in its action it showed a determination to purge religion of any foreign influence. Then it took away most of the property of the churches, stripped them of their educational and welfare activities, and restricted them to purely liturgical functions. It proceeded to imprison the major leaders of the Church, not officially on religious grounds but on grounds that they were attacking the revolution. It created bodies of pro-regime clergy and laity to help carry out these attacks on Church leaders. Finally, after having destroyed the Church's leadership, it appointed compliant successors. The goal was to make the Church a subservient, hollowed-out shell.[13]

Riberi was expelled from China in 1950 and almost all other foreign missionaries were expelled by 1952. Some of them were accused of espionage and subjected to brutal prison treatment. Some suffered greatly; Bishop Francis X. Ford of Maryknoll died of such treatment.[14] Their stories of mistreatment inspired devout Catholics in the West to take up the struggle for the faith against "godless communism." With missionaries gone, Chinese Catholic priests and laypeople were more vulnerable than ever. Nonetheless, many carried out staunch resistance, which only intensified the Communist cadres' determination to crush them. The government was especially harsh toward the Legion of Mary (the Chinese name, *jun*, translates as "army"), which they saw as a militant organization bent on destroying their regime. The Jesuits in Shanghai organized secret sodalities among their young college students, who took oaths signed in blood to defeat communism. After being arrested and subjected to torture, some of the priests gave up names of the secret sodality members as well as names of other priests and nuns who were opposed to the regime. The police promptly arrested such "counterrevolutionaries," and some of them would spend the next forty years in prison. By 1955, fifteen hundred Shanghai Catholics had been arrested, including Bishop Gong Pinmei, the most influential Catholic leader in China. Similar waves of arrest took place throughout the country.[15]

Meanwhile, beginning in 1950, the government was setting up local "Catholic reform committees," which by 1957 had become part of a nationwide "Catholic Patriotic Association," a government "mass organization" that served as a "transmission belt" between the government and Catholics. Most Catholic clergy and laity shunned this organization and in 1950 the Vatican issued a decree excommunicating all who participated. But a small number of clergy did participate, including five bishops, who then ordained other bishops (about forty-one of them by the early 1960s). By Church law these ordinations were "illicit but valid." Some of these collaborating clergy had helped the police identify and arrest other Catholics disloyal to the regime. Most Catholics wanted nothing to do with the Patriotic Association, nor any priests connected with it. The only liturgies that could be celebrated openly were those under the Patriotic Association, and few people attended them. But the faith was carried on quietly at the local level. Where possible, priests surreptitiously said Mass for their congregations. Where not possible, laypeople carried on the prayers themselves. Mothers and grandmothers baptized their children. Although its ecclesiastical structures were destroyed, the Catholic Church carried on as a communal religion.[16]

As noted earlier, evangelists since the sixteenth century had aimed not simply to convert individuals, but whole communities. By the mid-twentieth century whole villages, or at least whole lineages within villages, were Catholic, and in these local communities the faith was embedded in all realms of local life. In many villages Catholics made a distinction between "true-believing" and "lukewarm" Catholics. But as long as they remained in their local Catholic village—and by the late 1950s, communist residence policies made it extremely difficult for a villager to leave his or her home community—even lukewarm Catholics still retained their religious identity. Even if one had hardly ever practiced the faith, one would at least be buried with a Catholic funeral. How else could one connect with one's Catholic ancestors?[17]

Silent, isolated, and without any direct communication with Rome, the Chinese Catholic Church was nonetheless caught up in the vast global movement of the Cold War. From Pope Pius XII on down, Catholic leaders around the world cited the plight of the Chinese Catholic Church in their condemnations of global communism. Clergy and laity who had fled China after the Communist victory were as a whole especially strong in their hostility toward communism. From the viewpoint of both world public opinion and Chinese Communists, the Chinese Catholic Church had become firmly associated with the anticommunist cause of the Nationalist Party—all of which helped increase the suffering of Catholics actually living in China.

The Cold War shaped the pastoral care for the millions of refugees, including hundreds of thousands of Catholics, who fled China after 1949 to Taiwan, to the British colony of Hong Kong, and to the Portuguese colony of Macao. These places were deemed to be bulwarks of the "free world" in the struggle against communism, especially by the United States but also by Britain and the dictatorial Salazar regime in Portugal. Western countries were generous in dispersing foreign aid for the health and welfare of refugee populations, which might have destabilized these territories. Much of the aid was channeled through churches, including Catholic churches, with the help of intermediaries like Catholic Relief Services. Foreign missionaries expelled from China regrouped in Chinese-speaking enclaves outside the country to begin new ministries and provide the main connections to foreign sources of help. In Taiwan, every parish distributed US Agency for International Development relief goods, mainly surplus flour, bulgur, milk, butter oil, and used clothing. Church-run clinics and hospitals obtained medicines that made a big difference in public health.[18]

In Hong Kong the colonial government supplied money to foreign missionaries and religious orders to build elementary schools in the parishes established in the vast resettlement estates in Kowloon. About half of the primary schooling in Hong Kong was conducted through such state-sponsored but church-run schools. Government aid also supported church-affiliated hospitals and clinics. Donations from foreign Catholics helped establish Hong Kong Caritas, one of the largest and best-run comprehensive social service agencies in Hong Kong. Foreign help also enabled the establishment of elite middle schools like the Maryknoll Sisters High School, which turned out streams of elite civil servants, educators, and community leaders.[19] There were also Catholic colleges like the Jesuit-run Wai Yan, but the most prominent Christian colleges, like Chungchi, Lingnam, and Baptist, were sponsored by Protestant denominations. In the small colony of Macao, where Catholicism was the de facto established religion (and which saw itself as a branch of the Portuguese Church), most schools and social services were provided by the Church.[20]

In keeping with pre–Vatican II ecclesiology and the sociopolitical context of the time, the Church was an extremely paternalistic institution. Anxious, displaced, and materially deprived people were dependent on handouts from representatives of a hierarchical institution whose leaders were intermediaries for the material aid provided by national governments eager to facilitate anticommunist development. Some missionaries would eventually worry that they were producing "flour Christians," who only entered their local churches to receive relief goods. However, most of the aid—including education in Catholic schools—was given regardless of religious affiliation. The vulnerability induced into the Church by its role in relief distribution was not from producing nominal Catholics more concerned about food than faith. It was induced by the Church's paternalism. As life in Taiwan, Hong Kong, and Macao stabilized and people began to both cherish an experience of self-reliance and develop a sense of skepticism about established authority, the Church began to suffer setbacks. Numbers of conversions dropped and levels of practice declined. Furthermore, there began to appear limits in the engagement of global powers in Asia.[21]

The case of Taiwan best illustrates this trend. After crises in the Taiwan Straits that opened the possibility of a nuclear war with China, the United States modified its confrontational stance and pursued a policy of "containment," which meant that it was not going to provide military help to Taiwan's government to "retake the mainland." The powerful protector that had bolstered the paternalism of the Church in Taiwan was no longer seen as powerful, and ecclesiastical paternalism was also less credible and gradually less acceptable. A similar situation occurred with the British stance toward Hong Kong. Meanwhile, theological changes were coming that would undermine the justification for paternalism, weaken the rationale for a rigid anticommunism and begin to change the relationship between church and society in the territories on the periphery of Mainland China.[22]

Vatican II Globalization

In the 1960s, a second phase of this new era of globalization began. The Second Vatican Council proposed a new vision of Christian engagement with the world. Meanwhile, the world was changing, as decolonization disrupted Euro-American–centered political orders and new generations of youth challenged the cultures that had sustained these orders.

In its document on the Church, the Second Vatican Council offered a vision of the Church as a people of God, emphasizing the mutual responsibility of all Christians and called for dialogue rather than blind obedience between laity and hierarchy. In the document on religious freedom, the council affirmed the dignity and integrity of conscience and the right of persons in good conscience to follow beliefs that did not conform to Catholic orthodoxy. In its document regarding the Church in the modern world, the council called for the Church to attend to the "joys and the hopes, the griefs and anxieties of the people of this age, especially those who are poor or in any way afflicted, these are the joys and the hopes, the griefs and anxieties of the followers of Christ." The proclamation of these messages coincided with social movements sweeping Asia, as well as the rest of the world—movements against imperialism, racism, and unfettered capitalism. At this stage, the driving force in these movements were the young, especially university students. The vision of Vatican II was carried to such activists by a new generation of young priests and sisters who had become excited and inspired by the council during their religious training. How far and which directions this inculcation of the spirit of Vatican II led depended on local contexts.

In Hong Kong the result was prophetic engagement with student movements that challenged ruling establishments. The ignitor of the spark of Vatican II was Fr. James Hurley, SJ, a young Irish Jesuit who had been inspired in his youth by Patrick Pearse, one of the people executed by the British for helping lead the 1916 Easter Rebellion for Irish Independence, when as W. B. Yeats put it, "a terrible beauty was born." As a teacher of and chaplain to the students at Chu Hai College, Hurley became engaged with the Hong Kong Federation of Catholic Students. The Catholic students were by and large politically passive, focused on their studies and careers. Then in 1966 came a challenge: as the Cultural Revolution swept across Mainland China, riots broke out in Hong Kong, instigated by government officials but in response to local grievances against British colonial rule. Most members of the Catholic Federation of Students were silent and confused in the face of these events and refused to take a stand. Hurley later wrote, "This was my first encounter with the 'closed' Catholic mentality. Moreover, I could see how deeply entrenched it was. The liberation process, I felt, would be a long one and maybe quite painful." Just before the riots, Hurley had led about forty students in a week-long retreat to discuss the Vatican II document on the Church. The seeds of the change in mentality had been planted. At the end of the year students took part in a seminar of the Hong Kong Federation of Students on engagement in politics.[23]

Afterward there was continuing student activism and in the end, with the initially reluctant support of Bishop Francis Hsu, activist priests like Father Hurley, along with sisters and Catholic laity, began to take up an activist role.

Those wishing to respond to the "signs of the times" by participating in movements for social change were now able to network across Asia, often through meetings at the East Asian Pastoral Institute at the Ateneo de Manila in the Philippines. In 1972, four Hong Kong representatives took part in an Asian chaplain formation course in Bangalore, India—the first of its kind in Asia—bringing together chaplains from throughout the region. In their consensus statement the representatives said: "We are convinced that we would betray our trust as priests and as student advisors if we were not to stand by [the students], and struggle along with them in their active socio-political action towards the building of a new society."[24]

The activism begun among students did not stay with students. In Hong Kong, in the early 1970s, Maryknoll priests and sisters, together with other clergy, set up the Populorum

Progressio Center, named after the encyclical of Pope Paul VI by that name, which called for "integral human development." The center engaged with workers who were seeking better pay and working conditions. In 1974, the Justice and Peace Commission was established and eventually became a focal point for social involvement.[25]

At the same time that Vatican II seeds of prophetic activism were being planted in Hong Kong, the Church in Macao, the tiny Portuguese colony just a few hours from Hong Kong by fast boat, was facing its own challenge. In December 1966, large riots broke out, once again instigated by government officials but in response to local grievances with the colonial government. Eleven people were killed and more than two hundred were injured. The Chinese government demanded compensation and apologies and forced the Portuguese government into a humiliating surrender. This marked the de facto control of Macao by the Mainland Chinese government. "The Macao Catholic Church, though it had earned widespread good reputation for social services to both local people and incoming refugees during World War II and after establishment of the Communist regime in China, had lost its social support because of its die-hard support to the Macao colonial government in this incident."[26] Most Catholics in Macao were among the dominant Portuguese elite, and the bishop had always been Portuguese until the installation of Bishop Domingos Lam in 1988. There has never been a Justice and Peace Commission, but the Church has continued to be a major provider of health and educational services on the island.

In Taiwan the Nationalist government under Chiang Kai-shek kept all aspects of civil society under tight surveillance and control. Tens of thousands of dissidents and potential dissidents had been arrested or executed during the White Terror (1947 to late 1950s). Victims were mostly Native Taiwanese who had resisted exploitation by the Nationalist government, which had taken control in 1945, and by the newly arrived Chinese from the mainland who poured into the island after 1949. After 1966, in response to the anti-traditionalist Cultural Revolution in China, the Nationalist government in Taiwan launched the Great Renaissance of Chinese Culture movement, which promoted an authoritarian version of Confucianism. The Catholic Church was mostly passive in the midst of all of this. Most of the local clergy were Mainlanders loyal to the Nationalist government. There were many foreign missionaries, mostly people displaced from the Mainland. A new generation of young missionary clergy arrived in the mid-1960s, enthusiastic about Vatican II, but were often frustrated by the conservative attitudes of the "Old China Hands." Sometimes intense generational struggles took place within the church between younger and older generations and sometimes between Mainland Chinese and foreign clergy. This displaced energy that might have been directed to engaging with the "joys and hopes, the grief and anguish of the people of our time."[27]

Catholic and Protestant Churches had a relatively privileged position in Taiwan. For example, although no Buddhist or Daoist organizations were allowed to establish a university, the Catholics established Furen University in Taipei and the Protestants founded Donghai University in Taizhong. Using methods similar to those of the Communists on the Mainland, the Nationalist government heavily restricted most forms of religion—except for Christianity. During the Cold War, to maintain its fragile position vis-à-vis the People's Republic of China, the Taiwanese government needed the support of missionaries in the United States. But the

Christian churches realized that they could maintain their privileges only by not challenging the government or its elite supporters.[28]

However, the privileges of the Catholic Church were to become a liability. The strength of the American commitment began to wane as early as the mid-1960s. In 1971, President Richard Nixon announced that he would visit Beijing to begin a rapprochement with the Communist regime. At the end of 1971, Taiwan's government—called the Republic of China—was expelled from the United Nations and its seat given to the People's Republic of China. As Taiwan's ability to depend on America weakened, so also did the enthusiasm of people in Taiwan for the Catholic Church. A steep drop in new conversions began around 1965, along with a drifting away from practice by many Catholics.

The loss of reliance on American support combined with economic and, most importantly, theological factors to undermine the paternalistic ecclesiology that had been the foundation for the Taiwan Church. By 1960 the Taiwan economy had stabilized. There was not widespread wealth, at least by first world standards, but neither was there as much dire poverty as before. With less need for handouts of American surplus came a decrease in dependency on Church services.

Besides the relative loss of economic power, Catholic paternalism after the mid-1960s suffered from a loss of moral legitimacy brought about by the Vatican II vision of the Church as less a hierarchical institution and more a people of God. By 1965 clergy were holding workshops to study the Vatican II documents and preparing to implement them. But reaction toward Vatican II was mixed. Many older clergy objected; many younger ones boldly and sometimes recklessly pushed ahead. Even though ordinary people in Taiwan might not have comprehended the fine points of the Vatican II declarations, they could see the confusion and controversy it was causing within the Church. The image of the Church lost its old clarity and the foundations of its paternalism became shaky.[29]

If in anxious, unsettled times some Taiwanese were attracted to a Church that seemed like a strong paterfamilias, in somewhat more settled times such authoritarian strength could seem like a turnoff, especially when it emanated from a now somewhat fickle foreign power. Moreover, the paterfamilias was showing signs of disorientation and even dotage.

Although the Second Vatican Council inspired profound and sometimes unsettling changes in the churches on the periphery of the Chinese mainland, the council had no direct effect on Catholic life in the People's Republic of China. By the early 1960s communication with the outside world had been cut off, and the country was recovering from the terrible famine that had begun in 1958 in the wake of Mao Zedong's disastrous Great Leap Forward. Then, in 1964, Mao launched a series of violent political campaigns, culminating in the Cultural Revolution, which lasted from 1966 to 1976. Although these campaigns were primarily aimed at both real and imagined political enemies, a secondary target was religious life. In northern China, during the Socialist Education Campaign of 1964–65, a target was the lay leadership of village communities who had carried on their faith in the absence of ordained clergy. A special target was the charismatic lay leadership. Henrietta Harrison vividly describes attacks by Communist work teams on some women who claimed to have received apparitions of the Virgin Mary. Such apparitions were indeed not uncommon in rural communities troubled by the roiling political currents of the times.[30]

During the Cultural Revolution, persecution was even more intense. "Red Guards" destroyed many Catholic Churches, along with countless other temples and shrines. Churches that were not destroyed were shuttered, desecrated, or turned into warehouses. Almost all priests and nuns, including those who had joined the Catholic Patriotic Association, were maltreated—sometimes beaten to death—and sent to labor camps. Anyone who openly professed faith was liable for punishment.

Under these circumstances the main concern of Catholics was simple survival. And the Church did survive. Grandmothers secretly baptized their grandchildren. Families furtively said the rosary behind closed doors. The embeddedness of the faith in local community life, especially at the village level, helped it to survive. The belief in a holy hierarchy extending all the way to the successor of Saint Peter also helped sustain the faith. Even though bishops and priests were in jail, the hierarchy was God's creation and, washed with the blood of martyrs, would in God's good time be reconstituted.

Reform-Era Globalization

Mao Zedong died in September 1976, and shortly thereafter his core supporters were toppled in a coup. The leader who emerged was Deng Xiaoping, who twice had been purged by Mao during the Cultural Revolution. Deng consolidated his power by the end of 1978 and launched an era of reform and opening. This began a third phase of late twentieth-century globalization. The Cold War had ended and Chinese communism had been transformed into a kind of state-run capitalism. Led by a rapidly growing China, the world has become more economically interdependent than ever, but more culturally fragmented than in previous generations.

These developments in the Chinese and the global political economy had a deep impact on the situation of the Catholic Church in both Mainland China and the peripheral areas of Greater China. The new regime of the People's Republic loosened controls on religious practice. For the Catholic Church, this meant that many—but not all—priests and sisters would be released from prison and allowed to resume their ministries. Some churches could be reopened and dioceses could even get compensation for some—but not all—of their confiscated or damaged property.

Although the new regime opened up some space for private freedoms, the regime made very clear that it would not tolerate any challenge to the ruling Communist Party. As applied to the Church this meant that all activities had to be conducted under the auspices of the Catholic Patriotic Association, whose leaders were ultimately chosen and supervised by the Communist Party's United Front Department. (Direct supervision was carried out by the State Association for Religious Affairs.) One requirement for belonging to the Patriotic Association was a refusal to accept papal authority, especially in the matter of choosing new bishops. Many Catholics, both clergy and laity (perhaps two-thirds of China's estimated 10 million Catholics) refused to cooperate and formed what is called the "nonregistered" or "underground" Church. The growth of this part of the Church was facilitated by a special dispensation issued by the Vatican in 1978, titled "Faculties and Privileges Granted to Clergy and Laymen who Reside in China under Difficult Circumstances." In view of the difficulties of communicating with the Holy See, bishops in the "underground" were given permission to select other bishops without the need to vet the candidates through the standard Vatican process. They could also run clandestine seminaries without having Vatican-approved curricula. This latitude made possible a dynamic revival of parts of the Chinese Catholic Church not controlled by Rome. The underground distinguished itself from the officially registered part of the Church by its professed loyalty to papal authority, but for practical purposes it was outside the range of that authority.[31]

Understandably, given the persecution it had experienced, the underground harbored strongly anticommunist feelings and rejoiced to hear even limited information about the role the Catholic Church was playing in opposing communism in Poland and other parts of Eastern Europe. Many were inspired by the idea that they might help accomplish in China what the Church was accomplishing in Poland. The underground bishops held a clandestine meeting in the fall of 1989, but it was raided by the police and many of the bishops were jailed. Agitation over this exacerbated tensions between the unregistered and the registered parts of the Church. These tensions were hardened because much of the Church, especially in rural areas, was deeply embedded in local communities. As a result, tensions between underground and official factions often mirrored tensions between different villages or lineages.[32]

Meanwhile, the Vatican began to develop unofficial communications, often through Hong Kong, with Catholics on the ground in China. Through this process it began to give official approval, or an "apostolic mandate," to some of the bishops who had been ordained under the auspices of the Patriotic Association.[33] By 2017 the percentage of such Vatican-approved bishops had reached around 95 percent of all clergy in-country. Nonetheless, a split has persisted between the officially registered and unregistered parts of the Church.

Several negotiations between the Vatican and the Chinese government were held in the 1990s and early 2000s to normalize Vatican connections with the Chinese Church, but all failed. New negotiations began under Pope Francis in 2016 and resulted in a two-year "provisional agreement" reached in 2018, then extended in 2020 for an additional two years, and again in 2022. The main point of conflict is the appointment of bishops. The Chinese government wants control over who gets selected to be a bishop, but the Vatican also insists on control. The text of the provisional agreement remains secret but seems to allow for a process by which bishops nominated by the Chinese government are subject to Vatican disapproval. (The right to disapprove is probably less potent than an absolute veto power.) A small number of new bishops, agreeable to both sides, have been ordained under this new arrangement. From the Vatican side the hope has been that the agreement will build mutual confidence and will lead to better treatment for all Chinese Catholics, including those in the underground. Regrettably, the acceptance of the provisional agreement coincided with implementation of stricter controls on religion under the government policy of sinicization. This has led to tighter controls on all Catholics and new pressures against the underground. Vatican diplomats concede that the outcomes of the agreement have been disappointing, but they recognize some modest progress in episcopal appointments, which they consider better than nothing.[34]

Because of continued poor communication with the universal Church and because of constant local political pressures, the Church in China has been mainly on the defensive.

While growth in Chinese Protestant Christianity has been spectacular, increasing from fewer than a million in 1949 to perhaps sixty million today, Catholic growth has been stagnant, rising from three million in 1949 to about ten million today, not even keeping up with China's natural population increase. Although there was a surge in vocations to the priesthood and religious life in the late 1980s, vocations have now dwindled. However, through many exchange programs with Hong Kong, Taiwan, Europe, and the United States, the teachings of Vatican II have been disseminated. Until the 1980s, liturgies were mostly celebrated in Latin, but now they mostly use the vernacular. Churches in different dioceses have gradually been offering social services like clinics, orphanages, and lepersoria. The Northern Center for Promoting Virtue (Beifangjinde) is an NGO-like social service organization located in the city of Shijiazhuang that carries out poverty alleviation and health promotion programs throughout China.

Through improved communication made possible by rapid economic development, Catholics throughout China, both acknowledged and underground, are now aware of one another. They are also under the leadership of a reconstituted hierarchy, no matter how factionalized and how constrained by political pressure. This has led to a homogenization of Catholic teaching and practice. During periods of upheaval, when communities were out of communication with one another, they developed distinctive local expressions of piety. The Catholic landscape was like a multicolored quilt. Now it is a fabric with varying shades of gray. The parts connected with the official Church are perhaps a lighter shade: they are able to have more communication with global innovations arising from Vatican II and many of their younger priests, sisters, and bishops have studied abroad and are thus more in touch with cosmopolitan perspectives. Without these kinds of experiences the underground tends to be more conservative, clinging to more traditionalist forms of liturgy, harboring suspicion of modern science and philosophy, and using its conservative stance to differentiate itself from the official Church. The theological conservativism may also stem from the need for a strong moral anchor within and among beleaguered communities.[35]

As Mainland China's connections to the global economy increased, Hong Kong's role as a bridge to the global market and a conduit for global finance expanded. Hong Kong played a similar role for religion. The Hong Kong Holy Spirit Seminary opened its doors to train seminarians and priests from the mainland in the latest theology and pastoral practice. In 1979, the Holy Spirit Study Center was established on the seminary's premises with the mission of conducting research on the Church in China and being a node of communication with the Chinese Church. The staff included both foreign and Hong Kong Chinese clergy and laity. One of the founding members was Fr. John Tong, who eventually became Hong Kong's Cardinal Archbishop. In the fashion of classical "Pekingology," the center tried to glean information about the Church from official Chinese publications, but over time it also built up networks of contacts with Catholics throughout China. Another important source of information was the United Catholic Asian News service (UCAN), which through its office in Hong Kong was able to send correspondents to China who could speak the local languages and cultivate contacts.

The new globalizing world order also changed Hong Kong society. Most manufacturing jobs were relocated to the Mainland, especially the bordering Special Economic Zone of Shenzhen. Over time, investment by newly rich Mainland Chinese elite inflated prices in the Hong Kong real estate market, making adequate housing out of reach for a great many middle-class residents. A meager social welfare system increased the populace's feelings of insecurity. Immigrants from Mainland China and elsewhere had mostly been welcomed in the decades after 1949, but immigration was increasingly a controversial subject. Finally, in 1984 the British government conducted a negotiation with the Chinese government to hand Hong Kong back to Chinese sovereignty in 1997 under the proviso that Hong Kong's civil liberties would be preserved for fifty years thereafter. Public controversy about how and to what degree these liberties would be protected was expected, and those controversies exploded into mass protest movements in 2014 and 2019 and led to the passage of a National Security Law by the Beijing government. This new law has suppressed all movements for political freedoms. The Hong Kong Catholic Church was called to respond to these signs of the times.

As mentioned earlier, a network of Catholic activists had grown up in the early 1970s and, in keeping with the spirit of the times, had reached out to non-Catholic Justice and Peace activists throughout Asia with similar concerns. Every year since its founding, the Hong Kong Commission on Justice and Peace has published literature, organized workshops and training sessions, and supported local and international demonstrations for human rights, just pay, and safe working conditions, fair treatment for migrants, and adequate social welfare programs. A few examples include: support for the People's Power movements in the Philippines, which brought down the Marcos dictatorship; anti-globalization movements to protect the livelihood of farmers in Thailand; and protests against the Chinese Tiananmen crackdown in 1989. In the 1990s, a particular focus was on provisions in the Hong Kong Basic Law that would allow for the gradual establishment of democratic governance after Hong Kong returned to Chinese sovereignty.[36]

From 1974 to 2002, the bishop of Hong Kong was John Wu, who was made a cardinal in 1988. Born in Guangdong province but later ordained in Taiwan, Cardinal Wu was the first bishop of Hong Kong to visit the Mainland. He went twice, in 1985, with a delegation to visit churches in Beijing and Shanghai and later in 1986 to Guangdong province, which included a visit to his hometown and a reunion with his eighty-five-year-old mother. In 1989, he wrote a letter to all the bishops of the world requesting them to appeal for justice and democracy in China. At the end of that year he wrote a pastoral letter, "The Dawning of a New Decade," to Catholics in Hong Kong, urging their engagement in democratic civic process. He continued to issue letters on this theme. Because of such activities he never received another invitation to visit Mainland China—a sign of the concerns about Catholic social justice activism from a hardening authoritarian government in China.

In 1996. Joseph Zen was appointed the coadjutor bishop under Cardinal Wu. By personality, Zen is a much more confrontational person than Cardinal Wu and his forthright criticism of the Chinese government's policies has made him persona non grata in China. After Cardinal Wu's death in 2002, Bishop Zen took over leadership of the diocese and in 2006 was appointed a cardinal. Cardinal Zen eagerly engaged in actions for social justice, in particular in protests against the PRC's encroachment on the rule of law in Hong Kong. As a *New York Times* article put it, he has been a "thorn to Beijing" and he has continued this role even after retiring in 2009.[37] Zen has been consistently suspicious of any attempts by the Vatican to reach an accommodation with Beijing about control over the Church in China. In 2022, at the age of ninety-one, he was arrested for supporting activists in the 2019 democratic movement.

Cardinal Zen's successor, Bishop and later Cardinal John Tong, had a more diplomatic style than his predecessor but his approach to social issues and to relations with Mainland China are not fundamentally different in substance. In late 2017, Cardinal Tong retired and Michael Yeung Ming-cheung became the new archbishop. After Bishop Yeung's untimely death in 2019, Cardinal Tong served as an apostolic administrator until the appointment of Jesuit bishop Stephen Chow Sau-yan in 2021.

There are now about 547,000 Catholics in Hong Kong—about 7.7 percent of the total population. Although there is certainly a wide range of opinion among Catholic clergy and laity on social and political issues—top government leaders and prominent protesters have both been Catholic—highly visible organizations like the Justice and Peace Commission take a very active role in pursuit of economic justice and the rule of law, not only for Catholics but for all citizens, and not only in Hong Kong but through networks of concern throughout Asia. These activities will now be greatly curtailed under the National Security Law.

In contrast to Hong Kong's activism, the Church in Macao played a passive role throughout most of the generation after China's reform and opening. Although still formally under the control of Portugal, after the riots of 1966, Macao was in most respects under the control of Beijing and Church leaders did not dare to engage in actions that would meet the disapproval of the Chinese government. With the influx of new immigrants in the 1980s, however, new demands for social services arose and Macau Caritas began to play an innovative role in providing them. Still, there is little incentive for the Church to take up a prophetic role. It has never set up a justice and peace commission.[38]

Although the first Chinese bishop was installed in 1988, the Macao Catholic community remained dominated by a small set of interlocking Portuguese-Chinese families who prized social stability. After Macao formally returned to Chinese sovereignty, it developed into a mecca for the gambling industry and, along with it, lucrative businesses in prostitution and money laundering.

Some Catholic nuns have been leading demonstrations against violence against women, and a group of laity and priests, with help from Hong Kong, have recently organized formation courses on Catholic social teaching. Macau Caritas continues to provide valuable social services and Catholic schools are a mainstay of education. But the number of Catholics remains small—only 5 percent of the population, or about 28,000 in all—and is mostly confined to the Portuguese-Chinese part of the population, with churches confined to the old part of the territory and having little direct presence in the large bustling areas of the garish casinos and hotels.[39]

Finally, the Church stayed largely out of the public sphere during the dramatic changes that took place in Taiwan since the late 1970s. After Chiang Kai-shek died in 1975, his son, Chiang Ching-kuo, assumed power and began a gradual loosening of political constraints. At the same time, Taiwan's economy was beginning an economic takeoff that has brought it prosperity as a leading center for high-tech development in Asia. In this context various elements of an emerging civil society have began advocating for human rights. This movement is especially strong among Native Taiwanese rather than among the mainlanders who had come with Chiang Kai-shek and his Nationalist Party in 1949. But the Church leadership and indeed many of its most influential members were mainlanders. Some foreign missionaries, like the Maryknoll Fathers and Maryknoll Sisters had learned Taiwanese and preached in the local dialect and sympathized with the concerns among grassroots Taiwanese about the domination of the Nationalist Party. A few of them actually supported local activists and got expelled from Taiwan as a result. When three Maryknoll priests took part in an ecumenical prayer service for human rights organized by Presbyterians in Taizhong, they received an open letter signed by 215 Chinese priests that said "it sounds that you are striving for freedom and justice, but in fact you are destroying the unity of the Chinese people. . . . You are destroying the work of the Church. We ask you to leave our country and go to any place else where you could make your ideals come true."[40]

Meanwhile, an emerging middle class was becoming more desirous of establishing the protection of human rights. After a turbulent half decade, in 1987 Chiang Ching-kuo lifted the martial law that had justified authoritarian rule and opened the way to a transition to democracy. One consequence of this was a steady rise of a Taiwan national consciousness—a sense of the people in Taiwan, even those whose parents had come over from the mainland in 1949—that they were a separate people with a separate culture from China. Among the urban middle classes there took place a religious renaissance, but one mostly of Buddhism and Daoism, not of Christianity. People seemed to want a modernized religion with roots in Chinese traditions rather than a foreign religion that had enjoyed special privileges in the era of dictatorship. (One exception was support for the Presbyterian Church in Taiwan, which had long been a supporter of Taiwanese nationalism.) Participation in the Catholic Church declined. In 1970 there were about 300,000 Catholics out of a population of fifteen million, about 2 percent of the total population. Now, there are still only about 300,000 Catholics, but out of a population of 23 million—about 1.4 percent of the population. In many places, Sunday liturgies are now attended more by guest workers from the Philippines than by Native Taiwanese.[41]

The Taiwanese Catholic Church has been relatively passive in civic engagement, with a notable exception of support for workers' rights in the 1990s and, recently, advocacy about family and life issues. For a long time the hierarchy advocated (without much success) against Taiwan's liberal abortion laws and more recently against the death penalty. Recently the Church leadership cooperated with other religions in a failed attempt to block proposals in the legislature to legalize same-sex marriage. Compared with Hong Kong, however, the breadth and depth of Catholic involvement in public affairs has been relatively slight.[42]

Conclusion

The Third Globalization was made possible by political, economic, and social transformations of the last half of the twentieth century, as well as by the theological reformulations of the Church's identity and mission by the Second Vatican Council. Of course, the theological reformulation was absolutely critical, but its effects on the Church in Asia were affected by preexisting conditions and the direction of its progress over those years depended on ongoing transformations in those conditions.

The circumstances faced by the Church in the 1960s and 1970s, nevertheless, influenced the way local churches adapted to their new situation. After being strongly persecuted and cut off from the global Church, the Church in Mainland China in the past generation has undergone some transformation through the theology of Vatican II, but it remains defensive and relatively insular. All parts of the Chinese Church are suspicious of the Communist Party-State, but some parts more than others. There has been increased communication and interaction with the global Church, but the communication and interaction remain constrained and fraught in the context of political control. The Church in Hong Kong aims to be a bridge with the Church in the mainland, but it also has been engaged with local Hong Kong forces that are critical of the mainland and want to resist its pressure. The Church in Macao continues to be rather insular and passive but it has recently been engaging with issues of family life that are brought to the fore by the dominant entertainment industry. The Church in Taiwan has lost much of its membership due to the rise of a Taiwanese nationalism and slowness in responding to the aspirations of a rising educated middle class. All of the areas of the Chinese world share the same basic Chinese traditional culture, but differences in their political, social, and economic circumstances lead the same Catholic theology to be heard, practiced, and institutionalized in different ways. Modern global Catholicism is localized differently in the different localities of the Chinese world.

NOTES

1. Erik Zurcher, "China and the West: The Image of Europe and Its Impact," in Stephan Uhalley Jr. and Xiaoxin Wu, eds., *China and Christianity: Burdened Past, Hopeful Future* (Armonk, NY: M. E. Sharpe, 2001), 43–62.
2. Kwang-ching Liu, "Introduction," in Kwang-Ching Liu, ed., *Orthodoxy in Late Imperial China* (Berkeley: University of California Press, 1990), 1–24.
3. On the rites controversy, see George H. Dunne, SJ, *Generation of Giants: The Story of the Jesuits in China* (Notre Dame, IN: University of Notre Dame Press, 1962); George Minamiki, SJ, *The Chinese Rites Controversy: From its Beginnings to Modern Times* (Chicago: Loyola University Press, 1985); Donald F. St. Sure, SJ, trans., *100 Roman Documents Concerning the Rites Controversy (1645–1941)* (San Francisco: Ricci Institute, University of San Francisco, 1992); J. S. Cummins, *A Question of Rites: Friar Domingo Navarrete and the Jesuits in China* (Aldershot, UK: Scolar, 1993); D. E. Mungello, ed., *The Chinese Rites Controversy: Its History and Meaning* (Sankt Augustin, Germany: Monumenta Serica, 1994); and Andrew Ross, *A Vision Betrayed: The Jesuits in Japan and China* (Maryknoll, NY: Orbis, 1994). The papal decree of 1704 was reaffirmed and strengthened by Clement XI's 1715 apostolic constitution, Ex Illa Die; in 1742, Pope Benedict XIV issued the decree Ex quo singulari, which not only confirmed Clement XI's decision but prohibited any further discussion of the matter.
4. Richard Madsen, "Beyond Orthodoxy: Catholicism as Chinese Folk Religion," in Stephan Uhalley Jr. and Xiaoxin Wu, *China and Christianity: Burdened Past, Hopeful Future* (Armonk, NY: M. E. Sharpe, 2001), 233–47.
5. Robert E. Entemann, "Christian Virgins in Eighteenth Century Sichuan," in Daniel Bays, ed., *Christianity in China: From the Eighteenth Century to the Present* (Stanford, CA: Stanford University Press, 1996), 183–90.
6. See Henrietta Harrison, *The Missionary's Curse and Other Tales from a Chinese Catholic Village* (Berkeley: University of California Press, 2013), 41–64.

7. Ernest P. Young, *Ecclesiastical Colony: China's Catholic Church and the French Religious Protectorate* (New York: Oxford University Press, 2013), 1–14.
8. See Harrison, *The Missionary's Curse*, 65–91.
9. Harrison, 103; Richard Madsen, *China's Catholics: Tragedy and Hope in an Emerging Civil Society* (Berkeley: University of California Press, 1998), 62.
10. Young, *Ecclesiastical Colony*, 54–77. See Joseph W. Esherick, *The Origins of the Boxer Uprising* (Berkeley: University of California Press, 1987).
11. Young, *Ecclesiastical Colony*, 148–232.
12. Madsen, *China's Catholics*, 35–37. For more detail, see Kim-kwong Chan, *Struggling for Survival: The Catholic Church in China, 1949–1970* (Hong Kong: Christian Study Centre on Religion and Culture, 1992).
13. Richard Madsen, "Religion under Communism," in S. A. Smith, ed., *The Oxford Handbook of the History of Communism* (Oxford: Oxford University Press, 2014), 586–91.
14. Jean-Paul Wiest, *Maryknoll in China* (Armonk, NY: M. E. Sharpe, 1988), 395–400.
15. Paul P. Mariani, *Church Militant: Bishop Kung and Catholic Resistance in Communist Shanghai* (Cambridge, MA: Harvard University Press, 2011).
16. Madsen, *China's Catholics*, 34–39.
17. Madsen, 50–75.
18. Nicolas Standaert and R. G. Tiedemann, *Handbook of Christianity in China* (Leiden: Brill, 2009), 795–99.
19. Standaert and Tiedemann, 795–99.
20. Beatrice Leung, "The Portuguese Appeasement Policy in Macao's Church and State Relations," *Journal of Contemporary China* 19 (2010): 381–400; Hao Zhidong, *Macao: History and Society* (Hong Kong: Hong Kong University Press, 2011).
21. Richard Madsen, "Taiwan Tianzhujiaohuide Chengchang yu Shuaitui: yi Malinohuide Liangge Jiaoqu wei Li" (The growth and decline of the Catholic Church in Taiwan: Example of two dioceses of the Maryknoll Fathers), *Taiwan Xuezhi Journal of Taiwan Studies* 6 (2012): 53–76.
22. Madsen, "Taiwan Tianzhujiaohuide Chengchang yu Shuaitui."
23. James Hurley, SJ, *Option for the Deprived* (Hong Kong: Chinese University of Hong Kong Press, 2008), 26–27.
24. Hurley, 56.
25. Hong Kong Diocese, *Tianguodaoshang yu ruoshitongxing: sanshi zhounian jiwang tekan* (The way of heaven accompanying the poor: A special chronicle edition on the thirtieth anniversary) (Hong Kong: Justice and Peace Commission of the Hong Kong Catholic Diocese, 2008), 179–80.
26. Yik Fai Tam, "Macao Roman Catholic Church and Its Limited Involvement with Civil Society," paper presented at the International Conference on Civil Society and Christian Religion in Greater China, Hong Kong Baptist University, December 8, 2016.
27. Madsen, "Taiwan Tianzhujiaohuide Chengchang yu Shuaitui."
28. Richard Madsen, *Democracy's Dharma: Religious Renaissance and Political Development in Taiwan* (Berkeley: University of California Press, 2007), 1–16.
29. Madsen, "Taiwan Tianzhujiaohuide Chengchang yu Shuaitui."
30. Harrison, *The Missionary's Curse*, 145–71.
31. Madsen, *China's Catholics*, 39–45.
32. Madsen, 65–75.
33. Richard Madsen, "Saints and the State: Religious Evolution and Problems of Governance in China," *Asian Perspective* 25, no. 4 (2001): 187–211.
34. See Gerald O'Connell's interview of Archbishop Paul Gallagher, the Vatican secretary for relation with states, in *America Magazine*, July 19, 2022. For Archbishop Gallagher, "The balance sheet [on the Provisional Agreement for appointment of bishops] is not terribly impressive. We've had

six episcopal appointments. . . . So it's not without results. . . . I suppose we would have liked to see more results, and there's much work to be done."

35. Richard Madsen, "Anti-Modern Theology and Pre-Modern Practice: Catholic Indigenization from Below in Modern China," in Vincent Goosaert, Jan Kiely, and John Lagerway, eds., *Modern Chinese Religion* 2 (Leiden: Brill, 2014), 861–64.
36. Hong Kong Diocese, *Tianguodaoshang*.
37. Keith Bradsher, *New York Times*, July 7, 2006.
38. Yik Fai Tam, "Macao Roman Catholic Church."
39. Yik Fai Tam, "Macao Roman Catholic Church."
40. Madsen, "Taiwan Tianzhujiaohuide Chengchang yu Shuaitui."
41. Madsen, *Democracy's Dharma*, 137–39.
42. Kuo Wen-ban, "Christianity and Civic Participation in Taiwan: A Global Perspective," paper presented at the International Conference on Civil Society and Christian Religion in Greater China, Hong Kong Baptist University, December 8, 2016.

4

Going Global

The Transformation of the Korean Catholic Church

DENIS WOO-SEON KIM, SJ

Don't Cry, Tonj (*Uljima t'onjŭ*), a 2010 documentary film on the life of a deceased Korean Catholic missionary priest living in the Sudan, made its main character, Fr. Lee Tae-seok (Yi T'aesŏk), famous throughout South Korea (hereafter Korea). Lee was a priest and medical doctor sent to South Sudan (then Sudan) as a member of the Salesian Congregation, an international Catholic religious congregation. He worked in a village called Tonj, where he served villagers, from the youth to lepers, as a doctor, an educator, and a Catholic priest. He was stricken by cancer, however, and returned to Korea and died there, despite his wish to return to Tonj. His story was documented and aired on KBS (Korea Broadcasting System), a major TV network, and later shown in theaters to great popularity. His story inspired many Koreans to become interested in the Sudan and, more broadly, in international cooperation in developing countries. It spurred volunteers and funding inside and outside Catholic circles. The two governments of Korea and South Sudan sponsored several events and programs in his memory. As a missionary Father Lee served as a bridge between the two countries and seems also to have expanded Koreans' horizons and stimulated their sense of solidarity with others beyond Korea's borders.

Nowadays, Korean missionaries, mainly Protestant, are serving at locations across the globe, from neighboring China and Japan to other regions of Asia, to distant Africa, with some even serving in "Christian" Europe and the Americas, North and South. Of course, not all missionaries leave a legacy such as that of Father Lee. Despite their vast numbers and regional outreach, moreover, they have rarely been studied in fields beyond religious and theological circles oriented toward fostering Christian mission. A few studies have been undertaken of Korean Protestant missionaries, and their work has sometimes been negatively criticized as a form of religious exclusivism using terms such as "Korean Christian triumphalism" or "Korean moral superiority."[1] The work of these missionaries' Catholic counterparts, however, has rarely been examined.

The Catholic Church in South Korea (hereafter KCC) got its start in the late eighteenth century, with the first baptism in 1784. As of 2020, Catholics make up 11.2 percent of the Korean population. For this rapid growth, exceptional for Asia, Korea has been called the

"Asian tiger of Catholicism," highlighting its rapid growth.[2] Among the clergy, Koreans have replaced the missionaries from Europe and the United States: as of 2020, there were 5,382 Korean priests, as opposed to only 156 foreign missionary priests.[3] Thus the KCC has rapidly grown in both believers and clergy. Scholars of Korean Catholicism have examined this transformation in terms of "Koreanization," "indigenization," and "inculturation."[4]

However, a focus on Koreanization or indigenization can lead us to miss a significant transformation that has been taking place in the KCC. This change, already implied in Father Lee's story, is the KCC's globalization, that is, the increase of its international presence and influence.[5] The country has experienced an explosion of missionaries being sent to numerous other countries and it has become committed to collaboration in international development and in responding to emergency situations. For instance, the first Korean missionary priest was sent to Papua New Guinea in 1984. The number of Korean Catholic missionaries increased from 335 in 1996 to 567 in 2008, then to 873 in 2020 and covering eighty countries on six continents.[6] At the same time, the KCC has become dynamically involved in international assistance through emergency response as well as international development in cooperation with such organizations as Caritas International and the One Body and One Spirit Movement (Han maŭm han mom undong). Since the 1970s the KCC has stressed the mission spirit, as expressed in the motto "From a receiving church to a giving church." Though the motto captures the mission spirit of Christianity itself, it also epitomizes the history of the KCC, which could not have survived without the help of missionaries or the material support of the international Church, now grown to proudly assist other churches.

This transformation of the KCC has not earned much attention from academia. The absence of scholarly research implies that this transformation is a new phenomenon. The transformation of the KCC from being a receiving church into a giving one is exceptional for the Catholic Church in the non-Western world. It presupposes not only the growth of local clergy but also national economic development. The Catholic Church in other non-Western areas of the world cannot be said to have fulfilled these conditions. Most still depend on other churches in terms of receiving missionaries or financial support.

The absence of research on this phenomenon is also partly due to the theoretical and methodological approaches of existing research on the KCC (and on Christianity in the non-West in general). On the one side, research has been largely preoccupied with the question of how Catholicism has accommodated itself to Korean cultural and social realities; on the other, it is built on methodological nationalism. The former preoccupation is grounded in the classic stereotype of "Christian West versus Confucian Korea," which assumes a dichotomy of "Koreanized" versus European Catholicism.[7] The latter has resulted in limited research within the territory of Korea and thereby a failure to analyze the transnational flows of the KCC and its implications. These approaches prevent a proper understanding of the transformations that have taken place within the Catholic Church and ignore the dynamic interaction between the Church and globalization.

I here explore the question of what has contributed to the transformation of the KCC from a receiving church to a sending one, in terms of both missionaries and financial resources, with a review of contemporary phenomena and a brief historical account of the KCC. Drawing upon historical and statistical data and interviews, this review calls attention to the push-and-pull factors that led to social and ecclesial changes within the KCC and in particular argues that the KCC's transformation is driven not just by the mission spirit but also is embedded in broader changes within the Catholic Church at the global level. My aim is to help researchers move beyond methodological nationalism and attend to the recent global transformation of the Catholic Church. It begins with an overview of KCC history and a description of the globalization of the KCC, and follows with an examination of international and Korean social and ecclesial factors that have facilitated this transformation to contemplate the implications for contemporary Korea and Catholicism.

THE DYNAMISM BETWEEN GLOBAL AND LOCAL

Since Korea's Catholic community was formed in the late eighteenth century, the KCC has evolved from a sect-like community that endured persecutions, to a community trying to indigenize into Korea, and eventually to a community reaching out globally. This evolution has revealed the dynamic relationship between the global and local.

Korea's first contact with Catholicism was in the seventeenth century, and it came through books—called "Western Learning" (*sŏhak*)—but not by missionaries from the outside. The books were brought by Jesuit missionaries from China; they covered topics such as Western philosophy, science, and Catholicism. Against the backdrop of Neo-Confucianism, the state ideology of Chosŏn Korea, the response to the new learning occurred in three ways: rejection, acceptance, and both, that is, reception of science and technology but rejection of philosophy and religion. Koreans belonging to the "accepter" group progressively formed a faith community without any missionary. In 1784, this community sent Yi Sŭnghun to Beijing to be baptized. The first Catholic missionary to Korea, Fr. Zhou Wenmo, a Chinese priest, arrived in 1794. Thus, the KCC was formed from within. However, the KCC soon faced persecution. As a result, it became a sect-like community until persecutions ended nearly one hundred years later, in 1886.[8]

Among the new phenomena resulting from new ideas and worldviews brought by Catholicism was a new way of life for women. Inspired by the saintly stories of virtuous women, many women chose the status of "virgin" as their vocation, something Chosŏn Korea had never before encountered. This opened a new space for Korean women, where traditionally a woman could not be recognized as a subject without being linked to a husband or father.[9]

A direct and serious encounter with Catholicism was made via the entry of foreign missionaries in what José Casanova presents as the second phase of globalization, Western imperialistic globalization.[10] Following the first two Chinese missionaries in the late eighteenth century, the most missionaries came from the Société des Missions étrangères de Paris (MEP), which took charge of the newly established Chosŏn diocese in 1831. The next groups were German Benedictines in 1908, US Maryknolls in 1923, and Irish Columbans in 1933. The period was characterized by a radical political transformation occurring as well: the decline of Chosŏn Korea, the colonization by Japan (1910–45), and national independence and the Korean War (1950–53). In the history of the Catholic Church, this period of expansion coincided sometimes in collaboration with and sometimes in struggle against the modern world. During this time of turmoil in Korean history, the KCC gradually grew. Theologically, there is only one church, in essence joined with the Western Catholic Church; sociologically, the KCC was a church a transplant, mainly a form of French Catholicism. The leadership of the KCC was composed of missionaries until the first Korean bishop, Paul Roh, was appointed in 1942.[11] Church buildings were constructed in the imitation of the styles of French churches. A hierarchical relationship between clergy and laity was enhanced by the asymmetrical relationship between France and Chosŏn Korea.[12]

Despite the political changes in Korea prior to Vatican II, whether the country was a colonial state or a dictatorship, the Church generally tried to maintain the church-state relationship as a way of securing its institutional well-being. For this reason, some KCC leaders of the colonial period have been criticized for their collaboration with Japanese colonizers. Nevertheless, one must acknowledge the uniqueness of Korea's situation, having been colonized by Japan, not by a Western country whose major religion was Christianity. This exceptional situation prevented a direct link between Catholicism and colonialism commonly found in other colonized countries and constitutes a historical context wherein Koreans did not perceive the KCC as the religion of the colonizer and allowed the growth of the KCC after Vatican II without "historical bondage."

Until Vatican II, the interaction between the global and the local in the KCC was rather one-sided. The reception of Christianity in a given culture involves a dynamic process of interaction between Christianity and the receiving culture, as Christian beliefs and practices brought in by missionaries are taught and expressed in the local politico-cultural setting. Schreiter's three models of local theology—translation, adaptation, and contextual—is helpful for understanding this reception process.[13] The first two models place emphasis on the Christian tradition apart from a specific cultural setting. The translation model considers Christian revelation as the kernel and cultural setting as the husk; the adaptation model conceives of the gospel as the seed and the culture as the soil. For its part, the contextual model concentrates "more directly on cultural settings in which Christianity takes root and receives expression" in what Schreiter calls an ethnographic, liberation approach.[14] In his schema, Catholicism entered Korea as a new Western religion and institution and was received in line with the translation model, not the contextual one.

Three factors reinforced this tendency toward translation. First, from the Korean side, as a historical factor, suppression and persecution for about a century made it difficult for Korean Catholics to reflect upon its creative reception. This is not to ignore the agency Korean Catholics showed in developing Catholicism in accordance with their own needs and situation. They did not have much missionary oversight and had to be rather creative to sustain their faith community. The situation of Catholicism being labeled an evil cult, however, did not allow them the time and resources to deepen their understanding and expression of Catholicism.

Second, the MEP missionaries, who shaped the KCC, were not positive toward modernity—intellectual formation included—in the ecclesial context of the post–French Revolution and post–Enlightenment criticisms of religion.[15] This was manifested in the incident in which MEP Bishop Mutel, the crucial KCC leader from 1890 to 1933, declined An Chunggŭn's suggestion to establish a university to educate Koreans.[16] Finally, the pre–Vatican II Catholic Church did not appreciate but tried to civilize and evangelize the so-called local cultures.[17]

Vatican II brought about a Copernican revolution, not just to the Church at the global level but also to the KCC. Its important impact on the KCC was less about dogmatic issues and more about the Church's relationship with the world. For the KCC, a minor religion in a poor country, it did not matter whether the Church was identified with the hierarchy or with the people of God. Most Korean believers did not understand or care about such a distinction. There was no debate over Pope Paul VI's 1968 encyclical *Humanae Vitae*, which rejected artificial contraception and thus disappointed many liberal and progressive Catholic believers in Europe and North America. The Korean state had already been promoting family planning since 1961, and despite the Church hierarchy's opposition to abortion and artificial contraception, Korean Catholic believers' conformity to the state program did not differ much from other Koreans.[18] Nevertheless, Vatican II transformed the KCC from an inward-focused Church to an outward, engaging one. Vatican II enabled the KCC to reorient itself from the position of bystander or opportunist in Korean history to being an active engager. Based on Catholic social teachings, including *Gaudium et Spes* (Pastoral Constitution on the Church in the Modern World) that emerged from Vatican II, the KCC came to contribute to Korean democratization and the human and labor rights movements of the 1970s and 1980s.

A close analysis of the KCC's reception of Vatican II reveals a dynamic relationship between the global and the local. Vatican II at the global level did not automatically result in the KCC's transformation. The reception of Vatican II required more than a translation of its documents, namely, it necessitated the interpretation and application of those documents to the Korean context. This presupposes agents who are able to interpret and apply them in the concrete Korean context. KCC leaders, particularly Stephen Cardinal Kim, who observed Vatican II with keen eyes during his days of study in Germany, played a crucial role in this regard. A group of progressive priests who established the Catholic Priests' Association for Justice (CPAJ) was also important. The Korean sociopolitical context in which they struggled to adapt was that of a "developmental dictatorship," which justified both dictatorship and human rights violations in the cause of development. Reverend Se-woong Hahm, a founder of CPAJ and a theologian, poignantly describes how this context, of both oppressive dictatorship and participation in resistance, became a hermeneutical key to grasping Vatican II, especially *Gaudium et Spes*: "We learnt the spirit and the teaching of Vatican II not in the classroom or at school. We learnt them in concrete life, a life in anguish, in tears, being beaten, chased by police, or in prison. We learnt by experience on the sites of terrible oppression. Indeed, it was a precious experience."[19]

The KCC, led by Cardinal Kim and others, resisted the abuses of dictatorship and advocated for the rights of those marginalized in the process of development.[20] This participation in and contribution to democratization and human rights made the KCC a part of Korean history, a rare case in Asia, leading Catholicism to no longer be perceived as a religion from the West. In short, the KCC had become Koreanized. However, it should be emphasized that it was Koreanized owing to its contribution to Korean history rather than its quantitative growth or indigenization of a Korean clergy per se.

GLOBALIZATION OF THE KOREAN CATHOLIC CHURCH

Since the late twentieth century, the Korean Catholic Church has rapidly globalized. This globalization includes, on the one hand, the diversification of international communities within Korea, notably displayed in the multiplication of Filipino and Vietnamese migrant communities, and, on the other, of the growth of Korean Catholic communities internationally, such as among Korean immigrants in the United States. Globalization here refers to the KCC's outreach to other countries. The KCC has become a major missionary-sending church as well as a church involved in international humanitarian and developmental assistance.

Until the mid-twentieth century, it was mainly French missionaries of the MEP who enabled the survival of the KCC; they constituted its backbone. From its beginnings, the KCC was banned by the Chosŏn authorities and suffered several persecutions. Following these persecutions, the formation of Korean seminarians became possible within Korea. Not until 1944, however, did Korean clergy outnumber foreign missionaries. The first religious congregation of women came from France. The year 1888 saw the arrival of the Sisters of Saint Paul of Chartres, now one of the largest religious congregations in Korea. Put simply, in its early years the KCC depended upon the support of the French Church.

Since the mid-twentieth century, the number of Korean clergy has increased dramatically. There were 298 Korean clergy in 1962, at the start of Vatican II, increasing to 530 by 1970, to 916 by 1980, to 1,504 by 1990, to 2,891 by 2000, and to 5,382 by 2020 (see table 4.1). Today, the KCC has become a missionary-sending church. In 1975, while still a dependent church, the KCC founded the Korean Missionary Society and sent its first missionaries to Papua New Guinea in 1981. The number of Korean Catholic missionaries accelerated from 335 in 1996 to 873 in 2020, and they were serving in eighty countries on six continents. Traditionally Christian Europe and the Americas have received just under 45 percent of them (130 in Europe and 262 in the Americas), but Asia received the largest overall number, 364 (see table 4.2). Of the total number of missionaries, just over 86 percent come from religious congregations and societies—largely women's—with the remaining 14 percent coming from diocesan clergy, a number that steeply increased from 2010 to 2020. It is important to note, however, that Korean missionaries had been sent out even earlier than 1981 through various religious orders, congregations, and missionary societies. Although it is not easy to identify the first Korean missionary, it is clear that several Korean religious men and women were sent abroad for overseas missions. For instance, in 1968, Sr. Lucia Yu was missioned to Kenya as a Maryknoll sister. Figure 4.1 illustrates the recent rapid increase in Korean missionaries.

The transformation becomes even more vivid when examining the present "reversed mission flow" between France and Korea. In 1895, after religious freedom was granted in Korea, there were about 38 French priests, but not a single Korean one.[21] Contrariwise, in 2020 the French Church received 40 Korean missionaries, among whom were 11 priests and 29 nuns. This reversed mission flow dramatically manifests the explosive growth of the KCC as well as the French Catholic Church's own growing need for missionary support. It reveals as well the transformation of the overall landscape of global Catholicism.

The KCC sends abroad not only missionaries, but also financial resources. A survey published in 2012 reveals how the KCC's involvement in international humanitarian and

TABLE 4.1. Number of Catholic clergy in Korea, 1865–2020

	Korean clergy	Foreign clergy
1865	0	16
1895	0	38
1900	12	40
1910	15	47
1920	30	43
1930	85	51
1944	133	107
1962	298	251
1970	530	369
1975	709	294
1980	916	250
1985	1,130	234
1990	1,504	201
1995	2,208	203
2000	2,891	200
2010	4,314	176
2015	4,909	153
2020	5,382	156

Source: CBCK (Catholic Bishops' Conference of Korea). The CBCK collects sound statistical data and publishes it on its website. For data from prior to 2000 see the website's history section, http://www.cbck.or.kr/page/page.asp?p_code=K3100; for data from after 2000 see the data section, http://www.cbck.or.kr/bbs/bbs_list.asp?board_id=K7200; for 2020 see http://ebook.cbck.or.kr/gallery/view.asp?seq=214863, accessed August 8, 2022.

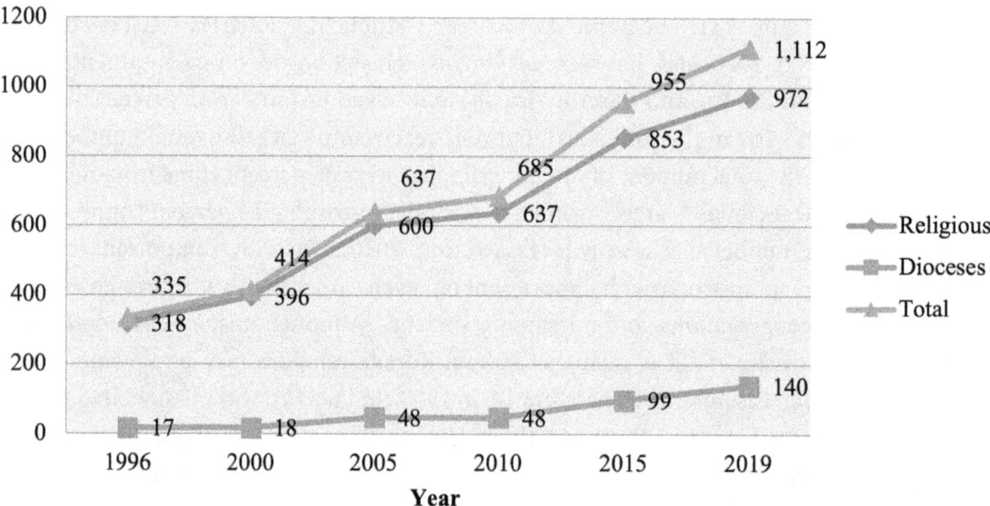

FIGURE 4.1. Religious and diocesan Korean missionaries (1996–2019). *Source:* Pontifical Mission Societies in Korea, "P'agyŏn hyŏnhwa" (Dispatch status), https://www.pmsk.net/missionary/status, accessed March 14, 2021.

developmental assistance began with assistance to Ethiopia by the Salesian Sisters of Don Bosco in 1983, followed by Caritas Korea (formerly called the Human Development Committee) in 1985.[22] In 1992, the Catholic Bishops' Conference of Korea (CBCK) officially committed the KCC to providing international developmental assistance, which began to work at the international level. During the period 2006–10, such assistance came to have multiple

TABLE 4.2. KCC mission countries and missionaries, by continent, 2020

Continent	Number of countries	Number of KCC missionaries
Asia	22	364
Africa	20	78
America (North and South)	19	262
Europe	14	130
Oceania	5	39
Total	**80**	**873**

Source: http://ebook.cbck.or.kr/gallery/view.asp?seq=214863, 50–52.

TABLE 4.3. Total KCC international development assistance, 2006–10

Actor	Project	Total assistance (wŏn)
Diocese	239	11,520,000,000
Religious congregations	277	10,450,000,000
Caritas Korea	151	6,570,000,000
General secretariat of CBCK	13	4,600,000,000
Other	142	10,140,000,000
Total	**822**	**43,280,000,000**

Source: Caritas Korea (2012), 28.

actors in the KCC: Caritas Korea, the General Secretariat of the Bishops' Conference, sixteen dioceses, thirty-six religious congregations, and five apostolic organizations among them. The total amount of financial assistance provided by the KCC during this period reached about 43 billion wŏn (US$37.5 million) (table 4.3).

Due to the multiple actors within the KCC, it is difficult to collect data on the historical trends of the Church's involvement in this area. Nonetheless it is useful to attempt to identify the major actors and examine the historical trends. Although thirty-six religious congregations are involved, the amount of assistance by each congregation is relatively small. Considering other individual organizations, the oldest and largest are Caritas Korea and the Seoul Archdiocese's One Body and One Spirit Movement (OBOS). Caritas Korea is a member of Caritas International, a confederation of about 160 Catholic relief, development, and social service organizations. Caritas Korea was established in 1975 by the CBCK and is formally known as the Human Development Committee. It began with overseas aid of 1,044,015,750 *wŏn* for 39 projects in 1993 and has expended to a total of 42 billion wŏn (about US$38.8 million) in 2015 for 815 projects in eighty-five countries (table 4.4).

Whereas Caritas Korea is run directly by the Korean Bishops' Conference, OBOS (established in 1989) is run primarily by the Seoul Archdiocese as part of its social and international ministries. Whereas Caritas Korea focuses solely on international development, OBOS—which conducted international outreach from its inception—also contributes to domestic social programs and a project for North Korea. Table 4.5 illustrates the historical growth of its international collaboration. Excluding 1989, when it was not yet ready to raise funds, OBOS's contributions to such collaboration from 1990 to 2015 increased more than threefold, from 83.6 million wŏn in 1990 to 2.8 billion wŏn (about US$2.6 million) in 2015.

TABLE 4.4. Caritas Korea development projects, 1993–2015

Year	Number of projects	Amount of assistance (wŏn)	Year	Number of projects	Amount of assistance (wŏn)
1993	39	1,044,015,750	2005	30	2,314,827,266
1994	53	1,016,193,600	2006	30	1,835,711,660
1995	36	1,156,345,158	2007	40	1,535,022,334
1996	32	1,338,282,839	2008	33	1,499,014,598
1997	29	606,789,100	2009	33	1,737,283,625
1998	29	924,338,955	2010	28	2,026,191,813
1999	33	1,032,072,051	2011	32	2,718,783,857
2000	40	1,038,566,498	2012	48	3,413,248,028
2001	18	1,183,051,960	2013	48	3,567,181,762
2002	22	906,217,394	2014	55	3,690,830,235
2003	23	1,300,221,998	2015	57	4,849,750,999
2004	27	1,460,651,708			
Total (1993–2015)				**815**	**42,194,593,188**

Source: Data for 1993 to 2014 provided by Caritas Korea; data for 2015 is the sum of emergency response and international development as shown on the Caritas Korea website (http://www.cbck.or.kr/page/page.asp?p_code=K2370).

TABLE 4.5. International development projects by One Body and One Spirit Movement, 1989–2015

Year	Total assistance (Korean wŏn)	Countries assisted	Number of projects
1989	2,100,000	1	1
1995	226,524,628	6	37
2000	303,000,000	5	5
2005	1,679,506,096	17	31
2010	2,854,725,257	11	28
2015	2,836,835,443	16	31
Total 1989–2015	**22,723,914,565**	**269**	**519**

Source: Data provided in a personal communication with One Body and One Spirit Movement.

An examination of the activities of just these two organizations, Caritas Korea and the One Body and One Spirit Movement, shows the rapid increase of the KCC's involvement in international development collaboration. The rapid globalization of the KCC over the past twenty-five years is thus manifested in both the surge of Korean Catholic missionary activities and the KCC's commitment to aiding international development.

What factors have contributed to this transformation of the KCC? The KCC itself understands the transformation within the framework of "from a receiving Church to a giving Church."[23] This motto is useful for mobilizing funds by drawing upon the pride of Koreans. However, one must not miss the motto's other implications of this motto: it well captures the international thrust of the Christian spirit. Christianity seeks to reach out for mission. It also reminds the faithful of the KCC's history as a church supported by other churches. Missionaries sustained the KCC in hard times. During the KCC's century of persecution, MEP missionaries went to Korea knowing that they likely would die there. Prior to the 1960s, when Korea was one of the world's poorest countries, many missionaries helped Korea by establishing medical or educational institutions. Some missionaries even played key roles in rural community development through entrepreneurship (what we today would call social entrepreneurship); two examples are the Isidore Farm established by Columban priests on Jeju in 1961, and Imsil Cheese, founded in 1969 by a Belgian missionary in Imsil. The motto "from receiving to giving" expresses this sense of indebtedness.

For researchers, however, one risks methodological nationalism in locating the KCC at the center of the research horizon. Doing so can miss the significance of the transnational flow already imbedded in the intrinsic international nature of the Catholic Church per se, which has been accelerated by the recent ethos of globalization. The giving nature of the KCC was already manifest in the outward missionary flow of its international religious congregations, as in the case of Sr. Lucia Yu in 1968 and in the international development collaboration of the Salesian Sisters' project in Ethiopia in 1983, which predated both Caritas Korea and OBOS. As a medical doctor, moreover, Sister Yu is a good example of the involvement of the Korean Church in international development. Moving beyond methodological nationalism, the historical and social context of push-and-pull factors within the universal Church itself are noteworthy: Korean national factors pushed the KCC to becoming globalized, but external factors pulled the KCC from abroad.

ECCLESIAL CONTEXT OF THE KCC'S GLOBALIZATION

Certain internal factors pushed the KCC to go global, and other factors pulled it from the outside, including transnational networks.

Push Factors

Although some have relativized the significance of the spirit of "from a receiving to a giving" Church, one cannot ignore that the sense of Christian mission constitutes a strong push factor. The establishment of the Korean Missionary Society (KMS) in 1975, when the KCC was still weak, manifests this spirit. In April 1982, the KMS sent the first Korean missionary priests to Papua New Guinea. The first KMS priest, Fr. Kim Dong-ki, later responded to some concerns that it was too early to send out Korean missionaries:

> It is necessary to examine the question of why we send priests abroad even though we lack them here [in Korea]. It was not only after they had traveled through all [villages] of Israel that the twelve apostles reached out abroad. [. . .] It is not the true spirit of the Church to give some left-overs to others [when we have enough]. In this sense, the spirit of moving beyond diocese and region is that of the Korean Missionary Society. In my view, it corresponds to the spirit of the Gospels.[24]

Father Kim conceived the catholic-universalistic spirit as a key aspect of Catholic identity. It was this spirit that led him to move beyond Korea's territorial and national boundaries.

Furthermore, the KCC's growth, in particular the explosive increase of Korean clergy and religious, has pushed it to move out toward overseas missions. In the case of international orders and congregations, openness to overseas mission is an essential element. The case of the diocesan clergy is different, for they are trained to serve within the diocese, primarily as pastors in local parishes. In the 1970s and 1980s, the diocesan clergy's options were limited to ministering to parish needs. Other ministries, such as educational, social, and spiritual ministries, were considered secondary. This pastoral orientation was one of the factors that led foreign missionaries, rather than the Korean diocesan clergy, to initiate major social ministries, such as those for workers, migrants, the urban poor, the addicted, and so forth. However, the upsurge in the number of diocesan clergy (see table 4.1) gave rise to an unintended consequence: a long delay for newly ordained priests becoming pastors with canonical administrative authority. The increase in the number of diocesan clergy surpassed that of parish priests, which meant that younger parish priests had to wait years to become pastors. This congestion led several major Korean dioceses to encourage overseas mission work. Father Song from the Archdiocese of Seoul, a missionary in Chile from 1999 to 2005, noted in the *Catholic Peace Times* how during one February 2013 meeting of priests in the Seoul Archdiocese, overseas mission was suggested as a way of easing the clergy personnel congestion of the archdiocese.[25] The rapid increase in the number of Korean priests partly explains the upsurge of missionary activities by diocesan clergy.

The case of religious orders is similar. The number of Korean religious missionaries increased from 318 in 1996 to 873 in 2020, with most coming from women's congregations. In the same period, the total number of Korean women religious increased from 7,584 in 1996 to 10,152 in 2020. As with the increase in diocesan clergy, the rapid increase of women religious has led to an unintended negative consequence: aging generation of nuns who continue to remain in leadership positions for long periods leads to communities lacking the ability to absorb the fresh spirit of their many young members. The frustration felt by the younger generation, imbued with the desire to pursue the ideal religious life, has thus led them to volunteer for overseas missions. Sisters of the younger generation feel checked by the hierarchical traditions of their congregations, enhanced by the Korean Confucian cultural legacy of respect for the elderly. Though many are already in their forties, they are treated as youths. Korean sisters have raised concerns about the hierarchical culture among the clergy; not surprisingly, however, they experience the same practices in their own congregations when they are treated as minors.

The explosive increase in the number of clergy and religious has pushed many of them to opt for overseas mission work. While the upsurge in numbers may be the immediate cause of this outward movement, it is mediated by the push factors of inner frustration and personnel congestion.

Pull Factors

The KCC's move toward the global is not merely a consequence of push factors. The contemporary transformation within the global Catholic Church has strongly pulled the KCC out of its national boundary. One aspect of this transformation is the rapid decline in the number of clergy and religious in the traditional Catholic countries in the West. Until the mid-twentieth century, it was the Church in the West that was able to send missionaries. However, both the rapid decline of vocations in the West and the growing Church in Asia and Africa have led to a demographic transition in the world of Catholic clergy and religious. The traditional missionary-sending countries have found themselves in dire need of missionaries and have searched to recruit them. It is no surprise, then, that the KCC has emerged as a sending country, symbolically manifested in the reversed missionary flow between France and Korea.

Not surprisingly, the largest group of Korean Catholic missionaries are sent to Asia (see table 4.2). Among them, the Philippines is the largest receiving country for Korean missionaries, followed by Vietnam, China, Japan, and Indonesia.[26] This shows that the KCC has sent its missionaries to geographically and culturally proximate countries. At the same time, and more importantly, it reveals that the KCC has been gradually taking over the region's missionary work, traditionally led by its Western counterparts. For instance, the Jesuit mission in Cambodia is under the responsibility of the Korean Province of the Society of Jesus. The KCC is also a key supporter of the nascent Mongolian Church.[27] Obviously, the Philippines, a "Catholic" country, has sent more missionaries than the KCC has.[28] However, owing to Korean economic power, the KCC not only sends missionaries but also provides financial assistance, which mainly funds medical and educational projects.

Transnational Networks

These push-and-pull factors expand the ecclesial context. However, it is the transnational networks at the various levels that connect the push-pull factors and catalyze their links. Particularly noticeable is the link to international orders and congregations. The first Korean missionary, Lucia Yu, was sent via the Maryknoll Sisters in 1968. The first foreign aid from the KCC came through the Salesian network established between Korea and Ethiopia. Diocesan clergy and religious from local congregations rely on these international congregations and the *fidei donum* (gift of faith) when they open a new mission.[29]

The increase of networks and upsurge in globalization has aided KCC's global outreach and has created a social environment that facilitates the work of the KCC for global needs. More young lay Catholics have come to work in these networks and receive professional training in the field; their skills, experiences in non-ecclesial NGOs and GOs (governmental organizations), and network connections have become a reservoir for supplying experienced professionals to the KCC system.

SOCIAL CONTEXT OF THE KCC'S GLOBALIZATION

The authors of the 2012 survey already mentioned rightly point to three factors that make possible the growth of the KCC's involvement in international development: the KCC's rapid development, Korea's overall economic growth, and the commitment of the KCC leadership.[30] In addition to the KCC's internal factors, the globalization of the KCC cannot be properly understood solely by Korea's economic growth. Obviously, since the 1990s Korea has been transformed from a recipient of official development assistance (or ODA) to a donator of it; and its economic development is the economic foundation for the KCC's international involvement.[31] However, one must see events within the KCC in the context of globalization of Korea as a whole. The nation has become globalized, and its globalization is the context in which the KCC exists.

A term often used to describe Korea's societal transformation is "compressed modernity," defined as "a civilizational condition in which economic, political, social and/or cultural changes occur in an extremely condensed manner in respect to both time and space, and in which the dynamic coexistence of mutually disparate historical and social elements leads to the construction and reconstruction of a highly complex and fluid social system."[32] This concept emphasizes not only the intensity of transformation, but also its consequent fluidity. This fluid condition has enhanced the "catch-up" spirit as a collective ethos of Koreans. Korea has endeavored to catch up with Japan and other advanced Western countries. In a similar pattern, social actors, whether organizations or individuals, have worked to catch up with whoever is perceived as being advanced. The KCC's globalization can be better understood in this sociocultural context.

Therefore, in order to understand the KCC's activities, we need to locate them within a broader context, that of the involvement of Korean NGOs in transnational activities. Despite its rapid growth, the amount of the KCC's international development cooperation constitutes a very small portion of the total amount of assistance delivered by Korean NGOs as a whole. For 2009, the KCC's international assistance amounted to 7.3 billion wŏn, a mere 4 percent of the 172 billion wŏn provided by the fifty other Korean NGOs that were surveyed by the Korean NGO Council for Overseas Development Cooperation.[33] Moreover, according to a 2017 survey, 135 out of 140 NGOs began operations since the 1990s[34] (see table 4.6). This means that one cannot appropriately comprehend the KCC's commitment to international development cooperation solely in terms of either the ecclesial factors of the Christian spirit or its prevailing transnational characteristics. Korea's economic development and globalization have created a social space and ethos in which many Koreans and Korean organizations have passionately engaged in international development. Although OBOS and Caritas Korea began their activities earlier than most Korean NGOs, they grew together with the growth of Korean globalization and reinforced that globalization. The fact that the KCC's contribution to international assistance amounts to only 4 percent of the total is noteworthy, since members of the KCC comprise 11.1 percent of the Korean population.

A comparison with one of the KCC's counterparts, the Korean Protestant Church, relativizes the rapid increase of Korean Catholic missionary activity. Korean Protestant missionaries abroad have grown remarkably, from only 93 in 1979 to nearly 15,000 in 2006, and 20,467 in 2014. In the same period, the number of target countries of Protestant missionaries increased from 26 to 168.[35] In the global Protestant Church, Korea is considered one of the top five missionary-sending countries. Considering that Koreans are a monoethnic and monocultural people, their active role in world mission work appears even more remarkable. Korean Protestant missionaries "have become known for aggressively going to . . . the hardest-to-evangelize corners of the world," even at times being "at odds with the foreign policy of South Korea's government." Some Korean Protestant missionaries have even been imprisoned in China, kidnapped in Afghanistan, and murdered in the Middle East. Despite some tragedies, a Protestant theologian has observed that "in most mission fields they are

TABLE 4.6. Expansion of Korean NGOs' international development projects

Years	Number of NGOs
1960–1969	1
1980–1989	4
1990–1999	34
2000–2009	60
2010–2017	41

Source: For pre-1990 data: "2013 Kukche kaebal hyŏmnyŏk NGO p'yŏllam 2013" (Korean International Development Cooperation CSO Statistics Handbook 2013), 15, available at http://www.ngokcoc.or.kr/bbs/board.php?bo_table=paper01&wr_id=72&&page=9. For post-1990 data: "Kukche kaebal hyŏmnyŏk NGO p'yŏllam 2017" (Korean International Development Cooperation CSO Statistics Handbook 2017), http://ngokcoc.or.kr/bbs/board.php?bo_table=paper01&wr_id=152.

more readily accepted by the local people than are Western missionaries, who may suffer from their own postcolonial guilt as well as from a perception of their being imperialistic."[36] In any case, in juxtaposition with Korean Protestant missionary activity, the rapid growth of the KCC's missionary work seems less impressive.

These two comparisons—with Korean NGOs' increasing international participation and then in light of what is occurring among Protestant missionaries—provide a glimpse of the overall picture of Korea's globalization in which the KCC's globalization has taken place. These comparisons do not imply that Korean NGOs' involvement in international development or the international deployment of Korean Protestant missionaries is a cause of the KCC's limited globalization. However, one must acknowledge that Korea's globalization has created a social environment wherein the KCC has been making efforts to go global.

PROSPECTS AND IMPLICATIONS

It is expected that the expansion of the KCC will continue for the time being, despite the recent decline in vocations to the priesthood and religious life in Korea. The recent decline may not instantly affect KCC expansion itself, but it could usher in a lay missionary movement. This prediction is based on the following two ecclesial and two nonecclesial observations.

First, the impact of the demographic transition of religious vocations being experienced by the global Church is very immediate. Many of the churches in mission areas, which have traditionally relied on the assistance of the Church in the West, still need external support. Even traditionally Christian Europe faces a shortage in the ministry, both priests and religious, and requires assistance from abroad. In his speech of Christmas greetings to Vatican officials in 2019, Pope Francis called to mind that the traditional distinction between "a Christian world and a world yet to be evangelized" is no longer relevant in the contemporary world.[37] Europe demands evangelization no less than Asia and Africa. In line with his predecessors John Paul II and Benedict XVI, Francis urges a new evangelization and re-evangelization.[38] Though he does not explicitly say so, this is surely a first, not only for non-Western areas but also for the West itself. Not surprisingly, in 2020, 130 out of 873 Korean Catholic missionaries were working in fourteen European countries, the majority in what were once termed Catholic countries, such as France, Italy, Spain, and Ireland.[39] The demographic changes in the numbers of priests and nuns in the global Church demand contributions from the Church in Asia and Africa. The Korean Catholic Church is one of the rare ones willing and able to send out missionaries and provide financial support.

Second, the history of the KCC is a factor enticing the Church in other countries to turn to Korea for help. Just as Korea's rapid economic development, often referred to as the "miracle on the Han," has attracted many developing countries, the KCC has its own historical factors that serve to attract churches from both the Western and non-Western world. The faith was initially planted in Korea not by outside missionaries, but by Koreans. Moreover, the KCC experienced a period of martyrdom, contributed to Korean history by its participation in movements for human rights and democratization, and transformed itself from a church dependent on foreign missionaries and aid to a church prepared to serve beyond its borders.

Finally, the KCC has a historical advantage in that Korea was colonized by Japan, and thus the KCC has no link to Western imperialism. This has freed the KCC from postcolonial guilt and imperialistic perceptions, an advantage akin to that possessed by Korean Protestant missionaries. The popularity of contemporary K-drama and K-pop also adds an element of soft power to this historical advantage.

It is not difficult to imagine that the KCC's growing presence and mission, especially in Asia, will add a "Korean-style" Catholicism to the local Church, just as French missionaries imparted many French attributes to the KCC. The Irish missions donated the practice of private confession to Europe, something that became universally practiced. Recently, an Indian style of meditation, such as that of Anthony de Mello, has become popular and globalized, adding a new element to the traditional recited or contemplative prayer. Although it is too early to identify what Korean trait might enrich universal Catholicism, one might point out some characteristics of Korean Catholicism. One of them would be organizational skills. Just as Korean development (and East Asian development) has been based on state-led development, the KCC's development has been led by effective administration and leadership at the diocesan and parish levels. The KCC's performance in this regard was well manifested in a series of mass rallies it organized, starting at the 150th anniversary of the establishment of the Chosŏn diocese in 1981, to one celebrating the bicentennial anniversary of the KCC in 1984, and to the most recent, the Papal mass for the beatification of 124 Korean martyrs in 2014. Although about a million had gathered in Seoul for that event, the mammoth plaza was clean after the rallies. The mass rally is an example of the mobilization and organizing of believers and resources. On a much smaller scale, it also requires certain organizing skills to run a parish or diocese. Despite many internal tensions, Korean parishes and dioceses have efficiently managed their growing bodies, demonstrating an ability to include small communities and diverse organizations that work for devotional and spiritual movements or social justice–oriented action. The KCC's organizational skills might be disseminated by those outreaching Korean missionaries.

However, the increase in missionaries and international development assistance does not merely mean the expansion of the KCC's influence; it can also have a "boomerang" effect, and bring about a new awareness of Koreanness or the KCC's cultural practices. One nun, who returned to Korea after living and working in Italy for sixteen years, describes her experiences:

> After I returned to Korea, it was not easy to readjust to Korea. Our community demanded too much conformity. To me, this was not based so much on our religious life, but rather on Korean style. It is a kind of a homogenization or standardization of everybody's life. [. . .] When I became a superior in a house, I tried to be a kind of coordinator rather than a superior, delegating some authority to other members.[40]

The contemporary notion of overseas mission tends to be understood not as a "going to and dying in" the mission country, but more as serving there for a certain number of years. This has been the pattern of most Korean overseas missionaries and implies that overseas missions will produce many "returnees." They will then accelerate the dynamic interaction, manifested in this sister's comments, between the global and the local in the KCC, but in a manner that is different from the way Western missionaries encountered Korea in the last century. As confirmed by a recent study by Ga-young Lee and the author on returnees from voluntary international service in a secular context, young Korean returnees, after serving for several years, have been reported to manifest a reconfiguration of their national identities, varying from refreshed Koreanness to a transnational, cosmopolitan identity.[41] For instance, some returnees come to affirm their Korean identity and want to commit themselves to building a better Korea. Others come to identify as more cosmopolitan and feel most in line with those of the region or country from which they returned. One returnee from Nepal offers a dramatic case. This returnee was more concerned about the 2015 earthquake victims in Nepal than the Korean victims of the 2014 Sewol ferry incident, which had given rise to fervent emotions among Koreans at the time.[42] If two or three years of international voluntary service transforms these volunteers in the secular context, it would not be difficult to imagine missionaries who spend more than five years, even some decades, in their commissioned region would lead to not just religious but also cultural transformation. In addition to individual missionary transformation, missionaries may have an influence on the larger communities around them—family, parish, and the supporters of the mission project. Their mission stories can link these Koreans with the local population in the foreign mission area. Therefore, the KCC's globalization means not merely a one-way expansion of the KCC, but also a new way of becoming both Korean and Catholic-universal.

CONCLUSION

The KCC has evolved from a sect-like community to a community that has become a major religion, and to a community trying to reach out globally—the Asian tiger of Catholicism. In this evolution since Vatican II, the KCC has been rapidly transformed in a dual sense: from inward- to outward-looking and from national to more catholic-universalistic. The KCC's globalization, on the one hand, challenges the widespread stereotype of the "Christian West versus Confucian East Asia." Contemporary Korea has felt the influence of Christianity—both Protestantism and Catholicism—no less than Confucianism and Buddhism. The KCC's globalization, on the other hand, suggests that Catholicism cannot be exhausted by the West. Korean Catholicism is not merely a receiver of Western Catholicism, but is also becoming an active contributor to the global Catholicism by enriching it with Korean cultural and religious elements. Just like the Church in the West, so is the Korean Church enriching global Catholicism.

The KCC's global movement invites scholarship that further investigates the mission activities of Korean Catholic missionaries, and how these activities differ from those caused by their Western counterparts during the period of Western hegemonic globalization. The latter activities have been criticized, if not as the "arms of Western imperialism" or cultural imperialism, but at least harmful to the local by the imposition of Western religion. The study of Korean missionaries may contribute to a deeper understanding of the development of Christian mission in the twenty-first century.

NOTES

This chapter is a slightly modified version of an earlier article titled "Going Global: The Transformation of the Korean Catholic Church" in *Journal of Korean Religions* 12, no. 1 (2021): 5–37.

1. Sung-Gun Kim, "Korean Christian Zionism: A Sociological Study of Mission," *International Review of Mission* 100, no. 1 (2011): 92. See also Yi Wŏngyu, "Chonggyojŏk hwaksan kwa munhwa kaldŭng: kidokkyo sŏngyo ŭi munje rŭl chungsim ŭro" (Religious diffusion and cultural conflict as related to the problem of Christian mission), *Hyŏnsang kwa insik* 32, no. 1–2 (2008): 59–82; and Kang Inch'ŏl, "Sŏn'gyo wa p'abyŏng ŭi ijungju: wihŏm ŭi sangsŭng chakyong, mimyohaejinŭn kukga—chonggyo kwan'gye" (Foreign mission and overseas dispatch of armed forces: Escalation of danger, distortion of religion-state relations), *Chonggyo munhwa yŏn'gu* 14 (2010): 137–68.
2. Deborah Ball and Jonathan Cheng, "Pope Francis Holds Mass to Huge Crowd in Seoul for Korean Catholic Martyrs," *Wall Street Journal*, August 16, 2014, http://www.wsj.com/articles/pope-leads-ceremony-honoring-korean-catholic-martyrs-1408157440. The expression "Asian tiger" in reference to religion has its origins in Sandro Magister, "South Korea, the Asian Tiger of the Church," *Expresso*, April 18, 2012, http://chiesa.espresso.repubblica.it/articolo/1350223bdc4.html?eng=y. In Asia, Catholicism is generally considered a minor Western religion. Only a few Asian countries are exceptional in terms of the percentage of Catholic faithful among the total population: the Philippines (79.5 percent as of 2015), Timor Leste (97.6 percent as of 2015), Vietnam (6.1 percent as of 2019), and Korea (11.2 percent as of 2020). Save for Korea, these are all former colonies of a Catholic or predominantly Catholic power—the Philippines of Spain, Timor Leste of Portugal, and Vietnam of France. Thus, the growth of Catholicism in Korea has stimulated the curiosity of scholars. For Korea, see Catholic Bishops' Conference of Korea, *Statistics of the Catholic Church in Korea 2020* (Seoul: CBCK, 2021), 7, http://ebook.cbck.or.kr/gallery/view.asp?seq=214912; for the other countries, see "CIA World Factbook," Central Intelligence Agency, accessed August 18, 2022, https://www.cia.gov/the-world-factbook/field/religions.
3. Catholic Bishops' Conference of Korea, *Statistics of the Catholic Church in Korea 2020* (Seoul: CBCK, 2021), 52, http://ebook.cbck.or.kr/gallery/view.asp?seq=214863.
4. Donald Baker, "The Transformation of the Catholic Church in Korea: From a Missionary Church to an Indigenous Church," *Journal of Korean Religions* 4, no. 1 (2013): 11–42; Kang

Inch'ŏl, *Han'guk ch'ŏnju kyohoe ŭi swaesin ŭl wihan sahoehakchŏk sŏngch'al* (Toward Renewing the Korean Catholic Church: A Sociological Reflection) (Seoul: Woori Theological Institute, 2007).

5. Globalization is a multilayered concept. This understanding here is that the KCC's globalization is embedded in the transformation of global Catholicism as well as in Korea's globalization, as characterized by the increase of interconnectedness in mind and structure. For an introductory discussion of globalization, see George Ritzer, *Globalization: A Basic Text* (Malden: Wiley-Blackwell, 2010).
6. The data of overseas Korean missions until 2019 were collected from the website of the Pontifical Mission Societies in Korea (PMSK). See "Dispatch Status," Pontifical Mission Societies in Korea, accessed July 16, 2020, https://www.pmsk.net/missionary/status. The 2020 data are from Catholic Bishops' Conference of Korea, 50–52. Though the number of missionaries in 2019 is greater than in 2020, the disparity seems to manifest the difference of collecting data between the two organizations rather than a growing trend itself.
7. The contemporary version of the stereotype of Christian West versus Confucian Korea is manifested in both the "clash of civilizations" thesis and in the discourse on the "rise of Confucian East Asia." See Samuel P. Huntington, *The Clash of Civilizations and the Remaking of World Order* (New Delhi: Penguin India, 1997); and Tu Weiming, "Implications of the Rise of 'Confucian' East Asia," *Daedalus* 129, no. 1 (2000): 195–218. Most discourses on indigenization and inculturation are preoccupied with this orientation, of Koreanized vs. European Catholicism. See Takako Frances Takagi, "Inculturation and Adaptation in Japan before and after Vatican Council II," *Catholic Historical Review* 79, no. 2 (1993): 246–67.
8. The France-Korea treaty of 1886 officially granted religious freedom to Catholics.
9. See Chŏng Pyŏngsŏl and Yi Suni, *Chukgŭm ŭl nŏmŏsŏ: sun'gyoja Yi Suni ŭi okjung p'yŏnji* (Beyond death: The prison letters of Martyr Yi Suni) (Seoul: Minum-sa, 2014); Song Chiyŏn, "Chosŏn sidae ch'ŏnjugyo yŏsŏng ŭi yŏksa tasi ilggi: tongjŏngnyŏ e taehan nonŭi rŭl chungsim ŭro" (Re-reading the history of Catholic female virgins in Chosŏn Korea), *Tongbang hakchi* 169 (2015): 33–73; and Yi Sŭnghŭi, "Chosŏn hugi ch'ŏnjugyo yuip kwa yŏsŏng ŭi ŭisik pyŏnhwa e taehan ilgoch'al" (A study on the change of awareness of Catholic women in the Late Chosŏn period), *Han'guk kojŏn yŏsŏng munhak yŏn'gu* 27 (2013): 121–49.
10. José Casanova, in "Locating Religion and Secularity in East Asia through Global Processes: Early Modern Jesuit Religious Encounters," *Religions* 9, no. 11 (2018): 349, categorizes globalization into three distinct phases. In East Asia the first phase of globalization, before Western hegemony, lasted from the mid-sixteenth to the late eighteenth century. The second phase, roughly from the end of the eighteenth century to the 1960s, is characterized by Western hegemony. Starting from the 1960s, the third phase is the contemporary global age of post-Western hegemony.
11. In comparison, the first native Chinese bishop was appointed in 1926 and the first Japanese one in 1927. The Vatican ambassador was sent to Korea in 1948 when the Korean government was internationally acknowledged, compared to this ambassador's dispatch to Japan in 1919 and to China in 1921.
12. After religious freedom was granted, French missionaries in Korea were referred to as "Western noblemen" (*yangdaein*) as a result of the asymmetric treaty between Chosŏn Korea and France.
13. Robert J. Schreiter, *Constructing Local Theologies* (Maryknoll: Orbis, 1997), 6–16.
14. Schreiter, *Constructing Local Theologies*, 12.
15. For the theological background of French missionaries in the nineteenth century, see Kevin M. Doak, "Introduction: Catholicism, Modernity, and Japanese Culture," in Kevin Doak, ed., *Xavier's Legacies: Catholicism in Modern Japanese Culture* (Vancouver: UBC Press, 2011), 5–12.
16. An, a fervent Catholic who later became a freedom fighter, assassinated Itō Hirobumi, the first Japanese resident-general of Korea, in 1909. Bishop Mutel condemned his action and even denied to An access to the sacrament prior to his execution. However, in 1993 Stephen Cardinal Kim

acknowledged An's action as a just defense, based on paragraph 79 of the Pastoral Constitution on the Church in the Modern World of the Second Vatican Council; he asked for the forgiveness of the Church's misjudgment of An's case. For the document, see Vatican II, Pastoral Constitution on the Church in the Modern World: *Gaudium et Spes*, December 7, 1965, https://www.vatican.va/archive/hist_councils/ii_vatican_council/documents/vat-ii_const_19651207_gaudium-et-spes_en.html.

17. The first history of the KCC reveals many cases of such perceptions and perspectives of missionaries of those days. See Charles Dallet, *Histoire de l'église de Corée: précédée d'une introduction de l'histoire, les institutions, la langue, les moeurs et coutumes Coréennes* (Paris: Victor Palmé, 1874), which was translated into Korean in 1979.
18. Quoted in Kang Inch'ŏl, "Saengmyŏng undong: ch'ŏnjugyo ŭi sin sahoe undong?" (Life movement: A Catholic new social movement?), *Hansin inmunhak yŏn'gu* 2 (2001): 290, 292. For a good overview of the Korean Catholic position on and response to the state's family planning program, see Pak Sŭngman, "Ch'ŏnyŏnhan chayŏn kwa wanjŏnhan chayŏn: 1970 nyŏndae chungban han'guk kattolik kajok kyehoek saŏp kwa chayŏn p'iimbŏp ŭi kyŏnghap" ("Innate nature" and "Complete nature": The Catholic natural family planning program and the competition of natural methods in mid-1970s Korea), *Ŭisahak* 29, no. 1 (2020): 81–119.
19. Hahm Seung, "Chŏng ŭi kuhyŏn undong ŭi sidaejŏk paegyŏng" (Historical context of the justice movement), in Kippŭm kwa hŭimang samok yŏn'guso, ed., *Amhŭk sok ŭi hwaetpul: 70, 80 nyŏndae imjuhwa undong ŭi chŭngŏn* (Torch in the Darkness: Witness to the Democratization Movement of the 1970s and 1980s), (Seoul: Gaudium et Spes Pastoral Institute, 1996), 5.
20. Denis Woo-Seon Kim, "For You and for All: Stephen Cardinal Kim, Church and Civil Society in Korea," *Gregorianum* 96 (2015): 345–63.
21. "History of the Korean Church, Part 2: The Course of the Church and the Passion of the Nation," Catholic Bishops' Conference of Korea, accessed August 18, 2022, http://www.cbck.or.kr/page/page.asp?p_code=K3122.
22. Caritas Korea, *Han'guk katollik kigwan, tanch'e haeoe wŏnjo hyŏnhwang pogosŏ 2006–2010* (Report on the Situation of Korean Catholic Organizations for International Development 2006–2010) (Seoul: Han'guk karit'asŭ int'ŏnaesyŏnŏl, 2012), 13.
23. Ch'oe Chaesŏn, "Han'guk ch'ŏnjugyo haeoe wŏnjo hyŏnhwang ŭl pat'ang ŭro han silch'ŏn kwaje" (Practical tasks for the Korean Catholic Church regarding international aid), paper presented at the symposium for Han'guk ch'ŏnjugyo haeoe wŏnjo hyŏnhwang kwa naagaya hal panghyang (Status and direction of international aid in the Korean Catholic Church), Seoul, 2010, 63–66.
24. Kim Dong-ki, "On illyurŭl wihan saje (A priest for all humanity)," *Kyŏnghyang chapji* 73, no. 12 (December 1981): 116–17.
25. Song Yŏngho, "'Pidei tonum' e chŏkkŭk nasŏja" (Let's join "Fidei Donum"), *Catholic Peace Times*, March 17, 2013, http://m.cpbc.co.kr/paper/view.php?cid=443327&path=201303.
26. Catholic Bishops' Conference of Korea, 52.
27. Union of Catholic Asian News, "First Mongolian Priest Ordained with Korean Support," *Union of Catholic Asian News*, September 1, 2016, http://www.ucanews.com/news/first-mongolian-priest-ordained-with-korean-support/77003.
28. In 2015, the Philippines sent 449 men and 1,115 women on foreign mission. See: "Religious and Lay Filipino Missionaries in the World are 'Christ First Witnesses,'" *AsiaNews*, July 16, 2015, http://www.asianews.it/news-en/Religious-and-lay-Filipino-missionaries-in-the-world-are-%E2%80%9CChrist-first-witnesses-34790.html.
29. *Fidei Donum*, (gift of faith) is the name of the encyclical of Pius XII of April 21, 1957, which called on all bishops to share his vision "to face the challenges of the universal mission of the Church." The mandate has facilitated in making diocesan priests available to other continents.
30. Caritas Korea, *Han'guk katollik kigwan*, 13; Ch'oe Chaesŏn, 63.

31. ODA refers to the flow of financial resources from central or local governments of donor countries and multilateral agencies to developing countries.
32. Kyung-Sup Chang, "The Second Modern Condition? Compressed Modernity as Internalized Reflexive Cosmopolitization," *British Journal of Sociology* 61, no. 3 (2010): 446. The term "compressed modernity" is widely used in Korean studies, but it is also applied to studies of Japan and China, which have also experienced economic, political, and social changes in a condensed manner.
33. Caritas Korea, *Han'guk katollik kigwan*, 75; Kukche kaebal hyŏmnyŏk min'gan hyŏpŭihoe (Korean NGO Council for Overseas Development Cooperation), *2009 Kukche kaebal hyŏmnyŏk NGO p'yŏllam* (2009 Korean NGOs for International Development Cooperation) (Seoul: KCOC Private Council for International Development Cooperation, 2010), 64, http://www.ngokcoc.or.kr/bbs/board.php?bo_table=paper01&wr_id=28&&sfl=wr_subject&stx=2009&sop=and.
34. Kukche kaebal hyŏmnyŏk min'gan hyŏpŭihoe (Korean NGO Council for Overseas Development Cooperation).
35. For 1979 and 2006, see Steven Sang-Cheol Moon, "The Protestant Missionary Movement in Korea: Current Growth and Development," *International Bulletin of Missionary Research* 32, no. 2 (2008): 59; for 2014, see Steven Sang-Cheol Moon, Hee-Joo You, and Eun-Mi Kim, "Missions from Korea 2015: Missionaries Unable to Continue Ministry in Their Country of Service," *International Bulletin of Missionary Research* 39, no. 2 (2015): 84.
36. Norimitsu Onishi, "Korean Missionaries Carrying Word to Hard-to-Sway Places," *New York Times*, November 1, 2004, https://www.nytimes.com/2004/11/01/world/asia/korean-missionaries-carrying-word-to-hardtosway-places.html, as quoted in Joon-Sik Park, "Korean Protestant Christianity: A Missiological Reflection," *International Bulletin of Missionary Research* 36, no. 2 (2012): 62.
37. Pope Francis, "Christmas Greetings to the Roman Curia," December 21, 2019, http://www.vatican.va/content/francesco/en/speeches/2019/december/documents/papa-francesco_20191221_curia-romana.html. Christmas greetings to Vatican officers have become an important vehicle for understanding Pope Francis's mind, beginning with his mention of the fifteen diseases of the Vatican, such as "spiritual Alzheimer's disease" and "existential schizophrenia" in 2014.
38. Pope Francis, "Christmas Greetings," December 21, 2019.
39. Catholic Bishops' Conference of Korea, 52.
40. Author interview of Korean nun, Seoul, August 30, 2016.
41. Lee Ga-young and Denis Woo-Seon Kim, "Naeburo put'ŏ ŭi segyehwa? Kukche chawŏn hwaldong kwihwan ch'ŏngnyŏndŭl ŭi t'alyŏngt'ohwa-cheyŏngt'ohwa twoen sam" (Globalization from within? De/re-territorialized lives of young Korean returnees from international voluntary service), *Kyŏngje wa sahoe* 116 (2017): 367–95.
42. Ga-young Lee and Denis Woo-Seoun Kim, "Naeburo put'ŏ ŭi segyehwa?," 381.

5

Filipino Catholicism in the Midst of Global Currents

Translation, Nationalism, Migration

JOSÉ MARIO C. FRANCISCO, SJ

Global forces brought sixteenth-century Spanish Catholicism to the seven-thousand-island archipelago bounded by the Pacific Ocean and East Asian seas, eventually named Filipinas after King Philip II. Interaction between the global and the local situates the journey of Philippine Catholicism in relation to "transnational flows of people, ideas, goods, and capital."[1] In navigating through these currents, Philippine Catholicism has used various platforms as modes of transmission and exchange. These platforms—conceptual paradigms as well as communication technologies, traditional and digital—have also shaped its meaning.

This chapter is divided into sections corresponding to the different platforms of translation, nationalism, and migration. The first deals with Philippine Catholicism emerging from the interaction between the Spanish and the archipelagic Native through the platform of local languages, the second with the twentieth-century transformation of Philippine Catholicism into a public religion, and the third with the various migrations and their impact on contemporary Philippine Catholicism.

This study is situated between two foci of contemporary discussions on religion: the "religion-globalization" nexus and the discourses on world Christianity.[2] The religion-globalization nexus typically unpacks the meaning of "religion" and interrogates related characterizations of modernity, secularization, and globalization. "Religion" has been differentiated into the personal and the social, the symbolic and the institutional, and the traditional and transformative. Furthermore, differing forms of modernity, secularization, and globalization are also recognized.[3] Many current studies also emphasize Christianity's demographic shift to the Global South and its diverse incarnations and transnational networks, thus preferring to speak of Christianity in the plural or as world Christianity.[4]

Though no clear consensus from these discussions has emerged, one observes the fundamental recognition of the historical nature of all religious traditions as well as the different concepts applied to them. Hence many studies stress personal and communal "lived religion" (instead of religion as monolithic) and investigate different nuances of Christianity in medieval Europe or today's Africa.[5] Moreover, they note that concepts generally applied to religious practice elsewhere have been rooted in European historical experience. For instance,

José Casanova acknowledges "Western centrism" and the neglect of "the transnational global dimensions" in his earlier work on public religion.[6]

Cognizant of these discussions, this chapter's exploration of Philippine Catholicism highlights its interaction with crucial globalizing forces and its transformation therewith and suggests how notions of secularization and modernization could be nuanced on the basis of the Philippine Catholic experience.

EMERGENCE OF PHILIPPINE CATHOLICISM: A MARITIME HUB BETWEEN EAST AND WEST

Philippine Catholicism emerged from complex multifaceted interactions of Native society with global forces from east and west. As a hub of maritime trade from West Asia and India beginning in the seventh century, the archipelago had been "a crossroads, a place where local and foreign ideas, goods, and people interact to produce cultural and social change."[7] Local settlements appropriately named *barangay* (boat) had trade and tribute relations, though they were intermittent due to political changes in China and elsewhere.[8] With subsequent migrations—Borneo Malays to twelfth-century Manila, Chinese traders and Arab missionaries to Sulu soon after, and the 1450s establishment of the Sulu sultanate—sixteenth-century Cebus traded in Native pearls and seashells, Mindanao deerskins and caged civet cats were destined for Japan, and Chinese wares including carabao horn, cotton blankets probably woven of Visayan cotton, fragrant boxes carved of Visayan sandalwood, even logs for ballast were aboard homebound Fujian junks.[9]

This extensive Asian network, recently recognized as the missing link in the history of New Spain, makes Spain's arrival "the first globalization" from Europe.[10] The country was henceforth connected to Spanish colonial transpacific expeditions navigating the South Sea and the American Pacific coast. The most significant link was provided by the galleons that connected the Asian Pacific with American viceroyalties and Spain from 1565 to 1815 and carried Latin American silver for Chinese silk, plus much more—indicated by the porcelain and jars of different materials and various metal armaments recovered from the sunken 1600 *San Diego*.[11] Even with the galleon's demise, nineteenth-century Philippine trade continued within an expanding agricultural export economy.

Aside from this commerce in goods, interaction between global and local forces involved colonial intent and Native resistance. Barangays were "reduced" to grid-patterned pueblos for political and economic purposes and for greater missionary access under the 1493 Patronato Real de Índias, thus intertwining the formation of the body politic and the body Catholic.[12] But this comprehensive intent was mitigated by the influence of Dominican Bartolome de las Casas, defender of Native rights and teacher of Manila's first bishop, Domingo de Salazar, and by the perennial lack of colonial personnel in what was initially considered a stepping stone to the Asian mainland.[13] Resistance took many forms: escape by those "who had, for one reason or another, remained unintegrated or had broken away from their communities," nativist protests against friar abuses or forced labor, and occasional unrest among the growing Chinese population due to vacillating immigration policies.[14] Protracted resistance came from Mindanao's Muslim settlements over maritime trade control and the Muslim slave trade.[15]

Beyond these conflicts, however, interaction between the global and the local shaped practically every aspect of Native life and society, from the *tamales*, a rice-and-meat dish boiled in coconut milk similar to Mexican *tamale* and Fujian *ma chang*, to churches with "a gargoyle scowling from a beam, a crocodile head supporting a choirloft, a pierced column resembling Chinese ivory work, [or] a *fu* dog in the patio, an image with large eyes resembling an idol rather than a Christian saint."[16] Surveying countless instances, Rene Javellana passes over essentialist conceptualization like "Orientalism" and appropriately describes the interaction as "weaving cultures" as seen from the postcolonial lens of *mestizaje*—a "complex and unfinished process" of communication that "transforms the sender and the receiver."[17]

Translating Catholicism Into and Through Native Languages

Evangelization of a native society was arguably the most significant locus of Spanish-Native interaction. Analogous to moving relics (referred to in Latin as *translatio*), the contact involved transplanting late-medieval post-Reformation Spanish Catholicism and required the necessary linguistic platform to transmit the Christian message.

Thus the 1582 Synod of Manila decision to evangelize in local languages called for a radical and multifaceted transformation of these Austronesian languages.[18] First, the Native *baybayin* (syllabary), necessary for conversation, recitation of folk forms, and short inscriptions like formal contracts, was transposed into the Roman alphabet. This change to grammar facilitated increased fluency for Europeans unfamiliar with deciphering consonant characters with vowel diacritical marks and the subsequent reproduction of Native texts through printing.[19] Furthermore, Native linguistic structures were straitjacketed into Latin and Spanish patterns.[20] Bilingual dictionaries standardized word usage, focusing on Spanish-local language entries to aid missionaries in learning these languages.

After this codification of grammar and usage, Christian texts in various Native languages were produced. The first book, the 1593 *Doctrina Cristiana* of Franciscan Juan de Plasencia, printed the Tagalog alphabet in Roman script plus basic Christian prayers and doctrines in Spanish, romanized Tagalog, and old syllabic script. Similar pamphlets called *caton* in other Native languages followed. European catechetical and doctrinal tracts, as well as novenas and devotional texts, were also translated. Sermon anthologies were written for recently arrived missionaries. Original Christian texts in Native languages were then written by Spanish missionaries and newly Christianized Natives; many employed Native forms for Christian purposes or European forms with Native influences.

In these texts, basic Christian terms were borrowed from Spanish (for example, *Dios* instead of the Tagalog *Bathala*) or rendered in Native equivalents (for example, using the Tagalog *binyag* of the Muslim purification rites when speaking of the Christian sacrament of baptism).[21] Even doctrinal formulations about body-soul relations or the ransom view of redemption took on Native nuances.[22] Moreover, many of these religious texts came alive in social rituals and contexts participated in or led by Christian Natives. Consequently, Native languages served not only as a medium for the Christian message, but also shaped this message through Native images, symbols, and stories.

The most popular and significant among these is the magisterial 1812 *Caysaysayan ng pasiong mahal* (Story of the Holy Passion), a revised and expanded version of Aquino de Belen's 1703 text, which itself was influenced by Spanish Catholic texts.[23] This text is communally chanted during Lent to fulfill a family tradition or a devotional promise for blessings received.

Many elements in both text and performance contributed to the emergence of a Philippine Catholicism distinct from its Spanish origins. Like other texts, it combined both foreign and Native vocabularies in religious discourse, described Christ and other characters with Native qualities and sensibilities, and drew from Native themes and values.[24]

Moreover, its mode of chanting engages the Native profoundly. As two groups chant antiphonally in traditional melodies or popular tunes, the roles of the faithful-Christian (narrator) and the sinful (narratee) in the text are alternated; thus no group assumes the voice of narrator or narratee exclusively, making each group both narrator and narratee.[25] This rhetorical dynamic, among other elements, contributes to the internalization of Catholicism, since the story of salvation becomes local and contemporary.[26] No longer is the preacher the Spanish missionary nor the penitent a passive Native. Salvation unfolds in the here and now, and the preacher and the preached-to are both Native. Given this, the *pasyon* functions as the Christian epic, replacing old "pagan" epics and, as Reynaldo Ileto suggests, gives "form and meaning to the people's struggle for liberation," providing the language for social and personal freedom movements for change, including the 1896–98 Philippine Revolution.[27]

Though certainly central, the pasyon is simply illustrative of the broader process of bringing Spanish Catholicism into Native hearts and society. One could best describe this process in terms of translation, understood not primarily as the transfer of sacred objects or of the Gospel in the abstract, as suggested in some views of inculturation, but as the mediation between cultures—the Spanish and the Native—which "involves the interface of languages, semiotic systems, cultural products, and systems of cultural organization, making manifest the differences and similarities of systems across cultures."[28]

The emergence of Philippine Catholicism through this process validates Lammin Sanneh's view of Christianity as "a vernacular translation movement."[29] Though performances of the pasyon tradition may decline due to altered social contexts or take on new modalities (such as found in YouTube videos), Philippine Catholicism remains an enduring substratum in Philippine society, not just measured by church affiliation and participation but materialized in religious statues found in homes and transport vehicles, located in popular shrines of the Santo Niño such as the Poong Nazareno (Black Nazarene) and the Blessed Virgin Mary, and articulated in Native symbolic idioms and popular forms.

NATIONALISM: IMAGINING A NATION OF FILIPINOS

Like its emergence, Philippine Catholicism was transformed into a public religion through interacting global and local forces. Historically, this transformation, which encompassed relations among the Church, the nation-state, and civil society, brought about the Catholic Church's dissociation from the colonial body politic and its complex engagement in the sphere of civil society.[30] Though seeds of this dissociation were sowed by chronic discontent with the colonial regime, the notion of a Filipino nation as an established state only grew in the late nineteenth century. Influenced by European ideas current then, disaffected Native constituencies initiated nationalist and revolutionary movements. The Philippine Revolution (1896–98), with its short-lived republic—characterized as "many revolutions within the one Revolution"—consisted of "the distinct views and interests of the liberal illustrados, the economic elite, the native clergy and the masses which were interwoven into the fabric of an 'imagined nation' at the outbreak of the Revolution."[31]

This Filipino nation as "imagined community" found its unifying language in European discussions on race, all of which "invited a kind of historical imagination in which the inhabitants of the islands before the arrival of the Spaniards were collective protagonists and actors, rather than occupants of an ahistorical pagan world that would only be brought into history by Catholicism's arrival."[32] Circulated in Spanish tracts and Tagalog commentaries, this articulation contrasted the colonial status quo with "both pre-Hispanic society (as established via ethnology, folklore, and linguistics) and early, more noble Spanish administration in the islands."[33] Thus "[European] models themselves were put to Filipino uses and defined by local political contexts and projects (always connected to the global)."[34] With this was born "a new historical person: the Filipino [into whom] disappeared, for most political purposes at least, the *indio*, the mestizo, and the *criollo*."[35]

Despite partisan Spanish missionaries and nationalist and revolutionary leaders with antireligious and anti-friar sentiments, the Church contributed to this birth of the Filipino. Most Native clergy advocated nationalist causes but kept their links with the wider Church, with the exception of Native priests like Gregorio Aglipay of the breakaway Iglesia Filipina Independiente (IFI). Some Native priests rallied others or actively participated in revolutionary campaigns and councils. Lay Christians shaped by Native Christian religiosity considered their involvement as solidarity (*pakikiramay*) with Christ toward *kalayaan* (freedom), as compared to the elites' aspiration for *independencia* (independence);[36] some reportedly spared friars and even offered Masses "for revolutionaries who had died in battle as for the Spaniards, inasmuch as . . . all were Christians."[37]

This contribution notwithstanding, the revolutionary Philippine Republic voted for the nonestablishment of the Catholic Church by a one-vote margin. This new arrangement became further entrenched in the aftermath of the global Spanish-American War, and despite promulgation of church-state separation, the victorious American nation-state was informed by a distinctly American Protestantism with the "manifest destiny" to "civilize and Christianize" Philippine Catholics. Thus Catholicism was both dissociated from the political realm based on the American Constitution and compelled to navigate in a public sphere subject to American geopolitics and other global forces.

With American neocolonial rule established after sporadic Native resistance, the Catholic Church had to negotiate with Filipino nationalists, Native clergy, Spanish missionaries, American civil and religious leaders, and the Holy See over complex issues: disposing friar personnel and estates, normalizing church life, and working under a different state framework, among others.[38] Furthermore, the IFI, progeny of the revolution, along with the newly arrived Protestant churches and organizations, made it more difficult for "the church [that was] in disarray," but that "remained essentially Spanish in language, culture, and outlook—its hierarchy, diocesan clergy, principal older religious orders, and the larger part of its educational system."[39] Hence, with the onslaught of American cultural ethos, "in the Church's rendering of the American-era . . . the dominant trope has been one of loss: lost opportunities for the Church to re-integrate itself with secular powers and the threat of the loss of the nation to secularism, Protestantism and breakaway religious movements."[40]

Simultaneous with this trope of loss, nationalist impulses persisted in Philippine society throughout the American neocolonial period and the post-1946 Philippine Republic. Though they often continued to be based on the late nineteenth-century concept of race (*lahing kayumanggi*)—a perspective uncovered by contemporary cultural studies as xenophobic—they became endemic because the sorry state of Philippine affairs was seen as the consequence of "the unfinished revolution" and "the aborted nation."[41]

Given all these, the Church remained wary of nationalism, and until Vatican II, resisted any form of nationalism within the Church, condemning the clamor of some Filipino religious priests in the 1960s who "call[ed] attention to the appallingly low rate of Filipino membership and leadership in men's religious congregations."[42] With this historical memory and the recent devastation from the Second World War, the Church "was principally concerned with the defense, protection, strengthening and furtherance of the vital interests of the Catholic Church as a social institution and of supernatural values."[43]

Imagining the Filipino Nation as Catholic/Christian

Given the de jure separation of church and state, Philippine Catholicism transformed into a public religion, thus reestablishing itself within Philippine society. Employing the same conceptual tool that severed its union with the state, its transformation consisted of imagining the Filipino nation as "a Catholic people" first expressed in the January 25, 1953, First Plenary Council, and as "the only Christian nation in the Orient" articulated with post–World War II global awareness, as expressed in the February 2, 1964, Fourth Centenary of Evangelization.[44] Social concern and devotional practice promoted this imaginary. In the late 1930s, Jesuit-educated students produced radio plays praising the Catholic nation-state similar to Salazar's praise in Portugal. Religious occasions such as the Holy Year (1950–51), the Marian Year (1954), and the second Eucharistic Congress (1956) were identified as "belong[ing] to the basic elements of our nationhood."[45]

Even Vatican II's iconic image of the Church as God's pilgrim people and the much-promoted strategy of building basic ecclesial communities were implicitly aligned with, if not coopted by, this imaginary. Church and political leaders and institutions used "*Para sa Diyos at para sa bayan* (For God and country) as the tagline for their respective purposes: the Church's perennial social work and later involvement in national development and politicians' appeal for populist support.[46]

The Catholic Church used this imaginary to respond to contemporary issues. The Catholic Welfare Organization (CWO, 1945–65) and the Catholic Bishops' Conference of the

Philippines (CBCP, 1967 onward) issued numerous statements on social issues of local, national, and global import, drawing both praise and criticism within and outside the Church.

Critical analysis of these statements shows how the imaginary facilitated setting boundaries of what and who are Christian and what different logics were at work in its application. All these uncover the inherent tension in the imaginary itself. On the one hand, the imaginary argued on the basis of the Filipino nation being Catholic or Christian; on the other, it critiqued the same nation, especially the nation-state, for being "un-Catholic." Bishops' statements on crucial social issues—education during the pre–Vatican II period, social injustice during and after Ferdinand Marcos's authoritarian regime (1965–86), and reproductive health from the 1990s on—illustrate this tension.

First, on the issue of education, the privileged realm for transmitting the Catholic faith, the CWO issued statements condemning the progeny of its nineteenth-century adversaries—the Masons, "false liberalism," and "the evil genius of atheistic Communism," the latter seen to be behind certain legislative proposals.[47] Given the thriving American-initiated public-school system and growing Protestant involvement in the country's education, the Church strongly lobbied for three things: 1) optional religious instruction in non-Catholic schools; 2) exclusion of nationalist books (e.g., Jose Rizal's novels) in the general curriculum; and 3) eligibility of foreigners, especially missionaries, for leadership positions in schools.

In the name of the imaginary, these adversaries were condemned for being "anti-Catholic." Behind the proposed nationalization of all schools was "the old Nazi dogma of racism, the kind of nationalism that ignited the Second World War."[48] Philippine Catholics were warned of its outcome, seen in the current state of "once-Christian nations stricken with domestic strife."[49] Rizal's novels had to be excluded from the general curriculum because they "were written when Dr. Jose Rizal, estranged for a time from our faith and religion, did contradict many of our Christian beliefs" and could compromise "the eternal salvation of immortal souls, souls for which We [the hierarchy] are answerable before the throne of Divine Justice."[50]

Second, with regard to Marcos's authoritarian regime, the Church's stance, like that of Philippine society, was not uniform. Though there was support from certain bishops, clergy, religious, and laypeople, others issued stinging criticisms against various groups associated with Marcos. The bishops' official stance was characterized as "critical collaboration with government," but as government oppression and violence became more intense and widespread, not sparing Church personnel or institutions, the substance and tone of their nine statements increasingly stressed the "critical" rather than the "collaboration."[51] All this culminated in the historic February 13, 1986, statement condemning systemic electoral fraud, subverting the moral legitimacy of the Marcos victory and finally urging people "to speak up," "to repair the wrong," and to do so in a "systematically organized" way.[52]

Even after the end of Marcos's rule, its September 16, 1997, critique of Philippine politics asks, "Why should this be so in a nation where the vast majority of the people are Catholic and Christian? Our faith in God has played a key role in major events of our history—even in a decidedly political matter like the People Power Revolution of EDSA. Yet politics as a whole has been strangely impervious to the Gospel. Our political culture denies, to our shame, our proud claim to the name Christian."[53]

Third, on the more recent reproductive health issue, new adversaries were identified: those espousing "a secular humanistic philosophy" or "a post-modern spirit" or "a secularist, materialist spirit that considers morality as a set of teachings from which [one] can choose, according to the spirit of the age."[54] Though not condemned, mainline and evangelical Protestants supportive of reproductive health were implicitly excluded from the imaginary of the nation as Christian.

Based on this imaginary also, the Church's condemnation of contrary views applied a different logical strategy. Though its position against abortion, contraception, and related programs was firmly based on Catholic teaching, the Church argued against them not for being anti-Catholic but for being anti-Filipino. Its July 9, 1995, statement considered these agendas contrary to "our own traditional Filipino-Christian values of true femininity that is based on the unique genius proper to women. The true Filipina, cognizant of her God-given mission, is able to successfully combine her role as a mother, wife and co-provider of the family with her own desire for self-fulfillment."[55]

When accused of imposing Catholic beliefs on others, the Church employed this strategic argument and pointed to its "commitment to the common good and to natural law as a path toward it accessible to all."[56] Conclusions that differed from its own, however, were judged as "un-Filipino" and derived from "the *western* ideology of feminism."[57]

These conflicting logics in the imaginary's application show the inherent tension within the imaginary itself. On the one hand, the Church used the nineteenth-century nationalist impulse in order to reestablish its place in Philippine society. On the other, it resisted or at least delayed, its implementation within the Church, as shown in its condemnation of Filipino members of international religious orders who lamented the absence of Filipino representation to their highest governing bodies.[58]

The ambiguous nature of the imaginary of the Philippines as a Catholic/Christian nation finds its iconic expression in the People Power Revolution against Marcos's regime (also known as EDSA I). The Church indeed played a crucial role leading to and during the actual event, and thus reads it as the "flowering of the Filipino Catholic faith, the blossoming of Filipino heroism."[59] But just like the "many revolutions with the one revolution" of 1896, EDSA I proved to be the conjuncture of open and covert interventions of various local and global actors aligned with or inimical to social development and Church interests. Hence its aftermath has seen the return of "cacique democracy" and even a revisionist reading of the Marcos regime.[60]

MIGRATION: LOCATING PHILIPPINE CATHOLICISM IN MULTIPLE SITES

In contrast to Philippine Catholicism's transformation into a public religion, migration—broadly understood as the movement of peoples, with all its material and social baggage—has located the faith in multiple sites, both in geographical and digital spaces. But since this globalizing force is as contemporary as it is pervasive, its impact on Philippine Catholicism is perhaps best described through illustrative examples.

Migration within the Catholic Church

Foreign Catholic missionaries have always been present in the Philippine Church—under the *patronato* they were European, mostly Spanish; from the American occupation onward they were of different nationalities unrelated to imperial Spanish traditions, fluent in English, and exposed to new educational perspectives and ministries.

Later arrivals contributed modern currents and practices to Philippine Catholicism, especially in education. After World War II, for instance, American and Filipino Jesuits as well as lay faculty studied empirical social sciences in American universities for a better understanding of Catholicism and Philippine society; hence the contributions of Jaime Bulatao's "split-level Christianity" and Frank Lynch's analysis of Philippine values.[61] Around the 1950s, psychological tests used by dioceses and religious orders abroad were introduced to assess local candidates for religious and priestly ministry.[62]

These globalizing influences, together with profound social changes in the world and the Church, greatly affected Philippine Catholicism from the 1960s. Although Philippine bishops at Vatican II (1964–68) generally voted with the curia-led conservative faction, Vatican II engendered engagement with modernity among Philippine Catholic clerics, religious, and laity.[63] On March 27, 1969, the Laymen's Association for Post–Vatican II Reforms (LAPVIIR) picketed Rufino Cardinal Santos's residence.[64] Filipina members of international religious orders—though "adhering to practices inside their communities that derived from European Catholicism and led by Europeans or North Americans [*sic*]"—were given by Vatican II "a vocabulary with which they tried to articulate a more meaningful spirituality" that, for some, entailed more direct social and political action.[65] But by the late twentieth century, with the ironic twist of "reverse mission" due to diminished European and American vocations, nuns and clergy were sent abroad, employing their Philippine Catholic experience to awaken greater social consciousness abroad.

Furthermore, this Philippine Catholic experience was shared in international organizations and conferences. The Federation of Asian Bishops' Conferences (FABC) was conceived at the 1970 Asian Bishops Meeting in Manila, with much participation from Filipinos, among them Jesuit theologian C. G. Arévalo.[66] It was later marked by the influence of Filipinos like Oblate Orlando Quevedo and Jesuit Francisco Claver. Through their participation on the global Catholic stage, Philippine Catholics encountered Latin American liberation theology and learned about interfaith issues from their Asian neighbors.

Local theological schools and formation houses have thus become internationalized with increasing numbers of Catholics from abroad, making the Philippines a hub of theological and religious formation. These international church personnel are often present in local ministries and communities, and at times the Vietnamese or Indonesians from Flores outnumber Philippine nationals. This migration to and from the Philippines opens an important new site where Philippine Catholicism interacts with others within the Church.

Migration of Evangelical and Charismatic Spirituality

Philippine Catholicism has also faced the entry of evangelical and charismatic groups—Protestant mainline, Protestant evangelical, and Catholic. In the early 1970s these groups organized prayer meetings in urban and semiurban centers.[67] Jesuit Herbert Schneider, a scripture professor at Loyola School of Theology with previous involvement in the Ann Arbor *Sword of the Spirit* community, became the moving spirit of the local Catholic charismatic movement and helped establish a pastoral and theological framework for smooth relations with local hierarchy and clergy. Thus, unlike in Latin America, charismatic Christianity in the Philippines has remained predominantly Catholic, as "70 percent of all Christians active in the [Charismatic] renewal identify themselves as Roman Catholic" and similarities of dogma among charismatic Evangelicals, Catholics, and Pentecostals appear to outweigh their differences.[68]

The Couples for Christ (CFC), a charismatic community founded in 1981 and headed by lay Catholics, established missions locally and abroad. Its aim, to promote "renewal within the Catholic Church," is focused on two areas: family life and global evangelization.[69] Convinced that a conversion of families to Christ is necessary to effectively renew society, CFC households are organized for prayer and formation as a working model for basic ecclesial communities (BECs). Moreover, the CFC believes that "what God started in the Philippines was not meant to be just for Filipinos, or just for Asia, but was to be an instrument of renewal for the whole world."[70] Thus it has spread to more than 150 nations and become "a mighty army, a multinational force, doing battle for the Lord and fighting tenaciously to firmly establish His reign on earth."[71] However, Gawad Kalinga (Providing care) (GK), initially CFC's arm to build housing for the poor, broke away in 2007. The organizations split because of GK's partnership with non-Catholics—Muslims, Mormons, and Pfizer, a manufacturer of Church-disapproved contraceptives. GK has continued its work in the Philippines and abroad to recruit volunteers and raise donations.

Despite these differences, both groups illustrate how evangelical and charismatic spirituality migrated from North America, then developed within the Philippine Catholic landscape and expanded worldwide.

Migration of Philippine Workers and Professionals

Migration of Philippine labor has become a global phenomenon—first, among farmhands in the 1930s and medical personnel in the 1960s (both to the United States); then among construction workers in the 1970s (to the Middle East); and, more recently, workers from practically any field to numerous countries. Thus the Philippine state has called migrants "new heroes" and the Church calls them "new missionaries." This mass movement has altered the social, economic, and cultural life of individuals, families, and the nation with beneficial and harmful effects.

Most of them have brought Philippine Catholic practices to new contexts, generating interaction with forces that shape the social and Catholic fabric of these contexts and challenging both migrants and local Catholics.

On the one hand, Catholicism, as its name suggests, bridges places of origin and of destination through international and local groups like the FABC or the Chinese Bishops' Conference of Taiwan.[72] Among others, the Filipino Catholic Center of the Archdiocese of Seoul provides many services.[73] On the other hand, the symbolic and organizational practices of local Catholics differ from the traditional Philippine religious ethos—represented by artifacts in their luggage and articulated in notions like "*nobena, panata, at paglalakbay* (novena, devotion, and pilgrimage)."[74]

Thus Philippine Catholic migrants live their Catholicism "between here and there," changing the Catholic practice at both ends of their journey. Philippine church communities at points of origin and destination become part of the migrant narrative, establishing pre-departure orientation and support programs for left-behind families and soliciting support for local church activities in the new realm. Migrants reenact Naga's fluvial procession in honor of Our Lady of Peñafrancia along the River Thames in the United Kingdom and hold Christmas novena Masses in countless parishes worldwide. These practices affect the local churches at these places. Some activities have been integrated in parish life with activities of other ethnic origins; others are simply given religious space and tolerance. Thus actual Catholic practice in the migrants' place of destination has become the subject of negotiation between migrants and locals and has provided a constant test of the Church's catholicity.

Migration through Media and Digital Technologies

Just as previous technologies played important roles in religious practice—for instance, the printing press for Protestantism—so too has new media influenced contemporary religion.[75] Given the impact of new platforms from mass media to digital communications, the Catholic Church has engaged social communications.

Church involvement in media has focused on content, that is, the preaching of the Gospel message. Thus it has created radio programs at crucial times—in the 1930s, *Kuwentong Kutsero,* promoting solutions to social problems based on Catholic social teaching rather than on "enlightened Masonry";[76] during the Marcos period, social commentary in different diocesan stations;[77] and, for today's issues, Radio Veritas or the Manila Archdiocese's TV Maria. Even with widespread digital communications, the content of the message remains primary in websites of church organizations and groups.

However, media's greater impact relates to how these platforms create new spaces for Philippine Christian practice. This new media-created religious space is illustrated by El Shaddai, an evangelical community founded by radio host Mariano "Bro. Mike" Velarde that is loosely linked to the Catholic Church. Velarde's preaching is influenced by the American "prosperity Gospel" but remains linked to traditional Native aspirations as expressed in petitions for personal healing, material blessings, and relief from poverty. It is broadcast through radio and television to those already present in public meeting grounds, those who are on their way, and those gathered in local parishes or neighborhoods, thereby expanding ritual space where "its message—and the healing power of the Holy Spirit—is easily transmitted into homes and into the hearts of the eager listeners."[78] Moreover, replays of the broadcasts circulate locally and among Philippine migrants and overseas workers, which are estimated to number nine to eleven million followers.[79]

Digital communications have provided these sites with even newer capabilities. Discussion of issues connected to religion has migrated to the various forms of social media and at times has played a subverting role. In the recent Reproductive Health (RH) controversy, when the CBCP used pastoral statements to deliver its message, Catholic laywomen and their supporters effectively used blog postings and chain emails in addition to the usual strategies of petitions and rallies to present their alternative position.[80] This use of digital platforms has contributed to greater support for the RH legislation among Catholics themselves.

These platforms have also been surprisingly employed for devotional purposes. One finds YouTube videos of family-sponsored pasyon chanting in some remote barrio, which are meant to be accessed by their relatives elsewhere. Funeral homes where families hold wakes of their deceased are now equipped with wifi connections so that others, especially those abroad, can pay their respects in "real time" digital space. With this, the time-honored Philippine Catholic practice of wakes and prayers has found a new site as *e-burol* (electronic wake).

DRAFTING THE JOURNEY'S LOG

Global currents have indelibly marked the journey of Philippine Catholicism—born through the interaction between the patronato Church and the sixteenth-century Native society that was linked to the Asian maritime network—and transformed it into a public religion, imagined as a "Christian nation" in response to twentieth-century geopolitics and social forces. Today it is located in multiple geographical and digital sites created by the migration of peoples, resources, and information.

Notwithstanding power differentials between Philippine Catholicism and carriers of global forces, interaction has been not unilateral but two-way, often producing unintended consequences. For instance, despite the totalizing intent of imperial powers and their religious collaborators, the Native force has employed "the weapons of the weak." The very emergence of Philippine Catholicism, distinct from Spanish Catholicism, was brought about not only by Native resistance and covert subversion but also by the infiltration of a Native ethos into Catholic practice through Native languages.

In an analogous way, Philippine Catholicism engaged the global platform of nationalism. It promoted nationalist sentiments: in the nineteenth century, by educating Philippine nationalists, including Native clergy, and by providing the language for liberation to those fighting for change; in the twentieth, by promoting social justice and freedom from authoritarianism. At the same time, it condemned nationalism through the imaginary of the Philippines as a Catholic nation in order to protect its interests regarding education and reproductive health and to exclude its perceived adversaries from the fold. These instances rehearse crucial issues in current religion-globalization discussions, Native agency in these interactions, opposition between personal autonomy and religious socialization, and the nature of secularization and modernization.

On one level the agency of the local–the Native–the colonized has been often ignored in Philippine Catholicism and globalization discussions. The characterization of Catholicism as a domesticating religion solely based on imperial intent distorts the multilateral nature of the interactions and promotes a derogatory image of the Filipino as utterly passive. From a postcolonial perspective, the multilateral nature of such interaction uncovers the historic formation of the Native—individual and people—as a subject who acts in appropriating Catholicism.

On another level, agency can also be applied to the Native culture asserting itself in the face of globalizing forces. One need not fall into linguistic or cultural determinism to acknowledge the substantive role of the Native symbolic world—idioms, images, and stories—in the emergence of Philippine Catholicism. Though this symbolic world changes, for instance, transforming from Tagalog to English to a mixture, these changes still become part of and thus both shape and are shaped by Catholic practice. Many Philippine Catholics then have not considered their Catholicism as non-Filipino.

Additionally, the opposition between personal commitment and institutional affiliation is not an adequate measure of the influence of Philippine Catholicism. Early secularization theories valorized personal autonomy and privatization of religion, especially with declining church participation in certain contexts and increasing religious choices available through communications digital platforms.

However, the journey of Philippine Catholicism interrogates such a perspective. The historic influence of Philippine Catholicism is not adequately measured by institutional participation nor does it undermine personal agency. Many of those who participated in the Philippine Revolution or EDSA I were formed by the popular Catholic ethos and did not regularly participate in church activities. Thus Philippine Catholicism speaks in many and often different voices. Official and lay Church leaders opposed President Rodrigo Duterte's desire to restore the death penalty, which many parishioners supported. Nongovernmental organizations with no Catholic affiliation are often informed by Catholic social teaching and led by committed Catholics.

Moreover, the stress on personal autonomy denigrates the value of religious socialization. Just like many in the Global South who are socialized into their traditions, a majority of Philippine citizens become Catholic in the same way. Though regional, ethnic, and class factors and varying links to the institutional Church shape this process, the insistence on conscious choice as the only authentic path to faith is more of an Enlightenment illusion. Historical studies of medieval women, peasants, and other laypeople show them as true agents of their religious practices, albeit in implicit and unthematized ways. Thus religious socialization and authentic faith need not be opposed to each other.

Furthermore, Philippine Catholicism displays the nuanced relationships between religion and secularization and between tradition and modernity. Differentiating the religious from what is seen as "secular" applies to setting borders between institutions: for example, the dissociation of the Catholic Church from the patronato state or the separation of church and state under American constitutionalism. But as borders always occasion disputes, the journey of Philippine Christianity has been fraught with border conflicts with the state over legislation on education or reproductive rights.

However, when "secular" applies to others areas of personal and social life, then borders become porous sites of negotiation and "the concept of the secular cannot do without the idea of religion."[81] Thus Philippine Catholicism is no longer tied only to the churches or plazas of traditional rural towns, the popular shrines across the Philippine landscape, or the new churches in cities and their suburbs. It is present in private homes as well as public places like airports, has crossed national borders through travel, and has found sites on the worldwide web, together creating participation through mutual exchanges in the formation of World Christianity. For example, Philippine Catholic migrants gathering at St. John's Catholic Cathedral in Kuala Lumpur see that "sacred communion and secular fun are connected in the Filipino migrant imaginary. The two most common activities among different Filipino groups, prayer and the sharing of a Sunday meal, are contiguous parts of a migrant's Sunday, when the communion of the Eucharist flows into the commensality of a Filipino meal."[82]

Within these multiple sites with porous borders, different constituencies of Philippine Catholicism—individuals of particular beliefs, devotions, and affiliations or institutional Church and religious groups—navigate their religious practice. Though changing or even declining in attendance at institutional activities, institutional forms of religion remain present and participate in these ongoing negotiations leading to change.

Given this situation, religion and modernity need not also be construed as inherently opposed. Philippine Catholicism has constantly changed through interaction with various global forces. But these modernizing changes, even those brought about by disruptive impulses such as anti-religious nationalism, have become embedded in some form within tradition. It has been suggested, for instance, that in the experience of young Philippine Catholics, "the coexistence of tradition maintenance and tradition construction" is at work, with "the result that religion becomes more personally meaningful and relevant."[83]

This journey of Philippine Catholicism amid tumultuous global currents is perhaps best told through the story of the "Our Mother of Perpetual Help" devotion.[84] In 1906, Australian and Irish Redemptorists enshrined the Cretan icon of Mary in Baclaran, a fishing village outside Manila. After World War II, when they introduced communal novena recitation every Wednesday, Baclaran began to attract thousands from all walks of life, and the practice has since been replicated in churches nationwide. Some devotees leave letters of petition and thanksgiving in a church depository. Reproductions and statues of the icon have become ubiquitous. But developments in church and society have also transformed the devotion. After Vatican II, novena prayers have been modified several times to reflect contemporary theology and Church life. Just as Baclaran has become a hectic commercial center with a significant Muslim population, the petitionary and thanksgiving letters now focus more on moral rather than sacramental concerns. This devotion has also migrated overseas and in digital spaces. Filipina domestic workers hold Wednesday novenas in a Marian grotto outside Beirut, Lebanon, which they call "Baclaran" and letters can now be submitted online.[85]

NOTES

1. Thomas Banchoff and José Casanova, eds., *The Jesuits and Globalization: Historical Legacies and Contemporary Challenges* (Washington, DC: Georgetown University Press, 2015), 1.
2. On the religion-globalization nexus, see David Lehmann, "Religion and Globalization," in Linda Woodhead et al., eds., *Religions in the Modern World: Traditions and Transformations* (London: Routledge, 2002); on discourses on world Christianity, see Peter C. Phan, ed., *Christianities in Asia* (West Sussex: Wiley-Blackwell, 2011), 426.
3. Ira Katznelson and Gareth Stedman Jones, eds., *Religion and the Political Imagination* (Cambridge: Cambridge University Press, 2010).

4. Dyron B. Daughrity, *To Whom Does Christianity Belong? Critical Issues in World Christianity* (Minneapolis, MN: Fortress, 2015).
5. Meredith B. McGuirre, *Lived Religion: Faith and Practice in Everyday Life* (Oxford: Oxford University Press, 2008).
6. José Casanova, "Public Religions Revisited," in Hent de Vries, ed., *Religion: Beyond the Concept* (New York: Fordham University Press, 2008), 102.
7. Patricio N. Abinales and Donna N. Amoroso, *State and Society in the Philippines* (Lanham, MD: Rowman & Littlefield, 2005), 24.
8. William H. Scott, *Barangay: Sixteenth-Century Philippine Culture and Society* (Quezon City: Ateneo de Manila University Press, 1994), 4–6.
9. Abinales and Amoroso, *State and Society in the Philippines*, xvii; Scott, *Barangay*, 76.
10. Banchoff and Casanova, *The Jesuits and Globalization*, 3.
11. Cuautémoc Villamar, "The Galleon in the Region of Asia," in Luis Gerardo Morales Moreno, ed., *Return Voyage: The China Galleon and the Baroque in Mexico 1565–1815* (Puebla: Museo Internacional del Barroco, 2004), 43–51; René B. Javellana, *Weaving Cultures: The Invention of Colonial Art and Culture in the Philippines, 1565–1850* (Quezon City: Ateneo de Manila University Press, 2017), 38–48.
12. Javellana, *Weaving Cultures*, 93; John N. Schumacher, *Readings in Philippine Church History* (Quezon City: Loyola School of Theology, 1979), 39.
13. Schumacher, *Readings in Philippine Church History*, 7–9; Linda A. Newson, "Old World Diseases in Early Colonial Philippines and Spanish America," in Daniel F. Doeppers and Peter Xenos, eds., *Population and History: The Demographic Origins of the Modern Philippines* (Quezon City: Ateneo de Manila University Press, 1998), 25.
14. Michael Cullinane, "Accounting for Souls: Ecclesiastical Sources for the Study of Philippine Demographic History," in Daniel F. Doeppers and Peter Xenos, eds., *Population and History: The Demographic Origins of the Modern Philippines* (Quezon City: Ateneo de Manila University Press, 1998), 323; Reynaldo C. Ileto, *Pasyon and Revolution: Popular Movements in the Philippines, 1840–1910* (Quezon City: Ateneo de Manila University Press, 1979); Richard T. Chu, *Chinese and Chinese Mestizos of Manila: Family, Identity, and Culture, 1869s–1930s* (Leiden: Brill, 2010), 57.
15. Abinales and Amoroso, *State and Society in the Philippines*, 70–71.
16. Javellana, *Weaving Cultures*, 85; René Javellana, *Fortress of Empire: Spanish Colonial Fortifications in the Philippines, 1565–1898* (Makati: Bookmark, 1993), 7.
17. Javellana, *Weaving Cultures*, 11–14.
18. Schumacher, *Readings in Philippine Church History*, 28–33.
19. Vicente L. Rafael, *Contracting Colonialism: Translation and Christian Conversion in Tagalog Society under Early Spanish Rule* (Quezon City: Ateneo de Manila University Press, 1988), 46–52; Javellana, *Weaving Cultures*, 51–55.
20. Bienvenido L. Lumbera, *Tagalog Poetry 1570–1898: Tradition and Influences in Its Development* (Quezon City: Ateneo de Manila University Press, 1986), 30–48.
21. Jose Mario C. Francisco, "Fidelity in Translating Religious Practice: Illustrations from Filipino Christianity," *Kritika Kultura* 21–22 (2013–14): 1–16.
22. Francisco, "Fidelity in Translating Religious Practice," 10.
23. Lumbera, *Tagalog Poetry*, 57–58.
24. René B. Javellana, ed., *Casaysayan nang pasiong mahal ni Jesucristong Panginoon natin na sucat ipag-alab nang puso nang sinomang babasa* (Quezon City: Ateneo de Manila University Press, 1988).
25. Fanella Cannell, "Reading as Gift and Writing as Theft," in Fanella Cannell, ed., *The Anthropology of Christianity* (Durham, NC: Duke University Press, 2006), 143.

26. Javellana, *Casaysayan nang pasiong mahal*, 30–33.
27. Ileto, *Pasyon and Revolution*, 316.
28. See Edwin Gentzler, *Contemporary Translation Theories* (London: Routledge, 1993), 188; and Maria Tymoczko, *Enlarging Translation, Empowering Translators* (Manchester: St. Jerome, 2010), 43.
29. Lammin Sanneh, *Translating the Message: The Missionary Impact on Culture* (Ossining, NY: Orbis, 1989), 7.
30. José Casanova, *Public Religions in the Modern World* (Chicago: University of Chicago Press, 1994).
31. John N. Schumacher, *Revolutionary Clergy: The Filipino Clergy and the Nationalist Movement, 1850–1903* (Quezon City: Ateneo de Manila University Press, 1981), 268–74.
32. Benedict Anderson, *Imagined Communities: Reflections on the Origin and Spread of Nationalism*, rev. ed. (Pasig City: Anvil, 1991); Megan C. Thomas, *Orientalists, Propagandists, and Illustrados* (Pasig City: Anvil, 2012), 201.
33. Thomas, *Orientalists, Propagandists, and Illustrados*, 202.
34. Thomas, 203.
35. Benedict Anderson, *The Spectre of Comparisons: Nationalism, Southeast Asia and the World* (London: Verso, 1998), 257.
36. Ileto, *Pasyon and Revolution*, 225.
37. Schumacher, *Revolutionary Clergy*, 52.
38. Michael J. Connolly, *Church Lands and Peasant Unrest in the Philippines: Agrarian Conflict in 20th-Century Luzon* (Quezon City: Ateneo de Manila University Press, 1992), 1–6.
39. Daniel Frankin Pilario, "Introduction: *Quae Mari Sinico* and the Church in Disarray," in Daniel Franklin Pilario and Gerardo Vibar, eds., *Philippine Local Churches after the Spanish Regime* (Manila: Adamson University, 2015), 1–16; John N. Schumacher, "A Hispanicized Clergy in an Americanized Country, 1910–1970," in John N. Schumacher, ed., *Growth and Decline: Essays on Philippine Church History* (Quezon City: Ateneo de Manila University Press, 2009), 251.
40. Coeli Barry, "Polyglot Catholicism: Genealogies and Reinterpretions of the Philippine Catholic Church," *Pilipinas* 32 (Spring 1999): 60.
41. Pnina Werbner and Tariq Modood, eds., *Debating Cultural Hybridity: Multi-Cultural Identities and the Politics of Anti-Racism* (London: Zed, 2000).
42. Barry, "Polyglot Catholicism," 61.
43. Pedro C. Quitorio III, ed., *Pastoral Letters, 1945–1995* (Manila: Catholic Bishops' Conference of the Philippines, 1996), 117.
44. Quitorio, xxiii, 237.
45. Quitorio, 227.
46. Quitorio, 161.
47. Quitorio, 123, 125.
48. Quitorio, 212.
49. Quitorio, 118.
50. Quitorio, 193, 194.
51. Robert L. Youngblood, *Marcos against the Church: Economic Development and Political Repression in the Philippines* (Ithaca, NY: Cornell University Press, 1990).
52. Quitorio, *Pastoral Letters*, 623.
53. Quitorio, 95.
54. CBCP, "Panigan ang buhay, tanggihan ang RH Bill (Liham Pastoral ng Kapulungan ng mga Katolikong Obispo ng Pilipinas)," accessed January 30, 2022, http://cbcponline.net/v2/?p=1166.
55. Quitorio, *Pastoral Letters*, 831.
56. CBCP, "Panigan ang buhay."
57. Quitorio, *Pastoral Letters*, 831 (emphasis added).

58. Coeli Barry, "The Limits of Conservative Church Reformism in the Democratic Philippines," in Tun-Jen Cheng and Deborah A. Brown, eds., *Religious Organizations and Democratization: Case Studies from Contemporary Asia* (Armonk, NY: M. E. Sharpe, 2006), 73.
59. Lisandro E. Claudio, *Taming People's Power: The EDSA Revolutions and Their Contradictions* (Quezon City: Ateneo de Manila University Press, 2013), 38.
60. Claudio, 11–15.
61. Jayeel S. Cornelio, "Popular Religión and the Turn to Everyday Authenticity: Reflections on the Contemporary Study of Philippine Catholicism," *Philippine Studies* 62, nos. 3–4 (2014): 475–77.
62. Coeli M. Barry, "Transformation of Politics and Religious Culture Inside the Philippine Catholic Church (1965–1990)," PhD diss., Cornell University, 1996.
63. James Kroeger, ed., "Appendix 2," in *The Documents of Vatican II* (Makati: Paulist Publications, 2011), 814–19.
64. Wilfredo Fabros, *The Church and Its Social Involvement in the Philippines, 1930–1972* (Quezon City: Ateneo de Manila University Press, 1988), 128.
65. Coeli M. Barry, "Women Religious and Sociopolitical Change in the Philippines, 1930s–1970s," *Philippine Studies* 62, nos. 3–4 (2014): 395.
66. C. G. Arévalo, "The Time of the Heirs," in Gaudencio Rosales and C. G. Arévalo, eds., *For All the Peoples of Asia: Federation of Asian Bishops' Conferences Documents from 1970–1991* (New York: Orbis, 1992), xv–xxii.
67. Christi Kessler and Jürgen Rüland, *Give Jesus a Hand! Charismatic Christians: Populist Religion in the Philippines* (Quezon City: Ateneo de Manila University Press, 2008), 126.
68. Christi Kessler, "Charismatic Christians: Genuinely Religious, Genuinely Modern," *Philippine Studies* 54, no. 4 (2006): 563.
69. Couples for Christ, introduction to "CFC as an Agent of Renewal within the Catholic Church," September 18, 1995, para. 1.
70. Couples for Christ, 40.
71. Couples for Christ, 50.
72. Lou Aldrich, "A Critical Evaluation of the Migrant Workers' Situation in Taiwan in Light of the Catholic Social Tradition," in Fabio Baggio and Agnes M. Brazal, eds., *Faith on the Move: Toward a Theology of Migration in Asia* (Quezon City: Ateneo de Manila University Press, 2008), 63–64.
73. Toshiko Tsujimoto, "Church Organization and Its Networks for the Filipino Migrants: Surviving and Empowering in Korea," in Mamoru Tsuda, ed., *Filipino Diaspora: Demography, Social Networks, Empowerment and Culture* (Quezon City: Philippine Social Science Council, 2003), 125–62.
74. Ibarra C. Mateo, "*Nobena, panata, at paglalakbay:* 'Importing' Religious Traditions from the Philippines to Japan," in Mamoru Tsuda, ed., *Filipino diaspora: Demography, Social Networks, Empowerment and Culture* (Quezon City: Philippine Social Science Council, 2003), 91.
75. Francis Khek Gee Lim, "Charismatic Technology," in Francis Khek Gee Lim, ed., *Mediating Piety: Technology and Religion in Contemporary Asia* (Leiden: Brill, 2009).
76. Vince Rafael, "Power, Pedagogy, and Play: Reading the Early Horacio de la Costa, SJ," in Soledad S. Reyes, ed., *Reading Horacio de la Costa, SJ: Views from the 21st Century* (Quezon City: Ateneo de Manila University Press, 2017), 102–8.
77. Youngblood, *Marcos against the Church.*
78. Coeli M. Barry, review of "Investing in Miracles: El Shaddai and the Transformation of Popular Catholicism in the Philippines," *Journal of Southeast Asian Studies* 37, no. 3 (2006): 566.
79. Katharine L. Wiegele, *Investing in Miracles: El Shaddai and the Transformation of Popular Catholicism in the Philippines* (Honolulu: University of Hawaii Press, 2006), 53; and Katharine L. Wiegele, "Catholics Rich in Spirit: El Shaddai's Modern Engagements," *Philippine Studies* 54, no. 4 (2005): 497.

80. Eric Marcelo O. Genilo, "The Catholic Church and the Reproductive Health Bill Debate: The Philippine Experience," *Heythrop Journal* 55, no. 6 (2014): 8–9.
81. Talal Asad, *Formations of the Secular: Christianity, Islam, Modernity* (Stanford, CA: Stanford University Press, 2003), 200.
82. Josefina Socorro Flores Tondo, "Sacred Enchantment, Transnational Lives, and Diasporic Identity: Filipino Domestic Workers at St. John Catholic Cathedral in Kuala Lumpur," *Philippine Studies* 62, no. 3–4 (2014): 464.
83. Jayeel Serrano Cornelio, *Being Catholic in the Contemporary Philippines: Young People Reinterpreting Religion* (London: Routledge, 2016), 138–39.
84. Manuel Victor J. Sapitula, "Marian Piety and Modernity: The Perpetual Help Devotion as Popular Religion in the Philippines," *Philippine Studies* 62, nos. 3–4 (2014): 399–424.
85. Manuel Victor J. Sapitula and Cheryll Ruth R. Soriano, "My Letter to Heaven via E-mail: Translocal Piety and Mediated Selves in Urban Marian Piety in the Philippines," in Sun Sun Lim and Cheryll Ruth R. Soriano, eds., *Asian Perspectives on Digital Culture: Emerging Phenomena, Enduring Concepts* (New York: Routledge, 2016), 38–39.

6

The Catholic Church and Globalization in Vietnam

PETER C. PHAN

A four-hundred-year-old history of an institution as multifaceted and complex as the Vietnamese Catholic Church can of course be told in several ways, depending on interest and perspective. It may be done, as was the common practice among older Church historians, by recounting what foreign missionaries, especially the hierarchy, did in the so-called mission lands. In this approach, expatriate missionaries are seen as the main, if not the exclusive actors and the local churches as more or less passive recipients and beneficiaries of foreign missions.

In recent times, ecclesiastical historiography has shifted the focus to the local Asian churches as active agents in the process of receiving and transforming the universal Christian message to suit their contexts. In Asia, the contexts are threefold. First, the narrative explores how Asian churches have contributed to the well-being of the local people, especially the poor and the oppressed (liberation and integral human development). Second, the narrative tells how Native Christians, especially the laity, have received and transformed the Christian message to reflect their Indigenous culture by instituting new ways of being church and constructing local theologies, a process referred to as "inculturation." Third, the new narrative studies how Asian Christians have related to the local religions by living together with their adherents, collaborating with them for the common good, carrying out theological discussions together, and sharing religious experiences (interreligious dialogue). These three modes of dialogue—liberation, inculturation, and interreligious dialogue—have been espoused by the Federation of Asian Bishops' Conferences (FABC) and Asian theologians to make the Christian faith into a reality not only *in* but also *of* Asia; in other words, to produce a Christianity with an Asian face.

While by focusing either on expatriate missionaries or on local Christians these historical accounts can each provide an informative overview of the Vietnamese Catholic Church, this chapter attempts to explore the narrative of Vietnamese Catholicism from the perspective of globalization. Globalization is here understood in its most generic sense, namely, the process by which countries and people interact and integrate across national boundaries on a global scale. This process of worldwide interaction and integration, often facilitated by technology, can and does take place in many intertwining areas, including economy, politics, culture, and religion. As a result, new global linkages, networks, and organizations of all types, and with them a new global consciousness, have emerged.

For the so-called world religions, globalization is their lifeblood. Through their missions and missionaries these religions spread and prosper precisely because of and thanks to both their globalization and "deterritorialization" and localization and indigenization. Through their religious faith, communal identity, ethical practices, and material resources they interact with the affairs of the world. Viewing the Vietnamese Catholic Church from this globalization perspective offers new insights into its history, especially in its multiple relations, not only with the state of Vietnam but also with other international organizations, both secular and religious.

In contemporary literature, globalization has been studied mainly in economic and political spheres, that is, in connection to the global spread of the market economy and democracy; its beginning is commonly tied to the rise of modernity in the West after the 1750s.[1] By contrast, it must be noted that, thanks to Catholic missions since the end of the fifteenth century, especially under the *padroado/patronato* of Portugal and Spain, the Catholic Church was, already in the premodern period, a powerful globalizing force. It disseminated throughout Latin America and Asia not only the Christian faith but also the material goods and the body of secular knowledge previously achieved in the West. Conversely, and no less significantly, Catholic missions also brought back to Europe the wealth and natural resources as well as the cultures and religions of these two continents, thus creating an international circulation of material and intellectual and spiritual cultures in all their forms, a genuine globalization *avant la lettre*. Viewing the history of Vietnamese Catholicism through the lens of globalization, though by no means the only way to gain an understanding of it, has the advantage of showing that globalization is not just a modern imperialistic and capitalistic expansion of Western economics, politics, and technology into other parts of the globe, but has also been the work, often with multiple positive results, of Catholic missions during the premodern age.[2]

The establishment of Catholicism in Vietnam was a part of this global and globalizing Christian movement. This chapter on Vietnamese Catholicism and globalization begins with a brief sketch of the background of seventeenth-century Vietnam. It then narrates the history of the Vietnamese Catholic Church according to its three phases of globalization: from the arrival of Jesuit missionaries in 1615 and later, of French missionaries of the Missions étrangères de Paris (MEP) in the second half of the seventeeth century to France's invasion of Vietnam in the second half of the nineteenth century; to French colonization of Vietnam in the 1850s to its end in 1954; and from the end of the First Indochina War to today.[3]

FIRST GLOBALIZATION: CATHOLIC MISSIONS UNDER PORTUGUESE *PADROADO* AND PROPAGANDA FIDE (1615–1850)

Before discussing globalization in Vietnam and the role of the Vietnamese Catholic Church within it, it would be useful to recall the real estate axiom: location, location, location. The geographical position of Vietnam, its eastern coast stretching from north to south along the Pacific Ocean (or the South China Sea) and its southernmost tip within easy reach from the Indian Ocean, makes the country one of the most coveted, strategically situated parts of the world for international trade. In the early phase of globalization it was a center of intense global rivalries for geopolitical supremacy, as successive imperial powers, from China to Portugal, Spain, Holland, Britain, France, Japan, and the United States, tried to occupy and annex it or at least carve out enclaves, treaty ports, and concessions for themselves. Furthermore, as Christopher Goscha has argued, the country that is known today as Vietnam has existed as a unified state in the current S-shaped land only for a total of some eighty-four years.[4] In other words, before there was *a* Vietnam, there had been *multiple* Vietnams, the history of which includes an imperial Vietnam, with its citizens "building and pushing their own empire southward, establishing protectorates over far-flung regions, promoting settlement colonies, alternating between 'direct' and 'indirect' methods of rule over distant, multiethnic peoples, testing cultural assimilation, and developing their own *mission civilisatrice*."[5] Thus, long before experiencing globalization from the West, Vietnam had been engaged in a kind of globalization of its own. This is not to deny that with the coming of Christianity at the dawn of the seventeeth century Vietnam entered a qualitatively different stage and kind of globalization, but only to recall that globalization in terms of economic and political international relations had already been at work in Vietnam centuries before the arrival of Western, especially French, colonialists and missionaries.

Though there had been sporadic visits to Vietnam by Spanish Franciscans and Dominicans from Malacca and the Philippines in the sixteenth century, Catholic missions to the country started only with the arrival of the Jesuits in the second decade of the seventeenth century. A brief word about the political context of seventeenth-century Vietnam is necessary to understand the many challenges facing the incipient Christian missions. In the early part of the century Vietnam, more precisely Đại Việt (Great Viet), the name of the country from 1428 to 1804 and known to the West as Annam, was divided into two parts: the north, called Đàng Ngoài (the Outer Region) and known to the West as Tonkin; and the south, called Đàng Trong (the Inner Region) and known to the West as Cochinchina. The dividing line was located slightly above the 17th parallel.[6] Politically, the country was under the Lê dynasty (1428–1788), but the Lê kings (*vua*) were puppets, with a largely ceremonial role. Real power was wielded by the lords (*chúa)* in the north by the Trịnh clan and in the South by the Nguyễn clan, both with dynastic ambitions. For almost fifty years (1627–72) seven wars were waged between the two regions, all ending in stalemate, with north and south coexisting as two independent parts of one country.

The Jesuits were entangled in this internecine rivalry when they first arrived in Cochinchina in 1615 and in Tonkin in 1627. Their missionary activities were favored or curtailed depending on their perceived usefulness to the political vicissitudes and military campaigns of the two ruling clans. The most influential early Jesuit missionaries include the French Alexandre de Rhodes (1593–1660) and the Italian Geronimo Maiorica (1589–1656), both of whom first came to Cochinchina in 1624. Jesuit missions in Vietnam ended in 1773 when the order was suppressed and did not resume until 1957.

Until this point, Catholic missions in Asia were carried out under the royal patronage (*padroado régio*) of Portugal, except in the Philippines, where missions were under the patronage of Spain. While Catholic missions undoubtedly enjoyed significant economic benefits from such royal patronages, they came with huge spiritual detriments as well, especially in matters of episcopal appointment. By the middle of the seventeenth century Portugal had lost its military and commercial hegemony in Asia to new Western colonial powers such as Holland and Britain and was no longer able to support Catholic missions effectively.

To wrestle control of the Catholic missions from the Portuguese padroado, in 1622 Rome founded the Congregation for the Propagation of the Faith, popularly known as Propaganda Fide. To rescue Catholic missions from the abuses and ineffectiveness of the Portuguese padroado, Propaganda Fide established "apostolic vicariates" (rather than full-fledged dioceses, which would require the consent of the Portuguese Crown) and appointed bishops as "apostolic vicars" to function not under the control of Spain or Portugal but under Propaganda Fide's direct supervision. Thanks to de Rhodes's interventions with Propaganda Fide after his return to Rome in 1649, a new group of French missionaries, members of the newly founded Société des Missions Étrangères de Paris (MEP), gained access to Vietnam. In 1659, Propaganda Fide established two apostolic vicariates and appointed two MEP members as bishops: François Pallu (1626–84) for Tonkin and Pierre Lambert de la Motte (1624–79) for Cochinchina. This ecclesiastical innovation proved to be of momentous consequence, at least for Vietnam, in four respects.

First, it created bitter and scandalous conflicts, which lasted until 1773, between the Jesuits and the new missionaries, the former refusing to acknowledge the authority of the latter on the grounds that they lacked the authorization of the Portuguese Crown. The new structure fomented rivalries among the religious orders for control of mission territories and the converts. Second, the new French missionaries brought with them a spirituality markedly different from the Iberian spirituality espoused by the Jesuits, with its new emphasis on popular devotions and which was more congenial to the Vietnamese temperament. Third, the MEP missionaries adopted a missionary method that is less receptive to local cultures and religious practices than the *modo suave* commended by Jesuits such as Alessandro Valignano and Matteo Ricci. Fourth, the predominant presence of new missionaries of French nationality tipped the balance of geopolitical interests and tragically, in light of later persecutions of French missionaries by the Nguyễn dynasty, it provided the convenient pretext of securing the safety of its citizens for the Louis-Napoléon Bonaparte III government to invade and eventually colonize Vietnam for a century (1858–1954).

It can reasonably be said that the period of the Jesuits' missions and other latecomers, such as the Dominicans, the Franciscans, the Augustinians, the Discalced Carmelites, and the MEP beginning in the early seventeenth century, represent the first phase of globalization in Vietnam.[7] Vietnam had by no means been a "hermit kingdom," totally cut off from transnational contacts, before the arrival of Catholic missionaries. On the contrary: for nearly a thousand years it had maintained relations of various types, at times vassalage, at times independence, with its giant neighbor to the north. Furthermore, from the second half of the fourteenth century to the end of the seventeenth century, Vietnam carried out what has been known as Nam Tiến (March to the south), by which it conquered and annexed the Cham Kingdom and the southernmost territory of Cambodia, thus tripling its original territory centered at the Red River Delta to its current size. In fact, Cochinchina, where the first Jesuits landed in 1615, had been part of the Cham Kingdom.

To be noted also is the fact that toward the end of the sixteenth century there began a new era of international commerce between Vietnam and other Asian countries, particularly with Japan, under the Tokugawa shogunate, and with European countries, particularly Portugal (with Malacca and Macao), Spain (with Manila), and Holland (with Batavia). The bulk of international commercial trading centered in Đàng Trong, which then boasted Hội An (known to Europeans as Faifo, today Đà Nẵng), the most important Southeast Asian port, where ships of Asian and European countries plied their trade. At the same time, Đàng Ngoài was constantly engaged in overland trade with China. However, at the beginning of the seventeenth century the Trịnh lords, who had not favored seaborne commerce, solicited trade relations with Japan, and later, in 1625, when Japan banned trade with Đàng Ngoài, the north began trading with the Dutch East India Company.[8]

Despite these and other extensive transnational interactions, it was Catholic missionaries, mostly Jesuits coming to Vietnam on Portuguese commercial ships, who promoted the first stage of globalization in Vietnam by carrying out a sustained process of linking Vietnam with Europe and vice versa, on a global scale. It is important to note that this first phase of globalization through missionary activities in Vietnam was devoid of economic, political, and military exploitative interests. It is a credible example of globalization without a colonialist agenda, which is of great importance, in light of the charge of colonialist collaboration that has often been leveled by secular historians against Catholic, especially French, missions in the country. Indeed, far from pursuing political and cultural domination, the Jesuits, while carrying out their missionary enterprise, were engaged in introducing, especially in Cochinchina, Western technical knowledge such as medicine, mathematics, physics, and astronomy. Several of them, including de Rhodes and Geronimo (Girolamo) Maiorica, also promoted local cultures by adopting them into Christian theology and liturgy.[9] In particular de Rhodes, making use of his confreres' efforts, perfected an alphabetized script, which is now Vietnam's national script. Missionaries produced numerous literary works in Vietnamese, in both the alphabetized and the demotic scripts (*chữ nôm*), such as dictionaries, grammars, catechisms, apologetical tracts, religious plays, prayers, and pious literature. In this way they made an immense and lasting contribution to the Vietnamese linguistic, cultural, and religious heritage. Furthermore, this process of globalization was a two-way street: not only did the Jesuit missionaries introduce the West to Vietnam, they also introduced Vietnam to the West, including its flora and fauna, political systems, cultural practices, and religious traditions through travelogues and historical reports.[10]

Dating the beginning of globalization in Vietnam to the premodern period, more precisely, during the Catholic missions in the seventeenth century, serves three important purposes: it decouples globalization from the quest for economic, political, and military hegemony of the Western colonialist enterprise and highlights the intimate connections between globalization on the one hand and culture and religion on the other. It further rejects the erroneous view, much in vogue in secular historiography, that there had been no real globalization in Vietnam before the coming of the "West," dated to the French colonization of the country in the middle of the nineteenth century, with its projects of "modernization" and "civilization." And it recognizes the significant and lasting contributions that the Catholic Church, especially through its expatriate missionaries, made during the first phase of globalization of Vietnam and continued to make to the development of the country in the second and third phases of globalization.

SECOND GLOBALIZATION: VIETNAM UNDER FRENCH COLONIZATION (1858–1954)

The second phase of globalization started with the French colonization of Vietnam in the second half of the nineteenth century. It began in 1858 when a Franco-Spanish fleet attacked Đà Nẵng; it began to fade in the middle of the twentieth century when, in 1945, the Democratic Republic of Vietnam was founded with Hồ Chí Minh as president; and it finally ended in 1954, when the French Army was defeated at the celebrated battle of Điện Biên Phủ and France was forced to relinquish its colonial rule over Vietnam.

To understand the role of Vietnamese Catholicism in this century-long phase of globalization, in many ways vastly different from and much more controversial than the first phase, it is imperative to recall the relations between the Vietnamese Catholic Church and the Nguyễn dynasty and the latter's many bloody persecutions of Catholics, both foreign and Native, especially under the reigns of emperors Minh Mạng (1820–41), Thiệu Trị (1841–47), and Tự Đức (1847–83). Indeed, it was the Nguyễns' persecutions of the Vietnamese Catholic Church, chiefly between 1825 and 1865, that provided Napoléon and then France's Third Republic with a convenient pretext to carry out their imperialist ambitions and to establish France's colonial rule over Vietnam.[11]

Thus, though it was only through the French colonization of Vietnam, effectively begun in 1862 with the Treaty of Saigon, that globalization in Vietnam entered a radically new and distinct phase; the roots of this second phase lie deep in the period preceding the founding of the Vietnamese last dynasty in 1802. Indeed, without the pivotal role of the French Catholic bishop Pierre Pigneaux de Béhaine (1741–99), there would in all likelihood have been no Nguyễn dynasty.[12] Thus, for good or ill, beginning in the late 1870s the Catholic Church was playing a large role in establishing new links between Vietnam and the West.

It would be a historical exaggeration to say that Pigneaux's military personnel and weaponry alone brought about Nguyễn Phúc Ánh's final victory over the Tây Sơn and the establishment of the Nguyễn dynasty. But it is not false, either, to say that these two events would most likely not have been possible without Pigneaux's and many other foreigners' considerable contributions. The bishop provided Ánh with war matériel, military expertise, and diplomatic connections when the latter was in dire straits.

Pigneaux's contributions to the Nguyễn's victory over the Tây Sơn were publicly acknowledged by Nguyễn Phúc Ánh and Prince Cảnh themselves in their funerary orations and, as a sign of the nascent nation's gratitude, they gave Pigneaux a national burial with full military honors on December 19, 1799. Pigneaux's military and diplomatic achievements are also recognized—albeit indirectly—by historians who are deeply critical of the alleged collusion between French missionaries and the French colonial government.

The point of mentioning Bishop Pigneaux is neither to defend nor to condemn his diplomatic and military activities on behalf of Nguyễn Phúc Ánh—there has been no lack of attempts at both—but simply to highlight his role and through him, as a spiritual leader of the Vietnamese Catholic Church, the establishment of a wide and effective network of diplomatic and military relations between France and Nguyễn Phúc Ánh, the future founder of the last Vietnamese dynasty.[13] The establishment of these international and intercontinental links, which included at the time not only France but also Portugal and Spain, is no doubt a momentous event in the process of globalization in Vietnam and Vietnamese Catholicism.

Given these pivotal contributions of the Vietnamese Catholic Church to the Nguyễn dynasty, there is deep irony—unconscionable ingratitude, some would argue—in the anti-Catholic policies of Nguyễn Phúc Ánh's immediate successors, namely, Minh Mạng, Thiệu Trị, and Tự Đức, and their bloody persecutions of Vietnamese Catholics. Extensive investigations into the three emperors' motives for their actions have been carried out, and there is no need to rehearse them here.[14] These motives ranged from perceived cultural to religious differences between Vietnam and Christianity, which was branded as *tà đạo* (heterodox/perverse religion). Political considerations also figured prominently in Minh Mạng's anti-Catholic policies.

Thiệu Trị, Minh Mạng's son, continued his father's anti-Catholic policies, but with a less severe impact on the Church due to the brevity of his reign, which lasted only seven years. Thiệu Trị's death at the age of forty-one precipitated a succession crisis when the court passed over his eldest son, Hồng Bảo, in favor of the twenty-year-old younger brother, Hồng Đức, who took the name Tự Đức. His thirty-six-year reign (1847–83) was plagued by a series of natural disasters of flood and drought that produced widespread famine and severely weakened the economy, and more than his two predecessors, Tự Đức undertook bloody persecutions of Catholics. Unfortunately, the last twenty-five years of Tự Đức's reign coincided with Napoléon's and the French Third Republic's (1789–1940) imperialist ambitions. France's colonization of Vietnam proceeded over the next fifty years. Begun in 1858, when its navy attacked Đà Nẵng, France's colonization of the six southern provinces of Vietnam, now called Cochinchina, was ratified by Tự Đức in the 1862 and 1864 Treaties of Saigon. By his death at the age of fifty-three on July 12, 1883, Vietnam as an independent country was reduced to an empty shell. Barely a month after Tự Đức's death, on August 25, France extended its rule over Vietnam by making protectorates of the north (Tonkin) and the center (Annam) through the 1883 Harmand Treaty, later ratified by the 1884 Patenôtre Treaty.

There is no need to narrate here all the political and military events between France and Vietnam, important but of no immediate relevance to our theme, until 1954, when France was forced to end its colonization of Vietnam. Obviously, Franco-Vietnamese relations in Cochinchina, a French colony, varied enormously from those in Annam and Tonkin, which were only French protectorates and over which the Huế court enjoyed a measure of control. Indeed, French authorities in Cochinchina were jealously defending its special status as a French colony and its financial autonomy from the encroachments of French authorities in the two protectorates of Annam and Hanoi. However these relations are evaluated, especially in terms of the tripartite dismemberment of Vietnam into Cochinchina, Annam, and Tonkin and in terms of Vietnam's independence, there is no doubt that they brought the process of the globalization of the country to a radically new level.

The immediate impact of the French colonialization of Vietnam was of course the globalization of the country through insertion into a wider international community that extended beyond northeast Asia (particularly China, Korea, and Japan), Southeast Asia (particularly Siam/Thailand, Laos, Cambodia, the Philippines, Malaysia, and Indonesia), and Europe and North America (Portugal, Spain, Holland, France, Britain, and even the United States).[15] For the first time Vietnam appeared on the global scene as a nation in the community of modern nations though, unfortunately, as one like many other Asian and African countries at the time, to be dominated and exploited by the West.

Vietnam did not, however, remain passive in this second phase of globalization. Rather, it tried to play an active role on the geopolitical scene, and Vietnamese Catholics were needed for these endeavors thanks to their linguistic skills, their Western education, their political savoir faire, and their religious contacts with the West. As early as 1840, in an attempt to build an alliance with European powers, the emperor Minh Mạng dispatched a delegation to France, headed by the mandarin Trương Minh Giảng and with the Catholic catechist Thomas Lê Hực as an interpreter, to offer France a trade monopoly. Prospects of success were hopeful when the delegation was received by the prime minister and the minister of commerce, but King Louis-Philippe, pressured by the MEP and the Vatican not to ally with "the enemy of religion," turned down the offer.[16]

In 1863, Tự Đức sent a seventy-strong embassy to France, headed by Phan Thanh Giản, with the mission of negotiating with France for the return of the three eastern provinces of southern Vietnam it had taken the year before. Three key members of the embassy were the Catholic priest Đặng Đức Tuấn, who served as interpreter; the lay Catholic writer Trương Vĩnh Ký, who also served as interpreter; and the French Vietnamese Catholic Nguyễn Văn Đức, also known as Michel Đức, the son of Jean-Baptiste Chaigneau (whose Vietnamese name is Nguyễn Văn Thắng) and his Vietnamese wife, who served as a go-between for Phan Thanh Giản and Paris. Napoléon initially agreed to the plea but changed his mind because of the vigorous objection of Chasseloup-Laubat, the minister of the navy and the Colonies. Despite the embassy's political failure, Phan Thanh Giản had the opportunity to witness France's technological advances, and upon his return urged Tự Đức to undertake educational reform and foster technological training to strengthen the country's position in a globalizing world.

In January 1867, Tự Đức sent another mission to France, one member of which was Nguyễn Trường Tộ, a prominent Catholic and Confucian scholar who was fluent in a dozen languages and well-versed in Western cultures, to recruit technicians and teachers for a Western-style school. Unfortunately, the project came to naught when in June of the same year France annexed the remaining three western provinces of southern Vietnam.

It is also to be noted that, despite its adoption of rigid Confucianism as the state political and moral philosophy, with the strong support of the anti-Western and anti-globalization mandarinate, and its bloody persecutions of Christianity, the royal court saw no irony in taking advantage of the technical expertise provided by French missionaries, among whom François Jaccard (1799–1838) figured prominently. The emperor Minh Mạng made extensive use of Jaccard as a translator of foreign-language materials and teacher of European languages to select students at the court. His execution in 1838, which Minh Mạng is said to have bitterly regretted, deprived the court of the only resource person capable of helping the court understand foreign-language documents and negotiate the complex political and cultural relations between the threatening European powers and the increasingly isolated Vietnam.[17]

As to how the Vietnamese Catholic Church contributed to its own globalization and that of Vietnam during the second phase of globalization, this can best be understood by distinguishing two kinds of Vietnamese Church during this time: the colonial Church and the emerging Indigenous Church. The colonial Church, which flourished throughout the nineteenth century, can be dated from Bishop Pierre Pigneaux's entanglements in the diplomatic and military relations between France and Nguyễn Phúc Ánh. No doubt the bishop pinned his hopes of rapid conversion of Vietnam on the eventual baptism of Crown Prince Nguyễn Phúc Cảnh. The bishop's early death of dysentery in 1799 at the age of fifty-eight and the prince's death from smallpox two years later at the age of nineteen brought Pigneaux's dream of a Vietnamese Constantine to naught. Furthermore, Nguyễn's persecutions of the Vietnamese Catholic Church and the later massacres of Vietnamese Catholics by the Văn Thân and Cần Vương movements, estimated in the tens of thousands, would have decimated the Vietnamese Catholic Church were it not for France's military protection and financial support from the middle of the nineteenth century to the middle of the twentieth century.[18]

Even if Pigneaux's hopes for a total Christianization of Vietnam through a Catholic emperor were dashed, the colonial Church during France's rule enjoyed extraordinary growth and took unprecedented steps toward globalization. This was due first of all to a revival of Catholic missions in France during the Restoration (1815–30), thanks in part to the Oeuvre de la Propagation de la Foi (Association for the propagation of the faith), founded in 1822, and the Oeuvre Pontificale de la Sainte-Enfance (Pontifical association of the Holy Childhood), founded in 1843, both of which raised huge sums of money to support French Catholic missions. In 1840–64, French missionaries in Vietnam received nearly three million francs from the Oeuvre de la Propagation de la Foi. With this financial boon, along with the funds coming from Rome, missionaries were able to expand dramatically, not only regarding evangelization of the people but also in the construction of churches, schools, and social services.[19]

From 1875 to 1933, the number of churches grew from 906 to 4,578, the most famous of which are the neo-Gothic style cathedrals built in Saigon (in 1880) and in Hanoi (in 1886) and the cathedral of Phát Diệm, the building of which was overseen by the Vietnamese priest Cụ Sáu and in a blend of European and Vietnamese architectural styles (built in 1892). Enormous progress was also achieved in education. Among high schools for boys, the most prestigious new schools were owned by the Brothers of Christian Schools (Frères des Écoles Chrétiennes), including the Lycée Puginier (in Hanoi), the École Pellerin (in Huế), the Collège d'Adran (in Da Lat), and the Institut Taberd (in Saigon). Elite schools for girls were run by the French Sisters of Saint Paul de Chartres, including the École Sainte Marie (Hanoi), the École Jeanne d'Arc (Huế), and the École Saint Paul (Saigon). The colonial Church also fostered social services, especially after the 1890s, by founding orphanages, hospitals, dispensaries, leprosaria, and homes for the elderly and the terminally ill. Such social-welfare and public-health services were rendered chiefly by the Sisters of Saint Paul de Chartres and the Vietnamese religious society Lovers of the Cross, the latter of which founded by Bishop Pierre de la Motte in 1670.[20]

These numerous and varied activities organized and carried out by foreign missionaries and religious orders, especially in the fields of education and health care, placed the Vietnamese Catholic Church on the global map in a way that had not been possible during the first phase of globalization. There was an exponential increase in the exchanges of money and material goods, in the promotion of Western education and health care systems, and in political and spiritual communications between Vietnam and the Vietnamese Catholic Church on the one hand and Europe and the French Church as well as the Vatican on the other. Of course, these globalizing activities were greatly facilitated and even financially supported by the French colonial rule.

However, expatriate missionaries and the French colonial government were not the only actors in this globalization of the Vietnamese colonial Church. Vietnamese-born Catholics themselves made significant contributions to the globalization, not only of the Vietnamese Church but also of Vietnam as a country, and in this way began forging an inculturated or Native Vietnamese Church. One important figure who made the Vietnamese Church known to the West and vice versa is the Jesuit priest whose Vietnamese name is Nguyễn Văn Bỉnh and whose religious name is Philiphê Bỉnh (1759–1833).[21] Bỉnh went to Portugal in 1796 to defend the heritage of Jesuit Portuguese padroado Catholicism against the Spanish Dominican and the MEP takeover and lived there until his death in 1833. During his thirty-seven-year exile in Lisbon, Bỉnh's intensely lobbied for a padroado bishop for his community back home in Tonkin and composed some sixteen works in alphabetized script to interpret Western culture and Christian spirituality to his compatriots back in Vietnam, placing the Vietnamese Catholic Church on the global scene.[22]

In addition to Bỉnh, other Vietnamese Catholics who have made lasting contributions to the modernization and globalization of Vietnam include four laymen: Nguyễn Trường Tộ (1828–71), Paulus Huỳnh Tịnh Của (1830–1908), Petrus Trương Vĩnh Ký (1837–98), and Nguyễn Hữu Bài (1863–1935). Nguyễn Trường Tộ, an ardent admirer of Western culture and technology, is known for the many petitions he submitted to the emperor Tự Đức advocating reforms in politics (including the separation of powers), economics, education, agriculture, and industry, all aimed at making Vietnam a modern nation among other nations. Huỳnh Tịnh Của, a polyglot and prolific writer, popularized the use of the alphabetized script and contributed to its eventual adoption as the *quốc ngữ* (national script). The popularization of the alphabetized script was also the work of Trương Vĩnh Ký, editor of *Gia Định Báo*, the first newspaper to use it.[23] Nguyễn Hữu Bài, a member of the privy council of the royal court and an officer of the French Légion d'honneur, traveled with Emperor Khải Định to France in 1922 and from there went to Rome, where he was granted an audience with Pope Pius XI. Bai presented four requests, the most significant of which was the creation of a Vietnamese hierarchy consisting of Native bishops.[24] Bài's request became a reality in 1933 when Pius XI ordained the first Vietnamese bishop, Nguyễn Bá Tòng, and even further in 1960, when Pope John XXIII established the Vietnamese Church hierarchy.

Lastly, the globalization movement during its second period was given a powerful push by the coming of a host of international religious orders and societies, both male and female, in addition to the Jesuits, Dominicans, Franciscans, Discalced Carmelites, and MEP who had arrived in the seventeenth century. These included the contemplative orders—the Carmelite nuns, in 1961; the Cistercians in 1934; the Poor Clares in 1935; the Benedictine monks in 1935; the Little Brothers of Jesus in 1939; and the Benedictine nuns in 1954—as well as the active orders—the Augustinians in 1701; the Redemptorists in 1925; the Lazarists or Vincentians in 1932; the Brothers of Christian Schools in 1866; the Sulpicians in 1929; the Chanoinesses de Saint Augustin in 1935; the Sisters of Divine Providence in 1876; the Daughters of Charity in 1928; the Franciscan Missionaries of Mary in 1932; the Salesians of Don Bosco in 1940; the Sisters of Saint Paul de Chartres in 1860; and many others. These religious orders and societies, diverse in their missions and activities, established and promoted international networks and institutions on a global scale hitherto unimaginable.

THIRD GLOBALIZATION: A GLOBAL CHURCH IN THE WORLD CHURCH AND THE COMMUNITY OF NATIONS, 1954–2020

The tempo of the globalization of Vietnamese Catholicism accelerated immeasurably in its third phase and at times even spun out of control under the pressure of unforeseeable and seismic political events. This third phase began with the 1954 Geneva Accords, which ended the First Indochina War (1946–54), then grew by leaps and bounds during the Second Indochina War or the Vietnam War (1965–75) and is currently taking on a truly transnational and intercontinental character thanks to the Vietnamese Catholic diaspora communities across the globe. A veritable avalanche of publications have been produced on the impact of the First and Second Indochina Wars and their aftermaths on Vietnam as a modern nation, but little research has been done on their profound impact on the globalization of the Vietnamese Catholic Church. Here I will focus on four momentous events during this sixty-six-year period that transformed Vietnamese Catholicism from a colonial and Indigenous Church to a global one.[25]

The first event of the third stage of globalization was the Geneva Accords (July 21, 1954). The Geneva Accords followed the defeat of the French Army by Gen. Võ Nguyên Giáp at the celebrated battle of Điện Biên Phủ and marked the end of the French colonization of Vietnam. It temporarily partitioned Vietnam into two zones at the 17th parallel as the military demarcation line, with North Vietnam under the control of the Communists and South Vietnam under the pro-Western government of Bảo Đại, the last emperor of the Nguyễn dynasty.[26] This political settlement stipulated that a plebiscite be held in 1956 to determine the type of political system for the to-be-unified country. It also provided for the possibility for people of each zone to freely move north or south according to their political preferences. This provision for internal migration proved to be a disaster for the northern Vietnamese Catholic Church, as it was decimated by the departure to the south of over 600,000 Catholics and clergy in 1954–55. The exodus brought the Vietnamese Catholic Church to the attention of the West, especially thanks to the publicity given to the work among migrants and the publication of the books of Navy lieutenant Dr. Thomas A. Dooley. Because the exodus was perceived as a Catholic rejection of communism, which Pope Pius XI's encyclical

Divini Redemptoris (1937) had condemned as "atheistic" and "a pseudo-ideal of justice" (no. 8), the Church received generous material assistance from Caritas Internationalis and the free world, especially the United States. From the perspective of Church organization, though this sudden influx of northern Catholics produced enormous pastoral challenges in the south, it also expanded the scope of the globalization of the Church insofar as it created political, economic, and spiritual linkages between the churches of the north and south but also between the Vietnamese Catholic Church and the universal Church.[27] This global connection was strengthened by Pope John XXIII's establishment of the ecclesiastical hierarchy in Vietnam in 1960 and the creation of three archdioceses (Hanoi, Huế, and Saigon) and seventeen dioceses.

The second globalization event was the Vietnam War (1965–75). The plebiscite stipulated in the Geneva Accords was never held, and soon a war erupted between North and South Vietnam, as part of the Cold War: the North was assisted by the People's Republic of China and the Soviet Union and the South by the United States. The conflict, with its gory images of death and destruction broadcast live daily on American television, made Vietnam a household word in the West and a rallying cry for geopolitical transformation by both the left and the right. For the first time, Vietnam had fully entered the global scene. The Vietnamese Catholic Church received much international, mostly negative, press because the first president of the Republic of Vietnam, Ngô Đình Diệm, was a devout Catholic whose regime was accused of being a dictatorship. His murder, along with his younger brother Ngô Đình Nhu, in November 1963 pushed the Vietnamese Catholic Church to the forefront of international news.

As the war progressed, global awareness of the country grew exponentially, thanks to print news and television broadcasts. After the United States entered the war, the massive presence of the American military inflamed the Communists' accusation against South Vietnam of collaboration with American imperialism and betrayal of the country. At the same time, Western goods flooded South Vietnam, creating an artificial consumerist economy, which enabled the population to have a taste of the Western lifestyle. Complex international networks were created with the communist world, especially China and the Soviet Union, and with several democratic Western countries. As a result, there arose a greater consciousness of the place of Vietnam in the global political scene. The Church for its part had to confront a war that pitted the opposing ideologies of communism and capitalism against each other. On the one hand, it had to adhere to the papal condemnation of communism and had no viable option to demand the end of the war and encourage reconciliation with the communist North to achieve the reunification of the country. On the other hand, it had to deal with the corruption and moral decadence that American capitalism produced among the Vietnamese people and within the Church itself.

Ecclesially, the Catholic Church was introduced to the international world of American non-Catholic churches and missionaries, especially the Christian and Missionary Alliance, the Baptists, the Church of Christ, the Assemblies of God, and Seventh-day Adventists. The presence of these missionaries and agencies created the need for ecumenical unity and collaboration, which is all the more urgent today because some of these denominations (e.g., house churches) are not registered with the government. They are enjoying phenomenal growth, especially among ethnic minorities in the highlands, and their evangelizing methods differ markedly from that of the Catholic Church.

The third event contributing to the globalization of the Vietnamese Catholic Church was the Second Vatican Ecumenical Council (1962–65). While the council had no impact on the Catholic Church in North Vietnam, which was cut off from all contact with the Vatican, the Church in the south benefited immensely from the council. In the decade 1965–75, a good number of Vietnamese priests and religious traveled abroad, especially to Rome and France, to earn graduate degrees in philosophy, theology, and canon law. Higher institutes of theology were founded within the country, such as the Pius X Pontifical Institute founded by the Jesuits in Đà Lạt. Numerous courses in the Bible, theology, and religious education were organized for the laity. There were very active and influential lay movements, such as Focolare and the Youth-Student-Worker Groups. Translations of Vatican II's documents into Vietnamese helped popularize the council's teachings and reforms. A scholarly translation of the Bible was produced. Liturgical innovations were introduced to adapt to cultural and religious customs. A plethora of religious orders, both male and female, were active in education, health care, and social service, and because these were international in origin and structure, they contributed greatly to the globalization of the Vietnamese Catholic Church.

The fourth event promoting the third globalization is the fall of the Republic of Vietnam (South Vietnam) to the communist north in April 1975. The internecine twenty-year war ended on April 30, 1975, and the country was reunified the following year under the name of the Socialist Republic of Vietnam. This event was both a bane and a boon for Vietnamese Christianity. On the one hand, the communist victory abruptly arrested the energetic growth of the Church in the south. The communist government sought to destroy many religious structures, Catholic as well as Protestant. On the other hand, with the unification of the country it was possible for the first time in twenty years for the Catholic Church to function as a single body and to establish regular contacts between the churches of the north and those of the south. In 1980, the Vietnamese Episcopal Conference was reestablished. Since then it has been able to hold its annual meetings and maintain contact with the episcopal conferences of other Asian countries, especially through the FABC. In December 2012, the FABC was allowed by the communist government to hold its tenth plenary assembly in Xuân Lộc, a town near Hồ Chí Minh City, with the attendance of seventy-one foreign cardinals and bishops from more than twenty countries, making the gathering a truly global event.

Another unintended consequence of the fall of South Vietnam in 1975 was the exodus of hundreds of thousands of Vietnamese Catholics to other countries, especially to the United States, Canada, and Australia. This truly international and transcontinental event created not only a Vietnamese diaspora but also a "Vietnamese Catholic Church in the Diaspora." Whenever possible, Vietnamese Catholics have organized themselves into ethnic parishes to preserve their cultural and religious customs. They have also contributed significantly to the building of the local Church. Currently there are Vietnamese bishops in all three countries of this diaspora. There are over one thousand Vietnamese priests and a large number of sisters in the United States alone. Vietnamese men currently make up 12 percent of the American seminary population. This overseas Vietnamese Catholic Church constitutes a powerful network of transnational and global communications and maintains a certain solidarity with the Catholic Church in Vietnam.

In retrospect, the globalization of the Vietnamese Catholic Church through its three phases—from the seventeenth to the twenty-first century—was not a well-planned project designed and undertaken by the Church alone. Rather, it was a collective response to the challenges of political and social events outside its control. No doubt, the fact that it is a part of the "one, holy, catholic, and apostolic" church has greatly facilitated the formation of global linkages, networks, and organizations of all types, and with them, a new global consciousness. But few could have predicted that the Vietnamese Catholic Church would be present throughout the world as it is today, contributing to the globalization of Christianity while preserving its cultural and religious heritage.

NOTES

1. The use of terms such as "modern," "modernity," and "globalization" are notoriously slippery and relying on them to periodize history is a highly controversial approach. In Western literature these terms commonly refer to the historical transformation in Europe and the United States, generally dated to the nineteenth century, a period that is characterized by a combination of the following factors: capitalism, scientific method, industrialization, technological progress, international trade, urbanization, bureaucratic rationalization, creation of the nation-state, and secularization. Most early studies of globalization focus on these elements alone and almost none focus on the impact of religion. Worth mentioning are two pioneering exceptions: John Tomlinson, *Globalization and Culture* (Chicago: University of Chicago Press, 1999); and Peter Beyer, *Religion and Globalization* (Thousand Oaks, CA: SAGE, 1994). Other than these two, a plethora of publications have focused on the mutual impact between globalization on the one hand and culture and the so-called world religions, in particular Christianity and Islam, on the other. One of the most significant studies is José Casanova, *Public Religions in the Modern World* (Chicago: University of Chicago Press, 1994).
2. It should be noted here that my historical account of the globalization/modernization of Vietnam differs significantly from the common treatment of the theme in Western, especially French and American, historical scholarship. First, it does not date this globalizing movement in Vietnam from the fateful year 1858, when the Franco-Spanish fleet attacked Đà Nẵng, presaging France's colonization of Vietnam. Indeed, in my view Vietnam's globalization, as the term is commonly understood today, was initiated at least as early as the first quarter of the seventeenth century. I concur with Christopher Goscha's proposal that we must eschew the Franco-centric approach to modernization of Vietnam. See his *Viet Nam: A New History* (New York: Basic, 2016), 1–11. Second, and of profound import for a general history of Vietnam, it is important to acknowledge the role of the Vietnamese Catholic Church, inclusive of foreign missionaries and Native Vietnamese Catholics, and its enormous contributions to this process of globalization. Secular and communist historiography of Vietnam, either out of ignorance or due to ideological bias, has not paid sufficient attention to this historical fact while lambasting the alleged collusion between the Vietnamese Catholic Church and colonial France.
3. Helpful single-volume comprehensive histories of Vietnam include Keith W. Taylor, *A History of the Vietnamese* (Cambridge: Cambridge University Press, 2013); Ben Kiernan, *Viet Nam: A History from Earliest Times to the Present* (Oxford: Oxford University Press, 2017); and Christopher Gosha, *Vietnam: A New History* (New York: Basic, 2016). On the relations between Vietnam and

the West, see Wynn Wilcox, ed., *Vietnam and the West: New Approaches* (Ithaca, NY: Cornell University Press, 2010).

4. See Goscha, *Viet Nam*, 4. Writing in 2016, Goscha put the number at eighty-three years and some months; I have rounded it up to eighty-four.
5. Goscha, *Viet Nam*, 9.
6. This bipartite division of the country should not be confused with the later tripartite division of the country during the French colonization, from the middle of the nineteenth century to the middle of the twentieth century, which was divided into three parts and known as Đại Việt (the Great Viet): the south, known as Cochinchina, which was a French colony and its main city was Saigon; the center, known as Annam, the capital city of which was Hue, where the Nguyen royal court was located; and the north, known as Tonkin, whose main city was Hanoi. Both Annam and Tonkin became French protectorates in 1883. In 1887 the three parts of Vietnam and Cambodia were formed into French Indochina, to which Laos was added in 1893.
7. This is the main thesis found in Brian Ostrowski, "The Rise of Christian Nôm Literature in Seventeenth-Century Vietnam: Fusing European Content and Local Expression," in Wynn Wilcox, ed., *Vietnam and the West: New Approaches* (Ithaca, NY: Cornell University Press, 2010), 19–39.
8. See Anthony Reed, *Southeast Asia in the Age of Commerce, 1450–1680, Vol. 1, The Lands below the Winds* (New Haven, CT: Yale University Press, 1988) and *Vol. 2, Expansion and Crisis* (New Haven, CT: Yale University Press, 1993).
9. On Alexandre de Rhodes, see Peter C. Phan, *Mission and Catechesis: Alexandre de Rhodes and Inculturation in Seventeenth-Century Vietnam* (Maryknoll, NY: Orbis, 1998). On Geronimo Maiorica, see Brian Eugene Ostrowski, "The Nôm Works of Geronimo Maiorica, SJ, (1589–1656) and Their Christology" (PhD diss., Cornell University, 2006). See also Ostrowski, "The Rise of Christian Nôm Literature." Noteworthy are Maiorica's forty-eight volumes written in *chu nom*, which are divided into four categories: lives of the saints, biblical narratives, sermons, and catechetics. These writings constitute an integral part of early premodern Vietnamese literature.
10. The importance of early missionaries' travelogues and annual reports on their missions as a rich source of historical knowledge of Vietnam cannot be overstated. For a list of Alexandre de Rhodes's works, see Phan, *Mission and Catechesis*, 206–7.
11. A helpful study of the Vietnamese Catholic Church from the mid-nineteenth century to the mid-twentieth century is Charles Keith, *Catholic Vietnam: A Church from Empire to Nation* (Berkeley: University of California Press, 2012).
12. On Pierre Joseph George Pigneaux (also spelled Pigneau), sometimes with the nobility-sounding designation "de Béhaine" added, see Frédéric Mantienne, *Monseigneur Pigneaux, évêque d'Adran, mandarin de Cochinchine (1741–1799)* (Paris: Les Indes savantes, 2012); and James P. Daughton, "Recasting Pigneau de Béhaine: Missionaries and the Politics of French Colonial History, 1894–1914," in Nhung Tuyet Tran and Anthony Reid, eds., *Viet Nam: Borderless Histories* (Madison: University of Wisconsin Press, 2006), 290–322.
13. On the relations between French missionaries and colonial authorities, see Cao Huy Thuan, *Les missionnaires et la politique coloniale française au Vietnam 1857–1914* (New Haven, CT: Council on Southeast Asia Studies, 1990); Nicole-Dominique Le, *Les Missions-Étrangères et la pénétration française au Viet-Nam* (Paris: Aubin, 1975); Patrick Tuck, *French Catholic Missionaries and the Politics of Imperialism in Vietnam, 1857–1914: A Documentary Survey* (Liverpool: University of Liverpool Press, 1987); and Etienne Võ Đức Hạnh, *La place du catholicisme dans les relations entre la France et le Viet-Nam de 1851 à 1870*, vols. 1 and 2 (Leiden: Brill, 1969); *La place du catholicisme dans les relations entre la France et le Viet-Nam de 1870 à 1886* (New York: Peter Lang, 1992); *La place du catholicisme dans les relations entre la France et le Viet-Nam de 1886 à 1903* (New York: Peter Lang, 2002).

14. On the martyrdom of Vietnamese Catholics, see Jacob Ramsay, *Mandarins and Martyrs: The Church and the Nguyen Dynasty in Early Nineteenth-Century Vietnam* (Stanford, CA: Stanford University Press, 2008).
15. In 1832, US president Andrew Jackson wrote a letter to Emperor Minh Mạng proposing trade between the two countries. The letter was carried by Capt. Edmund Roberts, who arrived in Da Nang on the HMS *Peacock*. The Minh Mạng court requested a Chinese translation of the letter, which Roberts was not able to produce; he then set sail for Macao. Three years later the *Peacock* returned. This time Minh Mạng was willing to welcome the Americans, hoping to use their power to curtail French influence. Unfortunately, Roberts died from illness and the *Peacock* left.
16. Minh Mạng also sent missions to Batavia, Calcutta, Goa, Malacca, Singapore, Jahor, and Semarang to search for trade and new technologies (for example, steamboats). Globalization had been in full force before the coming of France and the West more generally.
17. On the role of François Jaccard at the Huế court and his trial and condemnation to death, see Ramsay, *Mandarins and Martyrs*, 76–82.
18. Among the MEP bishops, only two openly promoted France's occupation of Vietnam: François Pellerin, bishop of Hue (1813–60), and Paul-François Puginier, bishop of Hanoi (1835–92). It is important to note that their motive was not to increase France's political colonial power but to protect Catholic missions, French missionaries, and Vietnamese Catholics. Furthermore, their political involvement was opposed by their own MEP confreres and the Spanish Dominicans, the latter seeing it as an attempt at promoting French national interests.
19. It is to be noted that the Vietnamese colonial Church was supported by the financial aid of the Church in France and Rome but also by the French government, which, though blatantly anticlerical, saw the work of French Catholic missions in Vietnam as a way to promote France's political interests and mission civilisatrice.
20. For these achievements, see Keith, *Catholic Vietnam*, 30–34.
21. On Philiphê Bỉnh, see George E. Dutton, *A Vietnamese Moses: Philiphê Bỉnh and the Geographies of Early Modern Catholicism* (Oakland: University of California Press, 2017). For a shorter study, see George Dutton, "Crossing Oceans, Crossing Boundaries: The Remarkable Life of Philiphê Bỉnh (1759–1832)," in Nhung Tuyết Trần and Anthony Reid, eds., *Viet Nam: Borderless Histories* (Madison: University of Wisconsin Press, 2006), 219–89.
22. George Dutton summarizes well the globalizing impact of Philiphê Bỉnh's journeys and writings: "In his journey to Portugal, Bỉnh stitched together significant portions of Catholic geographies of place and culture. . . . His presence in Lisbon and use of the trading networks that spanned the oceans between Tonkin and Europe created a connection between these two remote places" (262).
23. The adoption of the alphabetized script as *quốc ngữ,* in which Vietnamese Catholics played a key role, the rise of Catholic literature with new literary genres, the founding of Catholic newspapers, and the spread of Catholic publishing houses together exercised a huge impact on the globalization of Vietnam and the Vietnamese Catholic Church. See Keith, *Catholic Vietnam*, 118–46.
24. On Nguyễn Hữu Bài and his four requests, see Keith, *Catholic Vietnam*, 98–100.
25. I have discussed this third phase of globalization of the Vietnamese Catholic Church at length elsewhere. See "The Roman Catholic Church in the Socialist Republic of Vietnam, 1989–2005," in Klaus Koschorke, ed., *Falling Walls: The Year 1989/90 as a Turning Point in the History of World Christianity* (Wiesbaden: Harrassowitz Verlag, 2009), 243–57; and "Christianity in Vietnam: 1975–2013," *International Journal for the Study of the Christian Church* 14, no. 1 (2014): 1–19.
26. For a study of the Vietnamese Catholic Church during the war of independence from France, see Trần Thị Liên, "Les catholiques vietnamiens pendant la guerre d'indépendance (1945–1954) entre la reconquête coloniale et la résistance communiste" (PhD diss., Institut d'Études Politiques de Paris, 1996).

27. On this migration of Catholics of northern Vietnam to the south and its impact on the Church in the south, see Peter Hensen, "The Virgin Heads South: Northern Catholic Refugees in South Vietnam, 1954–1964" (PhD diss., Melbourne College of Divinity, 2008). According to *Informations catholiques internationales* 158 (December 15, 1961), there were 860,026 refugees from the north to the south. Of these, 80 percent (676,384) were Catholic, that is, almost half of the Catholic population of the Church in the north. The migrant group included 5 bishops and 700 priests (two-thirds of the total clergy of the north). In addition, almost all the male religious and a great part of the female religious of the northern Church also moved south. Remaining behind were 7 bishops, 374 priests, and a few religious serving 750,000 faithful in ten dioceses.

7

The Indo-Malayan Archipelago

JOHN MANSFORD PRIOR, SVD

THE FIFTEENTH TO TWENTIETH CENTURIES: DEFINED BY TRADE

The Indo-Malayan Archipelago has been a crossroads for pan-Asian trade for millennia, particularly from China to the north and India to the west. Indeed, the ancestors of the peoples of Southeast Asia can be traced to southern China and South Asia. Over millennia, waves of migrants mixed with the aboriginal inhabitants.[1] Maritime trade from Bengal Bay and the Arabian Peninsula to China of necessity passed through this equatorial island chain. China has been buying cloves from the Moluccas for medicines and food flavoring since at least the Han Dynasty (205 BCE–220 CE). Intercultural and interreligious exchange has thus been an ongoing experience long before recorded history, resulting in the mix of the hundreds of Austronesian and Melanesian languages and cultures found on the archipelago today.

But the Indo-Malayan Archipelago was not simply a hub of pan-Asian trade. Until the sixteenth century, the Malays themselves were primarily a maritime people, interacting and intermixing with peoples beyond Asia, for instance, through trade and migration to and from Madagascar off the east African coast.[2] To facilitate inter-island commerce, the Malay language, free of ethnic-exclusive baggage, grew into a practical lingua franca. Since the late nineteenth century, this thousand-year-old tongue has developed into the sophisticated national languages of Malaysia (Bahasa Malaysia or Bahasa Malay) and Indonesia (Bahasa Indonesia).

Traders brought not only their languages (Chinese, Sanskrit, Arabic), but their religions as well. And so Confucianism, Hinduism, and Buddhism spread peacefully within the court circles of Sumatra and Java and, through cultural osmosis, were absorbed by local Kejawen religiosity. The merchants and monks freely mixed with the local people throughout the four centuries of the Mahayana-Buddhist maritime empire of Sriwijaya (eighth to twelfth centuries), which controlled sea trade between India and China, and during the two centuries of the Hindu-Javanese Majapahit empire (thirteenth to fifteenth centuries).[3] Sriwijaya established its capital in Sumatra; Majapahit did the same in eastern Java. Both empires straddled parts of what is today Malaysia and Indonesia.

There are indications of a possible small Syriac Christian presence on the west coast of Sumatra in the eighth century, but recent scholars are more skeptical than earlier ones.[4] Franciscans may well have passed through the archipelago in the thirteenth century, but nothing remains of any Christian communities that may have formed in the coastal trading posts.

Islamization and Christianization, 1450–1680

The entire religious geography began to change radically during the mid-fifteenth century. By the end of the seventeenth century more than half the population of what are now Malaysia and Indonesia had been touched by Islam or Christianity "in some sense."[5] In the late thirteenth century, Melaka (or Malacca, Malaka) became Muslim. Melaka was the greatest port of the region, strategically placed as it was in the Strait of Melaka, making it possible to control the bottleneck between the Indian Ocean and the Java and South China Seas. Melaka was also the wealthiest Muslim sultanate on the peninsula.[6] Muslim port-states grew up along the spice route along northern Java to the Moluccas, and along northern Borneo to Manila. Islam settled along the coast, centered in the trading posts and ports.[7]

When Portuguese traders arrived and conquered Melaka in 1511, Islam had already been there and along the coasts of Malaya, Sumatra, and Java for fifty to eighty years.[8] The Portuguese conquest of Melaka did not bring about large-scale conversions to Catholicism, but it did galvanize the Muslim traders who opposed the Portuguese encroachment on their commercial interests.

The arrival of commercial rivals initiated a period of Islamization and Christianization. Periods of intense commercial competition, often brutal, led to both *dakwah* Islam and mass baptisms. Boundaries between the two religions, previously fairly porous, became sharply defined. Religious identity was shaped through rivalry. Later, after the Protestant Dutch had solidified their commercial monopoly in the region, religious boundaries again became more fluid. This pattern persists: competition and threat raise ideological walls and potential conflict, whereas times of common prosperity are marked by peaceful coexistence and a recognition of common local cultural roots. Hence, traders brought Islam and Christianity to the Indo-Malayan Archipelago, and their commercial competitors gave shape to religious identity and decided which location would be aligned to which religion. Trade, and later colonial, policy throughout these nearly five hundred years ensured that ethnicity and location became inexorably intertwined with religious identity.

In defiance of Portuguese encroachment, and to reassert its position, Islam developed direct commercial, religious, and military contacts with Mecca and the Ottoman caliphate. Meanwhile, Portuguese traders, more accurately described as pirates and plunderers (*fidalgos*), brought along Dominican and Jesuit chaplains.

Religion and trade, then, were part and parcel of a single package. In the words of Karel Steenbrink, "Religious export was a by-product of political and economic activities."[9] When trade with Gujarati Muslims became more favorable than trade with the Portuguese, ports of call would opt to become Muslim. When Portuguese were on the ascendant, their friars were free to baptize. When one side lost in battle, the trading ports were liable to switch their religious allegiance to the victor. Strength and victory were blessed, weakness and defeat not so. The Portuguese period was one marked by increasing polarization.

Founded in 1602, the Dutch East India Company (Vereenigde Oost-Indische Compagnie, or VOC) arrived on the scene and took over Melaka in 1641 after 130 years of Portuguese domination. These merchants conquered the entire commercial route to the Moluccan spice islands. By the 1680s there remained only sporadic revolts to be quashed. To ensure their loyalty, ordinary folk already Catholic were pressured to convert to the religion of their raja or sultan, becoming either Muslim or Protestant.[10] So ended the Jesuit mission in the Moluccas, and later, in the seventeenth century, the small Catholic community in Makassar.

The British assumed control over Melaka and the remainder of the Dutch territories in 1795, when the Dutch sided with Napoléon. While what is now Indonesia was returned to the Dutch after Napoléon's defeat in 1815, Melaka was exchanged for Riau on Sumatra, becoming a British colony in 1824. The arrival of the British coincided with the establishment of the first British Protestant overseas mission societies. Anglicans and Methodists followed in the traders' footsteps, and established schools.

Y. B. Mangunwijaya views the violent upheavals of these centuries not as primarily conflicts between Europe and Asia, nor between Christian and Muslim, but rather as yet another case of the ongoing manipulation and exploitation of the poor by the rich and powerful.[11] Indeed, economic and political motives were always to the fore. Precisely these forces define the way Catholicism and Islam tend to relate to each other today.

The Lesser Sunda Islands

Another pattern emerged in the Lesser Sunda Islands.[12] The virtual absence of Portuguese clergy allowed for a grafting of Portuguese popular Catholicism onto the local Austronesian cultures of Solor, Timor, and Flores. This marriage of popular religion and ethnic religious culture may well explain the persistence and continuing sustainability of Catholicism in the Lesser Sunda Islands over the centuries.[13] The most spectacular example of this vitality is the Holy Week processions from Palm Sunday to Holy Saturday of Tua Ma (the Sorrowing Mother) and Tua Ana (the Suffering Son).[14] Catholicism gave identity and strength to the people of Larantuka vis-à-vis whoever attempted to govern them, whether the Portuguese or the Dutch.[15] The lay Confreria Renha Rosari (Queen of the Rosary Association) has maintained its semi-independence until today. After a prolonged but useless struggle, the Catholic hierarchy has learned to come to terms with the Confreria and accept its role in organizing the processions.[16]

The institutional model of a church wherein alone salvation is to be found led to the actual baptism of many coastal communities. Frans Cornelissen concludes his survey by asking: "Were they all baptised? Did they really convert in any seriousness? Or were they entered in 'our' number, that is, on 'our' (Portuguese) side when they promised to become Christians on condition that they would have a fortress built for their 'protection' from enemies?"[17]

The Nineteenth-Century Colonization Process in British Malaya

Before the late nineteenth century, the British largely practiced a noninterventionist policy. British-dominated areas were administered in a highly decentralized manner, as the British East India Company was interested only in trading, and so tried to steer clear of

Malay politics.[18] Only in 1946 were the seven administrations of British Malaya united in the Malayan Union, which became the Federation of Malaya in 1948. With the defeat of the communist insurgency (ongoing from 1948) Malaysia achieved independence in 1957. Sarawak and Sabah joined the federation in 1963, while Singapore separated in 1965 to become an independent city-state. Similarly, what is today Indonesia was ruled from a single authority in Batavia (Jakarta) only for the last thirty-six years of Dutch rule, that is, from 1906 until the Japanese invasion of 1942.

To run its tin mines in Perak and Selangor, and later work the rubber plantations and build the railways, the British imported cheap labor from South Asia (mainly Tamils) and northeast Asia (Chinese). This single colonial policy largely determined the ethnic, racial, and religious composition of Malaysia today.[19] The Christian minority thrived among the ethnic minorities. In 2010, there were 1,007,643 Catholics in Malaysia—just over 3 percent of the total population, similar to the percentage of Catholics in Indonesia.

Dutch East Indies

As the Malay Peninsula and the northern coast of Borneo were coming under the authority of the British East India Company, in 1799 the VOC was declared bankrupt and taken over by the state. Thus began the formal colonization of much of the Indo-Malayan Archipelago by the Dutch government. The Dutch territories were no longer being run by an association of merchants, but by the Dutch Crown, and after 1849 increasingly by the Dutch parliament.[20]

In 1808, two Dutch Catholic priests were allowed into Java to minister to Catholic colonial troops in the cities. By 1842, an apostolic vicariate had been established, though pastoral work remained restricted to Catholics of European descent until the Jesuits arrived in 1859.

The Dutch Jesuits took over from the Dutch diocesan clergy. Through three-year primary schools, and also through carpentry and building workshops and residential cooking, sewing, and hygiene courses run by sisters for prospective teachers' wives, Catholicism slowly expanded. In central Java a real though limited expansion took place only at the turn of the century, when Frans van Lith, SJ, paid off the debt of a group of indebted laborers, bought them land, and helped them organize cooperatives. Van Lith gradually realized that Indonesia would become independent, so he took responsibility for the education of many of the first generation of Catholic politicians at the secondary school in Muntilan, which he directed. Prominent alumni include Ignasius J. Kasimo, the first president of the Catholic (political) Party, his replacement, Frans Seda, and Soegijapranata, SJ, the first Javanese archbishop (1940–63), who had converted from Islam while studying at Muntilan.[21] The Dutch State financed the Catholic Church on the same basis as the Protestant Church.

Slow Growth

Indigenous Catholics had been able to survive only in East Flores and the surrounding isles (Adonara, Solor), which had been under Portuguese authority until 1859. Of a total

Indonesian population of around 7 million, it is estimated that by 1859 just 0.7 were Christian, Protestant, or Catholic, while Muslims were at 85 percent, a percentage they have maintained until today. By 1900, non-European Catholics numbered 26,464 and Protestants about 25,000 in a population of around 30 million.[22] By the time of the Japanese invasion in 1942, some 3 percent of the population was Christian. Both numbers, but more interestingly the percentage of Christians, increased rapidly in the first years of independence, so that by the end of the twentieth century almost 10 percent of the Indonesian population was Christian, including not quite 4 percent who were Catholic and the remainder Protestant.[23]

The Catholic Church had preceded the Dutch in Flores, as had the Protestants in North Sumatra, while both Churches evangelized large areas of Papua before the Dutch established control. In these locations both churches fairly easily wedded into the identity and dignity of the local population. Whereas clergy and their village catechists evangelized from a catechism, the people tended to accept or reject Catholicism according to their own vision and their own needs. We can detect a "working misunderstanding" between the institutional Church and the convictions of a majority of the people.[24] A similar enculturated faith grew among the indigenous peoples of Sarawak and Sabah.[25] The Church, as the main employer, educator, and socioeconomic local provider until the early 1970s, played the major role modernizing the Catholic island of Flores (2016 population: 2 million). In all public areas of life, including the political and the economic, the people listened to the clergy. Today, Catholic leadership is simply one voice among many.

THE TWENTIETH-CENTURY POLITICAL AND RELIGIOUS RENAISSANCE

The early years of the twentieth century saw a national awakening and a Muslim rejuvenation. The mass educational Muhammadiyah movement, which endeavored to return to a purified Islam free of Javanese cultural accretions, was founded in 1912 and today numbers over 30 million members.[26] In reaction, the traditionalist "enculturated" village-based Nahdlatul Ulama (NU) was established in 1926, which today numbers over 40 million adherents. Meanwhile, the trading organization Sarekat Dagang Islam (est. 1905) evolved into the first explicitly Muslim political party, Sarekat Islam (est. 1913).

Muslim rejuvenation was accompanied on the Christian side by a great increase in foreign missionaries. While the Jesuits retained key areas such as the capital, Batavia, and central Java, other religious orders took over the rest of the country. No fewer than fifty-eight religious orders and congregations, the majority of them sisters, were active when the Japanese invaded in 1942.

As Muslim-Christian competition heated up, the SVD set about the systematic baptism of populations in the districts of East Nusa Tenggara, where Catholics were permitted, namely mid-Timor and the island of Flores. By 1951, over half of Indonesian Catholics came from East Nusa Tenggara. Due to expansion in Javanese cities through these baptisms, but also through large-scale migration, today only 30 percent of Catholics live in East Nusa Tenggara.[27]

Under the "New Order" Regime of General Suharto

The first Indonesia-born bishop, Soegijapranata, SJ, was a fervent nationalist and supporter of President Sukarno (1945–67). Unfortunately for Indonesia, the Second Vatican Council came a decade too late. When the Church opened up to the world after 1965, General Suharto was just coming to power. The military reduced the public role of religion to supporting the regime, allowing freedom only in internal matters of doctrine and ritual. To strengthen ideological control, Suharto had the *satu-satu asas Pancasila* law passed through parliament in 1985, whereby all organizations, including Islam and Christian, had to accept the national ideology as their one and only organizational basis. Religion was reduced to a matter of group identity and spiritual support for the individual and the family. Many Catholics became engaged with ecclesial movements and charismatics, while a few prophetic voices managed to make their expressions heard, such as the architect, journalist, novelist, human rights advocate, and diocesan priest Mangunwijaya.[28]

A massacre of perhaps more than a million Indonesians in late 1965 and early 1966 brought Suharto to power. For political and commercial reasons, this slaughter had the tacit, indeed active support of Washington, London, and Canberra.[29] Half a century later the nation, including most Catholics, has yet to acknowledge what actually happened, let alone be able to rehabilitate the victims and their families.[30] Hundreds of thousands of political prisoners were held without trial for up to fifteen years, many on the infamous penal island of Buru.[31] Without coming to terms with this tragedy, it is difficult to envision how the institutional Church can become a credible prophetic presence of peace and justice.[32]

The Suharto regime (1967–98) rejected the earlier model of socialist development promoted by the "1945 Generation," and opened up Indonesia to global capital. Over the next three decades many enjoyed general prosperity, and today less than 20 percent of Indonesians are below the poverty line. The global capitalist model ("casino capitalism") also brought with it a dramatic and growing gap between the super rich and ordinary folk.[33] Economically, Catholics in Indonesia are divided equally: 50 percent super-prosperous and 50 percent not so prosperous or poor.[34] In a not dissimilar way from Suharto, Mahathir Mohamad (1981–2003) spearheaded economic, technological, and social progress in Malaysia, which culminated in his "Vision 2000" of 1992.

While the Indonesian Church sought to protect its educational, health, and social institutions by conforming to the Suharto regime, the Malaysian Church was caught up in the interethnic violence of the late 1960s, when prominent Church personnel actively demonstrated and were briefly imprisoned. The ascendancy of Malay Islam when Singapore left the federation (1965), and later when prime minister Mahathir Mohamad engaged in positive discrimination in favor of the Malays, sidelined the Chinese and Tamil minorities. The Church soon lost control of its schools and has had to live with the increasing Islamization of the public law.[35] In 1990, a signature campaign against the imposition of Islamic law on non-Muslims was organized in Malaysia. The following year racial and religious polarization was debated during the election campaign. Where does this leave the Catholic Church of the archipelago in terms of globalization?

THE IMPACT OF INDONESIAN EPISCOPAL PRESENCE AT VATICAN II

Indonesia was one of only three bishops' conferences to submit a document of preconciliar *vota* (views).[36] This vota (submitted May 15, 1960) placed concern over world population growth at the head of Catholic concerns. Then followed headings on moral and pastoral theology, liturgical adaptation, Church law, and catechesis. The vota called for a curial office to dialogue with the World Council of Churches (WCC), collaboration between local churches, and participation of the entire Catholic world in Indonesia's central government. The bishops called for a constitution on the Church and clarity on the status of the laity. The Indonesian vota was ignored in the Vatican's Final Syntheses of Resolutions and Suggestions (March 12, 1960).

The apostolic vicar of Purkowerto suggested an organization of the council according to cultural areas with a calendar of meetings; seven geographical sections; a plenary council every fifty years; and a worldwide conference every twenty-five.

The apostolic vicar in Kalimantan founded and led the Vriendenclub—a loose network of around three hundred council members and expert advisors who constituted "His Majesty's Loyal Opposition." The SVD congregational leader, Johann Schütte, one of many chairmen of preparatory commissions (he chaired the final drafting of the mission schema), regularly consulted the Vriendenclub.

In early 1964, the Indonesian Conference (twenty-eight bishops) sent in its comments regarding the Schema on Revelation, which were "marked by the greatest fervour for renewal." In September 1965, the entire Indonesian presence (thirty-one bishops) joined with one hundred French bishops to underline the ontological basis of religious freedom, namely the obligation to seek the truth, which requires freedom from coercion.

A letter to the Commission on Seminaries from Darmajuwana, bishop of Semarang, in the name of the Indonesian Bishops' Conference, challenged two issues on priestly formation. They wanted the council to be open to move beyond the traditional seminary system and they called for an end to obligatory celibacy. This latter request was quashed by the intervention of Paul VI on October 11, 1965. They later unsuccessfully called for the removal of a hortatory paragraph calling for priestly holiness as the whole Church is called to holiness.

Two individual interventions stand out. First, during the first session on liturgical adaptation to local cultures, by Willem van Bekkum, SVD (Ruteng Diocese, Flores, secretary of the bishops' conference); all of van Bekkum's suggestions were incorporated into the *Sacrosantum Concilium*.[37] The other noteworthy intervention occurred during the third session by Anton Theijssen, SVD (Larantuka Diocese, Flores), regarding the need for a new Vatican body to advance relations with other religions. On Pentecost Sunday 1965, Paul VI established an interreligious secretariat.

As the council commenced there were just four Indonesia-born bishops and two Malaysians among the hierarchy of twenty-seven Dutch *episcopoi*.[38] The Indonesians held weekly meetings during each of the four council sessions, deciding issues such as a common policy on Catholic universities and institutes of higher education in Indonesia, future ecumenical and interfaith relationships, the need for socio-religious research (later undertaken by Atma Jaya Catholic University), and policies on socioeconomic development. For each concern, new bodies were established at the conference. They published a joint pastoral letter in February 1965 encouraging dialogue in the face of the confrontation with Malaysia and the increasing influence of the Indonesian Communist Party (PKI).[39]

Significant Ecclesiastical Changes

The post–Vatican II era in the Indo-Malayan Archipelago coincided with the worldwide postcolonial era. Political independence was proclaimed in Indonesia in 1945 and acknowledged internationally in 1949. Malaysia achieved independence a decade later in 1957—with Sarawak and Sabah joining the federation in 1963—while Singapore separated in 1965. The non-Block movement was founded in Bandung in 1956 under the leadership of India's prime minister Jawaharlal Nehru, Yugoslavia's president Josip Tito, and Indonesia's Sukarno. The churches of the Indo-Malayan Archipelago had to discover what it meant to be church, as their peoples were redefining themselves as independent and the Catholic Church was entering a process of *aggiornamento* (updating).

One important result from Vatican II was the development of the bishops' conferences of both countries. Formerly, each district was under a particular religious congregation, and bishops had more contact with their own religious headquarters than with each other. This forging of a common Catholic identity took time, but was galvanized by restrictive immigration policies concerning foreign Christian workers in Malaysia beginning in 1966 and in Indonesia a decade later.[40] This led to the rapid replacement of foreign church personnel, which paved the way to the birth of Indonesian- and Malaysian-led churches.

The shift from European to Indonesian and Malaysian Catholic Church personnel had been slow. The first Indonesian ordination to the priesthood came only in 1926 and the first Indonesian bishop in 1940, after war had broken out in Europe and Japan was preparing to invade. In 1940, only 16 priests were Indonesian (of a total of 570), just 3 percent. By the late 1970s, when the Indonesian government implemented the 1977 regulations that refused renewal of half of the visas of foreign missionaries, still only 42 percent of the clergy were Indonesian.[41] It was the restrictive 1966 regulations on foreign religious personnel in Malaysia and the similar 1977 law in Indonesia that jolted the institutional Church. The 1969 race riots in Kuala Lumpur resulted in a state of emergency, which was used in Sabah to expel foreign missionaries.[42] While ordinations to the priesthood as well as to the religious life in Malaysia decreased, departures increased.[43] However, in Indonesia, since the 1980s priestly and religious vocations have increased exponentially.[44] Mission is now reversed: over a thousand Indonesian missionary priests, the largest number coming from NTT Province, and almost as many sisters, are working in over forty countries throughout the world.[45]

Thus a collection of particular churches on each island or district, each with its own separate historical journey, became the Catholic Church of Malaysia and of Indonesia, both remaining as diverse as before yet now with overarching shared identities and common approaches to key issues.

Catholics, who had been viewed as belonging to branches of a foreign body, were now recognized by the general populace as faith communities rooted in Malaysian and Indonesian history, cultures, and concerns. This occurred through the gradual indigenization of the bishops' conferences and ordination of local ordained and religious personnel; through recognition by the majority community of the important role of Catholic institutions in education, health, and social outreach; through regular national gatherings of bishops and laity from locations across both countries; and through the adaptation of the Church's liturgy to local cultures with the use of national and local languages, garments, music, and dance.

Some of the Catholic minority are engaged with the wider society in Catholic and interfaith nongovernmental organizations (NGOs) through an ongoing struggle against systemic corruption, discrimination against religious and ethnic minorities, ecological issues, justice, peace, and gender and environmental advocacy. In terms of formal statements, these latter engagements have the support of both the Malaysian and the Indonesian Bishops' Conferences. For instance, in 1979 the Asian Bishops' Institute for Social Action met in Kuala Lumpur for dialogue on religions. In 1983, the Malaysian Consultative Council on Buddhism, Christianity, Hinduism, Sikhism (MCCBCHS) was formed to represent their interests with the authorities.

It became clear during the 1998 Synod for Asia that the Malaysian and Indonesian Churches were no longer simply subsidiaries of Rome but had become local churches in Asia. This transformation arose through multiple contacts with the Federation of Asian Bishops' Conferences (FABC); through local provinces of international religious congregations undergoing their won renewal and rejuvenation; and through participation in the ordinary and extraordinary synods of bishops in Rome, in particular the 1998 Synod for Asia. However, since the papacies of John Paul II (1978–2005) and Benedict XVI (2005–13), the churches have faced the challenge of re-Romanization and re-clericalization.

Indonesia

In Indonesia a series of meetings of the Sidang Agung Gereja Katolik Indonesia (SAGKI, the General Assembly of the Indonesian Catholic Church) have been held every five years since the fiftieth anniversary of Indonesia's independence in 1995. All the bishops participate alongside lay representatives from the parishes, dioceses, and Catholic organizations. SAGKI I in 1995 was titled The Engagement of the People of God in the History of the Nation. Two years later the bishops issued their famous Lenten pastoral letter denouncing the regime. With the fall of Suharto and turbulent political reforms in progress, in 2000 SAGKI took up the theme Empowering Basic Ecclesial Communities towards a New Indonesia. SAGKI III in 2005 took up the theme Rise Up and Get Moving!; SAGKI IV's in 2010 was "He Came that All Have Life in Its Fullness; and SAGKI V in 2015 was The Catholic Family and the Joy of the Gospel. While weeklong national gatherings give a great sense of hopeful identity and apostolic verve to participants, the danger of evolving into a routine exists. Individual dioceses are left to draw up strategic plans.

Malaysia

The most dramatic decision to bring the fruits of the Second Vatican Council to the archipelago was surely the shutting down of the Church in Malay Peninsula for the month of August 1976 so that the three bishops and all the clergy and religious could take part in the aggiornamento renewal program. Each of the three Peninsula dioceses discussed the program's core need and related requirements, and then combined them into a common program. They formulated the common core need as "Christ-Centred Communities at all levels with concern for 1) Unity among bishops, priests, religious, and laity in all fields, 2) Formation of all groups as an ongoing process to produce committed and motivated lay leaders, 3) Dialogue with Christian and non-Christians when and where possible, and 4) Integral human development of the poor."[46]

While the bishops published a joint pastoral letter, no common strategic plan was envisioned or drawn up. Ten years later, the first Peninsular Malaysia Pastoral Convention (PMPC I) was held to assess progress. The laity focused on the key need of prioritizing basic ecclesial communities, which was accepted as the core pastoral need. PMPC II was held a decade later. Apparently, basic ecclesial communities were largely misunderstood as merely task groups, just as in Indonesia they had devolved into administrative subunits of parishes. There was a renewed call for systematic and strategic planning and implementation. This time the convention itself issued the pastoral letter. The following year a vision-mission statement was released:

> Our vision is: to be rooted in the communion of the Trinity and among ourselves, to be in solidarity with the whole human family and creation. This vision leads us to live out our vocation to be at the service of the Kingdom of God. Our mission is to witness through basic ecclesial communities founded on Christ and thus transform our parishes into "communion of communities"; to proclaim and dialogue with cultures, religions and the poor. For us, this means journeying together towards a new way of being Church.[47]

One sees here the vision, indeed the language, of the Federation of Asian Bishops' Conferences (FABC).[48]

FABC

The Malaysian and Indonesian Churches were active in the birthing of the FABC in 1970 (first assembly in 1974) and remained so until the Synod for Asia in 1998. Key FABC office secretaries hailed from Malaysia, such as Anthony Rogers (Office for Human Development) and Edmund Chia (Office of Ecumenical and Inter-Religious Affairs). Hardawiryana (Hardo), who assisted the Indonesian bishops at Vatican II, was subsequently theological advisor to the bishops' conference for more than three decades (1965–99). Also serving in the FABC Office of Theological Concerns, Hardo encouraged the see-judge-act model of theologizing in Indonesia. It is a challenge to keep theology openly intercontextual, and bishops' conferences appointed by John Paul II and Benedict XVI led such engagement to become routinized and the FABC to become a largely neutered body.

Theological Trends

Indonesian and Malaysian theologies can be described as *tambal-sulam*, a "patchwork theology," or, employing Albert Widjaja's term, "beggarly theology." Liberationist, intercultural, and interfaith strands are all present in moderate quantities. *Liberationist strands* predominated during turbulent times in both countries. Pre–Vatican II *intercultural strands* were rooted in local cultures, while post–Vatican II ecumenical theology is broadly national. More recent intercultural theologies are returning to local issues as Indigenous cultures—facing the impact of globalization—are undergoing a dramatic revival, with ecological concerns coming to the fore.[49] *Multifaith strands* have emerged through practical and scholarly collaboration. *Feminist and gender strands* are mainstream in Protestant theologies, but slow to reenvision Catholic theologies; there are few openings for Catholic women to teach or practice theology full-time. By way of exception, the Archdiocese of Kucing sponsored the postgraduate theological studies in Louvain of husband-and-wife team Jeffrey Goh Choo Kee and Angelina Lim Chan Hian, allowing them space for full-time teaching and writing.[50] The Catholic feminist theological network Ecclesia of Women in Asia (EWA), founded in 2002, has a small but vocal membership from Malaysia and Indonesia.[51]

Interesting theological developments within Catholic and interfaith NGOs are taking place outside faculties and seminaries, including in the printed and electronic media, using language and ideas that are understandable to the Muslim majority. Theological thinking on political and human rights issues begins with practical involvement (protests, occupation of ecologically destructive mines, etc.), and so are broadly interdisciplinary in nature. What does this say about the public presence of Catholicism in the archipelago?

PUBLIC CATHOLICISM

Catholics earned an honorable place in public life in independent Indonesia through their active engagement in the struggle for independence (1945–49). For instance, Sisters' hospitals treated both wounded Indonesian guerrillas and Dutch soldiers. The first Indonesian archbishop, Soegijapranata, SJ, closely aligned with founding president Sukarno and coined the slogan "100 percent Catholic, 100 percent Indonesian." Catholics in Malaysia were naturally in favor of independence but were nevertheless apprehensive. East Malaysian bishops stated that success would depend upon four freedoms: of worship, of religious education, of Church personnel, and of freedom from communalism.[52] Malaysia has a secular constitution yet acknowledges Islam and identifies all ethnic Malays as Muslim. The founding generation of both countries supported a secular state. Indonesia is based on the five principles of *Pancasila*: belief in one God, a just and civilized humanity, the unity of Indonesia, democracy, and social justice. Indonesia is a secular state but all citizens must adhere to one of the six acknowledged religions: Islam, Protestant Christian, Catholic Christian, Hindu, Buddhist, and Confucian. The Pancasila state ideology provides a commonly accepted basis for interreligious dialogue.

Clearly, minority religions in both countries remain strong supporters of a secular state as well as of Liberal Islam.[53] Small but strong minorities in both countries have been gradually

Islamizing their culture and there is patchy Islamization of law in some districts. In Indonesia, *shariah* law is acknowledged only in Aceh Province—which brought an ongoing insurrection to a peaceful conclusion.

POLITICAL ENGAGEMENT

While Catholic political engagement in Malaysia is tied to ethnic minorities, in Indonesia Catholics formed their own political party in 1945, which was represented in local, district, and national parliaments and in Sukarno's cabinets. In 1972, Suharto forcefully merged the Catholic and Protestant Parties into the secular Indonesian Democratic Nationalist Party (PDI). Catholic politicians then divided between the PDI (the opposition) and Suharto's governing Party, Golkar. Golkar held sway until Suharto was ousted in May 1998. There were up to seven Catholics in some of Suharto's cabinets, including the head of the armed forces, Benny Moerdani (1988–93).

As Indonesia moved from the "guided democracy" of Sukarno to the military regime of Suharto, a key educator of Catholic militant cadres was the Jesuit Joop Beek, SJ.[54] Fervently anti-communist, Beek collaborated with the "brains" behind the Suharto regime, Ali Mertopo, and the Chinese Indonesian Jusuf Wanandi.[55] Beek and the Catholic hierarchy sided with the military.[56]

Under the Suharto regime the Church became largely preoccupied with internal issues and the prosperous classes involved themselves in ecclesial movements, a variety of devotions, and local and international pilgrimages. Similarly in Malaysia, the scope of the Church's educational and social outreach became severely limited as Church schools were increasingly controlled by the government. Only in Sarawak and Sabah, after a petition by the churches in 1995, did the state allow in schools any faith education besides Islam.

As the Suharto regime faltered in the late 1990s the Indonesian bishops finally came out with a clearly prophetic voice in their Lenten Pastoral (March 1997). Drafted by Mangunwijaya and Magnis-Suseno, the letter called out the regime on greed, corruption, and nepotism, and a complete disregard for human rights and appealed for a total moral transformation of social life. The Muslim mass organization Nahdlatul Ulama (NU) distributed twenty thousand copies of the letter among its members. With the onslaught of the monetary crisis the following year, the regime collapsed and Suharto was forced out on May 21, 1998.

Since 1998, a Catholic presence remains in the Indonesian parliament, but there is no common vision. The singular prophetic voice throughout the Suharto regime was the diocesan priest and social activist Mangunwijaya (1929–99). Catholic and interfaith NGOs quietly at work locally quickly surfaced after Suharto's fall. Today many religious orders are active in advocacy for human rights and ecological campaigns and against human trafficking, and they work to accompany HIV sufferers.[57]

From 1998 to the present, the Indonesian Bishops' Conference has issued periodic pastoral guidelines on social morality in politics (2003), on culture (2004), on economics (2006), and on the environment (2013). Each pastoral was composed with the aid of lay intellectuals during special "study days." The bishops have become teachers of social morality, drawing up guidelines in collaboration with academics.

EDUCATION, MEDIA PRESENCE, AND INTELLECTUAL ENGAGEMENT

Throughout the archipelago from the 1920s through to the 1970s, the Church identified with elite schools in the cities, many of which were ranked as among the best in the country, most run by congregations of sisters. The Church was also very much present in village schools and in wide-ranging health services and social projects. The Church in the outer islands identified not just with cult and creed, but with the modern world, introducing a market economy through cash crops and farming cooperatives and spearheading education, which produced personnel for the executive, legislative, and juridical branches of government at local, regional, and national levels.

In Indonesia, Catholic schools, largely but not entirely run by religious congregations of sisters, brothers, and pastors, still play an important role. With the development of national school systems in both countries, and of comprehensive Muslim networks from kindergarten to university, Catholic schools have lost the pivotal role of pre- and early independence times. Indonesia has a dozen Catholic universities, some with local branches. In Malaysia, Catholics schools have been taken over by the state. With the school curriculum in the hands of the state, the pastoral challenge is how to infuse education with faith-inspired public ethics.

In 1964, a group of Catholics in Jakarta founded *Kompas*, which quickly grew to become the biggest circulation quality daily broadsheet in Indonesia. Over the years, *Kompas* has developed into a major multimedia empire of published books, magazines, and DVDs, a network of bookshops, a TV channel, and an online presence. Catholics are prominent in many academic fields: linguistics, culture, sociology, and philosophy, and are found among well-regarded poets, novelists, and playwrights.[58]

CONCLUDING REMARKS: THE IMPACT OF GLOBALIZATION

The impact of globalization can be seen in five key transformations of the Catholic Church. First, as electronic and cyber communications have become available throughout the archipelago, local churches have shifted from ecclesial communities embedded in particular local, national, and international situations to become a host of diverse networks with very different mindsets beyond time and space, a process that expanded exponentially during the COVID pandemic of 2020. The pastoral challenge is how to replace, or at least balance, the geographical parish with more fluid networks and communities.

Second, through mass economic migrations throughout the archipelago and beyond, local churches have shifted from ethnically based and largely monocultural (or majority-cultural) communities to become ethnically mixed multicultural communities. The pastoral challenge is how to move beyond ethnicity and re-root uprooted migrants and urbanites in faith-based communities.

Third, the global economy has created an increasingly unbridgeable gap between the top 1 percent and everyone else. This economy has also created mass economic migration with a human trafficking underbelly. Meanwhile, global capitalist interests have taken over local, regional, and national economies. Within this complex of changes, Catholic Church members have shifted away from traditionally tight communities in village and towns, where farmers, teachers, government workers, factory and plantation workers, and entrepreneurs sensed a common engagement in economic and social life. The result is a breakdown of common goals and values. The pastoral challenge is to develop an alternative economy through people-centred cooperatives and networks, both local and global.

Fourth, through economic migration and the global impact on each religious constituency via cyber networks, the Church has shifted from religious communities largely ethnically and geographically based into multireligious communities with changing constituencies. The majority-Muslim community feels threatened and so has become politicized. The pastoral challenge is to reach out to Muslim communities as individuals and as groups and organizations at every level, forging friendship, understanding, and common goals.

Finally, through the rapid concentration of wealth in ever-fewer hands and those few hands' takeover of the economic and political spheres, we have moved from being democratic countries with the freedom and dignity inherent in citizens able to decide their common future to a neutered politics filled with impotent political parties. This has led to the religionization of politics and the politicization of religion and to everyone having to struggle on their own to achieve their own fate and future. The pastoral challenge is to participate in the reinvention of an ethical economics and politics from below, replacing a politics of fear with a politics of hope.

Key Challenges

Globalization brings four challenges to the fore:

Glocalization (global-local): Survival seems to depend on how deeply a local community is rooted in its cultural context. And yet, the great attraction of the Church in the twentieth century was that it introduced modernity, which in turn paved the way for Indigenous peoples to succeed in the wider world. Globalization has brought about mass economic migration, both domestic and international. With the digital age and universal access to hand phones and the internet, nowhere is isolated. Nonetheless, while information and collaboration are readily available, so is faux news that stokes prejudice. Also, the underbelly of migration is human trafficking, with Indonesia being a major source and Singapore and Malaysia among the destinations. Migration split families and is the major instigator for the rapid spread of the HIV virus.[59]

A Split Church: The Church is split between the prosperous and those barely surviving. Many active prosperous middle-class families lead a devotional life and are engaged in one of the charismatic movements. As the movements made headway in Javanese cities in the 1970s, so the first Catholic charismatic convention was organized in Ipoh on the Malay Peninsula in 1977. Meanwhile, the poor sought solace in the struggle for survival. Their devotions are closely tied to belief in spirits and they interact with the power of traditional village healers (*dukun*). For the strugglers there is great confidence in miracles and, for men, gambling is seen as a shortcut to an ever-elusive prosperity. Thus we have economically and ideologically "split Churches." We need to bring into dialogue grassroots JPIC networks and middle-class ecclesial movements. The one separates piety from social engagement; the other is in danger of losing its religious adherence and heart.

A Church from Below: Strategic planning is needed to implement changes of mentality and structure required to bring about the FABC vision of a "communion of communities," with basic ecclesial communities as their dynamic base. The vision is clear in writing, but pastoral planning and the willingness to let go of clerical control is still lacking.

Interfaith Encounter: These three named challenges coalesce into this most crucial one. Until the 1970s, educated Christians had remained convinced that Islam had little future in the modern world: shariah law was viewed as too rigid and popular Islam was rooted in "superstition." The past half century has proved how false this assumption was. History informs us that in an age of uncertainty, people who feel threatened tend to fall back on ethnic and religious identity. Basuki Tjahaja Purnama ("Ahok"), the governor of Jakarta, a Christian of Chinese descent, lost the 2017 election, not due to his policies, which were widely popular. Rather, he lost because the winner, Anies Baswedan, who was funded largely by Prabowo (a former and future presidential candidate) and SBY (a former president)—both army generals in the Suharto regime—manipulated ethnic and religious emotion among the public. This is the first time the exploitation of ethnic-religious sentiment by elements in the billionaire elite won an election in Indonesia. This, together with the progressive Islamization of civic society in Malaysia, does not augur well for the future.

To conclude: widespread economic insecurity accompanied by the globalization of consumeristic cultural values have led to a sharpening of ethnic and religious boundaries and led, almost inevitably, to interreligious strife. Hence the present model of globalization could well prove disastrous for communal harmony throughout the Indo-Malayan Archipelago. The challenge is to engage Islam through personal friendship and to collaborate on common social and human rights projects at every level. While a minority of extremists are sponsored and manipulated by former army generals, grassroots interfaith networks continue with courage and confidence. The latter, surely, are the custodians of the authentic soul of the archipelago, molded as it has been for millennia through a constant blending of peoples, beliefs, languages, and cultures, including that of Catholic communities.

NOTES

1. Gregor Neonbasu, *Citra Manusia Berbudaya: Sebuah Monografi tentang Timor dalam Perspektif Melanesia* (Jakarta: Antara, 2016).
2. The Malagasy language is closely related to Malay. For more on the pan-Asian trade and fascinating insights into the Malays' major shift from a maritime nation to an enclosed people during the sixteenth century, see the epic novel by Ananta Toer Pramoedy, *Arus Balik* (Jakarta: Hasta Mitra, 1995), composed while he was a political prisoner on Buru Island from 1969 to 1979.

3. Stefan Dietrich, "A Note on Galiyao and the Early History of the Solor-Alor Islands," *Bijdragen tot de Taal-, Land- en Volkenkunde* 140, no. 2–3 (1984): 317–26. Dietrich outlines elements in both oral tradition and documentation that indicate that Majapahit had contact with eastern Flores in the fourteenth century. Missionary linguists and ethnologists had long proposed this possibility.
4. Y. Bakker, "Umat Katolik Perintis di Indonesia: k.l. 645–1500," in M. P. M Muskens, ed., *Sejarah Gereja Katolik Indonesia, Vol. 1* (Ende: Penerbit Nusa Indah, 1974), 19–40; John C. England, *Hidden History of Christianity in Asia: Churches of the East Since 1500* (Dehli: ISPCK, 1996), 97–99; and Adolf Heuken, "Christianity in Pre-Colonial Indonesia," in Jan Sihar Aritonang and Karel Steenbrink, eds., *A History of Christianity in Indonesia* (Leiden: Brill, 2008), 3–7. Trade along the southern Silk Road in the seventh century makes this a plausible scenario. While Bakker and England are positive on the few extant sources, Heuken is more skeptical.
5. Anthony Reid, *Southeast Asia in the Age of Commerce 1450–1680, Vol. 2, Expansion and Crisis* (New Haven: Yale University Press, 1993), 132.
6. Charles Ralph Boxer, *The Portuguese Seaborne Empire, 1415–1825* (London: Hutchinson, 1969), 42–46.
7. Moluccas ("Maluku"), a name derived from the Arab traders' term for the region, and *Jazirat al-Muluk* ("the land of the kings").
8. Maria Melink-Roelofsz, *Asian Trade and European Influence in the Indonesian Archipelago between 1500 and about 1630* (The Hague: Martinus Nijhoff, 1962), 155.
9. Karel Steenbrink, "Dutch versus Portuguese Colonialism: Traders versus Crusaders?," in David Thomas and John Chesworth, eds., *Christian-Muslim Relations: A Bibliographical History*, vol. 8 (Leiden: Brill, 2016), 40.
10. For instance, Baabullah, Sultan of Ternate (1570–83), compelled Christian supporters of his Portuguese rivals to accept Islam as a sign of loyalty.
11. Y. B. Mangunwijaya, *Ikan-Ikan Hiu, Io, Homa* (Jakarta: Sinar Harapan, 1983); Steenbrink, "Dutch versus Portuguese Colonialism," 46–47.
12. For a recent account and evaluation of the Portuguese presence in the Lesser Sunda Islands see Maria Alice Marques Viola, "Presença histórica 'portuguesa' em Larantuka (séculos XVI e XVII) e suas implicações na contemporaneidade" (PhD diss., Faculdade de Ciências Sociais E Humanas, 2013).
13. Similarly, Islam rooted itself in Javanese popular culture despite waves of "Arabization" over the centuries.
14. See Paul Budi Kleden, "Salib Yesus–Penderitaan Maria: Devosi Maria dalam Ibadat Jalan Salib versi Solor–Lamaholot," *Jurnal Ledalero: Wacana Iman dan Kebudayaan* 10, no. 2 (2011): 161–87. Kleden analyzes the prayers and hymns of a contemporary Good Friday procession on Solor Island, concluding that while women identified with the suffering Jesus drawing strength for the daily struggle, there is no encouragement for social, let alone gender, transformation.
15. The recent commercialization of Holy Week in Larantuka is having more impact on the processions (now a major tourist attraction) than the 150 years of attempted clerical oversight.
16. Since the Second Vatican Council (1962–65), Confreria members have been given advisory status in parish councils in the Larantuka district.
17. M. P. M. Muskens, ed., *Sejarah Gereja Katolik Indonesia, Vol. 1* (Ende: Penerbit Nusa Indah, 1974), 378.
18. In 1895, the colonies on the Malay Peninsula were divided between the Federated Malay States (west) and the Unfederated Malay States (east). Melaka, Penang, and Singapore in 1826 became the Straits Settlements controlled by the East India Company. Sarawak and Sabah on British Borneo were administered separately.
19. In the 2010 census the population of Malaysia was 28.3 million. Bumiputera (Native) citizens, at 67.4 percent, are divided as ethnic Malay 63.1 percent and Indigenous citizens on North Borneo

(Iban 30.3 percent in Sarawak and Kadazan/Dusun 24.5 percent in Sabah). Chinese citizens amount to 24.6 percent, Indians to 7.3 percent, others 0.7 percent. The same census noted that 61.3 percent of the population practices Islam (all ethnic Malays are constitutionally considered Muslim), Buddhist 19.8 percent, Christian 9.2 percent, Hindu 6.3 percent, Confucian, Tao, and other Chinese religions 1.3 percent, unknown 1.0 percent, and no stated religion 0.7 percent. See *Preliminary Count Report, Population and Housing Census 2010* (Putrajaya: Malaysia Department of Statistics, 2011), 60–64. In the previous census (2000) some 76 percent of Chinese Malaysians are Buddhist, 10.6 percent are Tao, and 9.6 percent are Christian. Most Tamil-Malaysians are Hindu (84 percent), almost 8 percent are Christian, and just less than 4 percent are Muslim. Among the Indigenous population, 50 percent are Christian, 36 percent Muslim, and just over 7 percent Indigenous religion. In Indonesia, a minimalist count in 2005 found 6,439,000 Catholics (3.15 percent of the population); in Malaysia the number is 784,000 (3.17 percent of the population); in Timor Leste, 767,000 (93.2 percent); in Brunai Darussalem, 21,000 (6.05 percent).

20. Thomas Van den End, "1800–2005: A National Overview," in Jan Sihar Aritonang and Karel Steenbrink, eds., *A History of Christianity in Indonesia*, (Leiden: Brill, 2008), 137.
21. For van Lith, see Rosaniyanto Floribertus Hasto, *Father Franciscus van Lith, SJ (1863–1926): Turning Point of the Catholic Church's Approach in the Pluralistic Indonesian Society* (Rome: Pontifical Gregorian University, 1997); and Gerry van Klinken, "Power, Symbol and the Catholic Mission in Java: The Biography of Frans van Lith, SJ," *Docmentatieblad geschiedenis Nederlandse Zending en Overszeese Kerken* 4, no. 1 (1997). For IJ Kasimo, see Gerry van Klinken, "Kasimo and Moelia Welcome the Modern State," in Gerry van Klinken, ed., *Minorities, Modernity and the Emerging Nation* (Leiden: KITLV, 2003), 51–83; and Tim Wartawan Kompas, *IJ Kasimo: Hidup dan Perjuangannya* (Jakarta: Gramedia, 1980). For Frans Seda, see Daniel Dhakidae et al., eds., *Frans Seda, Simfoni Tanpa Henti: Ekonomi Politik Masyarakat Baru Indonesia* (Jakarta: Yayasan Atma Jaya, Gramedia, 1991); Leo Rahardian et al., eds., *Frans Seda, Ad Multos Annos* (Jakarta: Unika Atma Jaya, 1991); J. Phillip Gobang et al., eds., *Frans Seda, Kekuasaan dan Moral-Politik Ekonomi Masyarakat Indonesia Baru* (Jakarta: Gramedia, 1996); and E. P. da Gomez, ed., *Dr. Frans Seda: Catatan Perjalanan Seorang Pejuang* (Maumere: Yayasan Kasimo Cabang Sikka, 2006). In 2012, the Jesuit Catechetical center in Yogyakarta produced the film *Soegija* based on the book by Jesuit historian G. Budi Subanar, *Soegija si Anak Betlehem van Java: Biografi Mgr. Albertus Soegijapranata, SJ* (Yogyakarta: Pustaka Sejarah, Gadjah Mada University Press, 2003). Nirwan Dewanto, a prominent Muslim film star, played the role of the archbishop.
22. Van den End, "1800–2005," 161.
23. The most extensive history of the Catholic Church in Indonesia is the three-volume work of Karel Steenbrink, *Catholics in Indonesia: A Documented History*, 3 vols. (Leiden: KITLV, Brill, 2003–2015).
24. Prior, "Customary and Church Marriage in Eastern Indonesia: In Search of a Working Misunderstanding," in Patrick H. Gesch, ed., *Culture, Gospel and Church* (Madang: Divine World Institute, 1994), 51–91.
25. Maureen K. C. Chew, *The Journey of the Catholic Church in Malaysia, 1511–1996* (Kuala Lumpur: Catholic Research Centre, 2000), 122–61.
26. Muhammadiyah remains the largest Islamic educational network running schools, from kindergartens to universities, throughout the archipelago, including "Catholic" Flores.
27. Karel Steenbrink, "Old and New Christianity in the Southeastern Islands," in Jan Sihar Aritonang and Karel Steenbrink, eds., *A History of Christianity in Indonesia*, (Leiden: Brill, 2008), 237–44.
28. John Mansford Prior, "Portraying the Face of the Nazarene in Contemporary Indonesia: Literature as Frontier-Expanding Mission," *Pacifica* 14, no. 2 (2001): 172–90.
29. A memoir by Frank Mount details involvement of Australia-based extreme right-wing Catholic organizations led by B. A. Santamaria in early support of the Suharto regime. See Frank Mount, *Wrestling with Asia: A Memoir* (Ballan, Victoria: Connor Court, 2012).

30. There is in fact an increasing body of literature on the massacre that brought the army to power. Of particular note, see John Rossa et. al., *Tahun yang Tak Pernah Berakhir: Memahami Pengalaman Korban 65. Esai-Esai Sejarah Lisan* (Jakarta: ELSAM, 2004); and Tan Swie Ling, *G30S 1965, Perang Dingin & Kehancuran Nasionalisme: Pemikiran Cina Jelata Korban Orba* (Jakarta: Komunitas Bambu, 2010). Before withdrawn from the US government website, documents implicating the CIA in the massacre were downloaded, translated, and published by Hasta Mitra. See Hasta Mitra, ed., *Dokumen CIA: Melacak Penggulingan Sukarno dan Konspirasi G30S 1965* (Jakarta: Hasta Mitra, 2002). For this author's take on the spineless role of clergy in Flores, see John Mansford Prior, "Apa Kata Mereka? Memoar Empat Misionaris Belanda Generasi Akhir: Kersten, Wetzer, Kramer & Boumans. Bagian I: Formasi Seragam, Pribadi Beragam," *Jurnal Ledalero: Wacana Iman dan Kebudayaan* 5, no. 1 (2006): 103–18. Two films by director Joshua Oppenheimer—*The Act of Killing* (2012) and *The Look of Silence* (2014)—are based on interviews with perpetrators in North Sumatra and show how little, if any, remorse exists fifty years later. Both films are banned from general circulation in Indonesia. The weekly magazine *Tempo* interviewed seventy perpetrators from throughout Indonesia; not a single murderer was repentant. See Tim Wartawan, "Liputan Khusus: Kesaksian Algojo 1965," *Tempo*, October 7, 2012, 50–106.
31. One such prisoner was the brilliant novelist Pramoedya Ananda Toer. For his experience on Buru Island (1969–79), see Pramoedya Ananta Toer, *Nyanyian Sunyi Seorang Bisu I: Catatan-Catatan dari P. Buru* (Jakarta: Lentera, 1995); and Pramoedya Ananta Toer, *Nyanyian Sunyi Seorang Bisu II* (Jakarta: Lentera, 1997). For an appreciation of Pram's literary contribution, see Tofik Pram and Septia Wulan, *The Wisdom of Pramoedya Ananta Toer* (Depok, Jakarta: Edelweiss, 2014).
32. In 2015, STFK Ledalero in Maumere was the only Catholic institution to conduct a national seminar on the massacre. See Otto Gusti Madung and John Mansford Prior, eds., *Berani Berhenti Berbohong: 50 Tahun Pascaperistiwa 1965–1966* (Maumere: Penerbit Ledalero, 2015). Bookshops refused to distribute the book as "too sensitive." For seminar contributions, see Franz Magnis-Suseno, "Sesudah 50 Tahun Kita harus Berani Menghadap Apa yang Terjadi," in Otto Gusti Madung and John Mansford Prior, eds., *Berani Berhenti Berbohong: 50 Tahun Pascaperistiwa, 1965–1966* (Maumere: Penerbit Ledalero, 2015), 1–12; and John Mansford Prior, "'Masa Lalu Tak Pernah Mati, Bahkan Tak pernah Berlalu,' Catatan seputar Pembantaian Terencana di Maumere, Februari–April 1966," in Otto Gusti Madung and John Mansford Prior, eds., *Berani Berhenti Berbohong: 50 Tahun Pascaperistiwa, 1965–1966* (Maumere: Penerbit Ledalero, 2015), 38–68. The other chapters in the volume are a reprint of the June 2015 edition of *Jurnal Ledalero* with six articles on the massacre and its impact fifty years later. From Timor, Mery Kolimon reflects theologically on her father as a perpetrator in "Pelaku Mencari Penyembuhan: Berteologi dengan Narasi para Pelaku Tragedi '65 di Timor Barat," *Jurnal Ledalero: Wacana Iman dan Kebudayaan* 14, no. 1 (2015): 34–59; and Karen Campbell-Nelson writes on victims' families who are now finally speaking out in "Bear Witness: Dua Wacana tentang Kesaksian dan Kebenaran," *Jurnal Ledalero: Wacana Iman dan Kebudayaan* 14, no. 1 (2015): 60–82.
33. According to *Forbes* magazine, the wealth of Indonesia's fifty richest people dropped only slightly in 2020 despite the economic paralysis of the COVID-19 crisis, which caused the country's first recession since 1998 and dragged millions into unemployment and poverty. However, the collective wealth of those fifty tycoons only slipped to US$133 billion from $134.6 billion the year before. This figure is more than 48 percent of the country's 2020 gross domestic product and about 72 percent of the proposed state budget spending for 2021.
34. The Research Centre of Atma Jaya Catholic University under Huub Boelaars undertook ongoing quantitative analysis of the state of the Catholic Church in Indonesia in the 1970s and 1980s.
35. Chew, *Journey of the Catholic Church in Malaysia*, 211–15, 268–86.
36. The others were Germany and Mexico. Other vota, as requested by Rome, were submitted by individual bishops. For the Indonesian vota, see Giuseppe Alberigo and Joseph A. Komonchak, eds., *History of Vatican II*, vol. 1 (Ossining: Orbis, 1995), 102–7, 119–27, 263, 283. For interventions,

see Giuseppe Alberigo and Joseph A. Komonchak, eds., *History of Vatican II*, vol. 2 (Ossining: Orbis, 1997), 110–11, 134; and Giuseppe Alberigo and Joseph A. Komonchak, eds., *History of Vatican II*, vol. 4 (Ossining: Orbis, 2003), 242, 339, 362, 366–67, 381.

37. Van Bekkum pioneered "water buffalo Masses" (*Misa Kaba*) in his diocese and gave a resounding presentation at the first International Congress on Pastoral Liturgy (in Assisi, 1956). Van Bekkum was elected to the commission that prepared *Sacrosanctum Concilium* with no fewer than 1,338 of the 2,000 votes of the council participants. Djajasepoetra (from Jakarta) spoke in November 1962 in a similar vein, in the name of the Indonesian conference. The bishops published a decree on the implementation of the liturgical constitution taking effect on February 12, 1964. In fact, the council was simply recognizing widespread liturgical practice.
38. From Java: Djajasepoetra, archbishop of Jakarta, and Soegijapranata, SJ, archbishop of Semarang (first session only, succeeded in 1963 by Darmajuwana). From Nusa Tenggara: Paul Sani, SVD, bishop of Denpasar (Bali), and Gabriel Manek, SVD, archbishop of Ende (Flores). From Malaysia: Dominic Vendargon, bishop of Kuala Lumpur, and Francis Chan, bishop of Penang.
39. The PKI was annihilated after the military coup in late 1965.
40. Chew, *Journey of the Catholic Church in Malaysia*, 156–58, 203–4; Huub Boelaars, *Indonesianisasi: Dari Gereja Katolik di Indonesia menjadi Gereja Katolik Indonesia* (Yogyakarta: Kanisius, 2005), 233–99.
41. Boelaars, *Indonesianisasi*, 236.
42. For numbers of expulsions and refusal of new entrants, see the table in Chew, *Journey of the Catholic Church in Malaysia*, 157.
43. Chew, 197–211.
44. For a detailed analysis of statistical data from the sixteenth century through 1990, see Boelaars, *Indonesianisasi*.
45. Largely, but not exclusively, by SVD priests and brothers and SSpS sisters.
46. Chew, *Journey of the Catholic Church in Malaysia*, 253–61.
47. Chew, 291–313.
48. For the post–Vatican II Church in Malaysia, see Chew, 170–97. For a collection of twenty-nine rather sober reflections on the Indonesian Church fifty years after Vatican II, see Madya Utama and Ignatius L., eds., *Setelah Setengah Abad, Ke Mana Kita Melangkah?* (Yogyakarta: Kanisius, 2015).
49. For a recent example, see Adrianus Sunarko, *Teologi Kontekstual* (Jakarta: Obor, 2016).
50. Chew, *Journey of the Catholic Church in Malaysia*, 233.
51. See the website of the EWA, https://ecclesiaofwomenblog.wordpress.com/.
52. Chew, *Journey of the Catholic Church in Malaysia*, 153–56.
53. See Nurcholish Madjid, *Cendekiawan and Religiusitas Masyarakat* (Jakarta: Paramadina, 1999); Gregory Barton, *Gagasan Islam Liberal di Indonesia* (Jakarta: Pustaka Antara & Paramadia, 1999); Neng Dara Affiah, *Muslimah Feminis: Penjelalajahan Multi Identitas* (Jakarta: Nalar, 2009); and Zuly Qodir, *Islam Liberal: Varian-Varian Liberalisme Islam di Indonesia, 1991–2002* (Jakarta: LKIS, 2010).
54. J. B. Soedarmanta, *Pater Beek, SJ: Larut Tetapi Tidak Hanyut* (Jakarta: Yayasan Obor Indonesia, 2008); and Mount, *Wrestling with Asia*.
55. See Seri Buku Tempo, *Rahasia-Rahasia Ali Meortopo* (Jakarta: Gramedia, 2014); Jusuf Wanandi, *Shades of Grey: A Political Memoir of Modern Indonesia, 1965–1998* (Singapore: Equinox, 2012).
56. From 1968 to 1998, the Central Committee of the Indonesian Bishops' Conference reported to Suharto following each annual conference. Under pressure, the committee accepted the state Pancasila ideology as the one and only basis of the Church's organization (1985).
57. Many religious congregations collaborate for information and advocacy in NGOs, such as Franciscan International and Vivat International, both of which have representation at the International Human Rights Court in Geneva and at the United Nations in New York.

58. Daniel Dhakidae, *Cendekiawan dan Kekuasaan dalam Negara Orde Baru* (Jakarta: Gramedia, 2003); Menerjang Badai Kekuasaan (Jakarta: Kompas, 2015).
59. East Nusa Tenggara, where 30 percent of Indonesian Catholics live, is a major source of economic migration as well as one of the main sources of human trafficking. Data from the government Department of Health shows that over 90 percent of HIV infection is due to unsafe sex, mostly by migrants away from their families.

8

Indian Catholicism and Its Global Connections, from Early Modernity to the Present

CHANDRA MALLAMPALLI

Since the early 1500s, Catholics have maintained a dual participation in global networks and local societies of India. From era to era, changing social and political influences refashioned this dual participation. Under Portuguese rule, imperial ties to Lisbon and Jesuit missionary endeavors brought global Catholicism into dynamic encounter with Mughal rule. Jesuit-Mughal interactions during the reign of the emperor Akbar (1556–1605) illustrate both imperial and interreligious encounters. With the rise of British power in India, Catholics had to reorient themselves to a new framework for the global reality, this time mediated through a Protestant imperial power. The emergence of Catholic printing presses and newspapers nurtured in Indian Catholics a growing sense of their place in India and their ties to a wider Catholic world. In independent India, rising Hindu nationalism led to a vilification of Christians and Muslims as members of so-called "foreign religions." The current campaign to Hinduize India (Hindutva) has sparked a surge in anti-minority sentiments and violence. Hindutva has also led to greater awareness of the paradoxes of globalization, particularly its capacity to foment militant, exclusionary nationalism and heighten the vulnerability of minorities on account of their global ties.

Since the sixteenth century, Catholics have maintained ties to a wider Catholic world while rooting themselves within cultural contexts of the Indian subcontinent. In key respects their story reflects the larger story of India. India's geographical location positioned itself to interact with societies of the Indian Ocean and along overland trade routes (most notably the Silk Road), connecting to west and central Asia and China. Over time, elements that once seemed distant and alien to the subcontinent were woven into its richly textured fabric. From era to era sociopolitical changes in India posed new challenges for Catholics, especially as they attempted to maintain dual participation in the global and the local. During the early modern period, Portuguese imperial rule provided the context that introduced Catholicism in India. Jesuits and other missionary orders mapped India's nascent Catholic Church onto a global canvas of Catholic engagement with "Gentile" religions.

This "Indo-Portuguese moment" in Catholic history was followed by the rise of British power in India.[1] From the late 1700s to the early twentieth century, Catholics and their institutions had to reckon with their new status under Protestant rulers. This fractured the Church between those who maintained ties to the Portuguese and their royal patronage (*padroado*) and congregations who came under the auspices of the Propaganda Fide, the new missionary initiative of the Vatican. Life under British rule compelled Catholics to become more aware of their distinctive identity vis-à-vis the colonial government and the other religions of India. Toward the turn of the twentieth century, Catholic newspapers played a vital role in nurturing a new, Catholic community consciousness. Newspapers and other printed media bolstered the self-esteem of literate laypeople by nurturing their ties to universal Catholicism. These newspapers also shaped Indian Catholic attitudes toward rising Indian nationalism and the influence of leaders such as Mohandas K. Gandhi.

After Indian independence in 1947, Indian Catholics faced an added burden of securing their status as a minority within the Indian nation. Since the 1980s, a coalition of militant organizations have carried on a campaign to make India an officially Hindu nation as distinct from a secular one. This agenda to Hinduize India, known as *Hindutva*, was accompanied by a vilification of Christians and Muslims as members of "foreign religions" and a surge in anti-Christian and anti-Muslim violence. These developments continue to pose new challenges for Catholics and other Christians in India, particularly in light of their ties to the global Church and allegations that such ties make them less Indian. At stake in such heated rhetoric is India's long-standing tradition of accommodating cultural, linguistic, and religious differences.

EARLY MODERN GLOBALITY: FINDING PRESTER JOHN

Christians of the Iberian Peninsula had long aspired to discover in India a lost Christian kingdom ruled by a legendary figure named Prester John. Rumors of this kingdom not only gave them hopes of finding riches, but also of gaining a valuable political ally in the East. This need for an ally arose precisely at a time when Spanish and Portuguese colonial fleets were encountering new religious traditions in the Americas and in Asia, respectively.[2] Finding a Christian ally in India aligned itself with aspirations to advance the cause of Christendom in the face of Muslim dominance in the Mediterranean. Adding to a sense of Catholic vulnerability was the growing Protestant movement in Europe sparked by the Reformation. Protestant reformers criticized many Catholic practices, such as the centrality of sacraments, clerical hierarchy, and the veneration of images of saints. It was against this climate of a beleaguered Catholicism that a text known as "The Letters of Prester John" circulated throughout Europe.

The text describes a wise priest named Prester John who presided over an ideal Christian kingdom and a huge army in the East. The Latin text initially was discovered during the twelfth century and later it was translated into Italian, Dutch, German, and English to reach wide European audiences.[3] The myth of Prester John reveals rising Catholic anxiety over religious diversity, especially as Catholic empires encountered non-Christian societies of the Atlantic and Indian Ocean. Moreover, it reveals the paradoxical tendency to identify a common bond between Iberian and Eastern Christians on the one hand, while branding the latter as "Nestorian heretics" when confronted with their desire to retain their own clerical hierarchy and customs.[4]

Historians disagree over how the Prester John myth influenced Portuguese behavior upon their arrival in India. Did the myth incline them to stress similarities between Catholicism and the religious traditions of India? Did this impulse cause them to see a Christian presence in places that were not Christian? During Vasco da Gama's first voyage to India in 1498, members of his entourage entered a Hindu temple in Calicut but mistook it for a church and the image inside for the Virgin Mary. In the earliest narration of this event, a crew-member named Alvaro Velho provided details about the structure of the building—which he repeatedly calls "the church"—and the customs observed by the "Christians of this country." He described the smearing of ashes on the bodies of devotees. He also noted the appearance of "saints painted on the walls of the church, wearing crowns . . . painted variously, with teeth protruding an inch from the mouth, and four or five arms."[5] The historian Sanjay Subrahmanyam notes that the structure was not a church, but in fact a Vaishnava temple (for devotees of Vishnu and his incarnations).[6] Why would the Catholic visitors make such an error? And why would their local interlocutors not be aware of the difference between a Hindu and a Christian place of worship, especially considering the presence of Thomas Christians (the ancient Christian community in India that traces its origins to Jesus's apostle Thomas) in the region?

For some historians, this example illustrates how the Prester John myth inclined the Portuguese, at least initially, to search for similarities between Catholicism and the local religion. It is difficult, however, to reconcile this "search for the similar" with the hostility the Portuguese eventually directed toward both Muslims and Hindus and their designation of the Thomas Christians as heretics.[7] Some maintain that the Portuguese approach to India shifted from a posture of tolerance (based on similarity) to one of aggression (based on the awareness of difference). The cause of that shift, however, remains vague.[8] When the Portuguese discovered the presence of the Thomas Christians, they appear to have realized their hopes of finding a lost Christian community who shared their beliefs. It was only a matter of time, however, before they sensed ecclesiastical differences with this ancient community and attempted to "Latinize" them.

Early on, the Portuguese either mistook Hindus for Christians or identified similarities between their beliefs and local ones. The Portuguese chronicler Tome Pires essentially believed that Hindus were once Christian, but strayed from their faith under the influence of Islam. The merchant and linguist Duarte Barbosa saw resemblances between the beliefs of Brahmins (the highest, priestly caste) and the Christian doctrine of the Trinity. Others drew parallels between Hindu bathing practices and Christian baptism, and between local festivals and the celebration of Christ's birth.[9] It was not long before the Portuguese became more hostile toward local religions. The establishment of Goa as a diocese in 1534 gave rise to aggressive measures of the Estado da Índia (Portuguese state in India) toward Hindus. These included the destruction of temples and strong state incentives for conversion. The similarity motif, however, appears to have survived this transition toward aggression. It reemerged among the Jesuits and also arose among Protestant missionaries and merchants. The perception of theological similarity between religious traditions does not appear always to have coincided with greater degrees of political tolerance. In some cases the similarity motif even accompanied European war capitalism.

If the similarity motif and the anecdote about "Vasco da Gama's error" do not teach us much about the basis for Portuguese religious policies, they do offer glimpses into the Portugueses' conceptual mapping of India and the world. Jesuit approaches to Islam were riddled with prejudice arising from their memory of the Crusades, Spanish Reconquista, and the Inquisition. The Portuguese, according to the historian Sanjay Subrahmanyam, appeared only to have had two classes of people on their radar, namely, the so-called "lost" Eastern Christians, who most likely possessed deviant customs, and Muslims. "Anything that was not explicitly Islamic appeared, residually, to be Christian."[10] Accordingly, they divided Asia along two axes. Whereas Muslims controlled a northwest corridor leading to Arabia, Christians—potential Portuguese allies—occupied the southeast corridor, with the region of today's Kerala occupying a middle zone.[11] Only later would they realize the flaws of this geopolitical mapping, particularly its omission of various Hindu sects, whom they labeled "Gentoo" or "Gentile."

As another "religion of the book," Muslims through the eyes of Jesuits actually posed a greater threat to Christendom than so-called Gentiles.[12] Jerome Xavier, the Spanish Jesuit missionary to the Mughal court, wrote: "We deal with the Moors [Muslims], who agree with us about all that concerns the nature of God; and we come into conflict with them about that which we cannot prove with reasons, but only with miracles."[13] Their antipathy toward India's Muslims was informed by centuries of conflict with Muslims in Iberia. During the Reconquista, Catholic armies killed or expelled Muslim and Jewish minorities throughout Spain and Portugal in order to consolidate Catholic power. Portuguese traders extended this combatant, crusade-like mentality into their affairs in India. They competed with Muslims of the Malabar Coast for control over the lucrative pepper trade. They saw their efforts to subdue and defeat Indian Muslims as part of their quest for the triumph of the true faith.[14] As the first Europeans to conduct long-term trade in India, build fortified settlements, and wage war, the Portuguese wore the dual hats of trader and crusader.

This crusader mentality elicited defensive, even militant responses from a community of Muslims known as the Mappilas. Portuguese assaults on their coastal enclaves incited the Mappilas to become more organized and united in a holy war against the Portuguese. One Arabic text dated from the 1580s exhorted Muslims to wage jihad against the "Franks," a designation, distinct from *kafir* (infidel), that drew upon the Portuguese role in the Crusades during an earlier era.[15]

The control over port cities was vital to Portuguese economic success at dominating the sea. Across the Indian Ocean littoral, the Portuguese seized control over the most strategic centers of trade. Goa, Colombo, Melaka, Hurmuz, and Diu were prominent ports that had been largely controlled by Muslims. By the 1530s the Portuguese armadas had taken all of them. This interest in the ports brought them into conflict with Muslim traders and with those wishing to make the hajj across the Arabian Sea. Through Portuguese eyes, the seas were open to all, but this was interpreted to apply exclusively to "Christian nations" who observed Roman law. Hindus and Muslims operated beyond this law—that is, "the law of Jesus Christ"—and thus could claim no right of passage even on Asian waters.[16] Muslims deeply resented Portuguese interference with their trade and movement across the Arabian Sea. One famous poet from Kerala, Zain al-Din, denounced the manner in which the Portuguese had attacked other ships and violated Muslim women.[17] Just as the Portuguese had framed their involvement in the Indian Ocean as a Christian enterprise, Zain al-Din portrayed their violence as a means of producing Christians. The poet, however, also criticized the Hindus, especially their caste system. In his work *Tuhfat al-Mujahidin* he portrays Muslims of Kerala as a distinct community that are called to differentiate themselves from Hindu society. Hindus converted to Islam, he argues, in order to escape "the multitude of inconveniences" arising from the caste system.[18]

In contrast to their approach to Muslims, which was heavily informed by Catholic-Muslim conflict in the Iberian Peninsula, Catholic attitudes toward Hindu religious institutions varied. This is due to the sense among Portuguese Catholics that no single political system unified India and, as a result, there were "many Indias" to speak of.[19] They designated as "Gentiles" that vast social domain of the subcontinent that was not Christian, Jewish, or Muslim, and, in other words, "non-biblical" religions. Under the spell of the Prester John myth, the Portuguese initially regarded Hindus as the lost Christians, but this misunderstanding appears to have been short-lived and supplanted by heightened awareness of difference. Increasingly, Catholics drew attention to idolatry, caste distinctions (and the role of Brahmins), and belief in reincarnation as beliefs that separated them from India's so-called Gentiles.[20]

By designating India's non-biblical or Abrahamic religions as "Gentile," Europeans were essentially accommodating them within a familiar framework—one derived from first century encounters with the Greco-Roman world. Borrowing language from this ancient context enabled missionaries to channel the past into the present. The Portuguese became the "new Romans," Jesuits the "new apostles," and Indians the "new Gentiles," this time within the context of Asian conquests.[21] This manner of classifying the non-European Other to coincide with the amorphous category "Gentile" was taken a step further. It became a form of cultural appropriation, which related more to cultural politics unfolding in Europe than to Indian beliefs and practices. Encounters with Hindus in India provided resources for defending Catholicism against critiques from humanists of the European Enlightenment. The triumph of Catholicism over "pagan" practices in India enhanced their case for the global relevance of their faith and its enduring relevance back home.

During the seventeenth century an ideological climate in Europe gave rise to anti-clerical sentiments and with them an alternative reading of early Christian expansion. Some challenged the belief that the Christian gospel had prevailed over the power of demons in the pagan (Gentile) world and over oracles who were inspired by demons. Men like Bernard Le Bovier de Fontenelle (1657–1757) and Anthony van Dale (1638–1708) argued that oracles were human institutions (indeed, frauds) who falsely claimed access to supernatural power. The decline of oracles was not due to the triumph of Christian belief (since demons and oracles were not "real"), but to more secular factors associated with the rise of the Christian empire.[22] Against such critiques, the French Jesuit Jean Venant Bouchet (1655–1732) drew attention to spirit possession in India and used this as evidence of the early Church's triumph over very real influences of demons and oracles in the lands of the Mediterranean.

INDO-PORTUGUESE MEETS INDO-ISLAMIC

The Portuguese were not alone in their participation in networks that can be called global. During the sixteenth century the Mughal Empire also was building its empire in India through conquest and trade. The Mughals controlled much of northern India, from the Afghan frontier to Bengal, and promoted trade through overland and oceanic routes. They gradually moved southward to control parts of India's central plateau and Deccan region. Goa, however, remained beyond the pale of Mughal control. The Portuguese were able to use the colony as a valuable base for trade and Catholic missions, with little interference from the Mughals.

The Portuguese and the Mughals were very much aware of each other's presence on the subcontinent.[23] The Jesuit missions to the court of the Mughal emperor, Jalal al-Din Muhammad Akbar (r. 1556–1605) provide the earliest and most detailed accounts of European encounters with the Mughals (the Islamicate empire that ruled India for several centuries). Members of the First Mission to Akbar's court (1580–83) learned the Persian language in order to communicate not only with Akbar but also with his courtiers and resident clerics. Their ultimate aim was to persuade the emperor to embrace Christianity.

At one level the Jesuits appeared to have felt a racial affinity with the Mughals. The priest Rudolph Aquaviva, who headed the first mission, had referred to the Mughals as "white men like us," referencing the racial difference that separated both Portuguese and Mughals from the general Indian population.[24] The similarity, however, ended there. By 1573 their relations had become more strained, when Akbar annexed the western province of Gujarat and its port city of Surat. Even though Gujarat was located at a considerable distance to the north of Goa (roughly five hundred miles), the annexation drew their spheres of influence into closer proximity. It gave both empires control over key ports and access to trade across the Arabian Sea. Whereas the Mughals dominated overland trade routes, the Portuguese held the upper hand at sea because of their superior ships. Their naval dominance allowed them to require Muslims making the hajj by sea to pay taxes when crossing Portuguese ports and to carry a *cartaz* (a pass or license) stamped with the image of Christ and the Virgin Mary.[25] Some speculate, not unreasonably, that Akbar aspired eventually to expel the Portuguese from Goa. Upon encountering Portuguese traders in Gujarat, Akbar's chief minister is said to have regarded them as "a pack of savages."[26]

It was in this context of rising proximity and tension that Akbar, somewhat ironically, developed a sincere interest in learning about the religion of the Portuguese. Prior to 1580, when the Jesuits made their first official mission to his court, other Catholic priests had made a favorable impression upon Akbar. In Bengal in 1576 two Jesuits refused to administer the sacraments to Christian merchants who refused to pay taxes to the Mughal government. So impressed was Akbar by their action that he invited Julian Pereira, a Jesuit priest stationed at Satgaon, a port in southern Bengal, to his court at Fatehpur Sikri. Pereira engaged in dialogues with Muslim clerics at Akbar's court, some of whom were less than cordial. Not being a very learned Jesuit, Pereira recommended that Akbar extend an invitation to priests based at the College of St. Paul in Goa.

In his *farman* (royal invitation or decree) Akbar expressed his "kind disposition" toward the Jesuits and his desire to learn about the "Law and Gospel" of their religion from their learned priests.[27] After much deliberation, the bishops at Goa decided to send three Jesuit priests to Akbar's court, each representing a different nationality. Francis Henriques was a Persian from Hormuz and a convert from Islam. He was to assume the role of translator due to his knowledge of Persian, the official language of the Mughal court. Antony Monserrate, a Spaniard from Catalonia, was responsible for producing a detailed account of their journey from Goa to Fatehpur Sikri, of Akbar's military campaign at Kabul, and of the early dialogues of the priests with Akbar. Rudolph Aquaviva was a high-born and learned Italian who was trained at Rome in theology and philosophy. When he sailed from Rome to Lisbon to become ordained, he was accompanied by Matteo Ricci, the Jesuit who had made a similar mission to the imperial court at China.[28] After arriving in Goa at the age of thirty, Aquaviva volunteered to be a part of the mission to Akbar's court. Clearly impressed by his credentials, the bishops appointed him to lead it.[29]

After three years of interaction with Akbar and members of Akbar's court, this first Jesuit mission failed to achieve the ultimate goal of converting the emperor. Akbar's interest in dialogue eventually declined. The priests faced open hostility from Muslims in his court, which signaled that they needed to consider returning to Goa. Akbar himself, however, did not want the Jesuits to leave. This was not because of any interest of his in becoming a Christian, but rather because of an affinity he had developed for them. At one level Akbar appears to have been drawn to the intensity of their spiritual convictions and their capacity to feed his sporadic need for religious discussions. Lengthy conversations that never resulted in Akbar's conversion ultimately disappointed the Jesuits. Still, they left behind a rich and revealing account of their exchanges within this Indo-Persian domain.

THE MODERN PERIOD: THE FRENCH AND THE BRITISH

Besides Goa, another key center of Catholic power and influence was Pondicherry, an east coastal French colony located to the south of Madras. In Goa and Pondicherry, Catholics maintained unique ties to European imperial power and trade interests. Within the context of these ties to Catholic empires, the two locales also became venues for competition between Catholic orders, which in turn gave rise to jurisdictional controversies and conflicts associated with race and caste. These complex developments show that Indian Catholicism was anything but monolithic and often experienced turbulent relations with the local populations.

During the eighteenth century Pondicherry became a venue for disputes between Capuchins, Jesuits, and missionaries of the Missions étrangères de Paris (Society of Foreign Missions of Paris, or MEP). Intra-Catholic rivalry in India quite often enacted politics arising from within European contexts. For instance, tensions in France between the Catholic majority and the Huguenots (the Protestant/Calvinist minority) played out in India as Dutch traders competed with the Compagnie des Indes Orientales (French East India Company) for access to valuable trade ports in South India. Since 1674, when Pondicherry had come under French rule, the French had made every effort to establish Pondicherry as a Catholic city not unlike what the Portuguese had done at Goa.[30]

The French project of creating a strong Catholic domain in Pondicherry was riddled with problems. Catholic religious orders and societies competed for influence. Capuchins, an offshoot of the Franciscans, were the first order to arrive in Pondicherry after it had become a French colony. After having serviced Europeans and Indian converts in the colony for roughly twenty years, the Capuchins came to regard Pondicherry as a domain entrusted to their oversight.[31] Jesuits arrived in Pondicherry in 1689 and in 1691 constructed their first church, Église Notre-Dame-de-l'Immaculée-Conception. The third religious body, the MEP, was a society of secular priests, not a religious order as such, whose members came under the authority of the Propaganda Fide, the missionary establishment commissioned directly by the pope.[32] With the backing of Rome and powerful French patrons, the MEP also came to Pondicherry with the intention of making converts and overseeing Catholic congregations.[33]

These three groups adopted different attitudes toward local affairs in Pondicherry. The Jesuits, who had grown in influence in the courts of Europe, tended to adopt an aggressive posture toward Pondicherry's non-Christian residents. Keen on converting the local population to Catholicism, Jesuits did not want to see in Pondicherry a platform for other religions to flourish. Capuchins and MEP missionaries, by contrast, tended to oppose the efforts of the Jesuits. They sympathized with trader-officials and the concessions these officials wanted to extend to Hindu laborers.[34] These divisions became most evident in conflicts concerning religious freedom for the local population.

Instituting Catholicism in Pondicherry involved the aesthetic shaping of the urban landscape along Catholic lines. This entailed the construction of ornate cathedrals, compounds for religious orders, and chapels that served the French military. By necessity it also required that authorities curtail certain freedoms of Hindus. Catholic officials and missionaries contended constantly with the visible, and highly public, dimensions of Hindu religiosity (festivals, processions, temple construction, and music) and its claims to space. On one occasion Jesuits pressured local officials to eliminate a popular temple located near one of their compounds and a military fort. The French governor, Francois Martin, asked the Tamil worshipers to either tear down their own temple or leave town. The worshipers chose to "call Martin's bluff": they assembled at the city gate and threatened to leave the town.[35] These laborers consisted of cotton weavers, land laborers, domestic servants, and wealthier merchants. They threatened to "leave Pondicherry an empty town" and make it impossible for the French to benefit from trade in textiles and other commodities.[36] They effectively forced Martin to revoke his demands and make concessions. The effectiveness of their protests exposed the inherent contradiction between the trading interests of the French and their ambitions to make Pondicherry Catholic. Such conflicts also show how Catholicism was far from being either a monolithic political force in India or a religion that invariably blended with local religions. On the contrary, Catholicism was always beset with sharp internal differences tied to its different orders and their varying and complex ties to imperial power.

On the other side of peninsular India, the Catholic population of Bombay came to be splintered along lines of race, caste, and social class. As with Catholics of Pondicherry, Bombay's Catholics enjoyed the backing of a powerful European state. During the 1700s, however, Portuguese influence on India's west coast declined and with it the capacity to secure Catholic institutions under the royal patronage of the Portuguese Crown, or *padroado*. When the British East India Company became the dominant power in western India after the defeat of the Marathas (1818), Catholic congregations had to reconcile themselves to life under a Protestant power. Adding to their need for reorientation was the expanding scope of the Propaganda Fide, the papal missionary body that fell outside of Portuguese control. The British East India Company became increasingly determined to undermine padroado control in Bombay and tended to favor Propaganda priests. Conflict between the padroado and Propaganda Fide was accompanied by a fracturing of the Catholic population along lines of race and caste.

What we now call "Mumbai," or previously "Bombay," had once consisted of seven semi-autonomous islands.[37] By the early eighteenth century the Catholic population of Salsette Island (in the northern Bassein district of Bombay) numbered roughly thirty-seven thousand and contained some twenty-five parishes. This population resulted from a combination of Portuguese settlement and aggressive missionary activity by Jesuit and Franciscan orders. As had been done in Pondicherry, authorities restricted the religious freedom of Hindu and Muslim residents. The bishop at Goa had incited missionaries to destroy Hindu religious structures in Bassein.[38] Entire villages such as Bandra and Trindade (known as Tirandz on British maps) came under Jesuit oversight.[39]

Despite these efforts to create a soundly Catholic domain in Bombay, the Catholic population became profoundly fragmented along the lines of race and caste and came to be divided as well by padroado vs. Propaganda jurisdiction.[40] At the top of the social hierarchy were European-born Portuguese, known as *reinois*, and then the Indian-born persons of Portuguese descent, known as *casados* or *descendentes.* This class resembled the Creoles of South America and Mexico. Below them were Indian converts, who continued to retain their caste distinctions. Brahmin converts, for instance, resided in separate neighborhoods from lower-ranking castes. The latter included the Kunbi cultivators and Koli fishermen. They also included the Agri and the Bhandari, who made a living extracting toddy, the intoxicating substance found in certain palm trees. The Portuguese labeled Indian converts collectively as *naturais.*[41] Alongside the Indian converts were persons of mixed racial descent. The term "East Indians" was applied to them. The same designation was applied to Indian converts to Catholicism who adopted Portuguese names and assimilated into Portuguese society. Later on, the East Indian community included the last remaining Portuguese families in Bombay island, who had been marginalized under British rule. They retained their prejudices, however, toward the naturais who vastly outnumbered them. The segregation of descendentes and upper caste Catholics from lower-ranking castes is part of the legacy of Portuguese colonial Catholicism. Under British rule, this racial hierarchy was configured in new ways.

As the British expanded their influence, they enacted measures that sought to eliminate the influence of the Portuguese Crown in Bombay. They tended to regard padroado priests with great suspicion on account of their loyalty to Lisbon. Company administrators similarly distrusted persons of Portuguese ancestry and upper caste Indian Catholics who retained their allegiance to the Archdiocese of Goa. As they enacted measures to restrict the influence of the padroado priests on specific congregations in Bombay, the British, ironically, were aided by measures adopted by the Vatican. In 1839 a papal decree, Multa Praeclare, transferred the islands of Bombay and Salsette to the jurisdiction of the Propaganda Fide.

The partnership of the British and the Propaganda Fide in dismantling the padroado establishment had ripple effects throughout Catholic communities of India. Churches and properties that were once under padroado control appear to have been transferred overnight to the jurisdiction of the Vicars Apostolic (the appointed leaders of the Propaganda Fide in a given bishopric). These measures were met with fierce resistance by people committed to the vast network of Goan priests who up to this time had been officiating in various parts of South Asia, fearing that the transition to British rule and Propaganda oversight would entail the loss of jobs and ecclesiastical independence once entrusted to the padroado priests, not to mention the huge loss of Portuguese prestige.[42] Heated disputes between rival priests and parishioners erupted throughout South Asia.

Instances of jurisdictional conflict between the padroado and Propaganda Fide represent the eclipsing of the Indo-Portuguese phase of Indian Catholicism and the transition to British rule. As Indian Catholics were weaned from Portuguese imperial patronage and cultural heritage, they faced new challenges under British rule. The British, after all, were Protestants. The advent of British rule compelled Catholics to differentiate themselves from Protestant society and thrive as a community that could not rely on the backing of the government. This defensive posture led to new ways of asserting boundaries within Catholic institutions vis-à-vis Hindu society.

BRIDGING THE GLOBAL AND THE LOCAL: CATHOLIC NEWSPAPERS

The degree to which Indian Catholics were shaped by global connections varied according to social class, literacy level, and profession. The Catholic laity in India was a mixed population, comprised of educated urban professionals, shoreline fishing communities, and village laborers from lower castes. Illiterate, lower-ranking communities tended to be more oriented to affairs within their immediate vicinity. During the early twentieth century, Catholic bishops in South India were recruited primarily from France and Italy. They tended to be more oriented to Rome's priorities and less responsive to the currents of local South Indian politics. Urban and educated Catholics who read Catholic newspapers were more attuned to developments in transnational Catholicism. Lay professionals (lawyers, members of the assembly, scholars), who were respected as leaders within the Catholic Church, often helped to mediate teachings of the hierarchy to other sections of the laity.[43]

During the early twentieth century, Catholic newspapers and societies were established to articulate and defend Catholic interests amid rising Hindu nationalism. Early on, the Catholic Association of South India (also known as the Catholic Indian Association or CIA) served to bring grievances of the Catholic community to the attention of the government. These grievances included matters relating to religious education, the employment of Catholics in government service, the question of communal electorates, and the right to observe various Catholic holidays. In 1919, the Catholic Truth Society established a branch in the southern city of Trichinopoly. Its purpose was to define religious and moral positions on various issues and to "assist Catholics in counteracting prejudices against religion."[44] In 1930, the Catholic Truth Propagation League added its voice, establishing numerous libraries and reading rooms aimed at promoting a more literate and publicly conscious Catholic laity. As Catholics came to terms with their status as members of a minority community, both within India and within other national contexts, they sought out new ways to exercise influence. Occasionally, activities of the laity sparked conflicts with the hierarchy over the parameters of legitimate social and political involvement. The need for a united Catholic voice on public matters culminated in 1944 in the establishment of the Catholic Bishops' Conference of India (CBCI). Its aim was to "facilitate common action of the hierarchy in matters affecting the common interests of Indian Catholics."[45]

Catholic newspapers played an important role in shaping a sense of Catholic identity. Newspapers bridged local affairs in India to those affecting Catholics worldwide. They did so during a turbulent interwar period, when Catholics found themselves navigating the fault lines between competing ideologies and international conflicts. The Church viewed itself as being embroiled in an ideological battle with modernism and all of its derivatives: socialism, Nazism, communism, and, of course, Protestantism. By way of print media, ideological fault lines on the global scene were brought to bear on Indian localities. The differentiation of Catholics from various international "others" contributed to the fashioning of a distinctive Catholic identity in India, especially as Catholics came to terms with the politics of Indian nationalism and the towering influence of Gandhi. Catholics also had to position themselves in relation to mobilizations against upper caste domination in Indian society.

During the 1930s, Catholic newspapers were established to equip an emerging class of lay scholars, lawyers, local politicians, and other professionals to wield influence on behalf of the Catholic community at large. These newspapers helped formulate a Catholic point of view on hot-button issues of the day. One might imagine the primary focus of the Catholic press as involving confrontations with Hindu nationalism or the emergence of Muslims as a political force in society. But factoring far more prominently in Catholic media of the day was the importance for Catholics to differentiate themselves from Indian Protestants. Protestants represented a path of moral compromise and capitulation to secular nationhood. As much as Catholic elites wanted to oppose Hinduism as a false religion, they opted to avoid any frontal assault that would earn reprisals. They saw in Protestants a softer target whose main problem was their accommodation to the political and ideological winds of the day.[46]

The Bombay-based newspaper the *Examiner*, for instance, often criticized Protestant compromises with modernism, Hindu nationalism, and secular nationhood. Protestant attempts to make Christianity appear "more "Hindu" or Sanskritic in its cultural complexion demonstrated a tendency toward capitulation to the external pressure of Hindu nationalism on minorities. Editors at the same time chided Anglicans for adopting weak moral positions on birth control, marriage, and divorce at the 1930 Lambeth Conference. The editors similarly criticized a statement produced by Protestant ministers titled "Laymen's Foreign Missions Inquiry," which recommended a more irenic approach to other religions and a reconsideration of the belief in Christian exceptionalism. That Protestant missionaries had criticized the *Laymen's Inquiry* even more severely than Catholics did appeared irrelevant to their larger aim of presenting the Catholic Church as the guardian of the one, true ancient faith.[47]

Catholic newspapers drew upon the global character of Catholicism to bolster the self-esteem of Catholic minorities in India. A good example of this is the coverage of Gandhi's 1931 visit to Rome and his attempt to meet Pope Pius XI. By this time Gandhi had risen to the status of an All-India leader and even a world leader, renowned for his espousal of nonviolence. His attempt to meet with the pope, however, was unsuccessful, apparently because of the pope's observance of a day of silence on the Sunday when Gandhi had hoped to see him. Catholic newspapers portrayed the ordeal as a competition between Gandhi's charismatic authority and the authority of the pope, viewing the latter, of course, as vastly superior. For the *Glasgow Herald*, Gandhi's main interest in meeting with the pope was to enlist India's Catholic bishops in the pursuit of Indian independence. The *Herald* viewed the pope's refusal to meet with Gandhi as a rebuff, claiming that the pope had uttered privately that "Gandhi might be 'multo bravo' as an individual but that he didn't see any particular reason why he should see him at the present juncture."[48] The *Examiner* drew more attention to the charismatic authority of the pope as the head of the Catholic Church, which was an "international moral power." Gandhi's visit to Rome, in the views of the *Examiner*, revealed his recognition of the Church as a moral force both internationally and within India.[49]

Even before the visit, the Catholic press had tended to be more critical of Gandhi than the Protestant press. Resistance to Hinduism and Protestant accommodations to Hinduism were recurring tropes in Catholic media. If it was not Gandhi's Hindu persona, it was the liberal Protestant's veneration of Gandhi that irked the Catholic press. Gandhi in 1931 was reported to have stated that he would oppose Christian missions in India if they persisted in conversion activities and did not limit themselves to humanitarian work. In response, the Madras-based *Catholic Leader* (later known as the *New Leader*) claimed the statement shattered any hope that Gandhi was genuinely supportive of the ethical vision of Christianity and the work of Christian missions as a whole. The *Examiner*'s criticism of Gandhi was also a backhanded criticism of Protestant "illusions" about him. In particular, Gandhi's comments shattered the notion that he was essentially a Christian without the Christian label, a perspective espoused by the Methodist missionary E. Stanley Jones.[50]

FROM INDEPENDENCE TO THE PRESENT

If the sociopolitical climate of early twentieth-century India posed challenges for India's Catholics, the conditions of independent India made Catholics even more vulnerable as a minority. After India achieved independence in 1947, Prime Minister Jawaharlal Nehru set out to establish India as a secular, socialist democracy. A constituent assembly, chaired by the Dalit (literally, "broken or oppressed ones," formerly called "untouchables") activist Bhimrao Ramji Ambedkar (1891–1956), staged roughly four years (1946–50) of debate and deliberation. The assembly yielded a highly progressive constitution for the new country. Article 15 prohibited discrimination on the basis of religion, race, caste, sex, or place of birth. Article 25 upheld the principle of freedom of religion. It guaranteed that "all persons are equally entitled to freedom of conscience and the right to freely profess, practice, and propagate religion subject to public order, morality and health."[51] In a land of such immense diversity and riddled with a history of caste oppression and religious strife, such guarantees held out the promise of a more equitable and humane future.

It was not long before the issue of religious conversion among the poor and oppressed again drew the attention of state officials. Immediately after independence, the government prioritized issues of economic development. It was hoped that missionaries would advance the cause of development through education and humanitarian aid. In 1953 the home minister, Kailas Nath Katju, declared that missionary humanitarian aid was welcome in India but that missionaries should not engage in proselytization. He drew attention to allegations that missionaries were proselytizing members of tribal communities within certain districts in the state of Madhya Pradesh. This concern led Katju to call for an inquiry into whether such proselytizing violated Article 25 of the constitution.

The very idea of religious freedom was being interpreted in very different ways. For Catholics, it meant the freedom to propagate their faith and receive converts into the Church. For critics of conversion it meant that certain vulnerable communities should be protected from proselytizing, especially by foreigners or foreign-funded agencies. In 1954, the government established the Christian Missionary Activities Enquiry Committee, which was headed by retired Supreme Court chief justice Bhawani Shankar Niyogi. The findings of the Niyogi Report released by the committee emphasized how missionaries had used humanitarian aid (especially schools, hospitals, and orphanages) as inducements for conversion.[52] The report essentially reinforced Gandhi's critique of missionary work and resulted in significant restrictions on missionary visas for decades to come. Critics of the report, however, observed how it reenacts the paternalism of the Gandhian approach in denying Dalits or tribals of any choice or agency in the conversion process.[53]

Hindu nationalists and policy makers of independent India have bought into the idea that Christian conversion among the poor arises primarily from material inducements. The fact that such a large percentage of the Indian population (as much as 40 percent) is Dalit or tribal who live in poverty makes Hindu nationalists all the more fearful that humanitarian relief could lure them into other religions. The claim, however, that the offer of jobs, financial assistance, education, or medical services has lured the poor into converting is loaded with weighty assumptions about the differential rates of development of Catholic and non-Catholic Dalits or tribals and their different experiences of social discrimination.

Such assumptions of Hindu nationalists, ironically, find a precedent in the rhetoric of missionaries of the late colonial period. Missionaries at the time tried to make the case that conversion would lead to social transformation and a better quality of life in the here and now. This case was built not upon crude promises of financial assistance or jobs, but on changes of inner character and lifestyle that would impact a convert's quality of life. After the departure of foreign missionaries from independent India, such optimistic rhetoric was replaced by narrations of continued hardship by Dalits themselves—not simply at the hands of upper caste landlords, but also within Christian churches and institutions. Even as Christians, many continue to experience the stigma of untouchability and economic backwardness. Their persistent state of impoverishment places them in the curious position of having to prove that they remain disadvantaged despite their Christian identity.

Following the Second Vatican Council (1962–65), the Catholic hierarchy approached other religions of India with greater tolerance and respect. Much of this sprang from the tenets of the papal decree Nostra aetate, which recognized "a ray of that Truth" in these other religions:

> The Catholic Church rejects nothing that is true and holy in these religions. She regards with sincere reverence those ways of conduct and of life, those precepts and teachings which, though differing in many aspects from the ones she holds and sets forth, nonetheless often reflect a ray of that Truth which enlightens all men. Indeed, she proclaims, and ever must proclaim Christ "the way, the truth, and the life" (John 14:6), in whom men may find the fullness of religious life, in whom God has reconciled all things to Himself.[54]

Arising from this declaration was a greater emphasis on interfaith dialogue and inculturation in theological training in India. The sharp lines in the sand drawn by Catholic newspapers during the early twentieth century gradually became less pronounced and a new, conciliatory approach to other faiths was embraced by the Church hierarchy in India.

The Second Vatican Council also placed a stronger emphasis on the role of laypeople in the mission of the Church. This emboldened lay leaders to initiate gatherings that emphasized the capacity of each believer to experience God directly and without intermediaries. During the 1980s, the Vincentian Fathers of Potta hosted charismatic retreats, which promoted grassroots forms of spirituality akin to Pentecostalism. These retreats were highly appealing to Syrian Catholics (Pazhayakur). Lay leaders played an active role in promoting and leading these retreats and forming independent prayer units. They delivered sermons that stressed repentance and moral reform, outreach to the poor, and the outpouring of the Holy Spirit.[55] In some instances the role of these lay leaders even surpassed that of the hierarchy and eventually these modes of spiritual services drew Jacobite Thomas Christians as well and led to the establishment of independent churches.[56]

Since the 1980s, Catholics and other religious minorities in India have had to contend with the rise of militant Hindu nationalism in India. A coalition of Hindu nationalist organizations known as the Sangh Parivar (or Saffron Brotherhood) has advanced its agenda of hindutva or, literally, the pursuit of Hinduness in all aspects of national life. The hindutva agenda has placed India's secular democracy under severe stress and has heightened the vulnerability of many Christians and Muslims. The Sangh Parivar portrays adherents of these two religions as non-Indian and foreign, despite centuries of integration into the cultural fabric of the subcontinent. Hindu nationalists have long portrayed Christian conversion as an act of deracination and denationalization. They have introduced anti-conversion laws in several states and have launched campaigns to reconvert Christians and Muslims to Hinduism.[57]

The rise of hindutva has coincided with a surge in anti-Christian violence in India. From 1964 to 1996 the country registered only thirty-eight instances of such violence. By 1998, the number of instances of anti-Christian violence went up to ninety, and from 2001 to 2005 there were as many as two hundred documented instances of anti-Christian attacks.[58] During the late 1990s Indian news media and human rights groups reported on churches being destroyed, nuns being assaulted and raped, priests being hacked to death, and social relief organizations being solemnly warned not to engage in conversions.[59] Such events occurred in a variety of places, including Gujarat, Bihar, Odisha, and Madhya Pradesh amid allegations of indifference or complicity by state officials. In December 1998, a wave of attacks against tribal Christians in the Dangs District of Gujarat state drew the attention of political parties and national forums. Sonia Gandhi, then president of India's Congress Party, described the "extreme fear and tension" felt by Christian minorities in the region. Spokespersons for the United Christian Forum for Human Rights declared the attacks to be part of a "systematic and orchestrated" agenda of Hindu nationalists.[60]

Instances of anti-Christian violence increased significantly over the past decade and have drawn the attention of the U.S. Commission on International Religious Freedom and other international organizations. Under the reign of the BJP and Prime Minister Narendra Modi, roughly five hundred acts of anti-Christian violence have been documented in 2022 alone.[61] Hindu activists claim that Christian conversion threatens the unity and integrity of a Hindu nation. Despite Modi's meeting with Pope Francis in October 2021 and his invitation to the pope to visit India, Modi's regime has overseen a persistence of vigilante violence against Christians, which usually go unpunished. Such actions are related to the perception, propagated by the Hindu right, of Catholics as belonging to a "foreign" religion. To counter such stereotypes and accompanying violence, Indian Catholics have urged the Catholic Bishops' Commission of India (CBCI) to play a more active role in speaking out to state and federal authorities. The Forum for Justice and Peace, which consists of numerous Catholic communities in India, compared attacks against Christians with those against Muslims. The CBCI remained silent when Muslims were vilified and lynched by Hindu vigilante mobs. They are now paying the price for this silence, as similar acts of violence are increasingly directed against them.[62]

As Indianness is increasingly defined as "Hinduness," Catholics, like Muslims, find themselves burdened to explain that the global dimensions of their faith do not diminish their love for and participation in Indian society. Their global ties have accompanied centuries of acculturation to Indian society and commitment to the betterment of the nation through its social services, educational institutions, and message of hope.

NOTES

1. The phrase "Indo-Portuguese moment" is used by the historian Sanjay Subrahmanyam in *Europe's India: Words, People, Empires, 1500–1800* (Cambridge: Harvard University Press, 2017).
2. Joan-Pau Rubiés, "Ethnography and Cultural Translation in the Early Modern Missions," *Studies in Church History* 53 (2017): 274–75.
3. Alexander Henn, *Hindu-Catholic Encounters in Goa: Religion, Colonialism, and Modernity* (Bloomington: Indiana University Press, 2014), 26.
4. See Clara Joseph, *Christianity in India: An Anti-Colonial Turn* (London: Routledge, 2019), 35.
5. Ernest George Ravenstein, Alvaro Velho, and João de Sa, trans., *A Journal of the First Voyage of Vasco da Gama, 1497–1499* (London: Hakluty Society, 1898), 52–53.
6. He bases this on the appearance of a bird's figure on the *stambha* (a sacred or auspicious column) outside the temple. See Sanjay Subrahmanyam, *The Career and Legend of Vasco da Gama* (Cambridge: Cambridge University Press, 1997), 132.

7. Henn, *Hindu-Catholic Encounters in Goa*, 21.
8. See, for instance, M. N. Pearson, *The Portuguese in India* (Cambridge: Cambridge University Press, 1987), 116–17.
9. Pearson, *The Portuguese in India*; and Stephen Dale, "Communal Relations in Pre-Modern India: 16th Century Kerala," *Journal of the Social and Economic History of the Orient* 16, nos. 2–3 (December 1973): 319–27.
10. Henn, *Hindu-Catholic Encounters in Goa*, 133.
11. Sanjay Subrahmanyam, "The Birthpangs of Portuguese Asia: Revisiting the Fateful 'Long Decade,' 1498–1509," *Journal of Global History* 2 (2007): 262.
12. Paul Shore, "Contact, Confrontation, Accommodation: Jesuits and Islam, 1540–1770," *Al-Qantara* 36, no. 2 (July–December 2015): 434.
13. Jerome Xavier's letter, dated September 14, 1609, "Eulogy of Father Jerome Xavier," 120–21. Quote is taken from Faraz Anjam, "Islam and Hinduism in the Eyes of Early European Travellers to India," *Journal of the Research Society of Pakistan* 44, no. 2 (December 2007): 62.
14. M. N. Pearson, *The Indian Ocean* (London: Routledge, 2003), 127.
15. Richard Eaton, *India in the Persianate Age, 1000–1765* (Oakland: University of California Press, 2019), 189.
16. Pearson, *The Indian Ocean*, 122.
17. Pearson, 124.
18. Dale, "Communal Relations in Pre-Modern India," 323.
19. Exceptions would be the Mughals and the southern kingdom of Vijayanagara. These too were regional kingdoms and therefore contributed to a sense of India's cultural and religious complexity, not unity. See Joan-Pao Rubiés, *Travel and Ethnology in the Renaissance: South India through European Eyes* (Cambridge: Cambridge University Press, 2000), 7–10.
20. For a perceptive analysis of the relationship between Jesuit Orientalism and missionary work, see Francis Clooney, "Understanding in Order to be Understood, Refusing to Understand in Order to Convert," in Francis Clooney, ed., *Western Jesuit Scholars in India: Tracing Their Paths, Reassessing Their Goals* (Leiden: Brill, 2020), 112–26.
21. Ines Zupanov, "*Antiquissime Christianita*: Indian Religion or Idolatry?" *Journal of Early Modern History* 24 (2020): 472.
22. Francis Clooney, "Excerpts from Fr. Bouchet's India: An Eighteenth-Century Jesuit's Encounter with Hinduism," in Francis Clooney, ed., *Western Jesuit Scholars in India: Tracing Their Paths, Reassessing Their Goals* (Leiden: Brill, 2020), 148.
23. See Jorge Flores, *Unwanted Neighbors: The Mughals, the Portuguese, and Their Frontier Zones* (New Delhi: Oxford University Press, 2018). According to Hugh Cagle, "Portugal's empire in Asia depended on a vision that situated the Estado da Índia within an emerging metropolitan vision of nature globally—a cartographic vision recognizable to private traders, royal factors, and Crown advisors alike." See Cagle, *Assembling the Tropics: Science and Medicine in Portugal's Empire, 1450–1700* (Cambridge: Cambridge University Press, 2018), 148.
24. John Correia-Afonso, ed., *Letters from the Mughal Court: The First Jesuit Mission to Akbar, 1580–83* (St. Louis: Institute of Jesuit Sources, 1981), 56.
25. Al-Badaoni, *Muntakhab-ut-Tawarikh,* vol. 2, trans. W. H. Lowe (Calcutta: J. W. Thomas Baptist Mission Press, 1884), 206. See also Correia-Afonso, *Letters from the Mughal Court*, 96n4; and Agnieszka Kuczkiewicz-Fraś, "Akbar the Great (1542–1605) and Christianity: Between Religion and Politics," *Orientalia Christiana Cracoviensia* 3 (2011): 75n1.
26. Iris Macfarlane, "Akbar and the Jesuits," *History Today* 20, no. 7 (June 1, 1970): 466.
27. Edward Maclagan, *The Jesuits and the Great Mogul* (London: Burns Oates and Washbourne, 1932), 23–24.
28. Correia-Afonso, *Letters from the Mughal Court*, 7.
29. Maclagan, *The Jesuits and the Great Mogul*, 25.

30. Hugald Grafe, *History of Christianity in India, Vol. 4, Part 2, Tamilnadu in the Nineteenth and Twentieth Centuries* (Bangalore: Church History Association of India, 1990), 49.
31. Danna Agmon, "Striking Pondicherry: Religious Disputes and French Authority in an Indian Colony of the Ancien Regime," *French Historical Studies* 37, no. 3 (2014): 443.
32. Henriette Bugge, *Mission and Tamil Society: Social and Religious Change in South India, 1840–1900* (Richmond, Surrey: Curzon, 1994), 51.
33. Grafe, *History of Christianity in India*, 35–39.
34. Grafe, 445.
35. Danna Agmon, "Striking Pondicherry," 454.
36. Agmon, 437.
37. After capturing these islands in 1534, the Portuguese established a factory along the coast in order to advance the trade of spices and cotton and silk textiles, among other things. In due course the Portuguese were compelled to develop closer ties to the British, largely in hopes of countering Dutch aggression and expanding influence in the Indian Ocean trade. William Foster, "The East India Company, 1600–1740," in H. H. Dodwell, ed., *The Cambridge History of India, Vol. V, British India* (Cambridge: Cambridge University Press, 1929), 85–88.
38. Sidh Daniel Losa Mendiratta, "Framing Identity: Bombay's East Indian Community and Its Indo-Portuguese Historical Background, 1737–1928," *Anais de Historia de Alem-Mar* 18 (2017): 207–48.
39. Mendiratta, "Framing Identity."
40. See Kenneth Ballhatchet, *Caste, Class and Catholicism in India, 1789–1914* (Richmond, Surrey: Curzon, 1998).
41. Mendiratta, "Framing Identity," 212–13.
42. Mendiratta, 225.
43. Chandra Mallampalli, *Christians and Public Life in Colonial South India: Contending with Marginality* (London: RoutledgeCurzon, 2004), 88.
44. *The Catholic Laymen's Directory of India* (Mangalore: C. J. Varkey, 1933), 48, 164.
45. *The Catholic Directory of India for the Year of Our Lord 1969* (New Delhi: St. Paul, 1969), 6.
46. Mallampalli, *Christians and Public Life in Colonial South India*, 135.
47. Mallampalli, 35.
48. Mallampalli, 97.
49. Mallampalli, 98.
50. Mallampalli, 97.
51. See https://www.india.gov.in/my-government/constitution-india/constitution-india-full-text.
52. Sebastian Kim, *In Search of Identity: Debates on Religious Conversion in India* (New Delhi: Oxford University Press, 2003), 60–69.
53. K. W. Christopher, "Between Two Worlds: The Predicament of Dalit Christians in Bama's Works," *Journal of Commonwealth Literature* 47, no. 1 (2012): 7.
54. Nostra aetate: Declaration on the Relation of the Church to Non-Christian Religions, Proclaimed by His Holiness Pope Paul VI on October 28, 1965, https://www.vatican.va/archive/hist_councils/ii_vatican_council/documents/vat-ii_decl_19651028_nostra-aetate_en.html.
55. Joseph Pampackal, "Vincentian Congregation of the Syro-Malabar Church in Kerala (India)," *Vincentiana* 51, no. 6 (November–December 2007): 417–27.
56. Author personal consultation with Pius Malekandathil, July 27, 2020.
57. See "Foreign Swadeshi," *Frontline*, December 24, 2014, http://www.frontline.in/thenation/foreign swadeshi/article6715524.ece?homepage=true&css=print; and "Agra Reconversion Row: Uproar in Parliament as Opposition Seeks Prime Minister's Reply; UP Cops on High Alert," *Hindustan Times*, December 11, 2014, http://www.hindustantimes.com/india-news/agra-conversion-that-muslims-say-wasn-t-rocks-parliament-bsp-cong-target-bjp/article1-1295082.aspx.
58. These figures are drawn from Sarbeswar Sahoo, *Pentecostalism and Politics of Conversion in India* (Cambridge: Cambridge University Press, 2018), 5.

59. For a list of newspaper articles, see Mallampalli, *Christians and Public Life in Colonial South India*, 4n10.
60. "Sonia Gandhi Warns Gujarat Government," *The Hindu*, January 9, 1999.
61. Each incident is carefully documented in "Hate and Targeted Violence Against Christians in India, Yearly Report 2021" published by the Religious Liberty Commission of the Evangelical Fellowship of India.
62. "India's Catholic Bishops Urged to Highlight Anti-Christian Violence," *Catholic News Agency (CNA) Newsletter*, January 24, 2022, https://www.catholicnewsagency.com/news/250196/india-s-catholic-bishops-urged-to-highlight-anti-christian-violence.

9

Catholicism and Public Life in India

EVELYN MONTEIRO

Vatican II was a defining moment for the World Church. With its optimistic appraisal and validation of the modern world, the Church rose to the occasion and courageously enunciated its prophetic self-understanding in public life. In the pursuit of an updated public role, the Church revisited its governing structure, liturgical worship, relationship with other Christians, cultures, religions, and mission in the world. This occurrence effected a major advance for Asian theology and initiated dramatic changes in Asian Pacific Catholicism. This chapter examines some features of Vatican II that resulted in crucial "turns" in theological approaches and ecclesiological models that led to consequential pastoral implications for India. A new way of being Church and doing mission in India and an Asian Pacific Catholicism were in the making:

from centralism to communion of churches/communities
from one true religion to many religions
from Church to public sphere in the world

The triple dialogue with cultures, religions, and the poor, specific to the Asian Pacific context constitutes the theological framework here. This chapter will also discuss the dynamics of globalization and religions in India as part of the modern social system. "There are diverse views regarding the role of religion in global society as there are about globalization," opines the distinguished sociologist Peter Beyer.[1] Beyer understands religion as a phenomenon that manifests both the sociocultural particular and the global universal. He suggests "the globalization of society, while structurally favoring privatization in religion, also provides fertile ground for the renewed public influence of religion."[2] While Eastern cultures enjoy diversity and yet increasingly suffer due to them, the West has appropriated globalization and liberalization—as it had once arrogated to itself the "discovery" of countries only to be resented for its worldwide incursions and exploitation. But the global movement and exchange are not static and the Indian-Asian Church cannot preclude this aspect from its self-understanding and identity.

The significance of the communion of churches in the pluralistic context of India and Asia as well as India's plural landscape are examined in order to properly situate the emerging theological trends and Catholicism in India. A reimagining and restructuring of Catholic communion *ad intra* is also confronted, including the compelling presence of Catholicism in the public sphere.

COMMUNION OF CHURCHES AND COMMUNITIES

The modern missionary movements from the sixteenth century onward until Vatican II shows that the West exported a European brand of Catholicism "along with other elements of this supposedly superior culture and civilization [while] not really attempting to change the commodity."[3] That is why the "majority of the local Churches in Asia are not yet local Churches of Asia, but are extensions of Euro-American local Churches in Asia," noted the Sri Lankan theologian, Aloysius Pieris.[4] The catholicity of the Church is a spiritual reality grounded in its very "concrete 'earthing' within its own milieu," affirms the Federation of Asian Bishops' Conferences (FABC) and "in the witness of ecclesial communion which constitutes its very nature as Church."[5]

Since Vatican II, the Church's openness to pluralism of cultures reveals that a certain primacy attributed to the relationship of the Church with the world affords the necessary orientation for fresh and creative theological reflection on the catholicity of the Church in and through communion. Communion that welcomes pluralism, recognizes difference, and respects dignity and equality of all is a perceptible expression of Indian and Asian catholicity that embraces all peoples, cultures, and religions without resorting to labeling.[6] There is also a realization that seeking the communion of Christians with other human communities has its own merits per se, but such is required for enhancing public life too. Such communion will encourage solidarity of effort, promote the exchange of ideas and designs, and provide universal scientific and technological knowledge for solving human and social conflicts as well as economic problems.

The construction of a dynamic self-understanding of the Church as a communion of communities with pluralistic human communities of goodwill is indeed a challenging task. In the second half of the twentieth century the bewildering diversity of peoples, languages, tribes, cultures, and religions alongside the scandalous disparity in caste, class, ethnicity, race, and gender called for a reinvigorated Catholicism in India. This drive ignited a search for an Indian theology, an Indian rite, and a truly Indian Church. Indian Christianity has never been monolithic and Catholicism does not pretend to be so.

A theology that is attentive to the Spirit of the Pentecost would not be unable to address different churches not in perfect communion or as part of a pluralistic India. However, even some sort of union of local churches in India in all their diversity would stand as a concrete expression of the catholicity of the Church. This catholicity offsets feelings of superiority vis-à-vis the other and engages without begrudging difference. Indian theologians could assist in engendering this communion and have in fact assiduously engaged in theologizing on various themes relating to the role of religious plurality in India.

DEVELOPMENTS IN INDIAN THEOLOGY[7]

A brief overview of the development of Indian theology from its beginnings to its current movements follows.

India's Plural Landscape: A Brief Overview

India, a millennia-old civilization, has been endowed with a diversity of ethnicities, cultures, languages, and philosophical and religious traditions.[8] The original inhabitants of India were the pre-Dravidian aborigines.[9] The Dravidians and Aryans, who migrated from regions to the southwest and central Asia, respectively, gradually spread all over the subcontinent, pushing the aborigines and earlier settlers to the margins of society. The Aryans developed the Hindu religious traditions of the Vedic religion and the classical scriptures of the Vedas and Upanishads. Over the course of time the caste system emerged, with the upper castes assuming control of all socioeconomic, cultural, philosophical, and religious practices. Globalization is now creating a larger middle class as well as increasing numbers living below the poverty line.

India has been hailed as cradle of many religions, including prehistoric tribal religions that lie outside the pale of Hinduism.[10] Zoroastrianism, Judaism, Christianity, and Islam entered India at different periods. Alongside the mainline religious traditions, India is richly endowed with myriad forms of popular folk religious traditions. In the second half of the nineteenth century, Hindu social reformers sought to reform the social and religious traditions and tenets of Hinduism.[11] Notwithstanding "an overarching common culture, an Indian world-vision, which is unique for its specific contribution to the global human community" has been attributed to the country, along with its holistic view of life with no dichotomy between the sacred and the secular spheres or the spirit and the body.[12]

Motivated by a multicultural and religious context and inspired by Vatican II, Indian theologians founded what came to be called a "pluralism of theologies." Their theological trajectories pursued two main orientations, as identified by Felix Wilfred: 1) theologizing with a religiocultural orientation; and 2) theologizing with a sociopolitical orientation.[13]

What follows is far from being a comprehensive historical survey of the emerging trends in Indian theology.[14] Rather, it is an attempt to underline some major theological developments in Indian Catholicism that have already received global validation. Indian theologies have significantly contributed to Asian Catholicism and beyond, but they have also evoked apprehension in some circles. However, it is yet to be seen whether these Indian theological endeavors can stand the test of time and help to interpret and respond to diverse local concerns and contexts, as well as to globalization.

Theology of Religious Pluralism and Inculturation

The articulation of new theological developments that could distinguish themselves from the traditional theology and Western narratives constituted the major preoccupation of Indian theologians in the late nineteenth and early twentieth centuries. They used free and creative Indian concepts, symbols, and meanings in their search for an Indian face of Christ and an

Indian Church. Pioneering Indian Christian theologians attempted to discover Christ within the Hindu scriptures and traditions, and they systematically reasoned that Hinduism and Christianity are not adversaries.[15]

Brahmanandab Upadhyaya (1861–1907), a Catholic nationalist and *sanyasi*, for instance, worked passionately to introduce an indigenous liturgy and theology in the Church. He used the Vedanta philosophy to explain the Christian faith to Indian people, just as the early Church Fathers used Greek philosophy to convert the Hellenistic world. Another adaptationist was A. J. Appasamy (1891–1975), who emphasized a personal devotion to God based on the Hindu Bhakti tradition.[16] Many Indian Christians followed this path. Other contributors to Indian Christian theology were Pandipeddi Chenchaiah (1880–1958) and Vengal Chakkarai (1889–1959), both Hindu converts who outlined a Christo-centric theology for the renewal of the Church. These pioneers worked toward an inclusive theology that regarded all religions as *preparatio evangelica* or precursors of salvation history. All these religiocultural Indian theological movements emerged during the period of nationalism and the struggle for independence but gradually lost their steam, though they did initiate a new chapter in Christianity in India.

The pioneering work of theologizing in the Indian context was continued and further developed by contemporary Indian theologians like Raimon Panikkar (1918–2010), Stanley J. Samartha (1920–2001), and D. S. Amalorpavadass (1932–90), all of whom were proponents of interreligious dialogue and inculturation.[17] They interacted with the Indian religious traditions and scriptures and classical as well as modern Indian philosophical systems. Panikkar, for instance, views the whole of reality as *advaita* (nondualism), which he calls the *cosmotheandric* experience. He advocates that the cosmos, theos, and anthropos coexist and are three irreducible dimensions of reality that diminish neither divine transcendence nor the difference between God and world, just as analogously the trinitarian unity does not eliminate the difference among the three divine persons.[18]

Another great contribution to the development of an enculturated spiritual-contemplative approach to theology was the Christian Ashram movement modeled after the traditional Hindu and Buddhist ashrams.[19] These groundbreaking ashrams were meeting places for the adepts of Hinduism and Christianity and eventually they became venues for interreligious dialogue and prayer gatherings.

These pioneering and promising approaches paved the way for an Indian Christian theology. However, in their attempts to integrate spiritual practices and scriptures of the great religious traditions of India, popular religious traditions of grassroots people and the public sphere of Jesus Kingdom movements were sidelined or overlooked. The basic shortcoming of those theologizing movements was their exclusive appropriation of cultural, philosophical, and religious categories and symbols of the Hindu upper castes and their consequent adoption in the Church in India, when more than 70 percent of the Catholics had nothing to do with them. Besides, this theological trend seemed to focus on a spiritual other-worldly salvation and the "here and now" of the kingdom movements to establish a just human and cosmic order were not addressed.

In the immediate post–Vatican II times, Catholic theology in India continued to be academic, urban, and borrowed. It has been exclusively a domain of and for clerics and for those destined to lead the Church, and it remains so until now. The Church's position was expected to remain neither left nor right, which meant the preservation at any cost of the status quo. Consequently, Catholic theology got disconnected from and became hardly relevant to modern public life and civil society. The thrust continued to be proselytism, particularly of the poor, the adivasis (the Indigenous), the Dalits, and other disadvantaged groups in rural India who, on seeing the charity and social benefits that the Church offered, were more susceptible to conversion.

Greater interest in a theology of religions as a separate branch within Catholic theology developed in the latter part of the twentieth century as a result of unprecedented circulation of people across the globe. It brought members of various religions into daily face-to-face contact. When globalization, postmodernism, and the communication revolution began displacing traditional religiocultural beliefs, human relationships, and community values, an urgency arose to interpret and redefine them anew. As unsustainable urbanization continued to create cultural shocks, wars, environmental degradation, and ever-expanding human migration, a new cultural norm emerged, which the post–Vatican II Church could not afford to ignore if she wished to be loyal to the council's call for renewal and involvement. The new developments offered opportunities to Christian theologians to learn from the newly emerging theology of religious pluralism. But legitimizing other religions created apprehension in some, that the uniqueness of Jesus Christ as well as the historical claims of exclusivity of salvation in Christianity were being relativized. Theologians had an uphill task ahead.

Unconventional thinkers like Jacques Dupuis, Michael Amaladoss, Peter Phan, and Aloysius Pieris, significantly influenced by the Asian context of religious pluralism, are concerned with how Catholicism understands and relates to other religions. They argue that other religions such as Hinduism, Buddhism, and so forth are part of the divine plan and that God does not necessarily intend that everyone be a Christian. Amaladoss, for instance, while upholding the uniqueness of Jesus Christ, states that any spirituality today cutting across religious frontiers, must become countercultural or counterhegemonic communities as alternatives to global capitalism.[20]

The Church also encouraged the use of Indian liturgy, spirituality, and way of life. An experimental Indian liturgy was launched. The National Theological Seminar (1974) considered "the inspiration of non-Christian Scriptures as a distinct possibility" and suggested their use in liturgy and prayer. In addition, some Indian methods of prayer were upheld and propagated, but popular religious practices of the marginalized masses were yet ignored. Today, inculturation has engendered much theological debate, particularly with reference to liturgy, mission, and evangelization. But again, and always with Brahmanical leanings and cosmetics, it precludes any liberating, dynamic, or praxis-oriented discourses. Inculturation, obviously, needs to consider concerns other than mere "Indianization" or "Asianization" of local churches. It needs to be more than symbolism and must address and incorporate the creative application of faith to public life.

Liberation Theology in India

A new openness to world realities and a secular critique compelled the Church at Vatican II to rethink about the relationship between theology and society. "Liberal theology," which focused on individual freedom, combined with the postconciliar "social gospel" movement that perceived the inseparability between justice and faith and the Marxist class struggle approach, influenced the emergence of liberation theology in Latin America (1950–60). Liberation theology being essentially contextualized lent itself successfully to other similar parts of the world, and gave rise to Black theology in the United States and South Africa, Dalit theology in India, and Minjung theology in South Korea.

In the 1980s, when liberation theology made its appearance in Asia, the collaborative approach between some Christian intellectuals and social activists inspired an action-oriented theological reflection for social transformation as well as theological renewal. Liberation had become a keyword in Asian theology in the decades of the eighties and nineties.

Indian Jesuit theologians like S. Kappen (1924–93), George Soares-Prabhu (1929–95), Samuel Rayan (1930–2019), and M. M. Thomas (1916–96), the latter a lay Christian theologian made unique contributions toward an Indian theology of liberation.[21] They underscored the inherent force of the Gospel for social transformation. They argued that evangelization was more about proclaiming and establishing God's reign of love, justice, and freedom rather than proselytizing as was done in the past. The vital point of discussion for Rayan is the struggles of the people. He explains it thus: "Theology . . . is made, done, lived before it is spoken or written. Theology is born of theopraxy, which he translates as right action. All struggles for liberation, justice, dignity and community are right action, theopraxy."[22]

Those theologians outlined the contours of a theology of liberation based on Jesus's prophetic Kingdom movement and focused on the specific situation of India, with its pluriform religiosity, massive poverty, and unjust and dehumanizing caste system. The oppressive experiences and the struggles for liberation of the exploited subalterns formed the context for an Indian theology of liberation. Soares-Prabhu, a biblical scholar, advocates a social reading of the Bible "in the light of a liberating praxis among the socially oppressed, without succumbing to Marxian reductionism."[23] Kappen notes that by adding to its own narrative the resources that belong to all religions, cultures, ideologies, sciences, and technology in the struggle against oppression, liberation theology became sui generis.[24] Christ and His prophetic dissent is seen as part of the people's history of revolts for change, similar to the Buddhist and Bhakti traditions that opposed the Brahmanical upper caste hegemony.

In Asia, social and political consciousness sparked several protest movements among the oppressed groups demanding their human rights for upward socioeconomic and political mobility. Many Christians were actively involved in these struggles, which formed the discursive basis for liberation theology. Minjung theology in South Korea, the theology of struggle in the Philippines, and Dalit theology in India each produced its own discourse based on peoples' liberating praxis. Minjung theology, for instance, arose from the struggle of concerned South Korean Christians for social and political justice in the 1970s. At the peak of their struggle, South Korean Christians "were forced to reflect upon their Christian discipleship in basement interrogation rooms, in trials, facing court-martial tribunals, hearing the allegations of prosecutors, and in making their own final defence."[25] The struggles of the poor, the Dalits, the Scheduled Tribes, women, fisher people, and other Indigenous and marginalized groups constitute the *loci theologici* for liberation discourse in India.

Plurality of Contextual Theologies

Among contemporary liberationist theologies, the following need to be mentioned.

DALIT THEOLOGY

Dalit theology, unique to Indian theologizing, has significantly impacted theological thinking and also attained global attention.[26] The age-old experience of negativity—material deprivation, social ostracism, and political and religious exclusion, compounded by discrimination of Christian Dalits within the Church—has eroded the very essence of the Church as a community of equal discipleship and forced Dalits to stand up against such an obnoxious system and articulate their own distinctive theology.

Wilfred notes: "Immediacy, concreteness and a certain urgency characterizing Dalit theology have spared it from vacuous theoretical discussions and theological narcissism."[27] Its radicalism is seen in its unmasking of oppressive social constructs of purity and impurity and a rediscovery of Dalit history and traditions. Dalit theology is a rendition that underlies many forgotten myths, stories, poems, and rituals, all of which serve as substrata for reinterpreting Dalits' faith in the Paschal Christ and for restoring their battered dignity and identity.[28]

TRIBAL THEOLOGY

The term tribal theology was coined in the late 1980s as a response to different forms of ethnic conflict, atrocities, ecological destruction, and the philosophical and anthropocentric traditions of Christian theology. Its point of departure is liberation from the perspective of "creation/land," which is intrinsic to the tribal worldview, its culture, its religion and spirituality, and even the idea of God.[29] Land dispossession is not just a political or economic justice issue for the Scheduled Tribes in India or for the Indigenous people of the Pacific Islands and other parts of Asia.[30] It is, rather, an alienation from their "common home" in which their inseparable humanity and identity are rooted. When theologically interpreted with sound biblical exegesis, this understanding provides a powerful antidote against exploitation. Furthermore, a strong sense of communal solidarity sustains them against consumerism, individualism, and indifference. The enduring tribal wisdom of respecting and preserving a "common home" contributes authentically to the evolving theology of ecology.

Today, Scheduled Tribe communities are in transition and are being forcibly evacuated from their historic lands due to political upheavals, armed struggles, illegal development, modernity, and globalization. Tribal contextual theology has yet to develop counterhegemonic ideas and writings that will empower and enable them to salvage their lands and identities.

INDIAN FEMINIST THEOLOGY

At the time when Latin American liberation theology was being contextualized in different countries, feminist theologies were also taking shape in Asia. The first recognizable collective attempt to establish an Asian feminist theology can be traced to the late 1970s. Asian feminist theologians emphasized women's shared identity, and their experiences of social oppression and marginalization. In the 1990s, such theology widened its scope of understanding to include a vast range of women's situations and experiences with a critical consciousness.

In India, feminist theology addresses grassroots concerns, such as female foeticide, honor killings, sexual harassment, domestic violence, unequal wages, discriminatory inheritance laws, child labor, repression of the girl child, human trafficking, and other social and cultural issues. "Women's lives are the 'text' for interpretation and elucidation, compassion or celebration," says Pearl Drego.[31] Feminist theology also engages in unearthing women's dignity and role in Holy Scriptures, in challenging gender stereotypes in the Church and society, in reinterpreting sexuality, and in creating an inclusive spirituality and new ways of being *ecclesia.*

Indian feminist theology has made some breakthroughs in spite of the resistance it encounters from the patriarchal society and Church. There are many academically trained women theologians today, some of whom are professors in seminaries, theological institutes, and other centers of priestly formation. However, concern for women's distinct experiences, perspectives, insights, and intuitions still remain at the margins. Women theologizing in India also insist on networking with grassroots feminist movements. But they need to increasingly bring subaltern and rural communities into their reflections and actions and enhance their own visibility and contributions.

Against all odds, academic and grassroots women theologians in Asia are courageously organizing themselves and impacting the Church and society in a small but sure way. Notable among them are the ecumenical forums of the Ecumenical Association of Third World Theologians (EATWOT) and Indian Women in Theology (IWIT), as well as Indian Women Theological Forum (IWTF) and Ecclesia of Women in Asia (EWA).

Inspired by two FABC institutes, the Office of Laity for Lay Apostolate (est. 1986) and the Women's Desk (est. 1996) and the specific aims of Commission for Women of the Catholic Bishops' Conference of India (CBCI), in 2001 the latter called for the first meeting of Catholic women theologians in India to promote theological education for women and articulate a women's spirituality. The report from that meeting proposed to integrate gender sensitivity and a feminist approach in all branches of mainstream theology. The meeting was rechristened Indian Women Theologians Forum (IWTF) in 2003 and now functions as an autonomous body. It has done much groundwork to reflect on grassroots experiences of women in India in order to construct a methodology for an Indian feminist theology and initiate constructive steps in the public sphere to emancipate and empower women.

The idea for the creation of the Ecclesia of Women in Asia (EWA) was conceived at an Asian theological conference in India in 2001.[32] The group was born at Bangkok in 2002, when fifty-five Asian Catholic women theologians came together for the first historic EWA conference. The conference provides space to Asian Catholic women to engage in theological research, reflection, and writing and to create networks with different Asian and global feminist movements and academies that are Catholic, ecumenical, and interfaith. The EWA takes up contemporary concerns of Asian women and is impacting public life in Asia through its theological reflections and publications.

At this juncture it is noteworthy to place on record the significant contribution of the Indian Theological Association (ITA) toward contextual theologizing. The founding of the ITA (in 1976) marked the transition to a plurality of theologies, as mentioned earlier. The ITA offers to both women and men theologians a platform to reflect on issues affecting the country and the Church and to creatively respond to the challenges presented in the Indian, Asian, and global contexts. Some important themes dealt with are globalization, religious pluralism and dialogue, religious fundamentalism and communalism, growing marginalization of subaltern groups, and ecological crisis. The annual statements and publications of the ITA bear witness to the concerted efforts by Indian theologians to make faith publically relevant. Indian theologians collaborate with the CBCI doctrinal commission and engage in theological dialogue with the bishops on matters pertinent to the Church and the nation.[33]

Theology in India and Asia has become multidisciplinary, integrating methodologies from the social sciences. The use of a variety of approaches is intrinsic for theologizing today as is evident, for instance, in contemporary missiology that integrates religiocultural and socioeconomic knowledge. The Church's witness and proclamation, its commitment to liberation and humanization, and its dialogue and evangelization of cultures are integral parts of one and the same mission.

Since some of the theologies already discussed deviate in some ways from traditional Catholic theology, they have acquired a reputation of indulging in adventurous experimentation and have been subjected to doctrinal scrutiny. Theology of inculturation and religious pluralism are two cases in point. The vibrant inculturation movement in India received a jolt just fifteen years after Vatican II encouraged it. Liturgical experimentation slowed down. A letter from the Congregation for the Doctrine of the Faith (1989) warned Catholics against the "dangers" that the Asian methods of prayer could cause. This was after a caveat, issued in 1998, against the well-known writings of Anthony D'Mello, who endeavored to enrich Christian prayer with Asian spiritual traditions. The declaration Dominus Iesus (2000) released by the Congregation for the Doctrine of the Faith came close to barring theological discussions on inculturation and religious pluralism. Some Asian theologians have come under investigation. Obviously not all was gray.

With the further impetus given by the Asian synodal document Ecclesia in Asia (no. 21) in 1999 combined with Pope Francis's encouragement and welcome of honest dialogue, debate, and discussion, Indian and Asian theology has once again led to conversation within the public regarding the light of faith that is inseparable from social justice and dialogue.

WAY FORWARD IN PUBLIC THEOLOGY

Recently, some new theological movements have emerged in response to new sociopolitical situations.

New Challenges to Catholicism in Public Life

Pope Francis views the contemporary world from two perspectives, as seen in *Laudato Si'* (2015) and *Fratelli tutti* (2020). These two encyclicals deal with many politically disturbing current issues as well as trends relating to profound social divisions caused by the present global neoliberal economic and cultural systems. The documents promote utmost urgency in caring for our common home as well as all of humanity, since all of us are brothers and sisters.

These social encyclicals call for tangible ways to be more creative in our social relationships in order to build a more just, friendly, and communitarian world. Francis's prophetic insights challenge us to evolve constructive theologies for our situation. In this background, two vital theological concerns in public life stand out.

Migration and Theologizing

Migration is the new normal social phenomenon today. It is obvious that, historically, migration always existed. But the scale as well as the causes of it today are unprecedented. As far as India is concerned, all indications of migration suggest that it will play a vital role in the future of nation-state geopolitics. With a sharp rise in the internal movement of peoples, interregional and intraregional shifts create new problems but also new possibilities.

An obvious disturbing feature is the social composition of the migrant groups themselves, which makes them extremely vulnerable to political and social exploitation. A large number of migrants belong to a "younger, mobile and feminized workforce" from marginalized communities. Migration push factors are natural catastrophes, poverty, scarcity of cultivated land, low agricultural productivity, corporate takeover of natural resources, caste and gender discrimination in educational and work opportunities, and pandemic. The recent COVID-19 pandemic once again forced migrants to return to their villages due to the urban lockdown and slowdown in the economy. Communal hatred and clashes and religious persecutions are other present-day grounds for forced migration.[34]

This new worrying scenario urges the Church in India to develop a theology of migrants. How to place the vulnerable "crucified peoples" at the center of theological research and discourse is the real question. Theology needs to discover anew God's presence in the human experience of migrants walking on busy highways, waiting with hope on city roadways to be hired, working under precarious conditions on construction sites, living in dingy slums away from the comfort of their homes and land, or relying on urban parishes where they are just "faceless outsiders." A theology of migrants also raises issues relating to the model of modern development that ignores inequalities and disparities among socially uprooted people.

Migrants ought to be schooled to be "agents in their own redemption," for "migrants are not seen as entitled like others to participate in the life of society, and it is forgotten that they possess the same intrinsic dignity as any person" (*Fratelli tutti* no. 39).[35] This instruction needs to be integrated with the theological quest for God seen among His people on the move in the sacred scriptures, in early Church history and social teachings, and in Indian philosophy and other religious scriptures.

Theology of Democracy

Democratic governance is so far the best political system that a nation-state has at its disposal, and all nation-states should continue to promote it despite its weaknesses. However, democracy as a political institution is unable to withstand the upsurge of fascism of dictatorial leadership in several countries. Pope Francis laments that the twenty-first century "is witnessing a weakening of the power of nation-states" (*Fratelli tutti* no. 172) and the fact that concepts such as democracy, justice, freedom, and unity are being "bent and shaped to serve as tools for domination" (*Fratelli tutti* no. 14).

Indian democracy is also going through stormy waters and is on a steep decline. The politics currently being witnessed are a manipulation of the ideal of being "a people," with its growing sense of intolerant Hindu nationalism. The democratic values of multiculturalism of Indian existence and the capacious nature of the Indian constitution are seriously threatened. This is crucial because the nation's spontaneous social humanism itself is in danger. The pluralist idea of Indianness is being substituted with intolerant ideologies and a narrative that diversity is dangerous to the unity of the nation-state. Moreover, India's history of a vibrant and thriving democracy is being rewritten by the fundamentalists. Furthermore, with the Hindutva ideology taking center stage, religious affiliation becomes more decisive and divisive than ever. A politics of hatred has polarized people, facilitating populism and the "othering" processes that cause religious prejudices, suspicion, and even fear of the "other." Democracy, like an infected patient, is struggling to breathe in India. Catholicism in India needs to be politically alert to safeguard democracy and its values.

The Theological Framework for Democracy

Religions by and large affirm that God is the father and mother of all and that the dignity of every human being is sacred. Religions teach that we are all brothers and sisters living in a delicate common home and are co-travelers on life's journey to eternity. In such a situation, the Catholic Church has a large role to play beyond her private sphere. The Church has also a public role, to go out from her place of worship and journey with all people for "the art of peace involves all people to work together, side by side, in pursuing goals that benefit everyone (*Fratelli tutti* no. 228). A theology of democracy can help the Church and members of other religions to become agents of democracy, ensuring constitutional rights/duties and safeguarding civilizational humanistic values.

A theology of democracy is grounded in the Kingdom of God, which is the central theme of Jesus's preaching and ministry. His revolutionary mission was to proclaim and establish the Kingdom of God, a democratic ideal where the values of freedom, justice, and equality reign. The inseparable love of God and neighbor is the only discourse Jesus used to combat the unjust socioreligious and political practices of the Jewish and Roman powers. The public characteristic of God's reign is a love that transcends artificial and inhuman borders.

REIMAGINING CATHOLIC COMMUNION *AD INTRA*

In the wake of Vatican II's vision of *ecclesia* as a communion of churches, high on the agenda of the historic All India Seminar on the Church in India Today in 1969 was the imperative to localize the Church in India. The seminar discussed proactive ways to address liturgy, spirituality, evangelization, dialogue with other religions and cultures, education, socioeconomic activities, and civic and political life. The first constructive step toward establishing an Indian

Church on the model of communion of churches was reimagining and restructuring its colonial legacy. The evolving plurality of theologies responded and contributed toward it.

Catholic Diversity

The Catholic communion in India includes three branches—the Syro-Malabar Rite (founded in the first century), the Latin Rite (in the sixteenth century), and the Syro-Malakara Rite (in 1930). Each has its own distinct history, tradition, and approach to theology, spirituality, and liturgy. This multiritual Catholic community is the largest Christian Church within India. Since 1987, the three individual churches have their respective episcopal bodies with their own forms and ecclesiastical legislation: the Conference of the Catholic Bishops of India (CCBI) for the Latin Rite, the Syro-Malabar Bishops' Synod (SMBS), and the Holy Episcopal Synod for the Syro-Malankara Church. The CBCI, constituted in 1944, now represents the three individual churches. It is the face of the Catholic Church in India and deals with questions of common concern and of national and supraritual character.[36]

In many ways, Catholicism has adjusted to the complex and varied contexts of India. Beyond its traditional base in South India, Catholicism has spread particularly among the subaltern communities in other parts of India. As per the 2011 national census, there are over 20 million Catholics in India, representing around 1.55 percent of the total population of 1.34 billion. Despite its small percentage, India has the second-largest Catholic population in Asia after the Philippines.

The mission of evangelization among the Tribal and Dalit belts continues despite the aggressive Hindu nationalist movement, which objects to religious conversion. In northeast India, for instance, the mission of evangelizing is active and fruitful. Before Vatican II only two dioceses existed, whereas today there are fifteen, with a Catholic Tribal population close to 1.7 million.

By far Dalit Catholics, about 12 million, constitute the majority in the Catholic Church, but sadly their presence in leadership roles and in administering dioceses and religious orders is scarcely visible.[37] Within the Church they are seen as second-class Christians. Most diocesan and religious decision-making bodies are dominated by non-Dalits. Caste distinction and discrimination in the Catholic Church still runs deep. Intercaste communal meals and marriages are not yet accepted as normal. Subtle or overt discriminatory practices in seminaries and religious houses of formation as well as in common worship or burying the dead in cemeteries die hard.[38] "Christ and caste cannot go together," asserts Vincent Manoharan, convener of National Dalit Christian Watch. As the Dalit Christian Liberation Movement stated in 2019, "We want Pope Francis to exhort the bishops to take responsibility and accountability to eradicate the caste discrimination of Dalit people within the Church."[39]

Jesus did not commission the apostles to form an exclusive and elite group of disciples. He said: "Go and make disciples of all nations" (Mt. 28:19). In Christ we are all children of God, through faith we belong to an all-embracing communion of Christians, where "there is neither Jew nor Greek, there is neither slave nor free, there is neither male nor female"; for we are all one in Christ Jesus (Gal. 3:26–28).

Furthermore, in civil society the Dalit Christian population suffers from a lack of recognition. They are fighting for the cause of their Scheduled Caste status in society in the supreme court. While India has on the one hand one of the oldest Christian communities in the world—the Syrian Catholics in South India—on the other it has the largest emarginated Christian communities of Dalits and Tribals, who at every moment risk losing their scarce economic and political liberties.

Multiple religious identities are another unique feature in India. A case in point are the Kristu Bhaktas, who profess faith in Christ and venerate the Virgin Mary and Catholic saints but are never shy to worship Hindu deities as well.[40] For this reason baptism is not conferred on believers in this community, leaving them apparently in an obscure religious space.

Globalization promotes multicultural and religious communities the world over and Indian Catholic communities are no different. There is a growing migrant Catholic community in the country bearing multicultural and religious ritual identities. Such seismic transformation in the faith and culture of Catholics in India prompts myriad challenges to the Catholic mission. Perhaps for the first time in the history of Christianity the missionary enterprise encounters formidable philosophical and theological issues that are not easy to overcome.

Church of the People of God

The famed "People of God" conciliar portrait of the Church, dear to Pope Francis, departs from the centuries-old grandiose narrative of the Church as "hierarchology" and rediscovers the Church as a congregation of the faithful from every race (*Lumen Gentium* no. 13) and "a fellowship of life, charity and truth" (*Lumen Gentium* no. 9). This self-understanding provides a wide berth for lay participation in the Church, in consultative bodies in parishes and dioceses. The laity participates more actively in the liturgical celebrations using elements drawn from their traditions (e.g., music, dance, symbols, and images). Tribal Christian communities, for instance, evolved their own folk community-based ecospirituality and integrate it in their liturgical celebrations. In addition, a growing number of Christians use Asian forms of meditation like yoga, zen, and vipasana. However, what is conspicuously missing is the incorporation of people's popular devotions, which usually evolve from life experiences in the liturgy.

Popular devotions, a phenomenon characteristic of Asian people, evince the osmosis that exists between the dynamic power of the Gospel and the struggles of people. These practices facilitate people's encounter with the living God in the grounded realities of life. The theology of the people draws inspiration from a common culture, devotions, spirituality, and sense of justice. Popular religious practices have proved effective instruments for social liberation. People's popular devotions are not just a means for evoking, expressing, or sustaining faith, but can also be integrated to promote social equality, justice, and wholeness of life (Jn. 10:10; Lk. 4:16–18).

The Research Seminar and Pastoral Consultation at Bangalore in 1976, the Asian Colloquium on Ministries in the Church at Hong Kong in 1977, and a series of well-documented FABC papers on the laity in Asia have made many concrete proposals for greater lay involvement in the life and mission of the Church.[41] The laity's role began to be felt in parish councils, on pastoral and financial committees, and among various other diocesan and national commissions. Women's presence and participation increased. The Indian Church has made structural adjustments at the hierarchical level to celebrate the autonomy of individual churches. However, the laity plays only a consultative role, with almost no say in decision-making in church councils and commissions. Rampant clericalism within the hierarchy is relegating collegiality and impeding lay initiatives. While there is forced passivity and apathy among lay men and women in church life, on the other hand a larger number of Catholics are making significant contribution in public professions, the media, civil services, and the armed forces.

What is wanting today is theological formation and empowerment of the laity. Little is being done to make the laity "theology literate." Institutionalized Catholicism in India has not induced the laity to think and act as a People of God in exercising their triple functions of common priesthood (*Lumen Gentium* no. 9–13). The local churches in India have not properly formed the youth and young adults or capitalized on their wisdom and vitality for active and prophetic roles in the Church and in the public sphere. Pope Francis insists that the Church is a missionary community and that no Christian is exempted from the missionary responsibility of "going forth" (*Evangelii Gaudium* no. 20). The new evangelization calls for personal involvement of each of the baptized (*Evangelii Gaudium* no. 120) to communicate the joy of the Gospel with courage.

Restructuring Priestly Formation

Incarnating contextual local churches depends to a large extent on the clergy. In 1971, the CBCI took concrete steps toward enhancing the clergy with the Charter of Priestly Formation for India, which was revised with practical directives in 1984 and 2002. It encouraged adaptation "according to the needs and traditions of different Rites, Regions, diocesan and religious Houses of Formation."[42] Consequently, regional seminaries, philosophates, and theologates were started to increase the Church's exposure to public life. The language of the region is used; the culture and religion of the people are studied in depth, and their presence within the lives of the people, especially in rural India, is made possible.[43]

There is awareness that priestly formation needs further revamping in order to meet the demands of a rapidly changing society and the challenges of the emerging technocratic and consumeristic global culture. The typology of the three publics of theology that David Tracy presents—the wider society, the academy, and the Church—is useful for critically examining the theological program and its orientations in India.[44] Even though theology does not eschew openness to the world, it is still inaccessible and incomprehensible to the laity. Basically, theology continues to be the preserve of the clergy and professional theologians who are unable to inform the public about its relevance.

ENGAGING PRESENCE OF CATHOLICISM IN THE PUBLIC SPHERE

Globalization in the 1980s motivated religions to assert their social or public roles. José Casanova refers to this phenomenon as "deprivatization" of religion and buttresses his argument on globalization by signaling out three spheres where religion made a dent: on the state, on political society, and on civil society.[45]

Globalization is changing the religions in Asia as well as causing their revival. The religious revival in Asia, writes David Halloran Lumsdaine, has led to "the appearance of a more assertive Islam, a resurgent Hinduism, a more politically engaged Buddhism and an expanding evangelical Christianity."[46] The resurgence of religions and religious forces, often radicalized, is impacting many Asian countries today. While being minorities (except in the Philippines and East Timor), Catholicism in Asia is challenged to engage with specific issues to establish a transformative relationship with the state and build up a pluralist polity and initiate theologies in their own countries.

India's tolerant, nonviolent, multicultural and religious ethos is also undergoing severe interruptions, sometimes in the direction of exclusive identities. Interactions have shifted from spontaneous tolerance to inconclusive negotiation and even rivalries for domination. By resorting to caste mobilization to win elections, the Hindu hardliners have taken control of the very democratic institutions in India. The neoliberal capitalist economy has also created dehumanizing systems.[47] Catholicism in India faces the test of public relevance when encountering such radicalized groups, which often find institutional and state support. Further, the rapid growth of Pentecostalism and its mode of evangelism have become the primary target of violence and a matter of concern for the presence and mission of the Catholic Church. Indian and Asian Christians, without being let down by the minority complex, are challenged to become a prophetic and dynamic voice in bearing witness to the reign of God, as did the prophets and the disciples of Jesus, always a minority in their society.

Catholicism for Reconciliation and Harmony

The religious landscape of India is highly variegated. Secularism as enshrined in the Indian constitution guarantees every citizen "the right to freely profess, practice and propagate religion" (Art. 25/1). It views positively the role of religion in the public sphere and underlines its potential for promoting individual freedom and social development. The Hindu right wing, bolstered by its ideology of Hindu nationalism, is trying hard to abrogate this constitutional right. Sectarian communalism threatens to destroy the rich secular fabric of the country. Discrimination against and persecution of religious minorities, particularly of subaltern communities, as well as the destruction and desecration of churches and venues of popular devotion, attempts to rewrite the constitution of India and Indian history, and the manipulation of educational policies and the curriculum are some of the planned strategies of Hindu fundamentalists. One of the important concerns of Indian public theology is the interpretation and protection of the constitutional right of "freedom of religion" in the interest of democracy.

Religious conversion is a perennial issue confronting Catholicism. Hindu nationalism, a political child of postcolonialism, treats any conversion to Christianity or Islam as an act of "de-nationalizing" of Indians and anti-patriotic. The anti-conversion laws enacted in several regional states is a case in point. The governments, run by fundamentalists, suspect and interpret any social service by Christians as bait for conversions of members of the poor sections of society.[48] Organized radical groups urge and incentivize Christians from the fringes to reconvert to their allegedly original religion. Often enough there is violence of a planned nature against Christians.

While we place on record the fidelity and fortitude with which over a hundred Tribal Catholics stood for their faith and the recent move to canonize them as saints, the gruesome killings at Kandhamal in the Indian state of Odisha in 2007 will never be erased from Indian history. Their slain and mutilated bodies, found in forests, riversides, and paddy fields; the destroyed or vandalized churches, Catholic social services centers, schools, hostels, and orphanages; and over 50,000 Indian Christians bundled into ill-provided refugee camps were decried as a national shame.

Following the outbreak of violence in 2007–8, the CBCI Office for Justice, Peace and Development and the Christian community adopted various measures to ensure justice for the victims. Lobbying the federal ministers, internationalizing the issue by addressing the matter to the UN Human Rights Council, retrieving important documents of the victims (bank passbooks, land documents), and mobilizing economic support are some of the efforts initiated to mitigate their suffering and rebuild their lives.[49]

Networking with people of goodwill and faith-based organizations with the purpose of creating interreligious communities is the dire need of the times. Such a move would help counter the growing unfounded suspicion and fear of the "other," promote fraternity and social friendship, restore tolerance and harmony, validate human rights and justice, and heal our wounded humanity and "common home."

Catholicism for Compassion and Justice

A new thinking since Vatican II has enabled Catholics to proactively read the signs of modern times. After all, Catholicism began adapting when Paul challenged the Jerusalem Church not to impose circumcision on non-Jews. Today globalization dares Catholicism to walk the talk of Vatican II and engage with other religious groups to transform civil society.

Catholicism has been a significant player in Indian civil society, which is manifest in varied ways. Mass educational programs (formal and informal), including female education, liberated and empowered countless people from the oppressive feudal caste system and patriarchal structures.[50] The social uplift engendered by education made them aware of the values of egalitarianism, liberty, dignity, and self-respect and has provided them global opportunities.[51] Indian Catholicism is also actively present in rural India through its voluntary social welfare schemes, health programs, disaster management, support projects like water harvesting and self-help groups, and in advocacy roles for the empowerment of the disadvantaged.[52]

The enormously diverse Tribals constitute 8.2 percent of the Indian population. There are more than 461 Indigenous communities in India. Today the Tribals are being dispossessed of their lands and status in the name of public developmental projects, inducing large-scale displacement and migration and census distortion. Operation Green Hunt, insurgencies, and intratribal conflicts—at times with the connivance of local governments—have interrupted tribal life. Ironically, this "tribal cleansing" is being hailed as progress.[53] In this context the CBCI Committee for Tribal Affairs, created in 2006, strives to facilitate, coordinate, and network with other Christian churches, civil societies, and people's movements to empower tribal communities and safeguard their rights, lands, and identities.[54] The Indian Bishops' Labour Office has also set up an online service to register migrant workers, promote safe migration, and provide pastoral care, counseling, and welfare assistance.

The Catholic Church's initiative in social projects has been globally acknowledged. The Church has also entered in a big way into human capacity building and helps the disadvantaged to avail themselves of the benefits and grants offered by government schemes. Women religious, numbering over 120,000, are the "mission force" of the Church in India. They are engaged in risk-taking to provide humanitarian services and women-empowering projects, reaching out to the most oppressed and marginalized in remote areas. Several politically proactive women religious have been killed or sexually molested with the connivance of politicians, as the account of the life and murder of recently beatified Sr. Rani Maria attests.

Religious, linguistic, and social minorities (Scheduled Castes and Tribes and Other Backward Classes) have constitutional rights for protection of their religion, language, and identity. Some of these rights come in the form of "reservation" or preference in government educational institutions and employment posts. Unfortunately, the state denies such benefits to Christian Dalits and Other Backward Classes. These two groups' conversion to Christianity has made them twice losers on the social and economic fronts. The Church has been representing their case before the law too. For instance, the CBCI reiterated its stand regarding equal rights for Dalit Christians and demanded the repeal of the 1950 presidential order that denies Dalit Christians the benefits accorded to other Dalits.

The new perspectives provided by the Pontifical Council for Justice and Peace and explicated in the *Compendium of the Social Doctrine of the Church* (2004) encourage Catholics to a greater engagement in civil society. The Church in India is engaged in a variety of projects, such as developmental and social work, and issues related to justice, solidarity, animation, and empowerment.[55] In order to become a public religion, Catholicism requires that its faithful interact with people of other faiths and makes their voices heard in legislative assemblies and in public forums. It also implies, as Pope Francis urges, that engagement with the periphery and the poor be made central to the Catholic faith.

CONCLUSION

Numerous sociotheological issues confront Catholicism in modern India, many arising during the third phase of globalization but some known since the Vatican II period. If the council constitutes the most defining moment for Indian Catholicism, it is because it caused several ruptures with what preceded it. Vatican II as well as postcolonial exigencies and new forms of globalization caused stark interruptions and irreversible changes in the traditional trajectory of Catholicism. These can be assessed against the engaging images of the Church and theological trends in India.

Globalization that contravenes diversity of identity and multiculturalism is the greatest challenge in modern times. If appropriately seized, the council's call for updating or modernizing the Church, expressed in the famous "aggiornamento" and Pope Francis's repeated call to the Church to reform itself, could offer new paradigms of being Church and doing mission in India and Asia. Although the nexus between colonialism and Catholicism in the "mission lands" prevented the localization of Catholicism and its larger acceptance, the acknowledged mission of Catholicism as a stakeholder in social uplift of those in the periphery and as a vehicle for inclusive humanistic ideas and values must go on.

NOTES

1. See Peter Beyer, *Religions in Global Society* (New York: Routledge, 2006).
2. Beyer, *Religions in Global Society.*
3. Karl Rahner, *Concern for the Church* (New York: Herder and Herder, 1981), 78.
4. Aloysius Pieris, "A Theology of Liberation in Asian Churches?," in S. Arokiasamy and G. Gispert-Sauch, eds., *Liberation in Asia* (Anand: Gujarat Sahitya Prakash, 1987), 18.
5. FABC, *Theses on the Local Church*, FABC Papers 60 (1990): 12; Asian synodal document no. 25, "Ecclesia in Asia" (1999).
6. Evelyn Monteiro, *Church and Culture: Communion in Pluralism* (Delhi: ISPCK, 2004),198–99.
7. See Kuncheria Pathil, "Trends in Indian Theology: A Historical Overview," and Felix Wilfred, "Indian Theologies: Retrospect & Prospects," both in Victor Machado, ed., *Society and Church: Challenges to Theologizing in Indian Today* (Bangalore: Dharmaram 2004), 91–136 and 137–64, respectively.
8. The eighth schedule of the constitution recognizes twenty-two languages in India.
9. A Supreme Court judgment on January 5, 2011, delivered the historic thesis that India is largely a country of immigrants and the aborigines/Tribals are the original inhabitants.
10. According to the 2011 census, of the 1.2 billion Indian population, 80.5 percent are Hindus, 13.4 percent are Muslims, 2.3 percent are Christians, 1.9 percent are Sikhs, 0.80 percent are Buddhists, and 0.4 percent are Jains.
11. The modern Hindu renaissance of the nineteenth and twentieth centuries, influenced by Western civilization and education, Christianity, and secularization of religion in the second phase of globalization and pioneering reformers like Ram Mohan Roy (1772–1833), Swamy Vivekananda (1863–1902), Mahatma Gandhi (1869–1948), Vinoba Bhave (1895–1982), and others, has reformed Hinduism in a radical way. Rejecting rigid ritualism and casteism, Buddhism and Jainism were protest movements that emerged from within Hinduism; Sikhism is a modern religious reform religion.
12. Pathil, "Trends in Indian Theology," 94.
13. See Felix Wilfred, *Beyond Settled Foundations: The Journey of Indian Theology* (Madras: University of Madras, 1993). Other theologians, like Mathias Mundadan, suggest three major approaches in Indian theology: 1) the spiritual-contemplative approach and the Indian Christian Ashram movement; 2) the intellectual-theological approach by which scholars dialogue with the philosophical and religious traditions of India; and 3) the social spproach, which deals primarily with the common struggles of people and building a new society. See "Inter-faith Approaches: A Survey of Contemporary Indian Christian Literature," in Thomas Aykara, ed., *Meeting of Religions* (Bangalore: Dharmaram, 1978).
14. Several erudite authors, including Robin Boyd, M. M. Thomas, Antony Mookenthotam, Mathias Mundadan, and Felix Wilfred, have researched and written comprehensive histories of Indian theology.
15. See Kaj Baago, *Pioneers of Indigenous Christianity* (Madras: CLS, 1969); Robin Boyd, *An Introduction to Indian Christian Theology* (Madras: CLS, 1969; repr. 1979); and M. M. Thomas, *The Acknowledged Christ of the Indian Renaissance* (Madras: CLS, 1970).
16. The Bhakti tradition is a theistic devotional trend that emerged in medieval Hinduism in the eighth-century Tamil South India and spread northward.

17. For the works of these scholars, see Wilfred, *Beyond Settled Foundations*; and A. M. Mundadan, *Paths of Indian Theology* (Bangalore: Dharmaram, 1998).
18. See R. Pannikar, *The Cosmotheandric Experience: Emerging Religious Consciousness* (Maryknoll: Orbis, 1993).
19. Protestant Christians were the pioneers in this field. Gradually Catholic ashrams like those of Jules Monchanin, Abhishiktananda, Bede Griffiths, Vandana Mataji, Sara Grant, and Amalorpavadass joined the movement.
20. See Michael Amaladoss, *Making All Things New: Dialogue, Pluralism and Evangelization in Asia* (Maryknoll: Orbis, 1990).
21. See M. M. Thomas, *The Acknowledged Christ of the Indian Renaissance* (Madras: CLS, 1970). Thomas was a "Christian socialist" who understood the Church's mission as a diaconal one of humanization and social transformation that needed to help change the structures of society toward justice.
22. Samuel Rayan, "Analysis of Society and Indian Theology," in Kurien Kunnumpuram, ed., *Collected Writings of Samuel Rayan, SJ, Vol. 2, Doing Theology: Indian Christian Reflections on Theologizing in India Today* (Delhi: ISPCK, 2013), 160.
23. George M. Soares-Prabhu, "From Alienation to Inculturation: Some Reflections on Doing Theology in India Today," in T. K. John, ed., *Bread and Breath: Essays in Honour of Samuel Rayan* (Anand: Gujarat Sahitya Prakash, 1991), 68.
24. For the selected writings of S. Kappen, see S. Kappen, *Jesus and Cultural Revolution—An Asian Perspective* (Bombay: Build, 1983); and S. Painadath, ed., *Jesus and Culture*, vol. 1, *and Jesus and Society*, vol. 2 (Delhi: ISPCK, 2002).
25. David Kwang-sun Suh, "Minjung and Theology in Korea: A Biographical Sketch of an Asian Theological Consultation," in Yong-Bock Kim, ed., *Minjung Theology* (Singapore: Christian Conference of Asia, 1981), 18.
26. Dalits and innumerable subcastes classified as Other Scheduled Class (OBC) have a unique history and traditions. Among them, the term Dalits means "trampled upon" in Sanskrit and they are the most demeaned in the Hindu caste system and called by different names: Untouchables, *panchamas* (fifth caste), outcastes, and harijans (children of God).
27. Wilfred, "Indian Theologies," 140–41.
28. See Pathil, "Trends in Indian Theology," 121.
29. A. Wati Longchar, "An Emerging Tribal/Indigenous Theology: Prospect for Doing Asian Theology," *Journal of Theologies and Cultures in Asia* 1 (February 2002): 7–12.
30. The Scheduled Tribes constitute 8 percent of the total population. Many tribes have embraced Christianity in search of a new identity against the oppressive forces of feudal landlords.
31. Pearl Drego, "Women Theologizing: Beginnings of Feminist Theologies and Their Concerns," *Jeevadhara* 40, no. 237 (May 2010): 236–38.
32. Ecclesia of Women in Asia (EWA) evolved out of the glaring concern that there were only two Asian women theologians among the fifty participants at this Asian Conference. Annette Meuthrath, Asian minister at the Missio-Scientific Institute; Edmund Chia, then executive secretary of interreligious dialogue for the FABC; and myself discussed it, reflected, and took up the challenge of identifying and bringing together Asian women theologians.
33. Indian theologians also contribute their theological expertise to the FABC.
34. Cow lynching by Muslims, prohibition of interfaith marriages, and so forth are some examples of harassment.
35. Message for the 2020 World Day of Migrants and Refugees, May 13, 2020, in *L'Osservatore Romano*, May 16, 2020, 8.
36. The CBCI serves the three ecclesial bodies spread out among 174 dioceses and fourteen regional councils of bishops. It has several national centers that address various needs of the Church and country: CARITAS India, the social wing of the CBCI; St John's National Academy of Health Sciences; the National Biblical, Catechetical and Liturgical Centre (NBCLC); the National Vocation

Service Centre (NVSC); the National Institute of Social Communications, Research and Training (NISCORT); and the CBCI Society for Medical Education for North India.

37. Despite the Dalit community making up nearly two-thirds of India's Catholics, only 12 of the 174 Catholic dioceses are led by bishops of Dalit origin.
38. The CBCI declared years ago that the caste system is sinful, but no credible move has been made to abolish its practice within the Church. In December 2016, the CBCI promulgated a stringent policy of Dalit empowerment, clearly stating that Dalit Christians should be given dignity, equality, and positions at all levels of the Church. The Church has yet to come out with an affirmative action policy and ensure its implementation.
39. See https://www.ucanews.com/news/papal-intervention-sought-to-end-dalit-discrimination-in-india/86079, accessed August 6, 2021. Dalit Catholic leaders across India have threatened to start their own Indian Dalit church if their demand to end the caste system and discrimination within the Catholic Church is not met. See ucanews.com, September 7, 2020.
40. They are Hindus from the Scheduled Castes (SC) and Other Backward Classes (OBC) in the Benares region of Uttar Pradesh, North India.
41. See FABC, "Trusting, Entrusting the Laity," from the First Bishops' Institute for Lay Apostolate of the FABC, Taiwan, October 31–November 9, 1984; and FABC, "The Vocation and Mission of the Laity in the Church and in the World of Asia," from the Fourth Plenary Assembly of the FABC, Tokyo, 1986.
42. CBCI, *The Charter of Priestly Formation for India* (Delhi: CBCI, 1988), 4. Each individual church worked out a contextualized formation for India in keeping with its respective tradition and in the spirit of the communion of churches (*Optatam totius* 1).
43. Errol D'Lima, "Priestly Formation for Service to the World," in Jacob Kavunkal, Errol D'Lima, and Evelyn Monteiro, eds., *Vatican II: A Gift and A Task*, from the International Colloquium to Mark the 40th Anniversary of Vatican Council II (Mumbai: St. Paul's, 2006), 239.
44. David Tracy, *Analogical Imagination: Christian Theology and the Culture of Pluralism* (New York: Crossroad, 1981), 4.
45. See José Casanova, *Public Religions in the Modern World* (Chicago: University of Chicago Press, 1994); and José Casanova, "Rethinking Public Religions," in Timothy Samuel Shah, Alfred Stephan, and Monica Duffy Toft, eds., *Rethinking Religion and World Affairs* (Oxford: Oxford University Press, 2012), 27.
46. David Halloran Lumsdaine, *Evangelical Christianity and Democracy in Asia* (New York: Oxford University Press, 2009), 20.
47. Patrick Gnanapragasam, "Theologie publique en Asie: Avec un regard particulier sur le contexte indien," *Spiritus* 221 (December 2015), 424–36.
48. The hidden agenda behind their suspects is to maintain the hegemonic status quo of the caste system. Empowering the subalterns will destabilize the economic, political, and social power of the upper caste and class.
49. CBCI Office for Justice, Peace and Development, "Golden Jubilee Special Celebrating 50 Years of the CBCI Centre (1962–2012)," *Catholic India* 22 (July–December 2011): 32.
50. The CBCI education policy states: "The Catholic educational institutions are to provide inclusive and holistic education especially for the marginalized and girls enabling them to live life to the full and responsibly, thus transforming the individual and society." From CBCI General Body Meeting, "Final Statement of the 32nd Plenary Assembly, March 2–9, 2016, Bangalore," *Catholic India* 27, no. 1 (January–June 2016), 61. The Catholic Church has established a vast network of schools and colleges. Noteworthy is the fact that 59.3 percent of these institutions (schools and hostels) are located in rural areas and girls constitute 54 percent of the students. Our educational institutions are also characterized by an attractive heterogeneity of staff and students from all religions, castes, and cultures, and a majority of the beneficiaries (71.7 percent) come from other religious communities.

51. Most of the mass conversions in India to Buddhism, Christianity, and Sikhism have been public statements of opposition to the caste hierarchy. Apart from personal religiosity, there has been a social significance in conversion.
52. The range of healthcare services, most of them in rural areas, is immense, with 788 hospitals and numerous dispensaries and centers for mental health, leprosy, HIV/AIDS, and the terminally ill. All these centers are serving people irrespective of creed or caste.
53. The resultant influx of outsiders would change the Tribal demographics of the area.
54. Along with various secular and religious organizations and movements, it is lobbying with the National Commission for Scheduled Tribes, the Government of India, and others institutions for a constitutional amendment to Article 342, in view of a national list of Scheduled Tribes. In May 2017, the Indian Tribal Catholic bishops submitted a memorandum to the president of India to protect the land, forests, and sociocultural rights of Tribals.
55. S. Arokiasamy and John Chathanatt, eds., *Songs of Silence: Christians in Nation Building* (Delhi: Media House, 2000), 9.

10

Australian Catholicism in the Third Phase of Globalization: Demographic Shifts and Unceasing Challenges

ROBERT DIXON

Australian Catholicism is a product of globalization. It was the globalizing forces of exploration and trade, combined with the need for England to find a place for its expanding prison population after the American War of Independence, when it lost any chance of using the American colonies for that purpose, that brought the first Catholics to Australia. Catholicism arrived in Australia when European settlement began in 1788, the year before the start of the French Revolution. The birth of Australian Catholicism coincided with the beginning of the second phase of globalization.

This chapter concentrates on Australian Catholicism in the third phase of globalization, that is, from the early 1960s to the present, examining particularly the demographic shifts in the Catholic population that began around that time and some of the serious challenges for the Church that have arisen over those decades. First, however, it is important to point out that the origins of Catholicism in Australia are quite different from those of the other Asian and Pacific countries considered in this volume. There are four major differences.[1]

First, no Australian Catholicism existed in the first phase of globalization. European settlement of Australia and the arrival of the Catholic Church in Australia occurred much later than it did in most other countries of the Asia Pacific region. By that time, the first phase of globalization had concluded and there is virtually nothing to say about Australian Catholicism during that time.

Second, there was no initial mission to Australian Indigenous peoples. When Catholicism did arrive in Australia, it was not, as elsewhere, in the form of a missionary effort aimed at bringing the Gospel to Indigenous peoples.[2] It was fifty-five years before any systematic missionary activity was directed to Australia's Aboriginal peoples. Rather, Australian Catholicism began as a result of the British government's decision to establish a penal colony in the land that, in 1770, Capt. James Cook encountered and named New South Wales. The First Fleet, eleven ships sent from England to establish the penal colony, arrived in January 1778. No priests were aboard those ships, nor anyone with the authority, intention, or even opportunity to evangelize the Aboriginal people. Rather, the First Fleet Catholics were mainly Irish convicts. It was not until 1800 that the first priests arrived in the colony, and they, too, were convicts; any pastoral concern they had was directed to their compatriots.

A third difference is that Catholicism was brought to the region through the British and Irish, not through the Spanish, Portuguese, or French, the nations that had brought the faith to Asia and most of the rest of Oceania. The fact that the Catholic faith arrived as an Irish form had a profound long-term impact on Catholicism in Australia. Throughout the nineteenth century most of Australia's priests were Irish. Many Irish priests and most of the bishops as well saw their task in Australia as nurturing the growth of an offshoot of the Irish Church, one that would preserve the characteristics they had known at home. It was not until the 1930s that Australia-born priests outnumbered Ireland-born priests.[3] Irish priests continued to come to Australia throughout the twentieth century, a few arriving even in recent years. The dominance of Irish spirituality in Australian Catholicism was reinforced throughout the nineteenth century by the arrival of Irish religious orders. As Katharine Massam has noted, "genuine Catholic culture was assumed to be essentially uniform and Irish in origin."[4]

A fourth difference is that the faith was initially brought to Australia not by religious orders, but first by lay people and then primarily by secular priests. The Australian Church was at first a lay church. Despite the fact that until 1820 priests were only sporadically available to celebrate Mass and provide the sacraments, many Catholics diligently and courageously kept their faith alive. Australia's first vicar-general, William Ullathorne, and first bishop, John Bede Polding, were both English Benedictines, but they were a minority among secular Irish priests. Religious order priests were very few in number until late in the nineteenth century. Overwhelmingly, the task of providing the sacraments and pastoral care to the Irish Catholic population was left to the Irish secular clergy.

THE THIRD PHASE OF GLOBALIZATION

The effects of globalization, especially the mass movements of people, are very apparent when one looks at how the Catholic population of Australia changed in the postwar years and has continued to change to the present day. The early 1960s were years of growing prosperity, partly due to the huge numbers of "New Australians" who had arrived from Europe after the war—particularly Italians, Maltese, Croatians, and Dutch—to work in the manufacturing and construction industries and as laborers.

There was a quiet confidence about Australia and Australians at the beginning of the 1960s, a sense that much had been achieved and that a prosperous, stable, and comfortable future lay ahead. This confidence was shaken somewhat as the decade advanced and a period of rapid social change began, presenting Australians in general and Catholics in particular with many challenges.

Conscription was introduced in 1964, and Australia sent troops to Vietnam, triggering an antiwar movement that featured several huge moratoria in Melbourne and divided the Catholic community into anticommunist supporters of the war and those who opposed war and conscription on the basis of the Church's teaching about peace and justice. The 1960s also saw the rise of the women's liberation movement, as women sought to remove gender inequality and enjoy the same rights of men at work and in wider society. Like other Western societies, Australia experienced upheaval in attitudes to sexuality and authority, particularly among young people.

The dawn of the third phase of globalization was characterized by revolutions in information, communications, and transportation, leading to "accelerating transnational flows of people, ideas, goods, and capital."[5] More young people went to university than ever before, and new universities were established. Television ownership expanded rapidly, and air travel became an affordable reality for many people, so that by the end of the 1960s many more young Australians than ever before were able to visit places like London and Europe.[6]

The combined impact of many factors—massive immigration, expansion of television ownership, easier and cheaper travel, Australian soldiers serving in Vietnam and Vietnamese refugees arriving in Australia, news of student unrest in France, and even seemingly minor things like the growing presence of Italian pizza restaurants—led to a change in outlook among Australians as they became increasingly aware of living in and being influenced by a wider world. For many Australians, globalization took on a subjective dimension.[7] During this period, largely as a result of increased educational opportunities, Australian Catholics were moving more and more into mainstream society.

VATICAN II

For Catholics, another event of unprecedented importance happened as well: the Second Vatican Council, held in Rome over four sessions from 1962 to 1965. The council brought about major changes in the practices of the Church and the lives of its members. Changes included the celebration of the Mass in English, encouragement to read the Bible, a new recognition of the dignity and role of laypeople, and a new sense of engagement with the world. The council also led to the establishment of parish councils, women acting as readers at Mass, and a more open and positive attitude toward other Christian denominations.

The conciliar and postconciliar era saw a rich development of Catholic social teaching, partly through the council but primarily through a succession of papal encyclicals and Vatican documents, including *Pacem in Terris* (1962), *Gaudium et Spes* (1965), *Populorum Progressio* (1967), *Evangelii nuntiandi* (1975), and the 1971 synod statement, Justice in the World. These helped reorient the faith of many Australian Catholics from a focus on personal piety to a more outward-looking perspective with a concern for justice, peace, and development at home and abroad, particularly in Asia and the Pacific.

THE CATHOLIC POPULATION

The massive influx of European immigrants after the Second World War began the long and ongoing process of changing the face of the Australian Catholic Church from its overwhelmingly Irish nature to a multicultural, and increasingly Asian, one. In 1961, according to the

Commonwealth Census conducted in that year, 83 percent of Australia's total population were born in Australia, but only 77 percent of Catholics were.[8] The larger proportion of overseas-born Catholics was largely a result of the fact that Catholics made up more than half of the immigrants from Europe. Eighteen percent of Catholics had been born in continental Europe, and a further 3 percent were from the United Kingdom and Ireland, meaning that only 2 percent were from other countries, including only 0.4 percent from Asian countries and a mere 2,004 people from the Pacific Islands, including Papua and New Guinea. Among the total Australian population, the percentage born in Asian countries was almost the same: 0.5 percent. (It is probable that a good many of those born in Asia and Oceania were the children of English or Australian expatriates born in places such as India, Malaya, Singapore, and Papua.) These totals reflect the impact of the "White Australia policy" introduced by means of the Immigration Restriction Act, passed by the Australian government in 1901 with the intention of prohibiting "all alien coloured immigration."[9]

The White Australia policy was gradually relaxed after the Second World War, as the government intensified its efforts to increase the size of Australia's workforce; by the middle of the 1970s the policy had disappeared entirely. People from Asia and the Pacific were beginning to arrive in increasing numbers, so that by the time of the 1991 Census there were substantial numbers of Catholics of Asian and Pacific Island origin, as shown in table 10.1. At the time, people born in Asian countries made up 4.1 percent of Australia's Catholics, while Catholics from continental Europe accounted for 12.4 percent. Twenty-five years later the situation was markedly different. By 2016, when the Australian Catholic population neared 5.3 million, or 22.6 percent of the total population, the number of Catholics born in Asia had more than doubled, from 187,800 to 406,000, while the share coming from continental Europe had fallen to 7.3 percent of all Catholics. The numbers of Catholics born in Italy, Malta, Croatia and other countries of the former Yugoslavia, and the Netherlands, all fell by between 30 and 40 percent, whereas those from the Philippines, India, China, and Korea all increased by well over 100 percent. By 2016, the Philippines had overtaken Italy as the largest source of overseas-born Catholics. The number of Pacific Islanders among the Australian Catholic population also grew substantially, to about 17,000 in 1991 and then increasing to around 24,000 in 2016; the main source countries are, in diminishing order, Papua New Guinea, Samoa, Fiji, and Tonga. During the same period the number of Catholics born in the United Kingdom fell slightly, although the number born in the Republic of Ireland grew by 40 percent, so the overall percentage of the Australian Catholic population from the United Kingdom and Ireland changed only slightly, from 3.8 percent to 3.5 percent.

According to the 2016 Census, more than three-quarters of Catholics in Australia who were born in Italy and Malta had arrived prior to 1971, while only 7 percent and 2 percent, respectively, had arrived since 2001. Asian countries, especially South Korea, Vietnam, and the Philippines, provided a strong contrast, with only 0.1 percent, 0.3 percent, and 0.6 percent, respectively, having arrived before 1971, whereas 61 percent, 29 percent, and 57 percent, respectively, had arrived since 2001. The end of the Vietnam War precipitated the arrival of many Vietnamese Catholics: more than 26,500 of the Vietnamese Catholics in the 2016 Census had arrived in the twenty years between 1976 and 1995. Vietnam and South Korea did

TABLE 10.1. Country of birth of Australia's Catholics, 1991 and 2016

Country of birth	1991	2016	Change (%) 1991 to 2016
Australia	3,430,716	3,894,990	+14
New Zealand	41,917	68,837	+64
Other Oceania	17,003	23,927	+41
United Kingdom	134,002	131,373	−2
Ireland	38,219	53,679	+40
Italy	236,040	149,901	−36
Croatia and other former Yugoslavia	72,332	43,504	−40
Poland	51,906	31,968	−38
Malta	49,909	33,464	−33
Netherlands	33,393	21,039	−37
Germany	33,133	26,992	−19
Other Europe (incl. USSR / Russian Fedn)	94,888	77,401	−18
Philippines	61,548	174,601	+184
India	25,398	59,690	+135
Vietnam	27,128	44,222	+63
Sri Lanka	13,343	22,784	+71
Malaysia	12,932	17,608	+36
Indonesia	10,148	17,603	+73
Hong Kong	10,929	11,084	+1
South Korea	5,280	17,366	+229
China (excluding SARS and Taiwan)	4,417	12,043	+173
Other Asia	16,683	28,941	+73
Lebanon	27,667	26,858	−3
Other Middle East and North Africa	20,432	51,462	+152
North America	13,903	21,991	+58
Central America and South America	49,038	76,963	+57
South Africa	9,183	19,798	+116
Other countries	22,311	39,309	+76
Inadequately defined / Not stated	28,120	92,441	+229
Total Catholics	**4,591,918**	**5,291,839**	**+15.2**

Source: Australian Bureau of Statistics, Census of Population and Housing, 1991 and 2016.

not even appear in the extensive list of birthplaces of Australians in the 1961 report from the Bureau of Census and Statistics.

Overall in 2016, 18.7 percent of Catholics were born in a non-English-speaking country, and a further 5.5 percent were born overseas in an English-speaking country, meaning that nearly a quarter of Australia's Catholics were born overseas. In addition, there were 131,860 Catholics of Aboriginal and Torres Strait Islander origin, accounting for 2.5 percent of all Australia's Catholics and 20.5 percent of all Indigenous Australians.

While almost all of Australia's 5.3 million Catholics belong to the Latin Rite, there are also small numbers who belong to Eastern Rite churches, five of which are established with dioceses or eparchies in Australia. In order of their establishment in Australia, these are the Ukrainian Catholic Eparchy (1958), the Maronite Diocese (1973), the Melkite Greek Catholic Eparchy (1987), the Chaldean Diocese (2006), and the Syro-Malabar Eparchy (2013). According to the 2016 Census, about 60,300 people self-identified as belonging to one of these Eastern Rites.

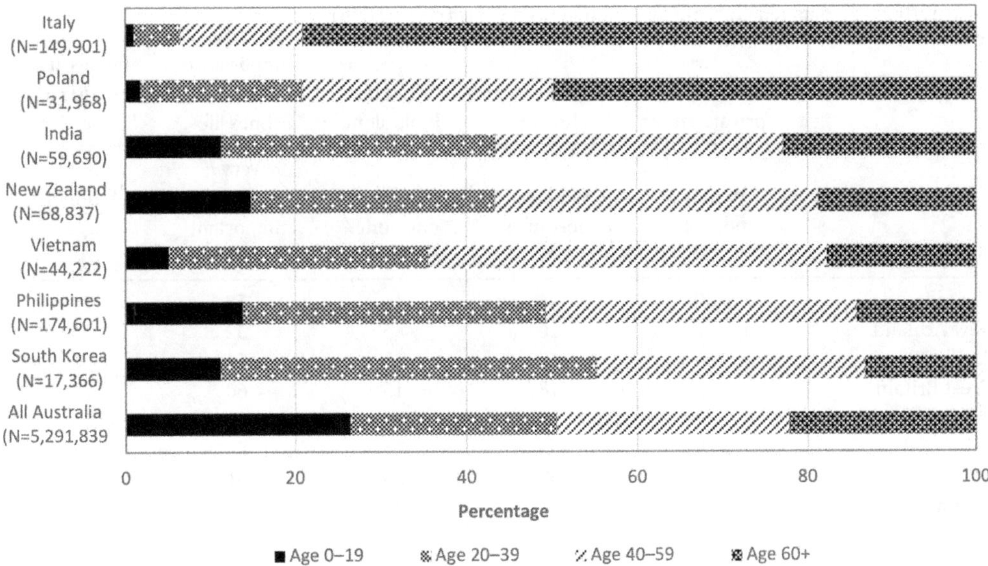

FIGURE 10.1. Age profiles of Catholics from selected countries of birth, 2016. *Source:* Australian Bureau of Statistics, Census of Population and Housing, 2016.

The age profiles of the main immigrant groups will ensure that the demographic shift away from a Catholic population of European origin and toward one of Asian origin will become even more marked in the future, as figure 10.1 illustrates. Almost four-fifths of Catholics from Italy were age 80 or older at the time of the 2016 Census, and only 1 percent were under age 20. The age profile for several other European postwar source countries was similar to that of Italians, although the situation for some others, such as Poland, was not as stark because of continued immigration in recent decades, albeit at lower levels than in the 1950s and 1960s. In contrast to European nations, the four Asian countries of birth shown in figure 10.1 all have much higher proportions under age 20 and very much lower proportions of Catholics age 80 or older. Compared to Australian Catholics as a whole, no source countries had as high a proportion of children and adolescents (age 0–19), reflecting the fact that most immigrants are likely to be young adults or, as is often the case with family reunion programs, older people.

CATHOLICS WHO ATTEND MASS

In 2016, the number of people in Australia attending Mass on a typical weekend was about 623,400, or 11.8 percent of the total Catholic population. Mass attenders are even more ethnically diverse than Catholics in general. In 2016, more than two-fifths of the people attending Mass in parishes (43 percent) were born overseas, including 37 percent who were born in non-English-speaking countries.[10] The demographic shift toward a more Asian Church is also evident here, with the percentage of attenders born in Asia more than doubling between 1996 and 2016, from 11 to 25 percent, with around 40 percent of the increase, or 10 percent of the total, coming from the Philippines. During the same period, the percentage of Mass attenders

TABLE 10.2. Personal religious practices and views, by birthplace (2016)

	Engage in private prayer	Say the Rosary	Read the Bible alone	Importance of parish in one's life	Believe it is a sin to miss Sunday Mass
Birthplace	Weekly or more often %	Weekly or more often %	Weekly or more often %	Very / Extremely important %	Agree / Strongly agree %
Australia	80	26	16	57	43
New Zealand	67	16	5	52	35
Pacific Islands	88	62	43	84	80
Great Britain	72	18	15	60	57
Ireland	72	34	11	32	35
Italy	89	36	23	56	47
Malta	88	50	10	61	60
Vietnam	77	61	27	71	68
Philippines	88	37	21	79	55
India and Sri Lanka	91	59	43	76	68
All Attenders	81	31	20	60	45

Source: National Church Life Survey 2016: Questionnaires S3 (N=2,591) and X (N=1,728).

born in the United Kingdom, Ireland, and Europe declined from 16 to 13 percent, and the percentage born in Australia fell from 69 to 57 percent. Migrants from particular countries tend to live in the same suburbs, and their parishes become the places where they gather for social events and community support as well as to attend Mass and receive the sacraments.[11]

There is considerable diversity of personal religious practice and spirituality among Mass attenders from different countries of birth, as the data in table 10.2 demonstrates. Italian and Maltese Mass attenders are well-known for their traditional piety and spirituality. As their presence in parish life diminishes, their place of primacy is being taken over by attenders from the Pacific Islands and Asia, who also demonstrate a commitment to strong personal religious practice and traditional spirituality. Asians and Pacific Islanders place great importance on the role of the parish in their lives, an indication of the strong communal dimension of their Catholic faith, and most regard it as a serious sin to miss Mass on Sunday without a compelling reason. Attenders from New Zealand, Great Britain, and Ireland score lowest on almost all the measures described in table 10.2.

One version of the 2016 National Church Life Survey (NCLS) used in Catholic parishes included questions about four key beliefs of the Catholic Church: the trinitarian nature of God, the Virgin Birth, transubstantiation, and the bodily resurrection of Christ. The totals in table 10.3 are the percentages of the national random sample of Mass attenders in the survey choosing the "Church's official teaching" or "orthodox" responses to the questions, all of which were phrased along the lines of: "Which of the following statements comes closest to expressing your belief."[12]

By and large, Mass-going Catholics display a high degree of orthodoxy, as indicated by the high levels of acceptance of the four key Catholic doctrines. Nine in ten (90 percent) said they believe that the consecrated bread and wine at Mass truly become the sacred Body and Blood

TABLE 10.3. Mass attenders' acceptance of key Catholic beliefs, by birthplace (2016)

	Belief about the Resurrection	Belief about God	Belief about the Eucharist	Belief about the Virgin Birth
Birthplace	Bodily resurrection %	As Father, Son, and Holy Spirit %	Bread and wine become Body and Blood %	Literal understanding %
Australia	71	83	89	75
New Zealand	47	86	95	70
Pacific Islands	91	100	100	79
Great Britain	74	80	87	80
Ireland	67	79	93	72
Italy	80	97	95	88
Malta	86	95	88	87
Vietnam	86	82	94	70
Philippines	73	95	98	67
India and Sri Lanka	90	93	96	82
All attenders	73	85	90	75

Source: National Church Life Survey 2016: Questionnaire S3 (N=2,591).

of Christ; 85 percent selected a trinitarian statement as best expressing their understanding of God; 75 percent expressed belief in the virginal conception of Jesus; and 73 percent assented to the statement that "Christ was raised by God's power from death to life—really, bodily, physically." This high level of orthodoxy is not unexpected among Mass-attending Catholics; what might be considered surprising is that the level of orthodoxy is not even higher.

Country of birth was found to have an influence on Mass attenders' responses to these questions about beliefs, in that attenders born in non-English-speaking countries tend to hold more orthodox views compared to attenders who were born in Australia, although it cannot be said that Mass attenders from any one country are more likely than attenders from another country to choose the orthodox response to all four questions (see table 10.3). Pacific Islanders seem to be the group most likely to hold orthodox beliefs. It is notable that differences by age are only moderate for each of the beliefs in question.

These numbers have varied only a little over the years since 1996 when the survey was first conducted. For three of the questions, the percentage of orthodox responses has increased, whereas for the question about the Resurrection the percentage has dropped. The most likely reason for the increased percentage of orthodox responses is that people with less orthodox beliefs have stopped going to Mass, but it's unclear why the percentage of orthodox responses to the question about the Resurrection has fallen while it has risen for the other three questions.

PRIESTS AND RELIGIOUS

Like the Catholic population in general, Australia's priests and religious also come from many different countries. Fourteen percent of overseas-born priests actually grew up in Australia or came to Australia as young adults, and only later decided to enter the seminary; 20 percent of the priests born in Vietnam are in this category. The others arrived already ordained as priests, either as migrants or to serve the Church for a few years before returning to their home countries. In 2014, there were about 600 overseas-born diocesan priests from fifty-eight different countries in Australia, roughly 32 percent of all diocesan priests. There were 150 diocesan priests from India, 89 from Vietnam, and 75 from the Philippines. Others came from Ireland (including Northern Ireland) (65), Nigeria (37), Malta (27), Great Britain (26), Poland (25), and Italy (23). Generally speaking, the Irish and Italian priests arrived in Australia many years ago, whereas the Filipino and Indian priests arrived more recently. Despite the strong presence of Asian-born priests, however, only two of the approximately 40 bishops currently in office in Australia were born in Asia, although another has Chinese ancestry.

A 2018 survey of Australia's religious orders found that 31 percent of all sisters, brothers, and religious order priests had come to Australia from (in diminishing order) Ireland (including Northern Ireland), Vietnam, New Zealand, Italy, India, Lebanon, the Philippines, Poland, Malta, Papua New Guinea, the Solomon Islands, Great Britain, and seventy-one other countries.[13] As a further sign of the increasingly multicultural nature of the Australian Church, just nine years earlier overseas-born religious had accounted for only 25 percent of all religious.[14]

UNCEASING CHALLENGES

Since the start of the third phase of globalization, the Catholic Church in Australia has been confronted with seemingly unceasing challenges. Among the first to arise were challenges related to sexual morality and, consequently, Church authority, which were initiated by the sexual revolution of the 1960s and the 1968 papal encyclical on birth control, *Humanae Vitae*. These were followed by, and were partly responsible for, a decrease in the number of priests and religious, caused by a drastic drop in the numbers entering the priesthood and religious life and the departure of existing members. The role of women in the Church became another area of challenge beginning late in the twentieth century. Most significant of all were the challenges presented by the child sexual abuse scandal and the findings and recommendations of the Royal Commission into Institutional Responses to Child Sexual Abuse, especially those recommendations relating to the Church's governance practices. About none of these issues can it be said that the challenges associated with them have been fully resolved. They persist, sometimes evolving into new forms, such as with sexual morality, where the issue of birth control has been largely displaced by the issues of same-sex marriage and the Church's teaching about LGBTQI people. And new challenges, such as the coronavirus pandemic of 2020, keep arising.

These issues and events or, in some cases, the Church's response to them, have precipitated further challenges. For example, the decline in the number of priests, coupled with Vatican II's renewed emphasis on the role of laypeople in the Church, resulted in experimentation with new modes of parish leadership.[15] The decline also prompted many bishops to recruit priests from overseas to work in parishes, which sometimes resulted in parishioners feeling frustrated because of a priest's heavy accent or angered by his unwillingness to work alongside women in parish leadership positions. Further outcomes of these challenges include falling attendances at Sunday Mass, the recent fall in the overall Catholic population, and a widespread lack of confidence and trust in Catholic Church authorities, even among its most loyal members—those who still attend Sunday Mass. Many of these challenges display a multicultural dimension.

SEXUAL MORALITY

Besides Vatican II, the other major event in the Catholic world in the 1960s was the promulgation of the papal encyclical *Humanae Vitae*, which reaffirmed the Church's prohibition against artificial means of birth control. Over the years, it has become clear that Catholics, even Mass-attending Catholics, vary a great deal in their views and practices, not only about contraception but about a range of issues related to marriage and sexuality. They do not always agree with or act according to the Church's teachings. Although it is true that contemporary attitudes and practices of Australian Catholics reflect and are strongly influenced by the views of secular society, it can be argued that the trigger that led to Catholics' independent thinking was the publication of *Humanae Vitae* in the new climate produced by Vatican II.

Results from the 2016 NCLS (see table 10.4) show that there is widespread dissent from the Church's positions on certain key moral issues, even among Mass attenders. While the official Church is opposed to the legalization of same-sex marriage, only about half of Mass attenders are opposed, just as fewer than half believe that premarital sex is always wrong. As well, fewer than half accept the Church's practice of refusing Communion to those who have remarried after divorce but without an annulment of the previous marriage. Less than a third of Mass attenders (31 percent) say that they always follow the teachings of the Church in making decisions about moral issues, while almost all the others (64 percent) say "I look to the teaching of the Church for guidance, but then I follow my own conscience." Only in relation to abortion did almost all (85 percent) attenders hold a position close to the Church's teaching, although many of those are prepared to allow abortion in extreme circumstances such as rape or risk to the mother's life. Often portrayed in the media as a Catholic position, this high level of opposition to abortion is reflected in most other Christian denominations in Australia as well.[16]

Responses to these moral issues vary considerably according to the birthplace of the respondent. Even among Pacific Islanders, who show themselves to be the most orthodox group in terms of Catholic belief (table 10.3), only 64 percent say they always follow the Church's moral teachings. Attenders from non-English-speaking countries tend to be more likely than attenders from English-speaking countries, including Australia, to accept the Church's position on same-sex marriage, premarital sex, and acceptance of the practice of refusing Communion to the divorced and remarried, and to say they always follow the teachings of the Church. The numbers do not always reflect internal consistency, however. For example, attenders born in Vietnam are the most likely to say they always follow the

TABLE 10.4. Mass attenders' views on sexual morality issues, by birthplace (2016)

Birthplace	Always follow Church teaching on moral issues %	Strongly oppose same-sex marriage %	Premarital sex always wrong %	Abortion always wrong or only permissible in extreme circumstances %	Agree, or agree with difficulty, with denial of Communion to divorced and remarried %
Australia	24	43	37	84	43
New Zealand	19	31	20	86	21
Pacific Islands	64	78	67	96	58
Great Britain	16	43	22	84	31
Ireland	19	35	33	86	43
Italy	47	32	61	91	47
Malta	40	44	55	90	47
Vietnam	65	36	52	80	56
Philippines	48	40	62	91	39
India and Sri Lanka	52	45	73	92	37
All attenders	31	41	44	85	41

Source: National Church Life Survey 2016: Questionnaires S3 (N=2,591) and X (N=1,728).

teachings of the Church, yet they also are among the least likely to be opposed to same-sex marriage and to say that premarital sex is always wrong. It is noteworthy that a high degree of orthodoxy (table 10.3) or a high level of personal religious practice (table 10.2) does not automatically translate to a high level of acceptance of the Church's authority to decide moral matters.

WOMEN IN THE CHURCH

In the 1990s, in response to the rise of the women's movement and the changing role of women in Western society and the Church, the Bishops' Commission for Justice, Development and Peace, in collaboration with Australian Catholic University and the Australian Conference of Leaders of Religious Institutes, carried out the Research Project on Women's Participation in the Catholic Church in Australia. The largest research project on a single issue ever undertaken by the Catholic Church in Australia, and far bigger than comparable government inquiries, the study aimed to gather information about the ways in which women participate in the Church and how their participation could be increased, as well as to help Church bodies reflect on and promote the gospel vision of the equal dignity of women and men.[17] The study, which resulted in the publication of the report *Woman and Man: One in Christ Jesus*, revealed a strong sense of pain and alienation among women and men alike, resulting from the Church's stance on women. The report highlighted the enormous contribution of women to all aspects of the life of the Church except in ordained ministry, leadership, and decision-making.[18] The project led in 2000 to the establishment of the Commission for Australian Catholic Women (later the Council for Australian Catholic Women) and the

Office for the Participation of Women. Together, the role of these two groups was to promote the participation of women, and particularly young women, in the life and mission of the Church, a role they carried out with some success, albeit limited by lack of resources.[19] That changed in December 2019, when the council was abolished and the office was closed, despite the release of an Australian Catholic Bishops Conference (ACBC) publication just one month earlier wherein the bishops claimed to be "still listening" and acknowledged that there was much "unfinished business" relating to the commitments they had made at the conclusion of the research project.[20] The actions by the bishops only served to reinforce the perception, noted by Sandie Cornish, that "while there have been advances in some areas, little seems to have changed in others, and in some matters, things seem to have gone backwards."[21] According to the media release announcing their decisions, the cutbacks were due to financial pressures caused by "current circumstances," which were understood to be falling attendance and the costs associated with redress for the crimes of many clergy.[22]

THE CLERGY SEXUAL ABUSE CRISIS

If Vatican II was the major twentieth-century event in the Catholic Church, it seems very likely that the clerical sexual abuse crisis will be the defining event of the twenty-first, in Australia as in numerous other countries, including Ireland, Germany, and the United States.[23] I recall that in 1986, while undertaking a course of study with German theologian Johann Baptist Metz, he would repeatedly remind us that it was not possible to do theology "with our backs turned to Auschwitz." Much the same can be said about Catholicism in Australia today: it is not possible for us to talk about the Catholic Church in Australia with our backs turned to the sexual abuse crisis or, in other words, to proceed as if the crisis can be disregarded as the Church exercises its ministry and mission now and in the future.

In response to the deplorable record of many institutions in this regard, not just the Catholic Church, in 2014 the Australian government established the Royal Commission into Institutional Responses to Child Sexual Abuse.[24] Twenty of the 57 case studies and 38 percent of the private sessions conducted by the commission involved the Catholic Church. The commission heard that between January 1980 and February 2015, 4,444 alleged incidents of child sexual abuse were made to ninety-three Catholic Church authorities. These claims related to over a thousand separate institutions and to a total of 1,880 alleged perpetrators, 32 percent of whom were religious brothers, 30 percent were priests, 29 percent were laypeople, and 5 percent were religious sisters. Of all alleged perpetrators, 90 percent were male and 10 percent were female.[25]

The final report of the commission consists of seventeen volumes and a 217-page executive summary. Volume 16, which deals with religious institutions, makes twenty-one recommendations specifically in relation to the Catholic Church and a further twenty-eight recommendations that relate to religious institutions generally. The Catholic-specific recommendations include that the ACBC should request the Holy See "to establish a transparent process for appointing bishops which includes the direct participation of lay people" (recommendation no. 16.8) and to "consider introducing voluntary celibacy for diocesan clergy" (no. 16.18).

Recommendation no. 16.26 urges the ACBC to consult with the Holy See in order to clarify whether, "if a person confesses during the sacrament of reconciliation to perpetrating child sexual abuse, absolution can and should be withheld until they report themselves to civil authorities." The Holy See's response to these recommendations was published on the Royal Commission's website in February 2020.[26]

LACK OF CONFIDENCE AND TRUST IN CHURCH AUTHORITIES

According to results from the 2016 NCLS, nearly two-thirds of those who attend Sunday Mass (64 percent) believe that the response of Church authorities to cases of sexual abuse by priests and religious "has been inadequate and shows a complete failure of responsibility" (see table 10.5). Also, three-fifths (59 percent) agree that their confidence in Church authorities has been damaged by these cases, and only 43 percent agree that Church authorities can be trusted when they speak about child sexual abuse.[27]

These questions suggest a natural progression in forming an opinion: those who believe that the Church's handling of sex abuse cases was inadequate and irresponsible are likely to have lost confidence in Church authorities and hence are wary about trusting what they say in the future. This is indeed the way it works for most people from the birthplaces listed in table 10.5: higher percentages saying the response was inadequate and that their confidence in authorities was damaged correspond to lower percentages saying that Church authorities can be trusted when they speak about child sexual abuse, and vice versa. It is not true, however, for attenders born in Asia and the Pacific Islands, who still register fairly high levels of trust in Church authorities even though they believe that the Church's response has been inadequate and that their confidence has been damaged. Attenders from Great Britain and

TABLE 10.5. Mass attenders' trust in Church authorities, by birthplace (2016)

	Church's response to sex abuse crisis inadequate	Confidence in Church authorities damaged	Church authorities can be trusted re: clergy abuse crisis
Birthplace	Agree / Strongly agree %	Agree / Strongly agree %	Agree / Strongly agree %
Australia	66	59	42
New Zealand	48	60	38
Pacific Islands	63	47	74
Great Britain	73	66	35
Ireland	85	68	36
Italy	64	55	46
Malta	61	55	44
Vietnam	46	50	69
Philippines	52	56	57
India and Sri Lanka	53	44	53
All attenders	64	59	43

Source: National Church Life Survey 2016: Questionnaire S3 (N=2,591).

Ireland are the most critical in their responses to these questions, with easily the highest percentages saying the Church's response was inadequate and that their confidence was damaged and the lowest percentage saying that Church authorities can be trusted.

DECLINE IN NUMBERS OF PRIESTS AND RELIGIOUS

Table 10.6 shows the number of diocesan priests, religious order priests, and religious sisters and brothers when numbers were at or near their peak in the 1960s and early 1970s, compared to totals in 2020. The number of diocesan priests has dropped by almost 600, but it has been fluctuating around 1,900 to 2,000 in recent years. The reason it has not continued to fall is that although there are fewer Australian priests being ordained, bishops are recruiting more and more priests from overseas. The drop in the number of priests belonging to a religious order has been less pronounced, partly because many of them belong to international orders whose members move from country to country. According to a 2018 survey of religious congregations, more than 50 percent of members of clerical religious institutes were born outside Australia.[28]

Australia had 1,892 diocesan priests in 2020 but, according to the 2020–21 *Official Directory*, 512 of those priests are listed as retired (27 percent), leaving a working population of 1,380 diocesan priests. It is estimated that a national seminary enrollment of around 320, an increase of 57 percent over 2019 enrollments, is required to maintain that number. If such a substantial increase in the number of seminarians cannot be achieved, the only way to maintain the current number of diocesan priests is by continuing to recruit priests from overseas, and this is what most of the bishops are doing. Even allowing for overseas recruitment, current numbers of those in active parish ministry are likely to continue to fall.

The number of religious sisters and brothers has declined at very similar rates: today's totals represent 25 percent and 22 percent, respectively, of the peak numbers. At the time of the 2009 survey, 30 percent of religious sisters were age 80 or older.[29] In the same survey, only 36 of the 851 members of orders of religious brothers were under age 50, and only 16 were under 45. That 2009 figure had already declined to 528 by 2020, a decline of 38 percent

TABLE 10.6. Number of clergy and religious, peak year and 2020

Clergy and religious	Peak year	Number in peak year	Number in 2020	Percentage change
Diocesan priests	1971	2,471	1,875	–24.1
Religious order priests	1971	1,424	1,006	–29.4
Religious sisters	1964	13,900	3,503	–74.8
Religious brothers	1968	2,376	528	–77.8

Note: Figures include active and retired priests and religious.

Source: For 1971 statistics of diocesan and religious order priests: *Official Year Book of the Catholic Church in Australia and Papua-New Guinea, New Zealand and the Pacific Islands, 1972* (Sydney: E. J. Dwyer). For 1964 statistics of religious sisters: *Official Year Book of the Catholic Church of Australia, New Zealand and Oceania, 1965–1966* (Sydney: E. J. Dwyer). For 1968 statistics of religious brothers: *Official Year Book of the Catholic Church of Australia, New Zealand and Oceania, 1969–1970* (Sydney: E. J. Dwyer). For 2020 statistics: *Official Directory of the Catholic Church in Australia, 2021–2022* (Belmont: National Council of Priests of Australia, 2021), 761–62.

in just eleven years. It is likely that numerous female orders and even some of the larger male orders such as the Marist Brothers, the Christian Brothers, and the De La Salle Brothers will cease to exist in Australia in the next 15 to 30 years. In response to this phenomenon, Catholic Religious Australia has recently established a new company, Emerging Futures Collaborative Limited, to facilitate the provision of the shared services and supports needed by the aging members of the congregations whose existence in Australia is coming to an end.[30]

DECLINING MASS ATTENDANCE

Mass attendance totals in Australia have been in decline since before the beginning of the third phase of globalization. Figure 10.2 shows the percentage of Catholics attending Mass weekly for the period 1947 to 2016.[31] Attendance rates reached a peak in the 1950s, when surveys at the time suggested that perhaps 70 percent or more of Catholics attended Mass every Sunday. But they have been declining fairly steadily ever since.

Given that the 2016 NCLS revealed that 43 percent of all attenders age 15 and older were between 60 and 79 years old, and that people age 80 or older made up a further 13 percent while those age 15 to 19 accounted for only 3 percent, there is little doubt that the downward trend in attendance will continue and that the percentage of people from non-English-speaking (and particularly Asian) backgrounds will continue to grow.

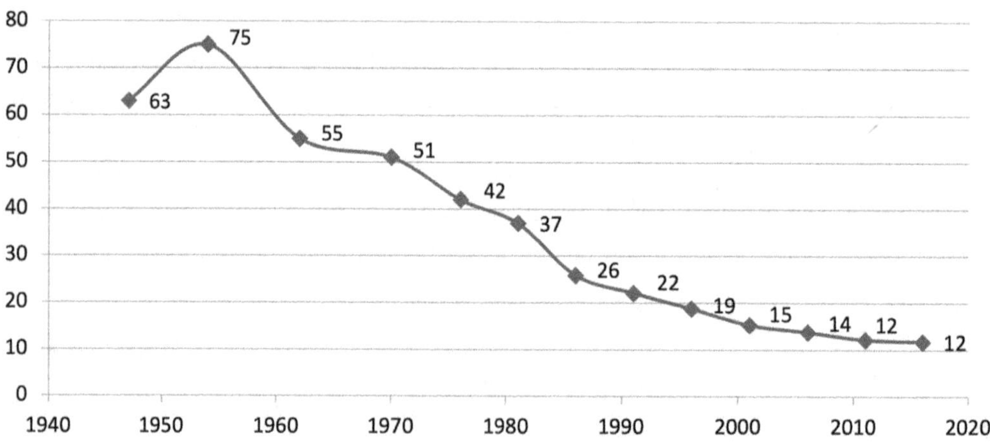

FIGURE 10.2. Mass attendance rates in Australia, 1947–2016. *Source:* Various surveys and attendance counts, 1947–2016. For detailed information about the sources and types of measure for each of the data points from 1947 to 1996, see Robert Dixon and Ruth Powell, "Vatican II: A Data-Based Analysis of Its Impact on Australian Catholic Life," in Neil Ormerod et al., eds., *Vatican II: Reception and Implementation in the Australian Church* (Mulgrave: Garratt, 2012), 27. For the data points from 2001 to 2016, the attendance rate is the total attendance for the whole of Australia, as determined by the National Count of Attendance, expressed as a percentage of the Catholic population according to the Australian Census.

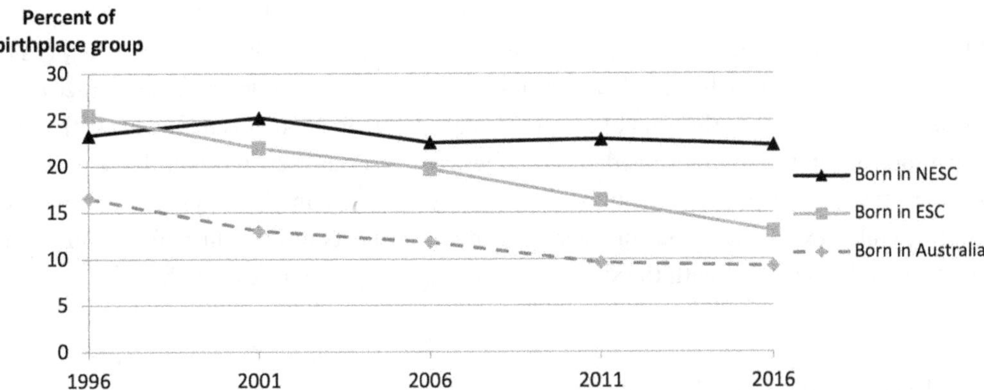

FIGURE 10.3. Mass attendance rates in Australia by birthplace group, 1996–2016. *Note:* NESC: Non-English-speaking countries; ESC: English-speaking countries. *Source:* Catholic Church Life Survey 1996 and National Church Life Survey 2001, 2006, 2011, and 2016; National Counts of Attendance 2001, 2006, 2011, and 2016; Mass attendance estimates 1996; Australian Bureau of Statistics: 1996–2016 Censuses of Population and Housing.

Between 1996 and 2016 the attendance rate of Australian-born Catholics fell from about 17 percent to 9 percent, and that of Catholics from other English-speaking countries fell from 26 percent to 13 percent. In contrast, the attendance rate of Catholics born in non-English-speaking countries remained reasonably steady, at around 22 or 23 percent (see figure 10.3).[32]

Reasons for the decline in Mass attendance are documented in a 2007 study of long-term Mass attenders who had stopped going to Mass.[33] The study identified ten reasons why people stopped attending. Chief among them was the view that the Church was out of touch with Australian society. In the eyes of almost all participants, "the Church had lost its ability to connect with the day-to-day lives of ordinary people and as a result they no longer regarded it as having the authority to guide them in living an authentic life."[34] At that time, the sex abuse crisis was found to have had only a very limited impact on people's decisions to stop attending; it is likely that it has been a much more significant factor in recent years, with the revelations of the Royal Commission contributing to the decline in confidence and trust in Church authorities.

DISIDENTIFICATION

The Catholic population grew at every Australian census from 1911 to 2011, but it dropped suddenly in 2016 despite 209,000 Catholic immigrants arriving between 2011 and 2016. The number of Australian-born Catholics fell by over 170,000.

The drop in the Australian-born Catholic population appears to be largely due to the phenomenon of disidentification. It is estimated that about 356,000 people age 15 and over at the time of the 2016 Census who had self-identified or who had been identified by their parents as Catholics in 2011 did not so identify in 2016. This was a large increase over the corresponding estimates for the two previous intercensal periods 2001–6 (107,000) and 2006–11 (189,000). Contributing to the increase was the growth in the number of people age 35 to 74 who ceased to self-identify as Catholics, from 31,000 in 2006 and 59,000 in 2011 to 162,000, or 45 percent of the total of people disidentifying, in 2016. It is highly likely that the sharp increase in the number disidentifying between 2011 and 2016 was in large part due to the revelations of the Royal Commission and the extensive media coverage of numerous cases of child sexual abuse, but disillusionment with aspects of the Church's teaching and practices and impatience with the slow pace of change may also have contributed.

RESPONDING TO THE CHALLENGES

All of these challenges have drawn responses from the ACBC and from individual bishops and other Church leaders. Some attempts to address challenges were promising and mildly successful for a period. For example, the Bishops Conference was an enthusiastic sponsor of the research on the participation of women in the Church and made strong efforts to implement the recommendations, but as time went on the bishops' commitment dissipated, culminating in the closure of the two new resulting organizations. In another example, in 2004 the bishops initiated research into why mature age Catholics who had been going to Mass all their lives had stopped attending.[35] The research resulted in a set of pastoral strategies designed to address this phenomenon for use in parishes and dioceses,[36] and led to the development of the Reconnect program for inactive Catholics, and Rewired, a program for the evangelization of young people.[37] That research also prompted the Pastoral Research Office to launch the Building Stronger Parishes project in 2010.[38] The aim of the project was to explore how twenty selected parishes from around Australia, conscious of their cultural and social context, had successfully developed programs or activities to overcome particular challenges facing them. The emphasis of the project was on the reproducibility of the initiatives: all of the programs and activities were capable of being adopted, with little or no modification, by other parishes.[39]

The Australian Church's handling of the demographic shifts described earlier, in themselves among the major challenges already facing the Church by 1960 and continuing ever since, has been largely successful. In general, immigrant Catholics have been made welcome in Australian parishes, just as Australians overall have consistently and strongly endorsed immigration and multiculturalism and rejected overt discrimination on the basis of race in immigrant selection.[40] Rather than establish national parishes for immigrants from particular countries, the usual practice of Australian bishops has been to prioritize territorial parishes, that is, parishes with specified geographical boundaries to which all the Catholics living within those boundaries automatically belong.[41] This means that it is not only the Catholic Church on a national scale that is multicultural; many parishes, particularly those located in major cities, are multicultural themselves. About twenty years ago my own large parish in suburban Melbourne conducted a survey of the people attending Mass and found that they had been born in sixty-six different countries. When visiting American sociologist of religion, the late Dean Hoge, accompanied me to Mass in the parish a few years later, I was able to point out to him people from fifteen different countries of birth sitting within a few pews of us. Similar anecdotes could be told about many of the larger parishes in Australia's major cities.

A CRISIS POINT

Although much about the Catholic Church in Australia today is strong and flourishing, especially in relation to Catholic education, social services, health, and care of the aged, the scale of the challenges facing the Church in Australia, together with the failed, inadequate, or temporary attempts to address them has brought the Church to a point of crisis that demands a far-reaching response. The crisis is multifaceted but has two major interconnected dimensions: a crisis of relevance, confidence, and trust, and a crisis of numbers.

The first dimension has been building for many years, but reached a peak as a result of the sexual abuse crisis and growing disaffection regarding the Church's teachings on sexual morality, particularly in relation to issues like same-sex marriage, so that it may now be said that the Church is experiencing a huge trust deficit, not only among Catholics but in Australian society generally. As Andrew P. Lynch has pointed out, the Church's hard-won acceptance in Australia's public sphere is at stake.[42]

The crisis of numbers refers to the declining number of people attending Mass, the increase in the number disidentifying as Catholics, and the falling number of priests and religious. While the causes of these are many and complex, there is no doubt that they are at least in part due to the crisis of relevance, confidence, and trust. Recognizing that these crises are not going to go away and are in fact becoming more severe, the bishops finally responded by convening a plenary council to be held in 2021.[43] (The first session was originally scheduled for October 2020 but was postponed due to the coronavirus pandemic.) This is only the fifth major assembly for the Catholic Church in Australia, the first in more than eighty years following the most recent one in 1937. Preparations for the Council involved extensive consultation, resulting in 17,457 written submissions representing the contributions of more than 222,000 people.[44] The consultation phase was followed by the establishment of groups to write six thematic discernment papers, eventually leading to the publication of an *Instrumentum Laboris* (working document) and agenda.[45] The reform group Catholics for Renewal has also provided the Council with its own comprehensive and widely publicized agenda and set of recommendations.[46] For the Council to have any credibility, it will need to be seen as transparent and open, with power to bring about real change in the way the Catholic Church in Australia operates. It offers the Australian Church an opportunity to address the crises and to begin the process of recovery and healing, but there is considerable doubt among concerned Catholics about whether the opportunity will be accepted.[47] Several bishops who are resistant to change have downplayed the importance of the Council. For many Catholics, perhaps, it is "the last throw of the dice."[48]

State governments around Australia responded to the pandemic by placing restrictions on people's movement and on attendance at church services, resulting in most parish Masses being suspended, except for perhaps one each weekend celebrated in the presence of a very small number of people. This situation illuminates both the crises noted earlier: it seems unlikely that church attendance will rebound to former levels once the pandemic is fully over and many former attenders will have discovered that they can survive quite well without Sunday Mass. They may decide to continue attending Mass online, or occasionally at their parish, or not at all. So far there is only anecdotal evidence about this. A National Count of Attendance was held in May 2021 and it will be interesting to see the results once they become available.

Smaller attendances mean lower income for parishes and less influence of Church authorities over the Catholic population, which is where the second crisis becomes apparent. Several Australian dioceses issued statements during the pandemic, indicating when Catholics in the diocese were dispensed from the obligation of Sunday Mass attendance and when the dispensation was rescinded and the obligation reimposed.[49] We have seen that Mass attenders of all ethnic backgrounds do not always follow the teachings of the Church in making decisions and have, to a greater or lesser extent, lost confidence in Church authorities and do not trust what they say, at least in relation to child sexual abuse. It is not difficult to imagine that their lack of confidence and trust at least partly extends to other statements made by Church authorities, so it is doubtful whether statements of this type will have any significant effect on numbers. Nor are they likely to demonstrate to the wider Catholic community that the bishops are really grappling with the current crises. It is noteworthy that the bishops who issue statements like this also tend to be the ones downplaying the importance of the Plenary Council.

The impact of globalization on the Australian Church has been profound, particularly in the way it has transformed so many aspects of the Catholic Church from a monocultural to a multicultural community. Yet the success of this transformation will count for little if the huge crises facing the contemporary Church are not successfully addressed, and soon.

NOTES

Data Sources: Australian Bureau of Statistics, 1991–2016: Customized data files from the Australia Censuses 1991–2016, prepared for the Australian Catholic Bishops Conference as part of the National Catholic Census Project; comprehensive demographic profiles of Australia's Catholic population for each census since 2006 are available from https://ncpr.catholic.org.au/catholic-social-profiles/. Ruth Powell, Sam Sterland, Robert Dixon, et al., 2016 (computer file): 2016 NCLS Attender Surveys: Catholic (versions S3 and X) (Sydney: NCLS Research).

1. These differences are discussed at greater length in Robert Dixon, "Australian Catholicism and Globalisation," in Beatrice Green and Keiti Ann Kanongata'a, eds., *Weaving Theology in Oceania: Culture, Context and Practice* (Newcastle upon Tyne: Cambridge Scholars, 2020).
2. Michael Hogan, *The Sectarian Strand* (Ringwood: Penguin, 1987). Hogan points out that the origins of European Australia were quite distinct from European colonial enterprises in the Americas in that Australian colonization had very little religious motivation. The duties of the officially appointed (Church of England) chaplain were to the colonizers, not a missionary endeavor among the Indigenous population.
3. Barry Dwyer and Graham English, *Faith of Our Fathers and Mothers: A Catholic Story* (Burwood: Collins Dove, 1990).

4. Katharine Massam, *Sacred Threads: Catholic Spirituality in Australia, 1922–1962* (Sydney: University of NSW Press, 1996), 21.
5. Thomas Banchoff and José Casanova, "Introduction: The Jesuits and Globalization," in Thomas Banchoff and José Casanova, eds., *The Jesuits and Globalization: Historical Legacies and Contemporary Challenges* (Washington, DC: Georgetown University Press, 2016), 2.
6. Kevin O'Connor, Robert Stimson, and Maurice Daly, *Australia's Changing Economic Geography: A Society Dividing* (New York: Oxford University Press, 2001).
7. José Casanova, "The Jesuits through the Prism of Globalization, Globalization through a Jesuit Prism," in Thomas Banchoff and José Casanova, eds., *The Jesuits and Globalization: Historical Legacies and Contemporary Challenges* (Washington, DC: Georgetown University Press. 2016), 261; O'Connor, Stimson, and Daly, *Australia's Changing Economic Geography*, 23.
8. 1961 census data is taken from Commonwealth Bureau of Census and Statistics, *Census of the Commonwealth of Australia, 30 June 1961: Volume 8—Australia, Part 1: Cross-Classifications of the Characteristics of the Population* (Canberra, 1965), available at https://www.abs.gov.au/AUSSTATS/abs@.nsf/DetailsPage/2107.01961?OpenDocument.
9. From a statement by Attorney-General Alfred Deakin, September 12, 1901. See National Museum of Australia, "White Australia Policy," https://www.nma.gov.au/defining-moments/resources/white-australia-policy.
10. This figure actually underrepresents non-English-speaking attenders because non-parish migrant centers celebrating Mass did not participate in the NCLS.
11. José Casanova, 'What Is a Public Religion," in Hugh Heclo and Wilfred M. McClay, eds., *Religion Returns to the Public Square: Faith and Policy in America* (Washington, DC: Woodrow Wilson Center Press, 2003), 118.
12. For a full discussion on Mass attenders' responses to these questions in surveys conducted between 1996 and 2011, see Robert Dixon, "Mixed Results for Orthodoxy: The Impact of Contemporary Cultural Change on the Acceptance of Key Catholic Beliefs and Moral Teachings by Australian Mass Attenders," in Giuseppe Giordan and William Swatos, eds., *Testing Pluralism: Globalizing Belief, Localizing Gods* (Leiden: Brill, 2013). See also Robert Dixon, "What Do Mass Attenders Believe," available at https://ncpr.catholic.org.au/what-do-mass-attenders-believe/. Catholic parishes did not take part in the 1996 NCLS but did engage in a parallel survey called the Catholic Church Life Survey. Between 2001 and 2016 the Catholic Church participated fully in the NCLS.
13. These soon-to-be-published figures come from a survey commissioned by Catholic Religious Australia and have been supplied courtesy of the National Centre for Pastoral Research.
14. Stephen Reid, Robert Dixon, and Noel Connolly, *See I Am Doing a New Thing: A Report on the 2009 Survey of Catholic Religious Institutes in Australia* (Mulgrave: Garratt, 2010).
15. Pastoral Leadership Task Group, *Tomorrow's Church Report: A Plan for Leadership* (Melbourne: Archdiocese of Melbourne, 1994). This was one example of many dioceses' efforts to address the challenges associated with declining numbers of priests and changes in the role of laypeople.
16. Nicole Hancock, Miriam Pepper, and Ruth Powell, "Attitudes to Abortion," NCLS Research Fact Sheet 14010 (Adelaide: Mirrabooka, 2014).
17. Marie Macdonald et al., *Woman and Man: One in Christ Jesus: Report on the Participation of Women in the Catholic Church in Australia* (Melbourne: HarperCollins, 1999), xi–xii.
18. Macdonald et al., viii.
19. Robert Dixon, *The Catholic Community in Australia* (Melbourne: Openbook, 2005), 38. See also www.opw.catholic.org.au/.
20. Sandie Cornish and Andrea Deane, eds., *Still Listening to the Spirit: Woman and Man 20 Years On* (Canberra: Office for Social Justice of the Australian Catholic Bishops Conference, 2019).
21. Sandie Cornish, "Introduction," in Sandie Cornish and Andrea Dean, eds., *Still Listening to the Spirit: Woman and Man 20 Years On* (Canberra: Office for Social Justice of the Australian Catholic

Bishops' Conference, 2019), xxvi. See also Tracy McEwan and Kathleen McPhillips, "Re-Framing Religious Identity and Belief: Gen X Women and the Catholic Church," *Journal for the Academic Study of Religion* 30, no. 3 (2017): 205–26.

22. Australian Catholic Bishops Conference 2019, "Malcolm Hart to lead National Centre for Evangelisation," media release, December 16, 2019, https://mediablog.catholic.org.au/malcolm-hart-to-lead-national-centre-for-evangelisation/.
23. See Marie Keenan, *Child Sexual Abuse in the Catholic Church: Gender, Power and Organizational Culture* (New York: Oxford University Press, 2012).
24. See https://www.childabuseroyalcommission.gov.au/. A royal commission is a government-instigated formal independent public inquiry.
25. Royal Commission into Institutional Responses to Child Sexual Abuse, "Analysis of Claims of Child Sexual Abuse Made with respect to Catholic Church Institutions in Australia," Sydney, June 2017, accessed September 14, 2017, at https://www.childabuseroyalcommission.gov.au/sites/default/files/CARC.0050.025.0001.pdf.
26. https://www.childabuseroyalcommissionresponse.gov.au/sites/default/files/2020-11/Response-Holy-See.pdf.
27. Robert Dixon and Stephen Reid, "Mass Attenders' Responses to the Clergy Sexual Abuse Crisis: A Report to the Truth Justice and Healing Council on Questions included in the 2016 National Church Life Survey" (Canberra: Australian Catholic Bishops Conference Pastoral Research Office, 2018).
28. This unpublished figure was provided by the National Centre for Pastoral Research.
29. Reid, Dixon, and Connolly, *See I Am Doing a New Thing*, 10.
30. Gabrielle McMullen, "Response to Bishop Vincent's 2021 Helder Camara Lecture," https://vox.divinity.edu.au/opinion/professor-gabrielle-mcmullens-response-to-bishop-vincents-2021-helder-camara-lecture/.
31. Note that sources for these compiled figures used different methods, so they are not strictly comparable. Nevertheless, they give a clear indication of the trend in attendance rates over the years.
32. Robert Dixon, Stephen Reid, and Marilyn Chee, *Mass Attendance in Australia: A Critical Moment* (Melbourne: ACBC Pastoral Research Office, 2013), 4.
33. Robert Dixon et al., "Research Project on Catholics Who Have Stopped Attending Mass: Final Report, February 2007" (Melbourne: Australian Catholic Bishops Conference, 2007), available at https://ncpr.catholic.org.au/research-project-on-catholics-who-have-ceased-attending-mass/.
34. Dixon et al., "Research Project on Catholics," 18.
35. Dixon et al., "Research Project on Catholics."
36. Pastoral Research Office, *Research Project on Catholics Who Have Stopped Attending Mass: Pastoral Strategies* (Melbourne: Australian Catholic Bishops Conference, 2007), available at https://ncpr.catholic.org.au/research-project-on-catholics-who-have-ceased-attending-mass/.
37. National Office for Evangelisation, *Reconnect: A Program for Inactive Catholics: Program Leaders Manual* (Canberra: Australian Catholic Bishops Conference, 2008); and National Office for Evangelisation, *Rewired: A Catholic Program for Evangelising Young People: Youth Leader's Manual* (Canberra: Australian Catholic Bishops Conference, 2008).
38. The Pastoral Research Office was renamed National Centre for Pastoral Research in 2018.
39. Trudy Dantis and Robert Dixon, *Building Stronger Parishes: Project Report* (Canberra: Australian Catholic Bishops Conference, 2015). This report and other documents relating to the project can be accessed at https://www.buildingstrongerparishes.catholic.org.au/research-publications/. See also Trudy Dantis, *A Handbook for Building Stronger Parishes* (Mulgrave: Garratt, 2016).
40. Andrew Markus, *Mapping Social Cohesion: The Scanlon Foundation Surveys, 2020* (Caulfield East: Scanlon Foundation and Monash University, 2021), available at https://scanloninstitute.org.au/report2020.
41. Robert Dixon, *The Catholic Community in Australia* (Adelaide: Openbook, 2005), 30.

42. Andrew P. Lynch, "Negotiating Social Inclusion: The Catholic Church in Australia and the Public Sphere," *Social Inclusion* 4, no. 2 (2016): 107–16.
43. See https://plenarycouncil.catholic.org.au/.
44. Trudy Dantis et al., *Listen to What the Spirit Is Saying: Final Report for the Plenary Council, Phase 1: Listening and Dialogue* (Canberra: Australian Catholic Bishops Conference, 2019).
45. All the documents referred to here can be accessed at https://plenarycouncil.catholic.org.au/keydocuments/.
46. Catholics for Renewal, *Getting Back on Mission: Reforming Our Church Together* (Mulgrave: Garratt, 2019).
47. See, for example, Terry Kean, "Reforming the Church and Australia's Plenary Council," *La Croix International*, February 22, 2021, https://international.la-croix.com/news/religion/reforming-the-church-and-australias-plenary-council/13838.
48. Vincent Long Van Nguyen, Bishop of Parramatta, "My Hope for the Plenary Council," Dom Helder Camara Lecture, Newman College, Parkville, Victoria, June 30, 2021, https://catholicoutlook.org/bishop-vincent-my-hope-for-the-plenary-council/.
49. "Come Home to Mass! On Returning to the Eucharist Following Easing of COVIDSafe Restrictions," Eighth Pastoral Letter of the Archbishop of Sydney to the Clergy and Faithful during the COVID-19 Pandemic, Third Sunday of Advent, December 13, 2020, available at https://www.sydneycatholic.org/coronavirus-updates/. See also Archdiocese of Hobart, "Obligation to Attend Sunday Mass Reinstated as of 26 October," at https://hobart.catholic.org.au/2020/10/23/obligation-to-attend-sunday-mass-reinstated-as-of-26-october/.

11

Global Influences in the Growth of the Catholic Church in the Pacific Region

PHILIP GIBBS, SVD

THE LIQUID CONTINENT

The Pacific is home to a much smaller human population than that of Asia, but it is sometimes called the "liquid continent" or the "sea of islands" because it covers almost a third of the earth's surface.[1] The term Pacific here refers to the Islands of Oceania (sometimes grouped as Micronesia, Melanesia, and Polynesia), which includes Aotearoa New Zealand in the south, the Mariana Islands in the northwest, Papua New Guinea in the west, Rapa Nui in the southeast, and Hawaii in the northeast. It does not include Australia, the Philippines, Taiwan, Japan, the Galápagos Islands, or the Aleutian Islands. (There is some ambiguity over West Papua, which has cultural links with Melanesia, but politically it is part of Indonesia.)

Today the Pacific Islands comprise twenty-five nations with varying political statuses, a reflection of colonial history from the eighteenth and nineteenth centuries. They are independent nations (Fiji, Kiribati, Nauru, Aotearoa New Zealand, Papua New Guinea, Samoa, Solomon Islands, Tuvalu, and Vanuatu), a US state (Hawaii), US territories (American Samoa, Guam), a free association with the United States (Marshall Islands), a US commonwealth (Northern Mariana Islands), free associations with New Zealand (Cook Islands, Niue), a New Zealand dependency (Tokelau), a federation (Federated States of Micronesia, Palau), and territories of France (Wallis and Futuna, New Caledonia, French Polynesia). Rapa Nui is a dependency of Chile, Pitcairn Island a British dependency, and West Papua a state of Indonesia. The complex and varied political status of these nations reflects a long history of global impact on the region.

In recent centuries the lives of people in the Pacific have been impacted by diverse global forces, mostly originating in Europe. It was not always so. The Pacific Islands have been settled in various migrations out of Southeast Asia. Fifty thousand years ago, when the earth was experiencing a cooler period and the ocean was more than 100 meters lower than its current level, it would have been possible for people in some parts to walk on dry land between what are islands today. Later oceangoing canoes enabled explorers to travel to distant islands,

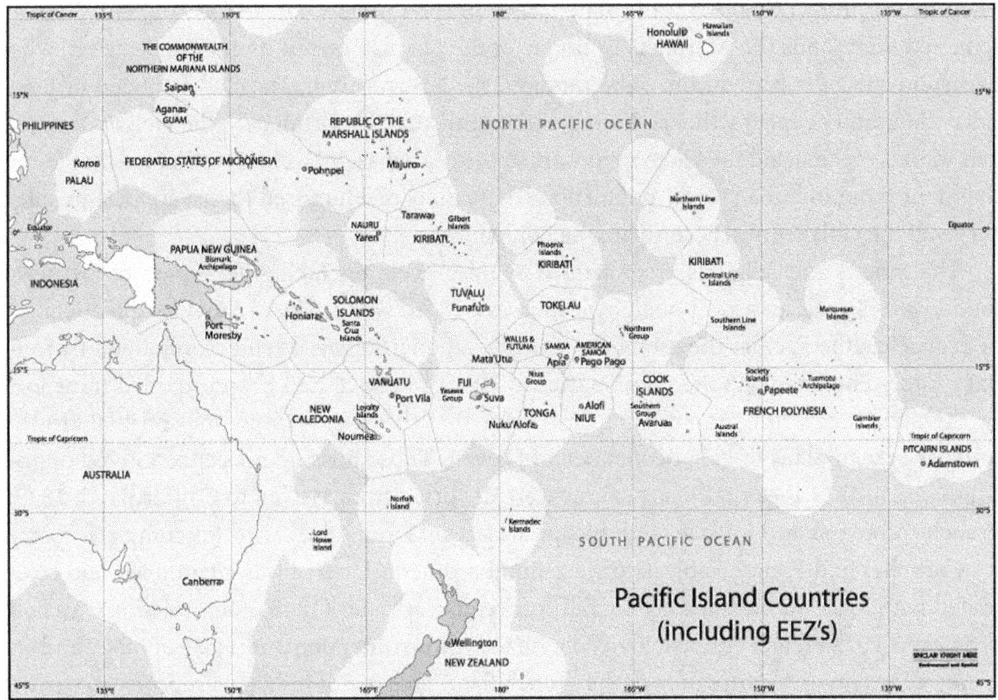

FIGURE 11.1. Map of Pacific Island Countries

leading to human settlement beginning in the Society Islands between AD 1025 and 1120 and in Aotearoa New Zealand between AD 1250 and 1300.

In 1493, with the papal bull Inter caetera, Alexander VI granted the right to the kings of Portugal and Spain to propagate the Catholic faith in the new territories they were opening up in the Americas. He did this by drawing a line pole to pole, dividing East from West through what is now Brazil, giving Portugal the right of royal patronage to the East and Spain to the West. The papal bull and the decision of the Treaty of Tordesillas the following year stirred European explorers into looking for a westward route to the "spice Islands" (Moluccas in Southeast Asia). In 1519, Portuguese explorer Ferdinand Magellan called the ocean "Pacifico" on finding calm waters after the stormy seas he encountered while rounding Cape Horn. He then traversed the Pacific, landing briefly on the island of Guam and arriving in the Philippines. Thus the two dominant kingdoms of Europe reached the Pacific from both west and east and at much the same time in the early sixteenth century.[2]

BEGINNING OF CHRISTIAN EVANGELIZATION IN THE PACIFIC

Christian evangelization in the Pacific began during the period of Iberian expansion when in 1668 Jesuit priests and brothers came from the Philippines to Guam—in what were then known as the Ladrones (Thieves) Islands. The missionaries accompanied a military garrison intended to protect Spanish trade. The leader of the mission, Diego Luis de San Vitores, renamed the islands the Marianas in honor of the Spanish queen mother and regent, who had sponsored the expedition.[3] The missionaries lost no time, and had baptized at least thirty thousand people by the beginning of the third year. Unfortunately, the violent death of San Vitores precipitated the Chamorro wars in the Marianas. It has been estimated that fewer than four thousand of a prewar population (of possibly one hundred thousand local people) survived the violence and accompanying epidemics.[4]

That priests and religious accompanied Spanish explorers taking possession of the new-found lands signals an aspect of globalization associated with many of the subsequent efforts to evangelize the Pacific: the establishment of Catholicism was often accompanied by military force. The first Catholic missionaries to Hawaii in 1828 had been provided transport by the French government, arousing suspicions that they were simply the spiritual arm of broader French plans to gain occupancy of Hawaii. Those missionaries encountered opposition and in 1831 the two Picpus priests were deported from Hawaii to California. In 1839, French commandant La Place, with his naval boat off Honolulu, called for complete liberty for Catholics and French subjects or face bombardment. Liberty was guaranteed and celebrated with Mass on Bastille Day. In Tahiti several years later (1848), after missionaries had been expelled, a French gunboat arrived with the commander demanding an apology and an honorific twenty-one-gun salute to the French flag.[5] This use of military firepower to ensure continued presence on some of the Pacific Islands prompted Marist missionary Jean-Xavier Montrouzier, in a letter to the Holy See, to ask whether on encountering new people it was necessary for the sailors accompanying them "to show themselves ready for battle."[6]

The use of military force by occupying powers was only one aspect of global politics impacting the lives of people in the Pacific. The Spanish were supplanted in the Pacific by incoming merchants, explorers, and scientific expeditions sent out by the Dutch, British, French, and Germans. The United States took over Guam after the Spanish-American War of 1898, and Spain sold the northern Mariana Islands and its other Micronesian "possessions" to Germany.[7] Global politics and mercantile maneuverings by whalers, traders, sandalwood buyers, and beachcombers, along with the accompanying spread of fatal diseases and the introduction of firearms, meant radical changes for people of the Pacific. The Church was founded in the midst of these changes.

COLONIAL EXPANSION AND THE CATHOLIC CHURCH

The growth of the Catholic Church in the nineteenth century closely follows colonial expansion in the region. Before official colonization, following the three exploratory voyages of Capt. James Cook between 1768 and 1779, British influence remained strong throughout much of the Pacific. British colonies were established in New Zealand in 1840 and in Fiji in 1872. The Gilbert and Ellice Islands were administered as a British protectorate from 1892 and Niue from 1900. Even before official colonization, national self-interest made it difficult for missionaries of one nationality to work in a territory controlled by a rival nation. At the time, with the restored papacy after the Napoleonic suppression, the restored monarchy of

France took over the missionary initiative from the older maritime Catholic powers of Portugal and Spain, and Catholic missionaries to the Pacific were predominantly French.

In 1844, France raised its flag on New Caledonia, but took it down two years later, prompting a suggestion that the pope might be interested in making New Caledonia a papal colony—after all, there were papal states in Europe, so why not a papal colony in the Pacific? Pope Pius IX declined, reasoning that "the pope is not and must not be a conquistador."[8] In 1854, France retook possession of New Caledonia, turning it into a penal colony from the 1860s to 1897, when prisoner transportations ended. With the declaration of a protectorate over Tahuata in 1842, France regarded the entire Marquesas Islands as French. These political moves opened the way for evangelization by Catholic missionaries, particularly those belonging to the Society of Mary, commonly known as Marists.

In Micronesia, missionary influence was very much dependent on the colonial interests of several nations. On the Micronesian island of Yap, Spanish Jesuit missionaries came in 1710 and again in 1731, at a time when Spain controlled shipping in the region. Their mission was interrupted when the missionaries were killed. A century and a half later, in 1886, with the intention of establishing a colonial government, Spain sent a governor to the Western Caroline Islands, with the support of fifty Filipino troops and a number of Filipino convicts. Six Spanish Capuchin missionaries accompanied them. Fourteen years later, after the sinking of a US battleship in Cuba, the resultant Spanish-American War ended with Spain selling the Caroline and Mariana Islands to Germany for 25 million pesetas in June 1899. With the exit of the Spanish, German missionaries began again the evangelization of Yap. Following the First World War, in 1921 Spanish Jesuits replaced the German Capuchin missionaries only to be replaced after the Second World War by American Jesuits.[9] Each change of political control brought about a change in Church personnel and their different approaches and varied degrees of access to resources.[10]

In the early nineteenth century came Catholic mission efforts that were coordinated and to a large extent controlled by the Congregation for the Propagation of the Faith based in Rome. The purpose of the Congregation was to organize and direct the missionary activity of the Catholic Church under the immediate supervision of the pope. Through the work of the Congregation, in 1825 Pope Leo XII approved the first official body of Church governance in the Pacific: the Prefecture Apostolic of the Sandwich (Hawaiian) Islands.[11] Four years later Pope Pius VIII established the Prefecture Apostolic of the South Sea Islands.

Jean-Baptiste-François Pompallier was a key person in founding the Catholic Church in the Pacific. In 1836, he was appointed as vicar apostolic of the new Vicariate of Western Oceania by Pope Gregory XVI.[12] Pompallier's initial plan was to visit the Tahiti and Tonga Islands and then go to New Guinea. Later he changed his plans, starting his mission in New Zealand.

With the political rivalry at the time between Great Britain and France, both nations had plans to establish colonies in New Zealand. In 1937, William Ullathorne, vicar general to the bishop of Sydney, had sent news to the English Benedictines that the British government had decided to colonize New Zealand and intended to send a Protestant bishop there.[13] In February 1840, the British governor conducted the Treaty of Waitangi, signed by representative of the British Crown and various Māori chiefs from the North Island of New Zealand. In July that same year, French captain Charles François Lavaud sailed to Banks Peninsula on the South Island of New Zealand in preparation for the founding of a French colony. An established English colony was nearby, and both colonies were being protected by vessels from their own countries. Bishop Pompallier found himself in a difficult position. The government officials were British and he spoke little English. He lived with a sense that "the only ones who love me cordially and have complete confidence in me are the New Zealanders [Māori]."[14] Aware of the Napoleonic Wars and the possibility of warfare breaking out locally between Britain and France, the bishop speculated that the British authorities in New Zealand might expel him, and he prepared to evacuate to islands to the north.

GLOBAL ECONOMIC TENSIONS

Global economic issues had a significant impact on initial missionary efforts, since French missionaries in the mid-nineteenth century relied almost entirely on funding from Europe. Isolated in New Zealand, Bishop Pompallier was running up debts, which brought him tension with the Marist administration in Europe. Father Jean-Claude Colin, the Marist superior, accused the bishop of getting "involved imprudently in a labyrinth of debts which compromise your honour and the mission itself and which reduce your co-workers to go begging even at the doors of the Protestants."[15] Economic instability in Europe also affected the Marist superior, who raised finances for the missions through the profits of a trading company. The company failed partly because of the 1848 revolution in France, which overthrew the French monarchy, precipitating a market crash.

The political and economic situation in Europe also affected the capacity of the Congregation for Evangelization in Rome. In 1870, the Italian state confiscated the patrimony of the Congregation, which was the source from which the Congregation drew its funds for missionary work.[16] The situation in the Pacific began to change only in the latter years of the nineteenth century, when German missionaries sought to be less reliant on funds from Europe and to generate funds locally by establishing commercial ventures such as coconut plantations.

TENSIONS STEMMING FROM THE REFORMATION IN EUROPE

Right from the start, animosity and prejudice already existing between Protestants and Catholics in America and Europe turned into a global issue affecting the local situation throughout the Pacific islands. In Polynesia, Protestant missions had been established long before the Catholic missionaries appeared. French Catholic missionaries arriving in the Marquesas Islands in 1834 were met with a letter from Rev. David Darling of the LMS: "My dear Gentlemen . . . We would like you to withdraw to some other group of islands, since we have taken possession of the Gambier Islands before you. . . . It should be up to you to leave them and go to some other Islands."[17] Not all exchanges between Protestant and Catholic were as polite. Tensions between missions flared up in New Caledonia in the 1860s, with Franco-British and Catholic-Protestant recriminations. In Hawaii, Protestant missionaries assisted King

Kamehameho II of the Sandwish Islands to establish an ordinance declaring that any ship's master transporting Catholic teachers would have the ship forfeited to the chiefs. In 1852, in Tonga there was a short civil war when Principal (and Methodist) Chief Taufa'sahou Tupou defeated chiefs on Tongatabu who had tried to use their Catholicism to be independent in the strongly Protestant kingdom.[18]

In some parts, civil authorities attempted to establish a comity agreement whereby mission boundaries were accepted but with different mission groups confined to specific areas. Catholic missionaries rejected this arrangement, claiming that it was interference in religious liberty and that it ran contrary to their mandate to bring the Church to all humanity.[19] While the transplanting of Reformation tensions from Europe and America to the Pacific had a weighty influence on the lives of early missionaries and the establishment and growth of the Church in the Pacific Islands, it did at times help motivate Catholic missionaries to seek new lands, such as the islands of Melanesia, as yet only evangelized by missionaries from other churches.

POWER AND THE UNDERSIDE OF HISTORY

Cultural and historical entanglements between local and global forces have impacted the interpretation of events, such as the violent death of some missionaries. In 1672, a Jesuit missionary in Guam, Fr. Diego Luis de San Vitores, was killed after he persisted in baptizing the chief's infant daughter against the chief's explicit warnings. The global version of the event is told in terms of genuine martyrdom as defined under the official Church discourse about martyrdom, including the negative historical and cultural representation of the Native people. However, today some local people in Guam question whether those who resisted the missionary must be seen as villains and whether the story should be differently seen as a narrative of the underside of history. Guam has been a site of global forces, both Western (Spanish and Catholic, followed by American) and Asian, notably Japanese imperial interests during World War II. Now some local Chamorros are consciously linking their social and political plight as a colony of the United States to a longer history of subjugation by the Catholic Church.[20]

Why people of the Pacific would accept a global religion has few clear answers. Historian John Garrett suggests a sociopolitical explanation: "Receptiveness to the new religion sprang from readiness to believe that the God of the newcomers, like the ships, must be more powerful than their own."[21] Visits of missionaries (and sailors) brought nails, iron tools, clothing, glass objects, and firearms, which local people found attractive. Some scholars consider this exchange resulted in the concept of "cargo" and the development of so-called cargo cults.[22] Material considerations were not the only concerns.[23] Throughout the Pacific, initial adoption of Christianity was often a choice by certain chiefs who imposed it on their subjects and used it to establish power over their rivals. In this sense there was a strong continuity with the past, as politics and religion operated in the same sphere of social life.

Adoption of religious practice does not necessarily mean conversion in a deeper sense. While there was rapid acceptance of outward elements of religious practice, such as introduced forms of clothing and attendance at church services, yet, at a different level, worldviews seldom change rapidly and in many cases an amalgam of two religious systems of interpreting the world was formed. For example, when biomedical explanations are given for the physical cause of death, the reasons behind death or misfortune could be attributed to sorcery or other occult forces. The very presence of the missionaries introduced Island people to new domains in terms of imagined spaces and mental mappings. People of Rooke Island near Papua New Guinea asked whether the priests and brothers had actually been born as babies, if there were white women, and whether white people died.[24] How much the missionaries changed people's imaginings and mental mappings at a deeper level through the experience of an encounter with people whose life experiences were very different from themselves is a matter for further consideration. Coming with belief that Pacific people are "savages" or people with "few ideas" presented an obstacle for some, but motivated others to study the language and life of the people.[25]

INCULTURATION OF THE GLOBAL TO THE LOCAL

Many missionaries saw their missionary work as a challenge to replace traditional customs with what, from their perspective, they considered new and better ones. In Palau, clubhouse prostitution, the ease of divorce and remarriage, and sorcery and spirit communication were among the main targets of the missionary campaign.[26] On Rooke Island in Melanesia, the missionaries tried unsuccessfully to oppose what they saw as the practice of infanticide.[27]

Catholic missionaries struggled to adapt aspects of ritual that were regarded as part of the Catholic faith but that did not fit with the local context. This meant the lengthy process of asking for dispensations through their superiors in Rome. For example, rubrics required them to use candles made of beeswax for Mass. However, beeswax was a rare commodity in the Pacific, but whaling was flourishing and whaling vessels were frequent visitors to the islands of Melanesia. A letter went to Rome with a request to use whale oil in the place of beeswax at Mass.[28] Other requests were made concerning the number of feast days to be celebrated and faculties for granting indulgences.[29] Even deciding how to determine the date was at times a source of controversy because of global concerns. The international date line runs through the middle of the Pacific with groups of islands not far distant being a day apart calendar-wise. Older missionaries insisted that their sabbath was set to coincide exactly with Jerusalem, whereas others followed the division based on the international date line.[30]

Use of local language was another issue referred to Rome. In 1852, French Marist priest Montrouzier asked for permission to use the local language for singing at all church services, noting that the local language had been banned by the Constitution *Annus quo* of Pope Benedict XIV and by a decree of the Congregation of Rites on March 24, 1653. Montrouzier pointed out how songs in the vernacular "captivate" the local people for the Church.[31] The existence of a tradition of songs in the vernacular indicates that the Roman response was positive. However, while words are in the vernacular, often they were used with tunes originating in Europe.

FROM COLONIALISM TO INDEPENDENCE

After the Second World War, the position of the Catholic Church in many parts of the Pacific was strongly influenced by the movement from colonialism to independence and the establishment of a local church. Moves for independence presented a new situation for the Catholic Church. France was engaged in nuclear testing in the Pacific and was insisting that its colonies remain as overseas French territories. Whereas a century before the links with Western powers, particularly France, had proved to be advantageous in forcing recognition of freedom of religion, now, in the postcolonial era, the Church found that links to Western powers provoked suspicion on the part of Indigenous people.[32]

Tongan writer Epeli Hau'ofa points out how nineteenth-century colonialism erected boundaries "that led to the contraction of Oceania, transforming a once boundless world into the Pacific islands states and territories that we know today." People were confined to their tiny islands, marked by artificial boundaries defined by others, when in fact they had sources of wealth and cultural enrichment across the whole ocean. "This is the historical basis of the view that our countries are small, poor and isolated. It is true only in so far as people are still fenced in and quarantined."[33] The colonial confines began to change with independence, and between 1962 and 1980 nine Pacific states achieved independence.[34] Such developments required not only a new national identity but in many ways also a new Christian identity. In this context former Catholic priest John Momis was among those stressing that people are meant to be the subjects or agents of history and that people in newly independent nations had the opportunity and responsibility to be involved in the actual process of molding society. This required a new attention to the public dimension of the Church's mission.[35]

Momis was not alone. Bishop Patelesio Finau of Tonga took the lead in working for structural change, particularly in the Kingdom of Tonga. He questioned not only the Church but the political establishment throughout the Pacific, noting how the Church was called to challenge the inequality supported by traditional elites and how the tradition of "the Pacific way" of respect and politeness can lead to people being so respectful that they refuse to name a culprit and sometimes fail to name a problem. This amounts to selling out on authenticity in favor of keeping up an image of being peaceful, polite, and respectful.[36]

CHURCH AND STATE

In the Pacific, religiosity is typically an orthodox and often taken-for-granted component of Pacific identity and, by extension, public life. Papua New Guinean Catholic philosopher and former cabinet minister Bernard Narokobi, author of the book *The Melanesian Way*, argues that differentiation between religious and nonreligious experiences is foreign to many people of Melanesia, who view the world as an integrated whole.[37] Thus many Pacific countries have not gone through the experience of modernity—distinguishing between sacred and secular—that has shaped modern European cultures and Christian faith.[38] While in theory there might be a separation of church and state, in practice such separation is far from the case. In Papua New Guinea (PNG), as in many Pacific nations, the secular has a negative connotation and religious language is notable in public discourse.[39] The public role of the church in Papua New Guinea is most probably aided by the fact that the Catholic Church plays an important role in wider society as a primary provider of over a third of educational and health facilities in the country, and often the exclusive provider in many isolated rural areas.

In Fiji, much of the debate in recent times over the new Fiji constitution has been whether Fiji is defined as a secular state or a Christian state, with the understanding by some that if the state is considered secular then God is absent. Many Taukei (Indigenous) Christians share conceptions about an active relationship between the Taukei community, the church, and the state.[40]

Manfred Ernst, editor of the most comprehensive volume on globalization in the Pacific, points out the downside of Pacific religious identity whereby Christian churches are an intimate part of the status quo such that there is little incentive for them to critique the negative aspects of globalization and the accompanying neocolonialist system.[41] Momis, now president of Bougainville, when writing as a priest at the time of PNG independence in 1975, was critical of the effects of the Church being so integrated in the structure of society. When the Church runs plantations and schools and hospitals it can end up making people dependent, and in doing so it becomes a part of an oppressive system.[42]

CHURCH VERSUS STATE IN VIOLENT CIVIL UNREST

Movements associated with independence have been far from peaceful in the Pacific. In New Caledonia, ex-priest Jean-Marie Tjibaou led the local Kanak population, half of whom are Catholic, to seek independence from French rule. Unrest led to bloodshed and Tjibaou was assassinated in 1989. Meanwhile, the Catholic Church—sometimes referred to as L'Église de Blancs—continued to minister to a population divided as to whether New Caledonia would remain with France or opt for independence (addressed in a referendum in 2018).[43]

Soon after independence in 1980, the new central government of Vanuatu had to call on the help of foreign troops to deal with secessionist movements on the islands of Santo and Tanna. The Catholic bishops of the Pacific tried unsuccessfully to get support from the Pacific Council of Churches for a statement of solidarity with the Christians of Vanuatu.[44]

Fiji achieved a relatively smooth transition to independence in 1970. However, since 1987 there have been several military coups. In the most recent, the Catholic Church, led by Archbishop Petero Mataca, played an important part in seeking a peaceful resolution to tensions.[45] Solomon Islands also had a serious outbreak of violence beginning in 1998, with fighting between the Malaita Eagle Force and the Isatabu Freedom Movement.

The most serious outbreak of violence was in Bougainville Island. On September 1, 1975, fifteen days before Papua New Guinea became independent from Australia, Bougainville raised its secessionist flag of the "Republic of North Solomons." The move was ignored by international interests. A decade later, in 1988, tensions over mining by Bougainville Copper Limited, a subsidiary of the Australian company Conzinc Rio Tinto, led to the Bougainville Crisis—the bloodiest war in the South Pacific since World War II. Over ten thousand people died in the conflict. The crisis was a major concern for the Catholic Church leadership in the region, perhaps partly because the majority of the Bougainville population are Catholic. Bishop Gregory Singkai declared his support for the will of the people of Bougainville, but was then seen as partisan by the Papua New Guinea and Australian governments. Later the bishop was taken hostage and humiliated.[46] There was tension between the government and the Church as the bishops insisted that the military option driven by the government was no solution, as it would only prolong the crisis and bring about more suffering and death. The bishops, highlighting the need to deal with fundamental issues such as ownership of resources, concern for the environment, political succession, and human rights, offered to facilitate dialogue.[47] However, it was only after a series of peace accords spearheaded by the New Zealand government that the killing ended. (The people of Bougainville called for a referendum on independence from Papua New Guinea in 2019.)

Such violent episodes are almost inevitable as people seek a change from being objects of colonial power to becoming the writers of their own history. These situations test the allegiance of the Church, caught between loyalty to international interests (and sources of funds) and commitment to the local churches and their concerns.

SECOND VATICAN COUNCIL

Twenty-seven bishops and vicars apostolic from the Pacific region and five bishops from New Zealand attended the Second Vatican Council (1963–65). Bishops from Oceania were only 2 percent of the bishops in attendance in the Council Hall, having little influence as a group.[48] Unlike some of the bishops' conferences from Europe, meetings by the Pacific bishops during the council were informal and there is little evidence of a common stand taken by the bishops from the region.[49] Their interventions reflect practicalities of life in Oceania. For example, Bishop Pierre-Paul-Émile Martin from New Caledonia wanted to move to the languages of the region and to have better adaptation of the rites of the sacraments and sacramentals to the customs and mentality of the Indigenous people.[50] Bishop Lemay of the North Solomons called for opening the doors and windows of the Church so that all people of goodwill might listen more attentively.[51] Pacific theologian Mikaele Paunga notes how the interventions and written observations of the Oceania bishops "clearly indicate their awareness that the Church is being sent to the contemporary world. It takes into account how people live and experience life in their cultural, socio-political and economic contexts."[52] Four themes from the council supported by the Oceania bishops come through strongly. First is the recognition of the indispensable ministry of the laity; second, ecumenism requires poverty of spirit and humility on behalf of the Church; third, inculturation; which links with the fourth, dialogue with the totality of life of people.

The years immediately following the Council saw big changes in the life of the Church in the Pacific region. One of the foremost was localization, with the ordination of priests, bishops, and religious born in the region. Louis Vangeke had been trained under the Jesuits in Madagascar before being ordained and later becoming bishop among his own people in Papua.[53] The first bishop of Samoa, Pio Taofinu'u, was ordained bishop in 1968 (and elevated to cardinal in 1973). Gregory Singkai was ordained bishop in the North Solomons in 1974,

Petero Mataca in Fiji was ordained bishop in 1974, and Paul Mea of Kiribati became bishop just before independence in 1979.

Religious sisters have provided invaluable service as well, particularly in health, education, and training of catechists. Initially they came as foreign missionaries, but in the twentieth century, particularly after Vatican II, their presence has rapidly become localized at all levels.

BISHOPS' CONFERENCES

The Catholic Church in the Pacific region has formed the Federation of Catholic Bishops Conferences of Oceania (FCBCO) to provide a forum through which members can share their interests and concerns and together plan for common pastoral action. The FCBCO is made up of the four bishops conferences: of Australia (ACBC), of New Zealand (NZCBC), of Papua New Guinea and Solomon Islands CBCPNG/SI, and the Catholic Bishops Conference of the Pacific (CEPAC). The FCBCO was established officially in 1990, though it claims the first meeting of the bishops of the region occurred during the visit of Pope Paul VI to Australia in 1970. The concept of such a body was discussed by the bishops in 1979 after seven bishops from various parts of Oceania were guests of the Federation of Asian Catholic Bishops' Conferences (FABC) while attending the Bishops' Institute for Social Action in the Philippines.

In an address to the FCBCO assembly in Rabaul in 2002, Cardinal Thomas Williams referred to factors that encouraged the establishment of the FCBCO.[54] Of particular importance was the practical matter of the cooperation of the Catholic development organizations and Catholic communication agencies. This required a direct link with a formal episcopal body for effective development in the region.

Documents from the federation indicates that the bishops were attentive particularly to *Gaudium et Spes* (Pastoral Constitution on Church in the Modern World) and Pope Paul VI's *Evangelii Nuntiandi* (Evangelization in the Modern World), both of which emphasized that the world is the concern of the Church in what amounts to a new understanding of the role of the Church in history.[55] The bishops were also inspired by the 1971 Synod of Bishops, which reminded them that it was time for the Church to interpret the signs of the age and proclaim prophetically a better and more humane future when confronted with ingrained structures of injustice. The bishops declared that they were "prepared to become actively involved in helping the peoples of the South Pacific in their struggle for national identity, legitimate self-determination, true freedom and real independence."[56] Work for human development was seen as an integral part of the Church's role. If Latin America would speak of liberation theology, in the Pacific it was a theology of integral human development, including justice and peace.

Integral human development became the principal object of the Pacific Partnership for Human Development (PPHD) initiated in 1972 and formally established by the Joint Bishops' Conference of Oceania meeting in Sydney in 1985. The PPHD was designed to complement similar forums of government development programs in the region.[57] The PPHD appeared to be an important body for involvement of the Church in global issues such as human rights, Indigenous peoples, HIV and AIDS, and models of development. Differing views of the latter issue caused considerable friction within the body when the Australian and

New Zealand delegates refused to support funding arrangements for school buildings and representatives from the Pacific Islands felt they were distrusted and misunderstood. The Pacific bishops wanted a true partnership of equals rather than a donor-receiver relationship. The PPHD was officially dissolved in 1996, with the Pacific bishops deciding to establish their own local development agencies and to give their support to Caritas Internationalis.

FULL MEMBERSHIP IN PACIFIC COUNCIL OF CHURCHES

After Vatican II, and following fruitful dialogue between and among members of several major churches, CEPAC in 1975 gained full membership in the Pacific Council of Churches (PCC). This was a unique and notable occurrence because in other cases worldwide the Catholic Church has had only observer status on such bodies, not full membership. The PCC held its third assembly at the University of Papua New Guinea on January 10–21, 1976, with the theme "God's Mission in the Changing Pacific Society." It was truly a time of change in Papua New Guinea, being less than a year after gaining independence. Bishop Finau from Tonga played a leading part in that meeting. Speaking about development, he called for real changes in church and society: "Discussing the problems of the Pacific means looking at the root problem of injustice because to develop people without justice is hopeless. . . . The emerging Pacific countries have to beware of still being colonial in mentality—of blindly and docilely accepting all the worst features of western materialism." He warned delegates "to beware of the new and old local oppressors whose oppressive roles are camouflages because they are local people." They "are worse than the western oppressors, and here we have to look at the chiefs and the nobles in our island societies."[58]

The PCC spoke out strongly against nuclear testing in the Pacific.[59] This presented a conflict of interest for bishops from countries that were still French territories. The presence of French military personnel contributed to the economy and their standard of living. Nevertheless, the PCC, along with Catholic Bishops participating, released strong statements reflecting the increasing impatience of Pacific Islanders with the leftovers of European colonialism and the worst features of globalization. They distributed resolutions such as the following: "We ask all our churches to bring together in thought and action those who seek personal evangelism with those who seek social justice, an end to racism, the preservation of our environment, the permanent departure of foreign troops and an end to nuclear testing. We also ask for watchfulness against exploitation of our countries by greedy commercial forces."[60]

Regrettably, in recent times the commitment to ecumenism has dramatically decreased in the region. The strong ecumenical spirit that flourished in the Pacific from the 1960s to the 1980s seems to have faded away, and in 2017 not a single national council is functioning well.[61] There have been disagreements in the past between the churches and the government on development issues. For example, the Churches Partnership Program (CPP) in Papua New Guinea is said to be an example of ecumenical cooperation, though there are limits because a program funded by the Australian government excludes debate on faith issues and Church matters. In reality, the CPP was not primarily about working cooperatively but about gaining access to Australian funds for Church projects. It could even be said that the program has weakened the Papua New Guinea Council of Churches when churches set up their own CPP offices.

The fact that newer churches are growing at the expense of the mainline churches has led to mistrust, suspicion, and a general trend toward denominationalism, whereby individual churches concentrate on the internal affairs of their own church in an effort to stop the outgoing decline of membership.[62]

SEARCH FOR A COMMON PASTORAL STRATEGY: THE SELF-STUDY IN PNG

The Self-Study of the Catholic Church in Papua New Guinea over three years (1972–75) was another major development in the Church in the Pacific following the Second Vatican Council. In 1968, the Tanzanian bishops launched a seminar study year to involve as many Catholics as possible in reflection upon the mission of the Church in Tanzania. In 1971, the director of the Melanesian Institute in Goroka, PNG, Fr. Herman Janssen, visited Tanzania and was impressed by the program there. He reported back to the Catholic bishops in PNG, who then decided to follow a process of self-reflection similar to what was taking place in Tanzania. Fr. Francis Murray, the organizer of the study year in Tanzania, was invited to guide the Catholic Church in Papua New Guinea in what came to be called a "self-study" of the Catholic Church.

Eighty-three position papers were written by specialists, as well as missionaries, seminarians, and catechists, in preparation for the two-week self-study workshop in November and December 1972. At that 1972 meeting Bishop Peter Korongku presented a paper with the title "The Indigenous Laity of Papua New Guinea Today Must Play a Greater Role in the Life of the Church by a Greater Share in the Decision-Making and in Responsibility within the Church."[63] Bishop Korongku argued that it is not enough to have local clergy for the Church to be considered indigenous. Rather, it is a matter of giving the administration of the Church to the (lay) people. "We taught our people to be silent and to accept things quietly. This is the price we now have to pay for being so mean and so selfish in not sharing our responsibilities with our lay people." He continued, "I am happy that people are working hard for indigenization, and I can say that we must make this indigenization an actualization and not just the object of a lot of theoretical talk and written words."

Papers from the 1972 conference were edited into the *Diocesan Seminar Handbook* containing thirty-five chosen papers. Controlled English and Pidgin texts were prepared, with 7,500 copies of each version printed. The self-study continued over three years, with meetings held in villages, hamlets, towns, and schools and among special organizations like teachers colleges, university faculty, and police and army groups. "From the middle of 1973 till the end of 1974 thousands of discussions took place in churches, halls, huts and under trees."[64] It is estimated that a third of all Catholic faithful in PNG (at least 250,000 people) participated in some way.[65]

During the years of the self-study, the PNG was preparing for self-governance and independence, so localization and indigenization were topics for debate. In a letter to the *Post Courier* newspaper, student leader at the UPNG Michael Mel supported statements made by Chief Minister Michael Somare, who had said that the Catholic Church should accept the challenge of self-government and independence. Mel wrote: "We think there are enough local priests to get at least another three bishops who will then look after four regions of the country.[66] He continued: "The Western clergy should now no longer call themselves missionaries, rather servants of the indigenous church. It means the church run by the indigenous people and in accordance to their way of life, and the white sector serving. After all they came to serve, not to be Masters."[67]

It became apparent during the years of the self-study that there was a positive (if limited) response to the call for indigenization within the Church. At the beginning of the self-study, in the aftermath of the colonial experience, catechists and church workers were found to be very dependent upon expatriate missionaries for initiative, advice, and organization, and few self-confident local leaders existed with the Christian community. This changed during the self-study. An observer from Australia, Cyril Halley, comments, "The most important achievement of the Self Study was the fact that thousands of villagers became aware that they are the Church and that it is not an organisation run by expatriate missionaries. Allied to this change in the people was the realisation by many of the expatriates of the same truth."[68]

The change was apparent when it came time for the national assembly held in May 1975. PNG had achieved self-government in 1973 and independence was only months away. Educated nationals had been drafting the constitution. The University of Papua New Guinea had started in 1968 and the first graduates were emerging. Many of these were Catholic, including a good number of ex-seminarians. If the people in Papua New Guinea had been consulted about the national constitution, then why not involve the people in planning for the future of the Church?

Unlike the workshop in 1972, where only three papers were written by national Papua New Guineans, three years later fifty-two of the seventy-eight official delegates at the assembly were national; forty were laypeople. Documents were written in Melanesian Pidgin and translated into controlled English. The chairmen were all nationals and the main language used was Tok Pidgin. The transition from global mission to Indigenous church is indicated by the top priority topic, which received 72 votes: "We Are Church."[69]

A SYNOD FOR OCEANIA

The 1998 Synod for Oceania was another special moment of identity for the Catholic Church in the Pacific.[70] Oceania was recognized by Church authorities in Rome as a region with its own identity. The original Roman plan in preparation for the Jubilee Year 2000 envisaged only four regional synods, with Oceania's being subsumed under Asia's. However, the appeal of the Oceania cardinals for a specifical Oceania synod was supported by the 1995 Consistory of Cardinals and accepted by Pope John Paul II.[71]

In November 1998, the Catholic bishops of Oceania—from Australia, New Zealand, the Pacific Islands, Papua New Guinea, and the Solomon Islands—traveled to Rome to attend the Special Assembly of the Synod of Bishops for Oceania. It was like the fruits of centuries of mission returning now to Rome to witness their coming of age as Church. There had been synods previous to this: for the bishops of Africa, Asia, and America and for Europe, which was in the final stages of preparation. But this synod for Oceania was special in a number of aspects. It was the shortest in duration, and the smallest of the synods in terms of number of attendees: 117 members, plus the pope, 19 auditors, and 14 additional personnel. This was the only synod in which all the bishops of the region had been invited; in fact, all except three of the bishops from the region participated. Most of the bishops already knew one another, many having met at the Federation of Catholic Bishops Conferences of Oceania (FCBCO) assembly in Auckland in 1994.

The impressive opening Mass in St. Peter's Basilica included dancing and music from the Pacific, notably Samoa. It seems that some Roman officials were rather critical of shirtless tattooed Samoan men in traditional dress dancing in the basilica. Perhaps it is symbolic of the cultural gulf when sights that are quite "normal" in the Pacific appear so scandalous to some members of the Roman Curia?

Talks presented by the bishops during the first week were pastorally oriented and very frank. For example, in his presentation referring to the shortage of priests, Bishop Ambrose Kiapseni of Kavieng, PNG, said that it seems the community's right to celebrate the Eucharist has become a rare privilege and that celebrations of the Word with Holy Communion distributed by a catechist or nonordained brother or sister are no substitute for the celebration of the Eucharist.[72] Bishop Kiapseni, without mentioning it explicitly in his intervention, touched on the issue of ordination of mature married men (*viri probati*). It seems that this was one of the "taboo" topics in Rome, but the synod was not deterred, and Synod Proposition 39 on "Communities without the Eucharist" asks that the "Holy Father continue to dialogue with the Bishops" on the matter. In his speech at the presentation of the papal exhortation Ecclesia in Oceania, Cardinal Williams from New Zealand (with many years of experience in Samoa) noted that community, inculturation, and a renewed proclamation of the Gospel in ways appropriate for the peoples of Oceania were the key themes and insights that had emerged from the 1998 Synod of Bishops for Oceania.[73]

DIRECTIONS FOR THE FEDERATION

As one who lives in Papua New Guinea but who travels occasionally to the Pacific and to New Zealand and Australia, I am struck by the cultural and socioeconomic diversity of the region. New Zealand and particularly Australia are relatively affluent nations with efficient modern infrastructure. Most of the other nations are so-called developing countries with modest infrastructure—some resource rich like Papua New Guinea—others environmentally vulnerable such as Kiribati, Tuvalu, and the Marshals. There is an even greater contrast in the public image of the Church with clergy sexual abuse scandals ruining the moral authority of the Catholic Church in New Zealand and Australia, while the Church retains a relatively high social and moral status within the CEPAC and PNG/SI territories. These different contexts affect the profile of the Church in the public sphere and bring diversity to the concerns of the churches of the FCBCO.

Topics of conversation at the federation assemblies since the Synod for Oceania reflect that diversity. At the 2002 assembly in Rabaul, PNG, topics included the post-synodal exhortation Ecclesia in Oceania, the issue of priests in politics, and the unlawful use of arms in the Solomon Islands. Four years later, in Suva, Fiji, there were sessions on pastoral care of people in remote areas, the life-giving gospel as an alternative to secular ideologies, HIV and AIDS, and climate change. In 2010 in Sydney, topics included the sacraments, the canonization of Australian sister Mary McKillop, the challenges and fruits of World Youth Day, and a workshop run by the migration and refugee office. At an assembly in Wellington, New Zealand, in 2014, the bishops reflected on topics such as Australian immigration policy and detention centers, pastoral planning and earthquakes, reading the signs of Fiji times, and responses to preparatory documents for the extraordinary Assembly of the Synod of Bishops. Another assembly, in Suva, Fiji, in February 2023, focused on sea level rise and climate change. Topics discussed in the almost twenty years since the Synod for Oceania reveal a desire on the part of the bishops to pursue an inductive pastoral theology that is capable of responding to issues in the world around them, whether it be evaluating World Youth Day in Australia, earthquakes in New Zealand, or military coups in Fiji.

The environment and climate change issue has emerged as a key one across the region covered by FCBCO. Campaigns in the 1980s against nuclear testing in the Pacific helped raise environmental awareness at the time. Even climate change sceptics like Cardinal George Pell did not distract the concern of the bishops for the environment at the Suva Assembly in 2006. The recent papal encyclical *Laudato Si'* has inspired new interest in all regions of the federation, particularly low-lying countries like Kiribati, whose people are concerned for their very existence. The effects of logging and mining concern the Church in places like Papua New Guinea and the Solomon Islands. "Eco" news appears in diocesan newsletters in New Zealand, and children at Catholic schools are being taught to care for nearby streams. People now question the use of plastic containers for holy oils at the Chrism Mass. It seems that environmental issues and climate change provide a concern for which all four bishop conferences in the federation can cooperate in promoting the social teaching of the Church.

Cardinal Williams has pointed out how it is not just for practical reasons that the bishops come together. They come together for "a journey intended to be travelled together in communion, in unity of faith and unity of love."[74] The formation of the FCBCO has meant that Oceania is recognized as a region in its own right and not simply as an appendage of Asia. It remains to be seen how the Church in Oceania will play an effective public role, standing witness to communion amid diversity, in a region where they are custodians of almost one-third of the earth's surface.

CONCLUSION

Catholicism entered the Pacific in the early modern phase of globalization with the first exploratory visits of Portuguese seafarers in the early sixteenth century and with evangelization by Spanish Jesuits that followed in the seventeenth century. Beginning in the mid-eighteenth century, and for two centuries following during a time of Western hegemonic colonial expansion, missionaries from Europe, mostly from France but later also from Germany, journeyed to Oceania on a "civilizing" mission that included conversion to Christianity. Their efforts were monitored by the Roman Congregation for the Propagation of the Faith. Political rivalries, economic instability, and religious tensions originating in Europe and the Americas had severe repercussions for the founding of the Church in far-off Oceania.

The evolutionary theories of civilization prevailing at the time influenced missionaries' attitude toward the Native people as "savages" who should be saved, or at least "civilized." Such ethnocentric attitudes, along with colonial economic interests, formed a background to the global interests impacting the lives of Pacific people. There were some successful attempts to learn local languages as a means to evangelization, but prior to Vatican II there was little emphasis on the intrinsic value of the local or substantial moves toward what today is referred to as "inculturation."

The years following the Second World War and the Second Vatican Council have seen major changes in the Catholic Church in the Pacific, with the establishment of an indigenous hierarchy and a federation of four episcopal conferences in the region. This occurred at a time of immense political and social change for Pacific people, as many nations both attained independence and faced issues such as nuclear testing and violent civil unrest. Tensions were inevitable, as people sought a change from being objects of colonial power to becoming subjects of their own history. The situation tested the allegiance of the Church, caught as she was between loyalty to international interests and commitment to the local church and its concerns. With countries becoming independent politically, the Catholic bishops were aware of the danger of becoming dependent economically in submission to global capitalism. Taking a public stance, they declared that they were prepared to become actively involved with the peoples of the Pacific in their struggle for national identity, legitimate self-determination, true freedom, and real independence. Work for human development based on local realities and concerns was seen as an integral part of the Church's role.

In the 1960s to the 1990s the theology and practice of integral human development became the liberation theology of the Pacific. However, in recent times, with the advance of globalization, the Church in Oceania is faced with the challenge of providing an alternative perspective to the one commonly found in larger industrialized nations, that the Pacific Islands are too small to be significant economic markets but small and poor enough to be sources of geopolitical instability.[75] The Church in Australia and New Zealand is becoming marginalized and is faced with providing an alternative to public opinion that the Church is authoritarian, dogmatic, discriminatory toward women, bigoted against homosexuals, and an obstacle to human progress.[76] Whether in those two relatively modernized nations or in the other developing countries of the Pacific, the challenge for the Church now is to foster visionary leadership that will provide a realistic alternative narrative to modern global trends and promote a credible moral discourse about what kind of societies people seek to collectively create in Oceania.

NOTES

1. See World Council of Churches, "Pacific Conference of Churches," accessed June 4, 2017, https://www.oikoumene.org/en/member-churhces/pacific/pcc; and Epeli Hau'ofa, *We Are the Ocean*: Selected Works (Honolulu: University of Hawaii Press, 2008).
2. Pedrode Valderama, a priest accompanying Magellan across the Pacific Ocean, celebrated the first Mass in the Philippines on March 31, 1521.
3. John Garrett, *To Live Among the Stars: Christian Origins in Oceania* (Suva, Fiji: Institute of Pacific Studies, 1982), 2.
4. Vincent Diaz, *Repositioning the Missionary. Rewriting the Histories of Colonialism, Native Catholicism, and Indigeneity in Guam* (Honolulu: University of Hawaii Press, 2010), 12.
5. Garrett, *To Live Among the Stars*, 254–55; Miriam Kahn, "Placing Tahitian Identities: Rooted in Land and Enmeshed in Representations," in Victoria Lockwood, ed., *Globalization and Culture Change in the Pacific Islands* (Upper Saddle River, NJ: Pearson Education, 2004), 292.
6. Ralph Wiltgen, *The Founding of the Roman Catholic Church in Melanesia and Micronesia, 1850–1875* (Eugene, OR: Pickwick, 2008), 123.
7. Diaz, *Repositioning the Missionary*, 12.
8. Wiltgen, *Founding of the Roman Catholic Church in Oceania*, 444.
9. Franz Hezel, *The Catholic Church in Micronesia: Historical Essays on the Catholic Church in the Caroline-Marshall Islands* (Chicago: Loyola University Press, 1991).
10. Other island groups in Micronesia experienced similar instability. See Hezel, *Catholic Church in Micronesia*.
11. Wiltgen, *Founding of the Roman Catholic Church in Oceania*.
12. Wiltgen, 126.
13. Wiltgen, 202.
14. Wiltgen, 325.
15. Wiltgen, 253.
16. Wiltgen, 496.
17. Wiltgen, 97.
18. Charles Forman, *The Island Churches of the South Pacific* (Maryknoll: Orbis, 1982), 4.
19. Garrett, *To Live Among the Stars*, 231, 243.
20. Diaz, *Repositioning*.
21. Garrett, *To Live Among the Stars*, 5.
22. Max Quanchi and Ron Adams, eds., *Culture and Contact in the Pacific* (Cambridge: Cambridge University Press, 1993), 79.
23. Francoise Douaire-Marsaudon and Gabriele Weichart, *Religious Dynamics in the Pacific: Contemporary Forms and Key Figures of Oceanian Spirituality* (Pacific Credo, 2010) 20, DOI: https://doi.org/10.1163/187489412X628046.
24. Wiltgen, *Founding of the Roman Catholic Church in Oceania*, 175.
25. The founder of the SVD New Guinea Mission gave his view that the missionaries should work with children in schools because the parents were sunk in *versumpftem Heidentum* (the swamps of heathenism). Patrick Gesch adds that "these hard words were soon accompanied by careful studies of many languages throughout the missionary area, and even by ethnological research which was prepared for publication." See Patrick Gesch, "There Can be Neither Black nor White: Relations between Missionaries and Sepik Villagers, *Verbum SVD* 37, nos. 1–2 (1996): 93–118.
26. Hezel, *Catholic Church in Micronesia*, 196.
27. Wiltgen, *Founding of the Roman Catholic Church in Oceania*, 179.
28. Wiltgen, 119.
29. Wiltgen, 125–26.

30. Garrett, *To Live Among the Stars*, 29.
31. Wiltgen, *Founding of the Roman Catholic Church in Oceania*, 129.
32. Philip Gibbs, "Politics and the Mission of the Church in Oceania," *East Asian Pastoral Review* 41, no. 3 (2004): 226.
33. Epeli Hau'ofa, "Our Sea of Islands," in Epeli Hau'ofa, ed., *We Are the Ocean: Selected Works* (Honolulu: University of Hawaii Press, 2008), 10.
34. French and English colonies had a different experience. Great Britain agreed to the gradual emancipation of its colonies and France tended to incorporate them into the French state. The only French possession that is independent is Vanuatu, whose independence was won after a nationalist struggle.
35. John Momis "Theology and Politics," *Catalyst* 5, no. 3 (1975): 9.
36. Patelesio Finau, "The Pacific Way and the South Pacific Commission," in David Mullins, ed., *Bishop Patelesio Finau, SM, of Tonga: He Spoke the Truth in Love: A Selection of His Writings and Speeches* (Auckland: Catholic Publications Centre, 1994). For the "Pacific way," see Ron Crocombe, dir., *The Pacific Way: An Emerging Identity* (Lotu Pasifika Productions, 1976); and Stephanie Lawson, "Postcolonialism, Neo-Colonialism and the 'Pacific Way': A Critique of (Un)Critical Approaches," SSGM Discussion Paper no. 4, Australian National University, 2010, https://dpa.bellschool.anu.edu.au/sites/default/files/publications/attachments/2015-12/2010_04_lawson_0.pdf.
37. Tom Otto, "After the 'Tidal Wave': Bernard Narokobi and the Creation of a Melanesian Way," in Tom Otto and Nicholas Thomas, eds., *Narratives of Nation in the South Pacific* (Amsterdam: Harwood Academic, 1997), 54.
38. José Casanova, "What Is Public Religion?" in Hugh Heclo and Wilfred M. McClay, eds., *Religion Returns to the Public Square: Faith and Policy in America* (Washington, DC: Woodrow Wilson Center Press, 2003), 132.
39. Philip Gibbs, "Political Discourse and Religious Narratives of Church and State in Papua New Guinea," SSGM Working Paper, Research School of Pacific and Asian Studies, Australian National University. Accessed December 20, 2017, https://openresearch-repository.anu.edu.au/handle/1885/43157.
40. Lynda Newland, "From Land to Sea: Christianity, Community, and the State in Fiji—and the 2014 Elections," in Steve Ratuva and Stephanie Lawson, eds., *The People Have Spoken: The 2014 Elections* (Canberra: ANU Press, 2015), 110.
41. Manfred Ernst, *Globalization the the Re-Shaping of Christianity in the Pacific Islands* (Suva, Fiji: Pacific Theological College, 2006), 747.
42. Momis "Theology and Politics," 11.
43. Denise Fisher, "Tjibaou's Kanak: Ethnic Identity as New Caledonia Prepares Its Future," SSGM Discussion Paper no. 4, Australian National University, 2014, https://dpa.bellschool.anu.edu.au/experts-publications/publications/1311/tjibaou%E2%80%99s-kanak-ethnic-identity-new-caledonia-prepares-its.
44. Minutes of CEPAC Tenth Plenary Assembly, Rarotonga, Vanuatu, April 1–6, 1981, 19.
45. Lawson, "Postcolonialism, Neocolonialism."
46. Elizabeth Momis, "The Bougainville Catholic Church and 'Indigenisation,'" in Anthony Regan and Helga-Maria Griffin, eds., *Bougainville before the Conflict* (Canberra: Australian National University Press, 2015), 324.
47. Media statement by Federation of Catholic Bishops Conferences of Oceania, May 1994.
48. Ralph Wiltgen, *The Rhine Flows into the Tiber: A History of Vatican II* (Gastonia, NC: TAN, 1991), 13. Hierarchy from the Pacific region who attended the Second Vatican Council were Bishops Arkfeld, Bernarding, Copas, Doggett, Doyle, Klein, Lemay, Noser, Wade, and Höhne from Papua New Guinea; Crawford and Stuyvenberg from the Solomon Islands; Baumgartner, Kennally, and Olano y Urteaga from Micronesia; and Bresson, Damancier, Foley, Guichet, Julliard, Lehman,

Martin, Mazé, Pearce, Poncet, Rogers, Terrienne, and Tirilly from the South Pacific. See www.catholic-hierarchy-org/event/ecv2-1-13.html.

49. Mikaele Paunga, *Oceania Bishops on Remote Preparation and Contribution to the Second Vatican Council, 1959–1965* (Suva, Fiji: Pacific Conference of Churches, 2006).
50. Paunga, 73.
51. Paunga, 93.
52. Paunga, 117.
53. John Garrett, *Where Nets Were Cast: Christianity in Oceania since World War II* (Suva, Fiji: University of South Pacific Institute of Pacific Studies, 1997), 168.
54. Cardinal Thomas Williams, "The Federation of Catholic Bishops Conferences of Oceania—The Journey So Far as an Expression Communio," address to the FCBCO General Assembly, Rabaul, Papua New Guinea, May 29, 2002.
55. Patrick Murphy, "Momis's Theology of Politics Interpreted," *Catalyst* 5, no. 3 (1975): 19–46.
56. "Statements and Resolutions from the Conference on the Catholic Church and the Development of Peoples in the South Pacific, held in Suva, Fiji, August 28–September 4, 1972," *Catalyst* 3, no. 2 (1973): 64.
57. Membership included not only representatives of the bishops of the region but also the Comite Catholique contre la Faim et pour le Dévelopment (France), the Catholic Fund for Overseas Development (CAFOD–England), Broederlijk Delen (Belgium), Trocaire (Ireland), and the Canadian Catholic Organisation for Development and Peace.
58. "Special Report by Pat Murphy," *Catalyst* 6, no. 2 (1976): 135.
59. More than three hundred nuclear tests were conducted in the Pacific between 1946 and 1996 by the United States, Britain, and France. See www.icanw.org/wp-content/uploads/2017/03/Pacific.pdf.
60. "Special Report by Pat Murphy," 136.
61. Manfred Ernst and Lydia Johnson, eds., *Navigating Troubled Waters: The Ecumenical Movement in the Pacific Islands since the 1980s* (Suva, Fiji: Pacific Theological College, 2017), 503.
62. Ernst and Johnson, 504.
63. "Self-Study National Workshop Position Papers," Alexishaven, Papua New Guinea, November 21–December 6, 1972, section 4, 1.
64. Hermann Janssen, "From Dar es Salaam to Goroka," *Catalyst* 5, no. 2 (1975): 5.
65. Fifteen dioceses participated; the diocese of Rabaul opted out.
66. At that time, 30 of 550 priests in the country were Papua New Guineans.
67. Letter to the Editor, "Action and Reaction," *Catalyst* 3, no. 3 (1973): 57.
68. Cyril Halley, "National Assembly of the Self Study of the Church in Papua New Guinea," unpublished manuscript in Melanesian Institute library, Goroka, Papua New Guinea.
69. The assembly allowed local people to express their thoughts openly and many did. For example, a proposition from the Dioceses of Kavieng and Wewak reads, "In Papua New Guinea there are black men and Europeans and mixed-race people. We want all of us to live well with one another. But there are some Europeans who look down on us, and say bad things to us and this bad way of some Europeans breaks the law of Christ."
70. Philip Gibbs, "The Reception of Ecclesia in Oceania," in Philip Gibbs, ed., *Alive in Christ, Point 30* (Papua New Guinea: Melanesian Institute, 2006): 160–81, http://pandora.nla.gov.au/pan/37047/20081020-1405/www.acu.edu.au/_data/assets/pdf_file/0004/92524/A_Synod_and_a_Pastoral_Plan.pdf.
71. Thomas Williams, "The Special Assembly of the Synod of Bishops for Oceania, 22 November to 12 December, 1998," paper presented in Rome on Cardinal Williams' behalf by Archbishop John A. Dew at the Synod on the Eucharist, 2005.
72. Ambrose Kiapseni, "Synod Intervention," reprinted as "Tradition and Inculturation" in *General Bulletin MSC*, December, 6, 1998, 10.

73. Thomas Williams, "Presentation of Cardinal Thomas Stafford Williams at the Promulgation of the Post-Synodal Letter," Vatican City, November, 22, 2001, 10.
74. Williams, "The Federation of Catholic Bishops Conferences of Oceania."
75. Ernst and Johnson, *Navigating Troubled Waters.*
76. Bishop Peter Cullinane, "Address to the FCBCO Assembly," Suva, Fiji, August, 9, 2006.

PART 2

Contemporary Challenges

12

Women in the Catholic Church in the Philippines during the Three Phases of Globalization

MARY JOHN MANANZAN, OSB

This chapter presents the situation of women in the Catholic Church in the Philippines throughout the three phases of globalization: the Age of Discovery, the end of Spanish rule, and modern globalization. During the first phase Spanish political, cultural, and religious beliefs and practices were brought to the land "discovered" by Spanish adventurers. Specifically, the cultural practices of the Spanish Moors were interwoven with the tenets of Christianity and affected the *mujer indigena* in the islands that the Spaniards would later name after their king, Philip II. During the second phase, which coincides with the end of Spanish rule in the Philippines and an influx of religious congregations, other European cultures were spreading globally, mostly through the religious congregations—especially the orders of religious women—that came into the country. During the third phase of globalization, when the momentous Second Vatican Council occurred, new perspectives were established regarding the role of the lay woman in the Church.

THE AGE OF DISCOVERY: THE IMPACT OF SPANISH COLONIZATION ON THE *MUJER INDIGENA*

The first phase of globalization was ushered in by the Age of Discovery. In Spain, it followed the Reconquista and the Conquista. During the reign of Charles I, grandson of Ferdinand and Isabella, the Philippines was "discovered" by Ferdinand Magellan in 1521. But it was not until the reign of Charles's son, Philip II, through the expedition of Miguel Lopez de Legazpi in 1565, that the systematic conquest and colonization of the islands, subsequently named after the reigning monarch, was formally launched. The colonizers brought Catholic Christianity to the islands they had "discovered."[1]

There is a general agreement that in the societies colonized and Christianized by Spain, the status of women was improved. In the Philippines, however, this was not the case. Let us first see the status of women in pre-Spanish society.

Women and Myth

The stories of a people are a reflection of the society in which they live. Myths and legends, especially creation stories, are usually etiologies that describe or rationalize existing conditions in a society. The creation story of pre-Spanish Filipinos illustrates a different relationship between men and women than the creation story of the Bible. The well-known Filipino version describes the beginning of humanity with a bird flying between the heavens and the sea. Becoming tired, it looked for a place to rest. It alighted on a piece of bamboo floating on the water. Hearing some sounds coming from the bamboo, it began to peck at it with its beak. As the bamboo split, "in the wink of an eye, man and woman slipped out of the joint, the man bowing politely to the woman." The woman gave recognition to the man. They walk away hand in hand.[2]

Not only was the woman not derived from the rib of man, the woman was for a long time regarded as the sole guardian of the preservation of the species, without external factors influencing the phenomenon of fecundity. For primitive tribes who put much value in the continuation of their progeny, the woman, who possessed the power of generation, enjoyed an elevated position—a reflection of some matriarchal elements in the pre-Spanish Filipino society.

The Precolonial Filipino Family

In Teresita Infante's well-documented study of women in the early Philippines and among tribal minorities, the following statements on the position of women in the Philippines before the coming of Spaniards may be gleaned from the author's conclusions:

1. Early Filipinos and non-Christian minorities attached equal importance to both male and female offspring.
2. Early Filipinos divided inheritance property equally among male and female children, distinguishing only primogeniture and legitimacy.
3. Training existed for both boys and girls in the family, although the roles assigned to girls were more distinct and specific.[3]

Furthermore, regarding the education of children, there was equal opportunity for both sexes. According to Antonio de Morga, writing in the mid-nineteenth century, "almost all the natives write in this language, men as well as women, and there were a very few who could not write well and with propriety."[4]

The Code of Kalantiaw prescribed sex education as one of the duties of a mother to her daughter. Regarding boy-girl relationships, there seems to have been few to no inhibitions: "In Luzon, the young girls are given a social liberty to deal with the best of the men. In the frequent feasts, the youth of both sexes learn to know and to fall in love with each other."[5] In fact, virginity in young girls was not valued among many tribes, with some exceptions, for example, among the Tagalogs. In any case, unwed mothers did not lose face in the community nor lose their chance for a good marriage because they were considered to have proved their capacity for motherhood. The law of custom, however, provided punishment for undue misbehavior between members of the opposite sex, thus preventing unrestricted promiscuity and the practice of prostitution."[6]

Prenuptial and Marriage Practices

Arranged marriages were a custom among pre-Spanish Filipinos. The groom usually gave a dowry to the bride's parents. In addition, the groom was wont to bestow presents upon the parents and relatives of the bride. There was also a bride service, which included work performed by the groom for the parents of the bride during a probationary period before the wedding. When married, the woman did not lose her name. In fact, among the Tagalogs, if the woman was especially distinguished, due to family connections or personal merits, the husband usually took her name. For example, one heard people talk of the "husband of Ninay or Isang."

There is a general consensus that Filipino wives were treated as companions, not as slaves. Robert Fox writes about the egalitarian character of pre-Spanish Filipino marriages: "Relationships between husband and wife were remarkably equalitarian; it is doubtful if even the term 'Patricentric' could be applied to the Pre-Spanish Filipino family. This was due also to the bilateral character of the family and kinship in which each spouse, after marriage, continued to maintain strong blood ties with his or her kinsmen. The property which the spouse brought to marriage remained an individual possession."[7]

The married woman not only exercised an equal share in the earning of livelihood in the family. With sagacity and innate managerial instinct, the married woman could play a key role in the economic stability of the family. The wife could also enjoy freedom in decision-making in the family; furthermore, a Filipina was free to have a baby and remain unmarried.

A woman's voice was not confined to domestic affairs. In fact, formal contracts were done only in her presence and if there was any choice of who could witness the contract, the wife was the first choice:

> She is at the same time the more serious and formal partner in the making of contracts. In truth, one can count the man who would dare to enter into them without the presence or consent of their wives. In these matters one needed the presence of the woman before the meeting, and in urgent cases, difficulties or impossibilities, one usually made the contract exclusively with her, being sure that she would fulfill totally and to the end what has been agreed upon.[8]

Divorce was universally practiced, especially before a child was born. The husband and wife had equal rights before the customary law in this matter, although in practice there was more limited cause for divorce for women and there was a stronger tendency to overlook or minimize a man's infidelity. Divorce entailed the return of the dowry by the wife's family if she was at fault. However, if the husband was at fault, he lost any right to the dowry's return. Legal responsibility for any children was divided equally between the two, regardless of sex. There was likewise a separation of conjugally acquired property. In some cases fines were also imposed on the guilty party.

Women's Role in Economic and Sociopolitical Processes

Women participated in economic processes that went beyond simple management of the domestic economy. In general, the woman bore the task of agricultural production once the ground had been prepared by the man. She also usually managed the local trading of the products and wares. Pedro Paterno explains how it was rare for a woman not to know how to manage the family's landholdings: "One sees very often young women directing on their own initiative, not only domestic but also commercial enterprises, one time dictating the correspondence, at other times making contracts and billings, and still at other times confirming, authorizing or endorsing the contracts of their husbands."[9]

The role of woman in the political field, especially her leadership in it, is a disputed point for those who contend that it was based merely on legend.[10] But this perspective fails to recognize the importance of myths, legends, and other oral traditions in societies where the "myth of history" has not been supplanted by the other forms of apprehending and recording reality. If one considers myths and legends as faithful mirrors of the existing conditions of the society that gave rise to them, there is ample evidence of women exercising leadership in the political field in pre-Spanish Filipino society. For instance, there are writings of Queen Maniwantiwan, whose permission was sought by her husband before selling his lands to Datu Puti. Also, in the seventh century Queen Sima is reported to have ruled Cotabato with integrity and justice and compassion.[11]

Father Bazaco writes of the legend of the first lawgiver in the islands, named Lubluban, the grandchild of the first man and woman. She established rules and regulations, especially concerning rituals, inheritance, and property.[12] The most famous of the women leaders of pre-Spanish society was Princesa Urduja of Pangasinan. She was known to be a beautiful "Amazon," courageous and knowledgeable of the culture and language of Old Asia and skilled in the use of weapons, along with an army of women who could fight as well as the men.[13]

The practice of primogeniture for inheritance regardless of sex gives a good basis to suppose that firstborn women could succeed their fathers as rulers of tribes.

Woman's Role as Religious Practitioner

It is in the religious field that the predominant role of the woman in pre-Spanish Filipino society is unquestioned. Living in a world believed to be inhabited by spirits, ancient Filipinos gave importance to one whom they believed to have the power to communicate with spirits and the supernatural being. This person, who had either special training or some special personal charisma, was called a religious practitioner (*babaylan*), in contrast to one who gains a certain right to perform ceremonies by mere training. Although differing in name, every tribe had its own women religious practitioners who were preferred to men. In fact, according to Marcelo de Ribadeneyra, such was the dominance of the female in the field that when a male performed the religious office of a *catalona,* he usually dressed as a woman.[14]

This role ranged from being the chief mourner of the dead and performer of ritual dances and songs to offering sacrifices and performing wedding ceremonies. Death was a significant event in the primitive Filipino society filled with semi-religious ceremonies led by women.

The principal wife of the deceased would lie down upon him and place her mouth, hands, and feet on the dead. The chief mourner took charge of dressing the corpse, cutting off the hair, and preparing the grave. She also presided in the wedding ceremonies of couples, performing elaborate rituals.[15]

The esteem for pre-Spanish Filipino women is much opposed to the Spaniards' disdain for the Indio. The Indio is described as indolent, taciturn, boastful, capricious, hard-headed, cowardly, fond of gambling, lascivious, and indifferent. He was seen to be forever suspicious and unsure of his convictions, and was frequently perceived as turning his back on this world. In contrast, the woman was highly regarded:

> Everyone recognizes the greater intellectual superiority of the indian woman to the indian man, of whatever class or social condition. She is the more serious and formal partner in making contracts.[16]

> In general the woman does not share the apathy shown by the man; industrious by nature and a devotee from childhood . . . her development surpasses that of the man in no little way.[17]

The Influence of Spanish Culture

There is no doubt that the Iberian conquerors brought along patriarchal values, structures, ideas, and customs to the colonies. The famous Augustinian missionary to the Philippines Fr. Casimiro Dias, in his instruction to the parish priests on the islands, warned:

> Woman is the most monstrous animal in the whole of nature, bad-tempered and worse spoken. To have this animal in the house is asking for trouble in the way of tattling, talebearing, malicious gossip, and controversies, for wherever a woman is, it would seem to be impossible to have peace and quiet. However, even this might be tolerated if it were not for the danger of unchastity. Not only should parish priests of Indians abstain from employing any woman in their home, but they should not allow any of them to enter, even if they are only paying a call.[18]

Though the missionaries were forced to acknowledge the *mujer indigena*'s superiority, which they could hardly deny, they nevertheless condemned as vice any behavior that they could not reconcile with the moral prescriptions for women in their mother country. Thus they praised the woman's intelligence, strong will, and practicality but also censured her for being too sensual and too free in her behavior. The missionaries made use of women's influence in society to be the vehicle of a more effective propagation of Christianity, while sparing no efforts in remolding her to the image and likeness of the perfect woman of the Iberian society of the time.

Manuals for young girls were either written or translated. Some well-known ones were Dr. Clemente's *Paginas de la Virtud: Lectura Moral Para Las Ninez*; Jose Ma. Chanco's *Reglamento o Regla de Vida que debe Seguir la Mujer, que Aspire a la Perfection*; and *Mga Tagubilin sa mga Dalaga*, which was a translation of Bishop Antonio Ma. Claret's *Los Avisos a las Doncellas Cristianas.*[19] All three were reminiscent of the works of the moralists in Spain, containing the values, concepts, and prescriptions regarding women, especially Juan Luis Vives's *Formacion de la Mujer Cristiana.*

In order to ensure that the *mujer indigena* learned to be a virtuous woman, the Spaniards established colleges for girls. The first one was the College of Saint Potenciana (est. 1669), which sheltered young girls, most of them illegitimate daughters of Spaniards and Native women. The founding of the college was welcomed because it was thought that girls would willingly accept moral guidance and not roam outside.

Another way of ensuring a young girl's virtue was the introduction of the cult of the Virgin Mary, albeit a Mary frozen in the Annunciation. Both Portuguese and Spanish conquistadores took this cult overseas with them in all the regions in which they settled. The Jesuits made it a point to develop congregations and sodalities of Mary in all their schools and colleges throughout the world.

The personification of the *doncella* as educated by the Spanish friar was Maria Clara, the heroine of Jose Rizal's novel *Noli Me Tangere*, a fictionized version of his real-life sweetheart, Leonore Rivera. Although Rizal may not have intended to portray her as the ideal woman, Philippine society during the Spanish times and onward enthroned Maria Clara as the model of the perfect Filipina: sweet, docile, obedient, and self-sacrificing.

But when one reflects on the fact that this "ideal form," with all her sweetness and beauty, never had the courage to share the fate of her beloved—being forced into an engagement with a Spaniard and choosing to enter the convent to flee from a loveless marriage, presenting a more permanent escape from vicissitudes of life as insanity—one can agree with Carmen Guerrero Nakpil that Maria Clara is "the greatest misfortune to have befallen Filipino women in the last one hundred years."[20]

Strangely enough, while taking all the efforts to protect the virtue of the *mujer indigena*, the Spaniards nevertheless suffered no qualms of conscience in robbing her of it. We have mentioned the numerous "orphans" that had to be sheltered in girls' colleges. This sexual exploitation was not confined to the lay male; the clergy was just as guilty. During the *ramo inquisición* in the Archivo General de Nación in Mexico, there is a remarkable frequency of entries of official complaints against Spanish friars for "*solicitationes*."

It is also curious to note that institutions sheltering young girls from the temptations of the world also housed "lewd women," albeit in separate quarters. Gemelli Caresi writes: "Married women are also admitted and lewd women put in by magistrates, but they have no communication with the sixteen orphans. The whores are maintained by the king and they are to work for him." Contrast this with Fr. Lorenzo Juan of Aringay's categorical statement: "*No existe la prostitución en las pueblas idolatras*." Prostitution seems to have come into practice precisely when purity and chastity of women were being assiduously preached in the islands.

Much later, during the Propaganda Movement, one of the most bitterly denounced abuses of the friars was the sexual exploitation of women. Members of the movement at the same time deplored the education given to them. Marcelo del Pilar exhorts his niece, Josefa Gatmaitan, not to confine herself to "lighting candles and mumbling novenas." Jose Rizal, in his famous letter to the women of Malolos, laments: "What could the offspring be of a woman whose only virtue is to murmur prayers, whose only knowledge is derived from *awit*, novena, prayer-books, and miraculous tales intended to fool men, with no other recreation but *panguingue* or frequent confession of the same sins?"[21]

In fact, despite the domesticating education Filipino women received during this period, many women broke through the mold to exert their influence in society just as their sisters in the Iberian Peninsula had done in various periods of their history. Women like Gabriela Silang, Tandang Sora, Gregoria de Jesus, and Maria Dizon played significant roles. And there are scores of unnamed women whose deeds made history, even if they themselves remained anonymous. For example, during the Ilocos Revolt of 1807, a Spanish parish priest of Batac who was trying to rally the people against the "rebels" indignantly reports on a woman who dared to preach against him:

> Last Sunday I preached again to the people exhorting them to their obligation and vassalage to the sovereign so that those who have remained faithful until then should maintain their sentiment without prevarication. While I was thus preaching, a woman had the nerve also to preach saying that they should not believe me, that everything I said was lies and that in the name of God and the Gospel, we do nothing but deceive them so that we Spaniards could fleece them, since we (the friars) are also Spaniards like all the others.[22]

Then there was one peasant woman of Kalamba who, though she was sick and had to care for her four children, vigorously fought against the Dominican lay brother who had come with soldiers to evict her from her home in the absence of her husband. Carlos Quirino, who related the story, observes: "Though she had to stay in bed the next four days to recover from her bruises, she had successfully defended the right to her home against the hated guardia civiles."[23] And there were the Young Women of Malolos, a group who led a protest movement on their own and preached that "it was dishonorable for a Filipino of either sex to follow the guidance of the priests."

THE STRUGGLE FOR NATIONAL INDEPENDENCE: NEO-COLONIALISM AND RELIGIOUS WOMEN CONGREGATIONS

The Political Situation

The second phase of globalization in Asia was marked by the rise of nationalism and the subsequent decolonization of Asia. It saw the gradual growth of independence movements on the Asian continent, leading ultimately to the retreat of foreign powers and the creation of a number of nation-states in the region, including the Philippines, Burma, Indonesia, Malaysia, Vietnam, Cambodia, and Sri Lanka, among others.

The colonialists who had to relinquish their political power over their colonies believed that these colonies would remain tied to their economic apron strings. In this situation, the old colonial powers, realizing fully the necessity of exploiting the resources of the new states for their own needs, were quick to devise new instruments of control. This led to the transformation of colonialism into neocolonialism.

In the Philippines, the Filipino revolutionaries prevailed over their Spanish colonialists. However, the latter, not wanting to surrender to their former colonial subjects, arranged with the United States to stage a mock battle at Manila Bay during the Spanish-American War in which Spain ceded the Philippines, along with Cuba, to the United States. In the Treaty of Paris of 1898, to which the Filipinos were not invited, the transfer of power was formalized, with the United States paying twenty-one million dollars to Spain. The Filipino revolutionaries continued fighting the new colonial master, but surrendered in 1902.

A Church in Disarray

The conflicts and wars and handover of power had disastrous effects on the Church in the Philippines, and it was decades before some sort of normalcy could be restored. First, the Church lost many of its leaders, as starting from 1898 few bishops were present in the dioceses. Once the religious congregations left, many parishes were left without priests. Of the remaining priests, many were judged to be unfit. This brings us to another problem that confronted the Philippine Church at the time: the arrival of Protestant missionaries.

The Introduction of Protestantism

Exacerbating the internal chaos in the Church was the influx of numerous Protestant missionaries from the United States, equipped with anti-Catholic biases that were characteristic of the time. The Protestant Board of Missions was one of the three strongest groups that strongly lobbied in the US Congress for the annexation of the Philippines. Between 1899 and 1905, various Protestant denominations established themselves in the Philippines, forming the Evangelical Union of the Philippine Islands. Just like the Spanish friars before them, these different denominations divided the islands among themselves. Protestant teachers, the Thomasites, established public schools all over the islands.

MASONRY

Even before the arrival of the Protestants, the Catholic Church authorities were already worried about the allegiance of many of the revolutionary leaders, especially the Ilustrados to Masonry, which a great many joined. This group was an offshoot of anticlericalism that arose during the latter part of the Spanish Rule. Until 1916, the principal Filipino Mason lodges had been affiliated with the Gran Oriente Español in Spain, to which the Filipino Propagandists in Spain had been affiliated. In 1912, the Grand Lodge of American Masonry was organized in the Philippines.

THE AGLIPAYAN CHURCH

A new threat to the Church was the establishment of a revolutionary church founded by Gregorio Aglipay, a Catholic priest who had joined the revolution against Spain and the United States. On October 20, 1898, General Aguinaldo appointed Aglipay as military vicar general of the revolutionaries. Aglipay interpreted this appointment as making him ecclesiastical superior to all Filipino priests who, as such, would all be appointed military chaplains for the duration of the war. Fighting broke out between the US and Filipino forces on February 4, 1899, which prompted Aglipay to withdraw to Ilocos Norte to organize an armed resistance. On April 29, 1899, Aglipay was excommunicated by Rome for usurpation of ecclesiastical jurisdiction.[24] Following the end of the war in 1902, Isabelo de los Reyes—a writer, politician, and political activist—was working toward the formation of a national church that would be independent of Rome. On August 3 of that year he suggested that Aglipay be its first bishop. Aglipay, a devout Catholic priest at the time, was reluctant, but accepted de los Reyes's offer to establish an independent church. On January 18, 1903, Aglipay was appointed supreme bishop of the "Philippine Independent Church."[25]

These three factors threatening Catholicism in the Philippines prompted Church authorities to appeal to the religious congregations in Europe and the United States to send missionaries to the Philippines. This ushered in the second wave of missionaries, including religious women congregations.

The First Religious Women Congregations

During Spanish colonial times in the Philippines, the major religious orders usually had three branches, also known as "orders." The first order is comprised of monks and friars, the second order is contemplative nuns, and the third order is affiliated laypersons. There were three types of members in the third order: a secular member who lives with her family; one who lived by herself like a hermit, did not wear a habit, and was not bound by vows; and one who lived in a community called a *beaterio*: she wore a habit and took simple vows during her lifetime or at the point of death. At the time, the beaterios were not considered religious, though they could be compared to active sisters of today.[26]

The first religious order of nuns founded in the Philippines were the Nuns of Santa Potenciana, who ministered to the first Spanish girls in Manila. A second school for Spanish orphan girls, Colegio de Santa Isabel, was established under the Daughters of Charity in 1632. These two monasteries were not allowed to accept Native vocations, because the royal foundations were specifically created for "pious Spanish women and daughters of the conquistadores who cannot marry properly," that is, no mention of Native women (and interpreted as a prohibition).[27] The *mujer indigena* could only enter the third order of the religious congregations as *beatas*. It was only in 1632 during the term of Mother Jeronima's successor—Madre Ana de Christo, a farmer's daughter—that a Native beata of the Third Order of St. Francis from Pampanga was given an exception to join the monastery.

Another woman from Pampanga, Sor Magdalena de la Concepción, became the second Filipino nun receiving the habit in the Manila monastery. Soon, the other monasteries of women started accepting Native vocations. There was another ban against the admission of Native women, due to the case of a woman called Sor Juana who claimed to be a visionary and was denounced for heresy to the Holy Office of Inquisition. It was only after two decades (1880) that Native women were again admitted to the religious congregations.[28]

Worthy of special mention is the Congregation of the Religious of the Virgin Mary, the oldest and largest Filipino congregation. This is the first all-Filipino religious congregation for women in the Philippines, founded by a Filipina, Venerable Mother Ignacia del Espíritu

Santo.[29] Mother Santo began her pioneering task in 1684, directed by divine inspiration and the wise guidance of her spiritual director, the Czech priest Pablo Clain, SJ.[30] At the age of twenty-one, Ignacia left her family and friends and gave herself without reserve entirely to the service of God by founding an institute whose first members were herself, her niece Cristina Gonzales, and two young girls, Teodora de Jesús and Ana Margarita. This small group formed the nucleus of the Beatas de la Compania de Jesús, which subsequently became the Congregation of the Religious of the Virgin Mary.[31]

New Congregations Arrive

The appeal of Church authorities to religious congregations in Europe and America reaped generous response, but the present focus is on religious congregations that came to the Philippines shortly before the American period and within twenty-five years of the new regime: The Daughters of Charity in 1862, the Augustinian Sisters of the Assumption in 1892, the Sisters of Saint Paul of Chartres in 1904, the Missionary Benedictine Sisters in 1906, the Missionary Sisters of the Immaculate Heart of Mary in 1910, the Franciscan Missionaries of Mary in 1912, the Sister Servants of the Holy Spirit in 1912, and the Maryknoll Sisters in 1925. Many more religious congregations of women came at later periods.

Whatever their special charisma, the congregations that came in the early period of American rule were all conscious of the goal to inculcate Christian Catholic values. To accomplish this, they all opened schools.

The daughters of prominent families were educated by these congregations and prepared not only for being good wives and mothers, but also for leadership roles in society. Corazon Aquino, for example, the first woman president of the Philippines, studied in Saint Scholastica's College; the country's second woman president, Gloria Macapagal Arroyo, graduated from Assumption Convent. In the context of martial law, several of these colleges adopted the same thrust: education for justice and for social transformation. They were also centers of excellence in various other disciplines. It is safe to say that many women leaders in a broad range of endeavor studied in convent schools run by women religious.

Health

The congregations of religious women lost no time in also addressing the health problems of the country. They established hospitals: the Holy Spirit Sisters established Lourdes Hospital; the Daughters of Charity Sisters started the San Juan de Dios Hospital; the Missionary Benedictine Sisters created the Divine Word Hospital in Tacloban and more recently the Saint Scholastica's Hospital in Pambujan, Northern Samar; the St. Paul Sisters took up the management of the Doctor's Hospital in Manila as well as many other health centers and clinics all over the country. Religious women who established the rural missionaries of the Philippines initiated the Community-Based Health Program and held responsible positions within it. Community-Based Health Program sites are now located all over the Philippines.

Social-Pastoral Work

Without religious women, parishes of today would be very limited in their services. Usually one or two communities of sisters manage activities in a parish, such as developing parochial schools, organizing and training catechists and fielding them in different parts of the parish, and building basic ecclesial communities. They also arrange the liturgical services, and some even manage the housekeeping of the priest's house and seminary (if one exists). They also run orphanages that are attached to the parish or diocese.

Current Issues of Women

There are many social issues that have become the focus of the commitment of religious women. Women religious are particularly sensitive to the many issues that disempower women, including the prevailing inequalities of the patriarchal society, domestic subordination, different forms of exploitation and violence, and human trafficking.

Religious congregations have founded shelters for women victims of violence, providing access to psychological and spiritual counseling, legal and medical advocacy, and economic empowerment of survivors. Two such organizations in which religious women have been active as founders or administrators are the Women Crisis (Care) Center and the Office of Women and Gender Concerns of the Association of Major Religious Superiors of the Philippines.

Religious women are also actively working to prevent human trafficking, especially involving women and children. A campaign called Talitha Kum was spearheaded by a Filipino Salesian sister, Sr. Estrella Castallone, when she worked at the English Section of the Union of Superior Generals in Rome (UISG). The program includes conscientization seminars and various forms of advocacy against human trafficking. The campaign has spread to countries all over the world. The first center for migrant workers, Tipanan, was established by the Missionary Benedictine Sisters in Madrid, Spain, in 1984, but was later transferred to Barcelona and renamed Tuluyan San Benito. Management of the center has since been given over to the organization of migrant workers, which the sisters helped to set up.

A school for women run by the Missionary Benedictine Sisters, Saint Scholastica's College, was also the first school to mainstream gender in the curriculum and established the Institute of Women's Studies to empower women through alternative feminist education. It has presented seminars to thousands of women, not only in the Philippines but in the many Asian countries that send participants to their long-term courses.

Environmental Advocacy

Religious women have been very active since the onset of ecological advocacy in the Philippines. One sister, Sr. Aida Velasquez, spearheaded a campaign in the 1970s against the development of a nuclear power plant, educating the whole village where it was supposed to be built. This grew into a national campaign, which succeeded in mothballing the nuclear power plant built in Bataan, which has never operated. Sisters were also involved in organizing the Nuclear-Free Philippines Coalition.

Many congregations of sisters have acquired farms to propagate organic farming and sustainable agriculture. Their schools have included environmental protection in the curriculum at all levels and encourage environmentally friendly practices with regard to waste management, anti-pollution, energy conservation, and reforestation.

The Role of Cloistered Nuns

The main orders of cloistered nuns in the Philippines are the Carmelites, the Adoration Sisters of Divine Mercy (Pink Sisters), the Contemplative Branch of the Good Shepherd Sisters, the La Consolacion Sisters, the Poor Clares, the Benedictine Nuns of the Eucharistic King, and, lately, the Trappistines. Cloistered nuns believe that their vocation is to witness the primacy of prayer in the Church, to serve as a reminder of the contemplative dimension in all lives, and to intervene for others before God. Besides being available to individual persons who seek their help and counsel, they bring the needs and sorrows of the world to God in their life of prayer. In spite of being cloistered, many contemplative communities have shown interest and concern for the burning issues of modern society. They sometimes also serve as a sanctuary for endangered people. For example, Corazon Aquino sought sanctuary among the Carmelite nuns when she ran for election against the dictator Ferdinand Marcos.

Filipino Missionaries to Foreign Lands

With the decline of vocations in many of the motherhouses of religious women congregations, Filipino nuns and sisters are now being sent to staff motherhouses and other mission houses all over the world. Besides being sent as a kind of reverse missionary activity to Europe and the United States, they are also sent to mission houses in Africa, India, and Latin America, especially to serve in leadership positions as prioresses, mother provincials, novice directresses, and principals of schools.

A Special Prophetic Role

During the martial law years in the Philippines (1972–86), many religious women became aware of the injustices and oppression of the people and became actively involved in addressing the struggles of the masses, including peasants, laborers, the urban poor, and Indigenous people.

In the 1970s, a movie entitled *Sister Stella L.* was shown in many theaters of the Philippines. It was all about a young sister, portrayed as the typical religious woman, who became aware of social issues and her commitment and involvement in the national liberation movement. The scriptwriter, Jose Lacaba, said that he based his character on the interviews he conducted with three religious women: Sr. Christine Tan, RGS (Good Shepherd Sister); Sr. Marianni Dimaranan, SFIC (Franciscan Sister of the Immaculate Concepcion, more popularly known as St. Joseph's Sisters); and this author, Sr. Mary John Mananzan, OSB (Missionary Benedictine Sister).

In a summary review of the film, Mina Roces writes:

> The fictionalised story of Sister Stella L. (played by film star Vilma Santos) depicted the militant nun's metamorphosis into political activist. It was the nuns' exposure to the victims of martial law that inspired them to speak out for political detainees, support labour strikes, report on the abuses of the regime and later act as human barricades in the front lines that faced the military. . . . The nuns were transformed into political activists almost immediately after martial law was declared in 1972. . . . Nuns were active from the very beginning of martial law, when most Filipinos, terrified of arrest, torture and death, kept quiet; when even the student radicals—so vehement in their demonstrations against President Marcos in the early 1970s—either went underground or kept silent. The mob of angry student protesters who filled the streets in the late 1960s quickly vanished, but the militant nuns, with far less noise and more courage, consistently took to the streets to champion human rights.[32]

THIRD PHASE OF GLOBALIZATION: LIBERAL CAPITALISM

The Economic-Political Situation

In the third phase of globalization, the term "globalization" is used primarily in an economic sense, referring to the integration of the economies of the whole world into the liberal capitalist market economy that is controlled by the Group of Seven. Although it promises much, this form of globalization has resulted in a greater gap between the rich and the poor, the surrender of local economic control, the devastation of the environment, and the creation of export-oriented, capital-dependent, debt-ridden local economies. The quantum leap in the development of communication made the world truly a global village.

The Church's Focus on the Laity

The most significant event in the Catholic Church during this phase was the Second Vatican Council that convened in 1965. This introduced radical changes in the life of the Church, including a shift in the perspective as a Church in the world. This provided the context for the rise of the laity in the Church. In the decree Apostolicam actuositatem, the Church Fathers pointed out the important role of the laity in the Church: "Our own times require of the laity no less zeal: in fact, modern conditions demand that their apostolate be broadened and intensified. With a constantly increasing population, continual progress in science and technology, and closer interpersonal relationships, the areas for the lay apostolate have been immensely widened particularly in fields that have been for the most part open to the laity alone."[33]

In the Philippines, the event that actually gave impetus to the rise of the laity was the Second Plenary Council of the Philippines (PCP II). In his address to the assembly of directors in 2006, Cardinal Orlando Quevedo succinctly states the vision of PCP II: "The general question that PCP-II grappled with in 1991 was: How can the Church be a more effective and credible evangelizer, given the present pastoral situation of the Philippines? The general answer was: by being a renewed Church and by being faithful to its mission of integral evangelization."[34] To properly implement the decrees of PCP II, the National Pastoral Commission on Church Renewal (NPCCR) was formed. Among the nine priorities outlined by the document released by the NPCCR, the empowerment of the laity was highlighted. To coordinate the programs of the laity, the commission founded Sangguniang Laiko ng Pilipinas (LAIKO) as the implementing arm of the Catholic Bishops' Conference of the Philippines (CBCP) in promoting nationwide initiatives and coordinating national programs of the laity.

The Emerging Role of Lay Women

Filipinos are a churchgoing people. It is safe to say that among churchgoers, about 80 percent are women. Thus, the first role of the lay woman in the Church is that of a *worshipper.* Perhaps in the eyes of God this is the most important role, but we live in a human society and there is a need to develop the active role of lay women in the pursuit of the Church's vision and mission. However, in pre–Vatican II times, the role of the lay woman consisted of participating in the choir (*manangs*), arranging the flowers on the altar, passing the collection bags after the offertory, and leading the rosary or novena prayers before or after Mass. After Vatican II, the lay woman could read the First and Second Readings, distribute Holy Communion, and act as commentator during the Mass. Girls could also be sacristans and Mass servers.

After PCP II, women started to join Church organizations that gave them opportunities for leadership and decision-making. They are not only active in Church-mandated women organizations like the Catholic Women's League or the Mother Butler Guild, but also in mixed organizations like Couples for Christ, Christian Family Movement, and Christian Life Community. Still, leadership in this mixed group is mainly in the hands of males.

To trace the role of lay women in the Church, it is helpful to give an example of someone who exemplifies the role of an active woman in the Church. Henrietta de Villa served in the secretariat of Cardinal Sin, convening international seminars hosted by the archdiocese and holding important positions such as the first Servant Leader of the Council of the Laity, the country's representative to the Plenary Council of the Laity in Rome, and president of the Mother Butler Guild. De Villa also received many awards, among them the prestigious Pro Deo et Patria in 2016. She became the first woman ambassador to the Vatican and was followed by two other women ambassadors. However, de Villa is most known for founding the Parish Pastoral Campaign for Responsible Voting (PPCRV). She led a group of laypeople to engage in the education of voters in parishes all across the Philippines. The group later developed into a national alternative canvasser of votes during elections, which still operates today.

The Phenomenon of Reverse Mission

With the rise of migration and migrant labor across the globe, a new task for the laity, especially women migrant workers, has emerged. Marx Oxbrow describes it this way:

> Another missionary force is also at work today, although it does not appear in the records of missionary activity or the databanks of specialists. It is the transcultural witnessing for Christ that takes place as people move around as migrants or refugees, just as in New Testament days. . . . They are missionaries "from below" who do not have the power, the prestige, or the money from a developed nation, and are not part of a missionary organisation. They are vulnerable in many ways, but have learnt the art of survival, supported by their faith in Jesus Christ.[35]

In the Center for Migrant Workers in Spain, the Tuluyan San Benito, a nanny once proudly shared how she "converted" the whole family she was working with. It seemed that when she went to Mass every Sunday, she would always bring her ward, a young boy, along with her. The boy later began to ask his parents why they were not going to church. The parents then started accompanying them and are now regular churchgoers.

When one attends church services in Europe and some non-Christian countries in Asia, one is immediately impressed by the fact that a great many of the faithful are Filipinos. One European said, "Without them, our churches are dead." Of course, they bring with them their devotions, like the Novena to the Perpetual Help, and even organize branches of Couples for Christ and El Shaddai.

Current Issues of Women in the Philippine Church

A recent controversy highlights a contemporary women's issue in the Church: the introduction and passage of a bill known as Republic Act No. 10354, also referred to as the "Responsible Parenthood and Reproductive Health Act of 2012." In general, it guarantees universal access to methods of contraception, fertility control, sexual education, and maternal care. The Filipino bishops launched a massive campaign against the bill, objecting mainly to the provision regarding contraceptives and sex education, while women organizations lobbied for it. One particularly notable group led by lay women called themselves Catholics for Reproductive Health. Nevertheless, and despite massive opposition, the bill was passed in 2012.

Another serious problem confronting the Church is the sexual abuse by the clergy, primarily targeting women and girls (although there are also male victims, in the case of pedophilia). Since the priests involved do not assume responsibility for the children born of these relationships, the women become single mothers and have to suffer, together with their children, the scorn of society in general. There is also no established procedure for prosecuting the erring priests, and most of them are simply transferred to other parishes.

On a positive note, there has been great progress in gender consciousness in the Philippines due to the strong women's movement. In fact many woman-friendly laws have been passed, including a Magna Carta exclusively for women. In 2015, the first memorandum of the year passed by the Commission on Higher Education (CHED) was to mainstream gender in all tertiary educational institutions. There has not been corresponding progress in the Church.

The Catholic Church still holds a conservative view of women. Church teachings on family life continue to emphasize the "obey your husband" dictum. It allows only the natural methods of family planning and has not lifted its ban on divorce. Many so-called happy marriages are built on the subordination of the woman, who simply keeps quiet "so there will be no trouble." In marital conflicts, confessors advise a too-early reconciliation without serious analysis of the conflict. The wife almost always has the exclusive burden of keeping the marriage intact, and abused women typically remain in such marriages so as not to have a "broken family."

The Church's moral theology still focuses on the "sins of the flesh," with a certain bias against women as "Eve the temptress." It offers the model of Mary as the Virgin Mother, which is difficult for Catholic women to emulate. The prevailing cult of virginity makes women who lose their virginity, even through no fault of their own, feel meaningless. Many women make a plunge into prostitution after losing their virginity either through rape or incest. The ideal woman image as one who is self-sacrificing, long-suffering, patient, and meek is actually a conditioning of a victim consciousness in women.

Although women are the most active people in Church service functions and activities, they are deprived of participation in the major decision-making processes and are denied full ministry in the Church. Celibate priests continue to make the rules and prescriptions governing marriage and family life. The structure is hierarchical and clerical, and women have no part in either. In the liturgy, there is still a sexist tone addressing the assembly as "brethren," praying for the salvation of "mankind," and exhortation to love one's "fellow man." There is also the sad reality of sexual abuse and sexual harassment of women and children.

Feminist Theology of Liberation

The women in the Philippines, both lay and religious, who are conscious of the continuing gender inequality in the Church have participated in the development of a feminist theology of liberation from the perspective of Asian women within the Ecumenical Association of Third World Theologians (EATWOT). Their avowed task is to deconstruct what is oppressive in the formal religion structure and to reconstruct what is liberating. They have participated in national, regional, and international conferences on feminist theology, delineating its methodology, defining its hermeneutic, and embarking on concrete projects like a feminist journal—*In God's Image*—and writing books on the gender aspects of theologizing, such as God-talk, Christology, mariology, ecclesiology, and missiology, among others. A new development is the establishment of a Catholic feminist theologians organization called ECCLESIA.

CONCLUSION: AN APPRAISAL

The three phases of globalization have had an impact on Filipino women in relation to the Catholic Church. The first phase of globalization ushered in the spread of Western culture as well as the patriarchal values of Spanish society brought over by the Spanish missionaries. These left a negative impact on the *mujer indigena*, who lost her status of equality and was domesticated by these values. Nevertheless, she has retained the subversive memory of her equality, which inspires the struggle of modern-day Filipino feminists.

The second stage of globalization widened the spread of Western culture; it was no longer confined to Spain, and included those of Europe and the Americas. There was a growth of religious congregations of women who played and still play an invaluable role in the life of the Catholic Church of the Philippines. More than the clergy, religious women have influenced the life of people living with them by caring for them, fighting for their causes, and working for their empowerment. It is not an exaggeration to say that the vitality of parish life is due mostly to religious women and their empowerment of laypeople. In the latter years, due to the crisis of vocations in the West, Filipino religious women have injected new life into their congregations by reinforcing the staffs in their motherhouses and by occupying leadership roles as superiors and formators in the mission houses of their congregations all over the world.

The third phase of globalization was a giant leap in information and communication technology, bringing countries into a global world and facilitating the spread of culture, ideas, and news at an unbelievable speed. The Second Vatican Council marked a turning point in the Church, most especially for the laity, who experienced an unprecedented involvement in the life and activities of the Church. In a special way, the increased participation of lay women in the leadership of lay organizations in the Church has given new life to parishes and dioceses. In the age of migration and overseas migrant work, migrant women workers (more so than migrant men) have sparked new life in the churches of the countries they are working in. Unintentionally, they have initiated a kind of reverse missionary movement, bringing back the faith to post-Christian countries.

However, there is still a virtual inequality of women in the Catholic Church despite the theoretical acceptance of her equality. The practice in the Church has not kept up with the progress of women's empowerment in larger society. There is no possibility of her having full ministry rights in the Church. This has given impetus to the development of a feminist theology from an Asian perspective, by people who are determined to see that the liberating factors in religion (Christianity) will at least to some extent neutralize its oppressive aspects.

NOTES

1. J. H. Elliot, *Imperial Spain* (London: Edward Arnold, 1963), 20.
2. Teofilo del Castillo y Tuazon, *Philippine Literature from Ancient Times to the Present* (Santa Mesa, Philippines: Teofilo Castillo and Sons, 1974), 22.
3. Teresita Infante, *The Woman in Early Philippines and Among Tribal Minorities* (Manila: UST Press, 1975), 59–61.
4. Antonio de Morga, *Sucesos de las Islas Filipinas* (London: Hakluyt Society, 1868), 241.
5. Pedro Paterno, *La antigua civilización Tagalog* (Madrid: Tipografía de Manuel G. Hernández, 1897), 222.
6. Infante, *The Woman in Early Philippines*, 6.
7. Robert Fox, "The Philippines in Pre-Historic Times," *Journal of History* 11, nos. 3–4 (1963): 457–58.
8. Pedro Chirino, *Relaciones de las Islas Filipinas* (Manila: Bookmark, 1969), 221.
9. Paterno, *La antigua civilización Tagalog*, 241.
10. Infante, *The Woman in Early Philippines*, 55.
11. Eufronio Alip, "The Barangay Through the Ages," *Journal of History* 29 (1974): 24.

12. Evaristo Bazaco, *Culture of the Early Filipinos* (Manila: UST Press, 1936), 49.
13. Gregorio Zaide, "Famous Women of History" (Unpublished manuscript, 1943), 11.
14. Marcelo de Ribadeneyra, *Historia de las Islas de Archipelago Filipino* (Madrid: Imprenta Saenz, 1947), 2.
15. Infante, *The Woman in Early Philippines*, 194.
16. R. Gonzáles y Martin, *Filipinas y sus habitantes* (Béjar: Establecimiento tipográfico de la viuda de Aguilar, 1896), 222.
17. Wenceslao Retana, *El Indio Batangueno* (Manila: Tipografia de Chafe, 1888), 51.
18. Quoted in Charles Ralph Boxer, *Women in Iberian Expansion Overseas, 1415–1815: Some Facts, Fancies, and Personalities* (New York: Oxford University Press, 1975) 97.
19. Antonio Maria Claret, *Avisos a las Doncellas Cristianas* (Tambobong, Philippines: Impreso del Asilo de Huerfano, 1890).
20. Carmen Guerrero Nakpil, quoted in Ma. Cristina Velez, *Images of the Filipina* (Manila: Ala-ala Foundation, 1975), 47.
21. José Rival, "Message to the Young Women of Malolos," in National Historical Commission, ed., *Political and Historical Writings: José Rival*, vol. 7 (Manila: Republic of the Philippines Department of Education National Historical Commission, 1972), 58.
22. Carlos Quirino and Abraham Laygo, *Regesto Guion Catalogo de los Documentos Existentes en Mexico Sobre Filipinas* (Manila: El Comite de Amistad Filipino-Mexico, 1965), 12.
23. Carlos Quirino, *The Great Malayan* (Manila: Philippine Foundation, 1940), 146.
24. James A. Robertson, "The Aglipay Schism in the Philippine Islands," *Catholic Historical Review* 4, no. 3 (October 1918): 326.
25. Robertson, "The Aglipay Schism."
26. See Luciano P. R. Santiago, *To Love and To Suffer: The Development of the Religious Congregations for Women in the Spanish Philippines, 1565–1898* (Quezon City: Ateneo de Manila University Press, 2005), 26–28.
27. Santiago, 66.
28. Santiago, 71.
29. Venerable Ignacia Del Espiritu Santo website, "Ignacia del Espiritu Santo," accessed 2015, http://motherignacia.info/index.cfm?fa=page.biography&menu_id=D794939F-57C2-4F09-A219-5C938B23BFD0.
30. Horacio de la Costa, SJ, *The Jesuits in the Philippines, 1581–1768* (Cambridge: Harvard University Press, 2013).
31. See Santiago, *To Love and To Suffer*, 122–25.
32. Mina Roces, "The Militant Nun as Political Activist and Feminist in Martial Law," *PORTAL: Journal of Multidisciplinary International Studies 1*, no. 1 (2004).
33. The Vatican, "Apostolicam actuositatem," November 18, 1965, https://www.vatican.va/archive/hist_councils/ii_vatican_council/documents/vat-ii_decree_19651118_apostolicam-actuositatem_en.html.
34. Orlando B. Quevedo, "PCP-II on a Renewed Church Pursuing Justice, Development and Peace," speech in Tagaytay, Philippines, March 23, 2006, found at Perspectives, http://abpquevedo.blogspot.com/2006/10/pcp-ii-on-renewed-church-pursuing.html.
35. Rev. Canon Mark Oxbrow, "Recovering Mission: Majority World Mission—A Return to Mission for the Majority," Lausanne World Pulse, January 2009, https://lausanneworldpulse.com/themedarticles-php/1071/01-2009.

13

Scattered and Gathered: Responses to Migration in the Context of Globalization

GEMMA TULUD CRUZ

The worldwide movement of people is as much a defining feature of globalization as the movement of goods, services, and capital. Like globalization, migration is not a new phenomenon. People have moved from one place to another since ancient times for much of the same reasons that encourage or compel people to move today, namely, economics, politics, and religiocultural conflicts. To be sure, patterns that connect the world have appeared from time to time throughout history and these have almost always resulted from or resulted in a wide-scale movement of people. In fact, nowhere is globalization's strongest impetus and enduring effects better illustrated than in population movements. This chapter provides a snapshot of the roots and routes, faces and facets of migrations in the context of globalization as experienced by Asians in general and Filipinos in particular.

ASIAN MIGRATION IN EARLY GLOBALIZATION

Asia has a long history of permanent, temporary, and cyclical migration due to various reasons. In precolonial times, nomadic tribes wandered the Asian continent in search of water and grazing lands. Prehistoric seafaring Malays are also said to have navigated the vast stretches of the uncharted Pacific long before the time of Columbus and Magellan, while Arab and Chinese traders formed part of the trade caravans that traveled on the renowned Silk Road.

The movement of Asian peoples intensified during the colonial period. The expansion of European empires across Asia not only brought soldiers and merchants but also missionaries who brought Christianity. The Spanish, Portuguese, and French empires, in particular, introduced Catholicism to countries such as the Philippines and Timor L'este (now Timor Leste or East Timor), which remain bastions of the Catholic faith in Asia. In addition, Asian converts on the move played an important role in the spread of Catholicism in the continent. There is, for example, the Japanese convert Yajiro (also called Anjiro) whom Francis Xavier met in Portuguese Malacca after the former fled Japan to escape punishment for a crime he had committed. Yajiro sought out Xavier, converted to Christianity, and returned to Japan as the interpreter for the first Jesuit mission to Japan, which included a Chinese who also had converted to Catholicism.[1] There is also the story of the returning Chinese migrants enlisted by French missionaries and the Korean envoy to China who brought Catholicism to Korea by bringing back books and articles on Christian doctrines upon his return to Korea from China.[2]

The "conquest" nature of the European expansion inevitably led to the abuse and exploitation of Asians through population movements, as territorial conquests and regulation of trade by European colonial regimes forced the migration of Asians as indentured laborers. The Dutch East India Company, for instance, transported thousands of slaves every year from the outer islands of the Indonesian Archipelago. Around this time Asian "coolies," or indentured laborers (mostly Indians and Chinese), also worked in plantations in Asia, Africa, and the Caribbean.[3] From 1834 to 1937 alone, some 30 million men and women from the Indian subcontinent were brought to Southeast Asia, Africa, the Caribbean, and the Pacific to work as indentured labor on British plantations.[4] International trade significantly expanded in this period, not just due to the extraction and exploitation of the colonized people's natural resources but also through the uprooting of the colonized peoples themselves to work as slaves or indentured laborers.[5] This combination of voluntary and involuntary migration went on for more than four centuries. As a result, more than one million people a year, or about 10 percent of the world's population, moved or were transported to the new world by the turn of the twentieth century. It could be argued that this period of migration laid considerable routes for the current phase of globalization because it is into these same routes and for the very same reasons, such as the search for better living conditions, that contemporary Asian labor migration finds some roots.

The Second World War picked up the pace of people's movements in and out of Asia. One notable player in these movements was Japan, whose expansionist interests brought thousands of Japanese into various Asian countries, notably Korea, China, and the Philippines, and triggered movements of people, primarily within national borders, in these countries. The war also propelled a significant migration of labor among Asians, as the colonizers used or recruited many of their former subjects to be foot soldiers in the war then lured more by opening their doors to immigrants to help rebuild their war-devastated economies. Americans, for instance, systematically recruited Filipinos, Chinese, and Japanese to work in their fruit plantations. Buoyed by a sense of familiarity with the colonizers' language and culture, other Asians also moved to their colonizers' home countries in search of a better life. Indians, Pakistanis, Sri Lankans, Bangladeshis, Malaysians, and Singaporeans moved to the United Kingdom, Indonesians went to the Netherlands, and Vietnamese and Cambodians settled in France, while Filipinos, Koreans, and Japanese as well as Vietnamese sought the American dream.

Political and economic crises, wars, and religiocultural conflicts in many Asian countries, combined with real and fabricated stories of a better life in the destination countries, encouraged many more Asians to migrate, both authorized and unauthorized, in the subsequent decades. Given their more accommodating policies on asylum and family reunification, Europe and North America became principal destinations. Today, despite European and North American countries' stricter border control and stringent immigration policies,

Asian migration to these areas continues to expand primarily due to the current phase of globalization.

FILIPINO MIGRATION IN THE EARLY PHASE

Migration is inextricably linked to the story of Filipinos. As a race, Filipinos themselves were born out of people's movements. One Filipino migration theory, known as the wave model associated with American anthropologist H. Otley Beyer, traces the evolution of Filipinos as a race to a series of migrations into what is now known as the Philippines. The first wave, according to the theory, was comprised of the Negritos who crossed the land bridges from Malay Peninsula, Borneo, and Australia. The second wave came with the maritime Indonesians, who arrived by boats after the submergence of the land bridges. The third wave was made up of the ancient Malays, who also came by boat in significant numbers from 200 BCE to 16 CE; these were the ancestors of most Filipinos today.[6]

Another migration theory, proposed by noted Filipino anthropologist F. Landa Jocano, disputes Beyer's model that Filipinos descended from Negritoes and Malays who migrated to the Philippines thousands of years ago. Jocano instead points to evolution theory and posits that the first people of Southeast Asia were products of a long process of evolution and migration.[7] According to Jocano, the early Filipinos were not just passive recipients but also active transmitters and synthesizers of cultures. For example, comparative studies of Pacific cultures show that some of the inhabitants of Micronesia, Polynesia, and other Pacific islands came from the Philippines.[8] Other notable movements of people in and out of the Philippines include the Chinese, whose interactions with Filipinos for trade purposes were recorded in the years 982 CE, 1001, 1225, 1373, and 1417. The Chinatown in Manila, often described as the oldest Chinatown in the world, was already a hub of Chinese commerce even before Spaniards established it as a settlement for Catholic Chinese in 1594. The first Filipino saint, Lorenzo Ruiz, a Chinese-Filipino martyred in Japan in the seventeenth century, and Venerable Mother Ignacia del Espiritu Santo (1663–1748), foundress of the first Native Filipino female religious congregation known as Religious of the Virgin Mary, lived in Chinatown.

Indeed, the Chinese and Arab traders that formed part of the trade caravans that traveled on the renowned Silk Road, the ancient network of trade routes that were central to cultural interaction through regions of the Asian continent connecting the West and East from China to the Mediterranean Sea, played an important role in the religiocultural history of Filipinos. In fact, Muslim traders from the Persian Gulf, South India, and, to a certain extent, the Malaysian Archipelago, brought Islam to the Philippines in the fourteenth century, a century earlier than Christianity, which was brought to the Philippines by its longest colonizer, Spain. Toma Pires's *Summa Oriental* (1515)—a history of the Portuguese in Asia containing the first mention by a European of the people from the Philippines—also notes the trade between Luzon, Borneo, and Malacca. Filipinos were referred to in the text as Luçoes (Luzones).[9]

In many ways, Spanish colonization brought the Philippines into contact with other parts of the world. Under Spanish rule, Manila maintained trade relations with Acapulco, thereby bringing Filipino seafarers to Mexico. Filipino migration to the United States also has roots in Spanish colonial times. The earliest Filipino migrants to the United States were the Manila men of the Saint Malo village in Louisiana. Called the Louisiana Community, the migrants were Filipino sailors who jumped from the Spanish vessels plying the Manila-Acapulco galleon trade during the Spanish colonization of the Philippines. While the galleon was docked on the west coast of Mexico, many Filipinos escaped the oppressive colonial conditions and traveled east to Vera Cruz, where they boarded another ship or traveled by land until reaching Louisiana.[10]

The American colonial period, meanwhile, brought a distinct group of Filipinos to the United States. In 1903, through the passage of the Pensionado Act, qualified Filipino students were sent to the United States to create a pool of qualified, highly educated civil servants embodying American ideals. These students were called *pensionados*, since they were scholars studying at the expense of the colonial government. The martial law years and, in particular, the economic policies of the late Filipino dictator Ferdinand Marcos, in the meantime, became a turning point for international migration among Filipinos, when labor migration took center stage well into the current phase of globalization.

WORKERS ON THE MOVE: THE CURRENT PHASE OF GLOBALIZATION

Migration has always been part of the story of the Asian region. Contemporary Asian and Filipino migration, however, is profound and distinct in that its volume and density is greater, its features more complex, and its ripple effects more comprehensive. No family, community, or nation-state is left untouched by it, primarily due to migration's deep imbrication with the current phase of globalization, which is more intense, more complex, and more widespread. It is to this breadth, intensity, and complexity that the focus now turns.

The Big Picture: Asia

Graeme Hugo noted in 2005 that migration flows within and from Asia had acquired an unprecedented scale, diversity, and significance.[11] Until the last decades of the twentieth century, labor migration was somehow minimal in the Asian region. Prior to this, political instability primarily accounted for Asian people's mobility, as wars and various forms of civil conflicts plagued the continent. Violent conflicts in Vietnam, Cambodia, Afghanistan, and Sri Lanka alone have created 6–7 million refugees. On top of this, 300,000 Rohingyas were forced to leave Myanmar in 1992 and 80,000 Nepalese have been forced out of Bhutan since 1991. Today, Asian mobility as a result of political instability remains a serious problem. When one factors in, for example, the 2.6 million Iraqis displaced at the end of 2008 plus the many more displaced by more current conflicts in Afghanistan, Pakistan, Sri Lanka, and other parts of Asia—notably the prolonged conflict in Syria and the brutal campaign of the Myanmar military in 2017, which drove out more than 740,000 Rohingyas into Bangladesh—Asians share a sizable number of the June 2022 record of 27.1 million refugees reported by the UNHCR (United Nations High Commissioner for Refugees).[12] Tied to this phenomenon is the growing issue of environmental displacement in the region. In 2010 alone, 249.2 million people in the Asian region were affected by extreme weather events.[13]

There is, however, an indisputable dominant face of contemporary Asians on the move: the migrant worker. The International Labor Organization estimates at least 30 million migrant workers in the Asia Pacific region, and that their numbers are increasing. Without a doubt, the current phase of globalization, which has uplifted some Asian economies and further marginalized the rest, is changing the volume, nature, face, and direction of Asian labor migration.[14] For one, there is a palpable shift in destination in recent decades, from Europe and North America to countries in Asia.[15] This large-scale and multidirectional migration within the Asian region is attributed to two developments, namely, the oil boom of the mid 1970s, which induced an immense investment in infrastructures by Middle Eastern countries, and the emergence of the so-called Asian tiger economies, namely, South Korea, Singapore, Thailand, Taiwan, Hong Kong, and Malaysia. These countries' increased economic development, coupled with industrialized Japan's needs, created a massive demand for cheap labor, which people from the many poor Asian countries readily filled out of dire need. The continuing demand for skilled and unskilled labor in these Asian countries, together with affluent Western countries' increasing need for replacements for its diminishing pool of workers (due to a high level of an aging population and low level of fertility rates), has fueled a steady increase of labor migration by Asians.[16]

In keeping with the trajectories of international labor migration, particularly as created by the current process of economic globalization, the majority of the Asian global workforce is undeniably in unskilled work.[17] The history and makeup of foreign labor of the Middle East, whose migration system is as alive now as it was in the 1980s, reflect this dominance of unskilled work.[18] Before the oil boom migrant workers in Middle Eastern countries almost exclusively came from neighboring Arab countries. When oil profits lifted these countries' economies they progressively turned to Southeast Asians (Pakistanis and Indians, then South Koreans, Thais, and Filipinos), first, because the British oil companies brought their Asian workers in Burma to the Gulf region; second, because Middle Eastern countries became worried about depending only on a few source countries; and third, because these host countries liked the concept of project-tied migration brought by large multinational contractors and commercial recruiters. When an oil price crisis occurred in the mid-1980s and the Middle Eastern economies survived and continued to flourish thanks to the revenues gained from their investments in industrialized countries, the demand for foreign labor shifted to service and production workers. The shift to these occupations reflected the trends of the global job market, not only in terms of volume and expansion but also in the way the shift was characterized by declining wages and other terms and conditions of employment (which often applied only to foreign workers, hence were less fair). The situation evolved from having almost exclusively oil and construction workers in the 1970s and early 1980s who came from India, Pakistan, South Korea, Thailand, and the Philippines, to an expanded foreign labor pool dominated by women domestic workers, hotel workers, mechanics, personal drivers, and sanitation and farm workers who came from Bangladesh, Sri Lanka, Indonesia, and, more recently, China and Vietnam.[19] This period started the outflow of women workers in considerable numbers, leading to the increasing feminization of Asian labor migration, with women constituting 42 percent of migrant workers in Asia by 2013.[20]

Of course, there are also Asian migrants in skilled work. There has been, in fact, a progressively larger number of professional- and managerial-level Asians working in the Gulf region, most of whom are actually hired to replace westerners and nonnational Arabs because they were willing to work for much less pay.[21] Indeed, while there are many skilled Asian workers who get better and fairer pay in other parts of the world, such as doctors, computer experts, scientists, engineers, and dentists, there are also a number of skilled workers who take on underemployment because, aside from other perceived benefits of migration, overseas work pay is still high when compared to the salary potential in their home countries (e.g., Filipino teachers who take on migrant jobs as domestic workers). On top of this are skilled Asian migrant workers who belong to the different breed of skilled migrants created by contemporary global integration: the "skilled transients," or corporate managers, consultants, and technicians who hop or get transferred from one international branch of a transnational company to another.[22]

The movement of skilled workers, including "skilled transients," is particularly strong into and from East Asia and, more recently, into and from India. Additionally, the movement involves three streams: 1) Asians who leave home for the first time to work inside other parts of Asia or outside of Asia; 2) Asians who previously migrated and settled in other (often industrialized) countries who return to their home countries on the basis of improved social and labor conditions; and 3) westerners who are lured not just by adventure but also by higher salaries and positions offered by more affluent Asian countries. For example, a reverse flow of Australian skilled workers (both Native and naturalized Australians from East Asia and Malaysia) to Singapore, Hong Kong, and Malaysia has been on the rise in the past decade.[23] Statistical records of foreign workers in Malaysia under the expatriate category (professional and technical workers) even shows the UK taking the fourth-highest spot (8.9 percent of the approximately 32,609 expatriates).[24]

From a general perspective, labor migration inside and outside of Asia can be organized into four systems: the Middle East, which has a strong dependency on foreign labor hired through the sponsorship system; East Asia, which reluctantly admits unskilled workers; Southeast Asia, which is both a region of origin and of destination; and South Asia, which is mostly a region of origin. The contexts and statistics already laid out also reveal that migration in Asia should be seen in a historical context; that the volume of migration is expanding; and that women, as independent migrants, constitute a significant share of current labor migration.[25]

Labor Exporter Par Excellence: The Filipino Experience

The distinct pattern of movements of the historical and continued outflow of Filipino migrant workers is enshrined in what are called the four waves of Filipino labor migration.[26] The first wave, in the 1900s, saw Filipino men migrating to work in sugar and pineapple plantations in Hawaii and later to the US mainland as apple pickers.[27] This first group of Filipino migrants originated mostly from northern Luzon and parts of Visayas, both of which have a history of migration to other parts of the country due to land problems.[28] In 1906, the first 15 Filipino laborers, all men, came to Hawaii, followed by 150 in 1907 and another 639 in 1909. There were 2,915 migrant Filipino workers in Hawaii by 1910 and from 1911 to 1920 an estimated 3,000 workers arrived yearly. In 1919, Hawaii recorded 24,791 Japanese workers and 10,354 Filipinos, representing 54.7 percent and 22.9 percent, respectively, of the total plantation labor force. By the 1930s, Filipinos had replaced the Japanese as the largest ethnic group of workers on the plantations despite a temporary halt in the influx of Filipino migrants due to the Great Depression. In fact, a total of 7,300 *sakadas* (sugarcane laborer or planter) were repatriated to the Philippines because of the Depression.[29] The last significant wave of Filipino plantation workers in Hawaii occurred in 1946, when Hawaii brought in around 6,000 men, 446 women, and 915 children to work as sakadas after the transfer of many plantation workers to defense industry work during World War II.[30]

In the postwar period, a different pattern of Filipino migration to the United States emerged. Groups consisted of immediate families of migrant Filipinos already in the United States, more professionals, and more women and children. This second wave (1940–60) brought the movement of thousands of Filipinos to the United States, Canada, and Europe as war brides and highly skilled workers, primarily as a result of more open immigration policies. This wave of labor migration included a variety of professionals, from doctors, accountants, and nutritionists to physical therapists and others. This group also included women, who worked mostly as nurses or hospital staff. This new batch has a distinct characteristic in the sense that most of the migrants were better-educated and skilled, arguably marking this period as a "brain drain" period of Filipino out-migration.

An economic downturn and high unemployment rate in the country due to the 1970s oil crisis, combined with then president Marcos's illicit use of foreign aid money, led to the third wave, which peaked in the 1980s. Seeing a significant source of national income in the remittances of OFWs (overseas Filipino workers), Marcos institutionalized labor migration in the mid-1970s through the Labor Export Program (LEP). The "trade" covered almost all occupational groups: doctors, engineers, teachers, nurses, seafarers, band singers, domestic helpers, chambermaids, and construction workers. This period also saw the expansion of sea-based work, from the shipping industry to the fishing industry. If the second wave was marked by a "brain drain" of the skilled and the intellectuals of the Philippines, the third wave went a little further by exporting both the "brains" and the "brawns" of Filipino society.[31] This period of labor migration was marked as well by the dramatic expansion of destination countries to the Middle Eastern Gulf States, due to the growth of the oil industry.

The current phase of globalization ushered in a shift in destination, that is, from Europe and America to the tiger economies in Asia. With its concomitant international division of labor and the expansion of the service sector, the current phase also created areas of job concentration, particularly in hospitality and service- or care-oriented work. This resulted in an unprecedented out-migration of Filipino women, mainly as nurses, entertainers, and domestic workers, which led to the fourth wave in the 1990s, which was characterized by the feminization of Filipino laborers.[32] This female domination peaked in 2001, when more than 90 percent of all OCWs (overseas contract workers) were women.[33] Continuing economic woes of the country propped by a culture of migration and, in particular, a commercialized and institutionalized migration industry saw a record 1 million OCWs in 2006.[34] In 2015, there were about 2.4 million OCWs, 51.1 percent of whom were women and 48.9 percent men. A full 97 percent of these OCWs worked with an existing labor contract, while 2.9 percent worked without a contract.[35] Today at least 10 million Filipinos work or live in more than two hundred countries as nurses, caregivers, domestic helpers, welders, carpenters, plumbers, electricians, engineers, or factory workers, among others. They are hailed as *bagong bayani* (new heroes) largely on account of their remittances' significant contributions to the country's economy. In 2006 alone, OFWs sent $22 billion, even exceeding by 25 percent the country's national budget for the same year. In 2011, meanwhile, remittances totaled 12 percent of GDP in the Philippines.[36] The goldmine that remittances represent continues to strongly motivate the Philippine government to promote labor out-migration.

Migration is deeply woven into contemporary Filipino life; it is said that about 70 percent of the population is affected by it. Many Filipinos have a parent (in some cases both parents), a sibling, a relative, a friend, or a neighbor who works or lives overseas. In a number of cases it is intergenerational; in some cases it involves almost entire clans. Labor migration, in particular, has become so much a part of Filipino society that "OFW," "OCW," and other words associated with particular overseas work(ers) have entered the Filipino vocabulary (e.g., "*katas* ng Saudi" or fruit of labor from Saudi Arabia; "DH" for domestic helper; and "*japayuki*" for Filipina entertainer in Japan).

SACRAMENT OF FAITH AND SOLIDARITY: PUBLIC CATHOLICISM AMONG MIGRANTS

Philip Jenkins's book *The Next Christendom: The Coming of Global Christianity,* the first in his trilogy on the future of Christianity, has been hailed as a landmark text in our understanding of modern Christianity.[37] One of the important points Jenkins raised in the book is how contemporary migration is reshaping and redefining not just human geography but also the religious features and landscapes of the world, particularly Christianity.[38] Jenkins notes how the survival, future, and vitality of churches in destination countries are significantly influenced by immigrant churches germinated in the Global South. Having sketched the Asian and Filipino migration landscape in the context of the key phases of Asian globalization, we now turn to the public role that Catholicism assumes in such a landscape.

A common public face of Catholicism among migrants is a deep and in some cases defiant witness to their Catholic faith. The first Filipino saint, Lorenzo Ruiz, who ended up on a ship bound for Japan in the company of two Dominican friars and a leper, was canonized for his deep faith in the face of torture and martyrdom in Japan in 1637. Refusing to recant his faith, Ruiz's famous last words were: "I am a Catholic and wholeheartedly do accept death for God. Had I a thousand lives, all these to Him I shall offer."

The late Filipino bishop Francisco Claver points out that, for all their defects and faults, ordinary Filipinos are a deeply religious people and their religiosity migrates with them into their new places of residence and work. Claver writes:

> It is a common enough phenomenon, but everywhere OFWs go they bring their religiosity along with them and they seem to be more faithful to their practice of religion than they show back in the Philippines—at least where weekly church-going is concerned . . . in the unfamiliar ultimate surroundings of their migrant situation, it is the Catholic faith and its rituals that make them feel at home amid the strangeness of all other aspects of their new life.[39]

Speaking primarily from his experience with Filipina migrants in Hong Kong, Singapore, and Japan, noted Filipino sociologist Randy David echoes Claver's observation by attributing what he regards as the legendary resilience of OCWs to their spirituality. David shares:

> I once visited a bar in a suburb of Tokyo where the hostesses were very young *Pinays*. I was very impressed with the way they dealt with the more aggressive among their Japanese customers. These girls were in total command of themselves and of the situation, even if their Japanese was barely understandable. One of them told me that all five of them prayed together at the beginning and at the end of every night—before an image of the *Santo Niño* (Infant Jesus) which was magnificently enshrined right among the cognac and whisky bottles. I also remember sitting in a plane beside a sexily dressed Filipina bound for Japan. She must have carried with her more than a dozen novenas to various saints. She did nothing but mumble her magical prayers through the entire trip, her contemplative pose only occasionally disturbed by the chatter of her Japanese recruiter. I asked her if she was nervous and if this was her first time to leave the country. No, she was not, and this was her third time.[40]

In Canada and elsewhere, Roman Catholic churches are centers of Filipino social interaction outside the confines of their homes.[41] The loneliness and isolation and, consequently, the need to connect, especially to people and rituals that remind them of home, strongly account for weekly church attendance. As one Filipina live-in caregiver bemoaned, "I will go crazy if I cannot go to church."[42] Such deep religiosity, made more relevant and intense by various problems associated with their lives as migrants, helps them keep their faith even in adverse circumstances. It is well-known, for example, that many Arab destination countries frown upon public display of religion other than Islam. This is particularly true in Saudi Arabia, where a puritanical brand of Islam is observed and strictly enforced by the religious police. Most, if not all, Filipino migrant workers bound for the Middle East know this restriction against public display of religion other than Islam. I have personally heard this information being relayed to Middle East–bound Filipina migrant domestic workers while attending a required PDOS (predeparture orientation seminar) as part of an exposure activity. The religious sister who was conducting the session told the participants not to bring articles of faith, particularly the Bible or rosary. Despite such training and warning, Delia, a former migrant worker who credits her faith for surviving an ordeal in the hands of Iraqi soldiers during their occupation of Kuwait, brought a Bible, rosary beads, and a prayer book at her own peril.[43] Mark Johnson writes that for many Filipinos in Saudi Arabia it is the "religious police" rather than the regular police who are perceived to be the prime agents of state surveillance and cause the most anxiety on a daily basis. There are stories of Filipino migrants who had trouble entering or leaving the country because the "religious police" found prohibited materials, such as the Bible.[44]

Unfortunately, this central role of the Church and religious activities does not always work well for migrants, since a church itself sometimes becomes the very place where they are hunted, chased, and arrested. For example, in Malaysia and Taiwan, where police and immigration agents are authorized to ask for documents in public places, churches are not immune to organized raids by agents. This is reflected in what happened in St. John's Cathedral (Malaysia) and St. Christopher's Church (Taiwan), when churchgoers, particularly migrant women domestic workers, were required to show proper legal documentation.[45] In 2010, Saudi Arabia arrested 14 overseas Filipino workers for participating in a Mass.[46] Felipe Muncada writes that in Japan, many undocumented Filipinos do not go to church because of fear that the church may be raided by immigration officials, since such incidents have happened in the past.[47]

As has been the case for generations of migrants, public Catholicism among Asian and Filipino migrants also has an ethnic face. Filipino migrants, for example, carry and observe in public their popular devotions all over the world, from the prayer circles in Florida (US), the Santacruzan in Tel Aviv (Israel), and the Simbang Gabi in Penang (Malaysia), to the various feast day celebrations for their hometown saints and other religious festivals.[48] Like Filipinos, Vietnamese Catholics are also known for bringing their Marian devotions, particularly to Our Lady of La Vhang. When the Vietnamese community in the suburbs of Washington, DC, had an opportunity to build a church for their own community, they chose not to build in the style reminiscent of the French colonial church buildings in Vietnam. Our Lady of Vietnam Parish is more in the style of Buddhist and Confucian temples in Vietnam. Robert Schreiter contends that this church is a notable example of church architecture being enculturated, expressing the religious identity of an immigrant group.[49]

Public Catholicism is also expressed by Asian and Filipino migrants through their missionary activities. Filipino migrants who practice their faith in myriad ways, such as attending Sunday Mass and devotional worship, subtly embody the Christian mission of evangelization.[50] As the world's largest group of foreign migrant workers, Filipinos are considered by the Lausanne Committee for World Evangelization as "God's secret weapon" in facilitating the global spread of Christianity.[51] The extraordinary opening of a Catholic Church in Dubai, for example, is strongly credited to Catholic migrant workers from the Philippines, Sri Lanka, and other Asian countries.[52] Bishop Claver points to the contribution of the many OFWs employed as caretakers of Arab children in the thawing of Muslim resistance to Christian presence. Claver muses, "When one hears of Arab mothers complaining that their children are learning from Filipina maids how to pray the Our Father and the Hail Mary, one can't help wondering what these children will carry into their adult life as a result of their experience with Filipina care-givers."[53] Quoting an Italian couple reflecting on how their daughter learned to go to church by joining her Filipina nanny, who never fails to go to Mass on Sundays, Claver points to reverse mission among Filipino migrants:

> This is what Filipinos are doing around the world, without any fuss, without strong statements, and just by their own presence. If centuries ago European colonizers went abroad far and wide to conquer countries and peoples with the sword, a new colonization is taking place today, and no one knows about it. But it's just as powerful and effective even if they are often dismissed as "maids" or "nurses." Yes maids, nurses, seafarers, but with a soul that can change everything around them.[54]

Last, but not least, public Catholicism is expressed among Asian and Filipino migrants by their transnational religious practices. Stephen Cherry speaks along these lines, based on his study of the impact of Roman Catholicism as a cultural framework and mediating institution on US Catholic civic life for first generation Filipino Catholic communities in Houston, Texas. Cherry argues that there is a relationship between the religiosity of Filipino Catholics and transnational civic engagement.[55] Jeremiah Opiniano echoes this Catholicism-related transnational philanthropy among Filipinos and cites Gawad Kalinga, the development arm of the Filipino charismatic group Couples for Christ, which has branches overseas and has raised more than 25 million pesos from overseas Filipinos, aimed at building low-cost housing for poor Filipinos.[56] Asuncion Fresnoza-Flot also mentions the church-related transnational humanitarian activities practiced by Filipina migrants in France, particularly fundraising for victims of natural disasters in the Philippines.[57]

To be sure, (im)migrant churches often contribute significant sums of money to community development in their sending communities. For example, in a survey containing more than two thousand randomly sampled responses from first-generation and second-generation Filipino Catholic (im)migrants from fifty churches in the ecclesiastical dioceses of San Francisco, Oakland, and San Jose, about 1,674 respondents declared themselves as prayers and senders, that is, they help families, communities, and churches back in their Philippine hometowns.[58] As Thomas Csordas contends, religious transnationalism, in the case of migrant believers, is linked with the processes of missionization, migration, mediatization, and mobility.[59]

A PAN-ASIAN CATHOLIC CHURCH IN THE CONTEXT OF MIGRATION

In the context of globalization, the experience of Asian migrants, particularly migrant workers, is clearly characterized by gifts and challenges. Not surprisingly, the Special Assembly of the Synod of Bishops for Asia, which was held at the Vatican in 1998, has urged that special attention must be paid to the millions of migrant workers who leave their families to earn their livelihoods in other countries. The synod fathers also stressed the urgent need of pastoral care for migrants in their own ecclesial traditions.[60] Hence, to make the most out of the gifts as well as address the challenges associated with migration, the Church in Asia must provide various forms of pastoral response within and across national borders.

The most common form of pastoral response is the provision of a chaplain with the same cultural background as the migrants. Consequently, the provision of the Mass in the migrants' language is a common form of pastoral response. For example, the Japanese Church provides Masses in Portuguese for its Brazilian migrants in the same way that many churches offer services in Indonesian, Korean, Spanish, Tagalog, and Vietnamese.[61] In some cases religious leaders from countries of origin regularly conduct pastoral visits. For example, earlier meetings between representatives of Cambodian Catholic communities in Australia and New Zealand often coincided with the visit of Bishop Ramousse or one of the French priests who had worked in the Cambodian Church before 1975.[62]

Catholic social teachings and advocacy, particularly through the Federation of Asian Bishops' Conference (FABC), also figure prominently in the pan-Asian response to the plight of contemporary migrants. For instance, even when the FABC had not yet issued formal statements on migration, the bishops of the Philippines and Taiwan had already released their own statements on migration in 1998 and 1989, respectively. In 1993, the Korean Church also addressed the issue of undocumented migrants and their problems through a statement of its Justice and Peace Committee, which emphasized the need to look at the issue from a human rights perspective and go beyond a national approach to embrace a "mature citizens' consciousness and conscious solidarity with the global family."[63]

It was in its final statement for its Fifth Plenary Assembly (1990) that the FABC makes a clear link for the first time between poverty and migration.[64] Subsequent plenary assemblies included discussions and references to migration, urging special attention to the displaced (e.g., political and ecological refugees and migrant workers). The sixth FABC Assembly statement exhorts the faithful to welcome these marginalized and exploited people, for "in welcoming them we expose the cause of their displacement, work toward conditions for a more human living in community, experience the universal dimension of the Kingdom (Gal. 3:28) and appreciate new opportunities for evangelization and intercultural dialogue."[65] While the FABC has generally emphasized the economic causes of migration, it has increasingly advocated for the rights of migrants as well. For example, the 1993 symposium on Filipino migrant workers organized by the now-defunct Office of Human Development (OHD) critiqued the economic system's "violent aggression on the rights of the Asian poor to live with human dignity as sons and daughters of God" and concluded that receiving countries do benefit from migrant workers but the benefit to the Philippines "remains questionable."[66]

Indeed, the Asian Church has not remained silent on the exploitation of migrant workers. The Chinese Bishops' Conference of Taiwan went as far as listing twenty-two instances of Taiwan's original laws or practices regarding migrant workers that contradict the UN document on human rights. These include exploitatively high broker fees, brokers breaking terms of original contract, and a prohibition against women migrant workers getting pregnant, marrying, or bringing family members.[67] The first Bishops' Institute for Christian Advocacy (BICA) in 2006, in the meantime, addressed solidarity with migrants and refugees and generated nine pastoral recommendations that integrate pastoral care and work for justice. The recommendations include: the establishment of a help desk to link home and host countries; the preparation of a video clip showing the life of migrants in the host country as part of a preparation kit to promote awareness of the rights of migrants and refugees; a dialogue with recruitment, employment, and government agencies concerning contracts; creation of welcoming committees in host countries and visits by chaplains from home countries;

communications with host countries to facilitate exchanges between migrant workers and their families; implementation of Migration Sunday in countries of origin; advocating and lobbying with local governments; country-specific recommendations; and regular dialogues with host countries on the specific issue of marriages, legal implications, laws of the host country, and the problem of producing baptismal certificates. The seventh Plenary Assembly in 2000 also gave prominence to migrants and refugees, with a special workshop devoted to the pastoral challenge they pose. In fact, that assembly's final statement included a lengthy section on sea-based and land-based migrants and refugees.[68] The eighth Plenary Assembly in 2004 addressed the phenomenon of Asian migration, particularly as it affects family life. The BICA in 2007 picked up that pastoral concern for migrant families.[69]

Social teachings and advocacies are complemented by concrete pastoral initiatives. These include special meetings, conferences, and symposia such as the FABC-OHD symposium on Filipino migrant workers. There was also the Faith Encounters in Social Action's (FEISA) fifth gathering, entitled "From Distrust to Respect . . . Reject to Welcome: Study Days on Undocumented Migrants and Refugees."[70] In the Philippines, the Church proposed a Day for Migrants (in 1970) and the hierarchy formally established in 1982 the annual celebration of National Migrants Sunday.

The creation of ecclesial structures and practices directly related to the pastoral care of people on the move is another way in which the Asian Church responds to contemporary migration. Regionally, as can be seen in its sponsorship and leadership in migration-related meetings, the FABC's OHD has played a public role on issues concerning people on the move. Nationally, a few bishops' conferences have an episcopal commission for migrants. The Catholic Bishops' Conference of the Philippines, for example, has the ECMI (Episcopal Commission for Migrants and Itinerant Peoples). In addition, various dioceses have pastoral offices or centers specifically catering to migrants. I have seen firsthand, for instance, the various initiatives by the Diocesan Pastoral Center for Filipinos in Hong Kong. The center offers a variety of services, from the more basic needs such as language classes to the more urgent services such as hotlines and legal assistance for those in distress, and the more strategic services such as livelihood and reintegration programs. The center also assists in the civic participation of migrant domestic workers, not just for their fellow migrants but also for the local community, especially through volunteer work.

Lay-led Catholic organizations with offices in Asia and with links to the institutional Church also form part of the pan-Asian pastoral response. These include the International Catholic Migration Commission (ICMC), whose mission is "to protect and serve uprooted people, including refugees, asylum seekers, internally displaced people, victims of human trafficking, and migrants—regardless of faith, race, ethnicity or nationality," using "needs-first and right-based approaches."[71] The ICMC's current activities—operations, advocacy, and Church networking—and current four focus areas—protection and prevention, humanitarian assistance, refugee resettlement, and migration and development—testify to how far the Church has come in its public support of and commitment to people on the move, evolving from a focus on migrants' spiritual care to an expansion into pastoral care that includes a social justice perspective.[72] Not to be outdone is the valuable work among migrants by various religious congregations and numerous faith-based organizations across the Asian Pacific. For instance, there is the Columban-run Hope Workers' Center in Taiwan and three Jesuit centers in receiving countries in Asia that provide casework, medical and legal help, and social and learning activities, as well as accompaniment for migrants: the Rerum Novarum Centre in Taiwan, the Yiutsari Jesuit Migrant Centre in South Korea, and the Jesuit Social Centre in Japan. The Scalabrinians play an important role through their research centers in New York and Manila and the Scalabrini International Migration Institute in Rome. In 1996, Filipino missionaries in Japan (priests, brothers, sisters, layworkers, and seminarians) formed a loose association called PhilMiss (Philippine Missionaries in Japan) for networking and support.[73] Then there are the Catholic educational institutions that provide pioneering efforts in putting a spotlight on migration, such as the Migration Theology Program offering a certificate in pastoral care of migrants at Loyola School of Theology in Manila.

In some cases lay-founded and lay-led Catholic groups or organizations with a global presence provide a vital source of support in dealing with problematic working conditions among migrants. Couples for Christ (CFC) and El Shaddai, for instance, are formidable sources of religious involvement and support for Filipino migrants all over the world, sometimes even providing assistance in looking for another employer because of abuse.[74] Last but not least are millions of Catholic individuals, the unsung heroes and heroines who come to the aid of migrants in need and actively participate in advocacies and public protests on behalf of migrants and refugees.[75] Everywhere in the world, many Filipinos in distress rely on the goodness of other migrants, particularly Filipinos, who not only generously share their time, energy, money, and talents but, in the case of the Middle East and war-torn countries, sometimes risk their jobs and their lives to help.[76] The story is the same for other Asian Catholic migrants and migrant communities in various parts of the world and such "critical" acts cannot be ignored.[77]

CONCLUSION

Based on the preceding discussion, one could say that in the context of contemporary global migration, transnational faith, solidarity, and justice characterize the Asian Church in general and the Filipino Church in particular. This is not surprising, since the Catholic Church itself is the single largest international religious organization in the world and is arguably the oldest globalized institution on earth. As seen in its history, the Church's global character and hierarchical as well as international structure is well-positioned to engage in multi-stranded and cross-border ties. Its hundreds of religious orders, which have members and missions scattered across the planet, have been heralds of a globalized world for centuries.

Today such transnational missionary activity is increasingly practiced by millions of Catholic migrants all over the world, including Filipinos, by connecting with and helping one another in ways that are reinvigorating the Church in the world. It is because of these Asian, notably Filipino, migrants and their plight that the Catholic Church, particularly the Asian Church, has slowly and increasingly responded in equal measure by taking on a more public role to become a house for all peoples and a sacrament of justice and solidarity. Pope Francis puts in a nutshell the practical vision and inspiration that is embedded in the Asian Church's pastoral response in the context of migration:

> Migrants and refugees . . . are an occasion that Providence gives us to help build a more just society, a more perfect democracy, a more united country, a more fraternal world and a more open and evangelical Christian community. Migration can offer possibilities for a new evangelization, open vistas for the growth of a new humanity foreshadowed in the paschal mystery: a humanity for which every foreign country is a homeland and every homeland is a foreign country.[78]

By articulating a vision of community that supersedes national boundaries and within which religious transnational civil society agents take center stage, Francis encourages members' sense of belonging in multiple settings. It is inevitably a, if not *the*, way of being and becoming Church in the context of migration in this age of globalization. Catholicism therefore gathers what globalization scatters.

The problem is that the term "Asian" itself does not really refer to a single, homogenous enclave but a panethnic category that includes persons, cultures, and languages from a vast geographical area that includes at least fifty-three countries. The ethnolinguistic diversity that characterizes Asian peoples themselves is staggering. Even the term "Filipino" could be considered a pan-ethnic category, as Filipinos are comprised of twelve lowland groups in addition to more or less a hundred communities known collectively as "Indigenous people." While Philippine languages share common Malayo-Polynesian roots, members of these groups do not necessarily understand each other's languages.

Robert Schreiter contends that, on the one hand, a pan-Asian perspective poses a hurdle, as more specific identities such as the Hmong from Vietnam or even national identities such as Filipino are amalgamated into a single Asian classification. Schreiter notes how within a continent as vast and varied as Asia, it is hard to see what a Korean and an Indonesian have in common. There is not even a common language that provides some bonding together, as is the case for peoples coming from Latin America. On the other hand, Schreiter points to the positive side of a pan-Asian approach, especially when one sees it in terms of how second-generation immigrants from Asia frequently join pan-Asian Christian congregations and parishes. These pan-Asian religious spaces, Schreiter submits, allow those of the second generation to negotiate between their national or ethnic identity and a larger identity that takes them beyond specific identifications.[79]

Indeed, such an approach or perspective has more appeal and is more frequently practiced among younger and second-generation immigrant Asians, as doing so allows them to not only remain faithful to their parents' religious identity but also to seek out and negotiate a religious identity more suitable to their own needs (e.g., using English in pan-Asian parishes).[80] As the generation who connects more strongly with the American side of their identity, explicit reminders of the home their parents have left (or were forced to leave) could elicit negative reactions.

Tito Cruz, a Filipino American Catholic priest and theologian, affirms the issues that a pan-Asian approach engenders. Cruz writes: "Whenever we use panethnic categories like

Asian, Pacific, Latino, Anglo, or Black we take the risk of naming people in ways that they don't use themselves." Cruz notes that just as most "Latinos" self-identify using their specific national or regional name, persons from Asia and the Pacific generally do the same. It is important not to sideline this practice, asserts Cruz, as "these names represent distinct narratives that connect us to our myths, symbols, and rituals. They call us to examine critically our colonial history, teach us to embrace persons who call themselves by other names, impels us to work for peace and justice, and encourage us in faith to strive toward a more abundant life in a new land."[81] At the same time, Cruz acknowledges that some Asian Americans prefer a hyphenated term like "Chinese-American" to designate their being between two cultures and being in both. Pastorally and theologically, a pan-Asian approach and perspective has gifts and challenges that warrant further investigation and discussion.

NOTES

1. Samuel Hugh Moffett, *A History of Christianity in Asia*, vol. 2 (New York: Orbis, 2005), 69–70.
2. Jean-Paul Wiest, "Catholic Mission Theory and Practice: Lessons from the Work of the Paris Foreign Mission Society and Maryknoll in Guangdong and Guangxi Provinces," *Missiology: An International Review* 10, no. 2 (April 1982): 179–80; Andrew Eungi Kim, "South Korea," in Peter Phan, ed., *Christianities in Asia* (West Sussex, UK: Wiley-Blackwell, 2011), 219.
3. Pieter C. Emmer, "We Are Here, Because You Were There: European Colonialism and Intercontinental Migration," in Dietmar Mieth and Lisa Sowle Cahill, eds., *Migrants and Refugees* (Maryknoll, NY: Orbis 1993): 45–48.
4. Manolo Abella and Lin Lean Lim, "The Movement of People in Asia: Internal, Intra-Regional and International Migration," in Christian Conference of Asia, ed., *Uprooted People in Asia* (Hong Kong: CCA, 1995): 12.
5. The Spanish conquistadors, for example, enriched themselves by connecting the Spanish empire in Latin America with the Asian market via the Philippines. Gold bullions were extracted by the Spaniards in Latin America and exchanged for silk, spices, and tea from Asia using the *galleon* trade, which utilized indentured labor from its colonies like Mexico and the Philippines.
6. See Sonia Zaide, *The Philippines: A Unique Nation*, 2nd ed. (All Nations, 1999), 32–34.
7. See "The First Filipinos" at http://www.philippine-history.org/early-filipinos.htm, accessed August 28, 2016.
8. See, for example, F. Landa Jocano, *Filipino Prehistory: Rediscovering Precolonial Heritage* (Quezon City, Philippines: Punlad Research House, 1998).
9. Damon Woods, *The Philippines: A Global Studies Handbook* (Santa Barbara, CA: ABC-CLIO, 2006): 187–88.
10. See the website of Philippine History, "Introduction," http://opmanong.ssc.hawaii.edu/filipino/labor.html, accessed April 30, 2016.
11. Graeme Hugo, "Migration in the Asia Pacific Region" (Global Commission on International Migration, 2005), 2, available at http://www.iom.int/jahia/webdav/site/myjahiasite/shared/shared/mainsite/policy_and_research/gcim/rs/RS2.pdf, accessed October 10, 2016.
12. For more on Sri Lanka, see Abella and Lim, "The Movement of People in Asia," 14, 16. Myanmar's treatment of the Rohingyas received renewed global attention with the declaration by US president Joe Biden on March 21, 2022, that the campaign was genocide and amounted to crimes against humanity. See "Myanmar: Momentum for Justice as US to Label Rohingya Crackdown Genocide," https://www.amnesty.org/en/latest/news/2022/03/us-myanmar-rohingya-genocide/,

accessed August 27, 2022. For UNHCR numbers, see UNHCR, "Figures at a Glance," https://www.unhcr.org/figures-at-a-glance.html, accessed August 27, 2022.

13. International Organization for Migration, *World Migration Report 2011: Communicating Effectively About Migration* (Geneva: IOM, 2011), 68.
14. It is among Asians, for instance, that we find the largest diaspora in the world, i.e., Chinese. See Jerold W. Huguet, "Towards a Migration Information System in Asia: Statistics and the Public Discourse on International Migration," *Asian and Pacific Migration Journal* 17, nos. 3–4 (2008): 247.
15. Abella and Lim, "The Movement of People in Asia," 11.
16. For a statistical sense of this increase see Huguet, "Towards a Migration Information System in Asia," 248–49.
17. Of the 2 million workers that Malaysia legally accepted in 2006, for instance, 1.9 million were unskilled laborers. Huguet, "Towards a Migration Information System in Asia," 248.
18. Abella and Lim attribute this continued demand for foreign labor to three factors: 1) profits derived from huge investments in Western countries on top of oil profits; 2) emergence of welfarism, which successfully raises the level of education among the Native populations but at the same time discourages them from doing manual work; and 3) the sponsorship recruitment system (*kafala* or *khafel*), a form of franchise to import foreign labor granted to loyal subjects that thrives on bringing in ever-increasing numbers of foreign workers willing to pay money for their jobs ("The Movement of People in Asia," 19).
19. Abella and Lim, "The Movement of People in Asia," 18–19.
20. See http://ilo.org/asia/areas/labour-migration/lang-en/index.htm, accessed December 23, 2014.
21. Abella and Lim, "The Movement of People in Asia," 19.
22. Nikos Papastergiadis points out that the circulation of "skilled transients" offers a clearer link between the globalization of the economy and the international labor market in that it resembles the current flows of capital. See Nikos Papastergiadis, *The Turbulence of Migration* (Cambridge: Polity, 2000), 40.
23. Abella and Lim, "The Movement of People in Asia," 30.
24. Vijayakumari Kanapathy, "Malaysia," *Asian and Pacific Migration Journal* 17, nos. 3–4 (2008): 336.
25. The July 1997 Asian financial crisis that plagued much of labor-importing East Asian countries is a case in point. South Korea deported 300,000 overseas workers, Thailand deported thousands of Myanmarese laborers, and Malaysia expelled 10,000 workers. In the case of OFWs, at least 3,000 Filipino engineers, draftsmen, architects, and others in the construction industry were laid off in Korea and 2,000 OFWs in Malaysia were retrenched. See Peter Tran, "Migrant Workers in Asia: The Call by the Synod for Asia to Assist Migrants," *Migration World Magazine* 26, no. 5 (1998): 32–34. See also Huguet, "Towards a Migration Information System in Asia," 247.
26. See Catholic Institute for International Relations, *The Labor Trade: Filipino Migrant Workers around the World* (London: CIIR, 1987).
27. Kanlungan Center Foundation, *Destination: Middle East: A Handbook for Filipino Women Domestic Workers* (Quezon City, Philippines: KCFI, 1997), 8.
28. See Mission for Filipino Migrant Workers, *The Filipino Maids in Hong Kong: MFMW Documentation Series No. 1* (Hong Kong: MFMW, March 1983).
29. To sustain the constant demand for labor, the Hawaiian Sugar Planters Association conducted a systematic, organized recruitment of Filipino laborers. Labor recruiters went to the Philippines and set up recruitment centers in Vigan, Ilocos Sur, and Cebu. See Philippine History Site, "Labor Migration in Hawaii," http://opmanong.ssc.hawaii.edu/filipino/labor.html, accessed April 30, 2016.
30. See Philippine History Site, "Sakada 46," http://opmanong.ssc.hawaii.edu/filipino/labor.html, accessed April 30, 2016.

31. The latter primarily has to do with the massive recruitment of men for construction work in the petro-dollar rich Middle East, particularly Saudi Arabia.
32. Ruby Beltran and Aurora Javate de Dios, *Filipino Women OCW's... At What Cost* (Manila: Women in Development Foundation, 1992), vii.
33. Kathleen Nadeau, "Out-Migration from the Philippines with a Focus on the Middle East: A Case Study," *East Asian Pastoral Review* 45, no. 3 (2008): 263.
34. Maruja Asis, "Philippines," *Asian and Pacific Migration Journal* 17, nos. 3–4 (2008): 367.
35. Philippine Statistics Authority, "Total Number of OFWs estimated at 2.4. million," https://psa.gov.ph/content/total-number-ofws-estimated-24-million-results-2015-survey-overseas-filipinos, accessed October 11, 2016.
36. International Organization for Migration, *World Migration Report 2011: Communicating Effectively About Migration* (Geneva: IOM, 2011), 69.
37. Philip Jenkins, *The Next Christendom: The Coming of Global Christianity*, 3rd. ed. (Oxford: Oxford University Press, 2011).
38. The other two books in the series are *The New Faces of Christianity: Believing the Bible in the Global South* (Oxford: Oxford University Press, 2008) and *God's Continent: Christianity, Islam, and Europe's Religious Crisis* (Oxford: Oxford University Press, 2007).
39. Francisco Claver, "Philippine Migrant Labor: The Challenge to Their Religious Identity," *Forum Mission* 5 (2009): 62–63.
40. Randy David, *Public Lives: Essays on Selfhood and Social Solidarity* (Pasig City: Anvil, 1998), 51–52.
41. Glenda Tibe Bonifacio and Vivienne S. M. Angeles, "Building Communities Through Faith: Filipino Catholics in Philadelphia and Alberta," in Glenda Tibe Bonifacio and Vivienne S. M. Angeles, eds., *Gender, Religion and Migration: Pathways of Integration* (Lanham, MD: Lexington, 2010): 265–66.
42. Employers of caregivers who live in rural outskirts often give them a ride to the church on Sundays. Bonifacio and Angeles, "Building Communities Through Faith," 266.
43. Kathleen Nadeau, "Out-Migration from the Philippines with a Focus on the Middle East: A Case Study," *East Asian Pastoral Review* 45, no. 3 (2008): 267.
44. Mark Johnson, "Surveillance, Pastoral Power and Embodied Infrastructures of Care among Migrant Filipinos in the Kingdom of Saudi Arabia," *Surveillance and Society* 13, no. 2 (2015): 256.
45. Graziano Battistela, "Irregular Migration: Issues from the Asian Experience," in Pontifical Council for the Pastoral Care of Migrants and Itinerant People, *Migration at the Threshold of the Third Millennium: Proceedings of the IV World Congress on the Pastoral Care of Migrants and Refugees*, Vatican, October 5–10, 1998, 152. See also Paul Allen, "Interview with Irene Fernandez," http://www.newint.org/columns/makingwaves/2006/04/01/irene-fernandez/, accessed October 20, 2016.
46. See "12 OFWs Arrested in KSA for Performing Christian Worship," http://www.gmanetwork.com/news/story/202695/news/pinoyabroad/12-ofws-arrested-in-ksa-for-performing-christian-worship, accessed October 6, 2016.
47. See Felipe Muncada, "Japan and Philippines: Migration Turning Points," in Fabio Baggio and Agnes Brazal, eds., *Faith on the Move: Toward a Theology of Migration in Asia* (Quezon City, Philippines: Ateneo de Manila University Press, 2008), 39n19.
48. Simbang Gabi refers to the nine-day novena Masses held December 16–24 in connection with Christmas. See Rachel Bundang, "May You Storm Heaven with Your Prayers: Devotions to Mary and Jesus in Filipino-American Catholic Life," in Rita Nakashima Brock et al., eds., *Off the Menu: Asian and Asian North American Women's Religion and Theology* (Louisville, KY: WJK, 2007), 87–105. See also Marisa Roque, "Fil-Canadians bring *Flores de Mayo* Tradition to Their Local Parish," http://globalnation.inquirer.net/122998/fil-canadians-bring-flores-de-mayo-tradition-to-their-local-parish, accessed October 16, 2016.

49. Robert Schreiter, "Spaces for Religion and Migrant Religious Identity," *Forum Mission* 5 (2009): 162.
50. See Luis Pantoja Jr., Sadiri Joy Tira, and Enoch Wan, *Scattered: The Filipino Global Presence* (Manila: Life Changing, 2004).
51. Lausanne Committee for World Evangelization, "The New People Next Door," *Lausanne Occasional Paper* 55 (2005), https://www.lausanne.org/wp-content/uploads/2007/06/LOP55_IG26.pdf, accessed October 16, 2016.
52. Claver, "Philippine Migrant Labor," 63–64.
53. Claver, 64.
54. Claver, 65–66. The story, which comes from an executive of Fiat whose marriage, family, and spirituality was transformed partly because of his experience of faith among Filipino migrants, came to light when the executive called the late Cardinal Sin in one of his visits to Rome to tell him the story.
55. Stephen Cherry, *Faith, Family and Filipino American Community Life* (New Brunswick, NJ: Rutgers University Press, 2013).
56. Jeremiah Opiniano, "Filipinos Doing Diaspora Philanthropy: The Development Potential of Transnational Migration," *Asian and Pacific Migration Journal* 14, nos. 1–2 (2005): 231, 235.
57. Asuncion Fresnoza-Flot, "The Catholic Church in the Lives of Irregular Migrant Filipinas in France: Identity Formation, Empowerment and Social Control," *Asia Pacific Journal of Anthropology* 11, nos. 3–4 (2010): 353.
58. Joaquin Jay Gonzalez III, "Second-Generation Filipino American Faithful: Are They 'Praying and Sending?'" in Carolyn Chen and Russell Jeung, eds., *Sustaining Faith Traditions: Race, Ethnicity and Religion among the Latino and Asian-American Second Generation* (New York: New York University Press, 2012), 160.
59. See Thomas Csordas, *Transnational Transcendence: Essays on Religion and Globalization* (Berkeley: University of California Press, 2009).
60. As cited in Peter Tran, "Migrant Workers in Asia: The Call by the Synod for Asia to Assist Migrants," *Migration World Magazine* 26, no. 5 (1998): 32. The synodal document Ecclesia in Asia addresses migration issues in numbers 7, 22, and 34.
61. Kanan Kitani, "Brazilian Migrants in Japan: Welcoming New Christian Members to Society and Its Potential Impact on the Japanese Church," *CTC Bulletin* 28, no. 1 (2012): 90.
62. Andrew Hamilton, SJ, "Catholic Cambodian and Laotian Communities in Melbourne," in Helen Richmond and Myong Duk Yang, eds., *Crossing Borders: Shaping Faith, Mission and Identity in Multicultural Australia* (Sydney: UCA Assembly and NSW Board of Mission, 2006), 169.
63. As quoted in Graziano Battistella, "The Poor in Motion: Reflections on Unauthorized Migration," *Asian Christian Review* 4, no. 2 (Winter 2010): 76.
64. Gaudencio Rosales and Catalino Arévalo, eds., *For All the Peoples of Asia: Federation of Asian Bishops' Conferences, Documents from 1970–1991*, vol. 1 (New York: Orbis, 1992): 276–77.
65. Franz-Josef Eilers, ed., *For All the Peoples of Asia: Federation of Asian Bishops' Conferences, Documents from 1992–1996*, vol. 2 (Quezon City, Philippines: Claretian, 1997), 11.
66. Sixth Plenary Assembly background paper, "Journeying Together in Faith with Migrant Workers in Asia," FABC Papers no. 73 (Hong Kong: FABC, 1995), 3, 8.
67. Chinese Bishops' Conference of Taiwan, "Loving Our Neighbors as Ourselves," *Asian Migrant Forum* (December 1993): 31–32, as cited in Lou Aldrich, SJ, "A Critical Evaluation of the Migrant Workers' Situation in Taiwan in Light of the Catholic Social Tradition," in Fabio Baggio and Agnes Brazal, eds., *Faith on the Move, Toward a Theology of Migration in Asia* (Quezon City, Philippines: Ateneo de Manila University Press, 2008), 63.
68. FABC, "A Renewed Church in Asia: A Mission of Love and Service," in Franz-Josef Eilers, SVD, ed., *For All the Peoples of Asia*, vol. 3 (Quezon City, Philippines: Claretian, 2002), 11.

69. FABC, "Plenary Assembly VIII Final Statement the Asian Family Towards a Culture of Integral Life," in Franz-Josef Eilers, ed., *For All the Peoples of Asia* (Quezon City, Philippines: Claretian, 2006), 15–18.
70. For a more comprehensive treatment of the FABC and migration see Jonathan Tan, "An Asian Theology of Migration," in Peter Phan and Elaine Padilla, eds., *Contemporary Issues of Migration and Theology* (New York: Palgrave Macmillan, 2014): 121–38.
71. See http://www.icmc.net/about/vision-and-mission, accessed October 19, 2016. Founded in 1951, the ICMC was initiated by the joint efforts of Pope Pius XII, Msgr. Giovanni Battista Montini (Vatican secretary for relations with states and future Pope Paul VI), and layman James J. Norris to support Catholic organizations in responding to the needs of displaced persons and refugees.
72. In 1970, Pope Paul VI, in his *Apostolicae Caritatis*, reorganized and coalesced various Church initiatives for migrants into the Pontifical Commission for the Spiritual Care of Migrants and Itinerant People. In a sign of the growing recognition of its importance, in 1988 Pope John Paul II elevated the commission to the status of a Pontifical Council in his *Pastor Bonus* and gave it equal juridical status with the other dicasteries of the Roman Curia. The council came to be known as the Pontifical Council for the Pastoral Care of Migrants and Itinerant People until 2016, when Pope Francis merged the Vatican departments on justice and peace, migration, charity, and health into the Dicastery for Promoting Integral Human Development in order to further draw attention to the social justice dimension of the departments. What is noteworthy to mention in this development is that a section dedicated to refugees and migrants will be led *ad tempus* (for the time being) directly by the pope himself.
73. Muncada, "Japan and Philippines," 40.
74. In Canada, for example, CFC members meet in small groups in households every week, where they share gospel readings, food, and information. See Bonifacio and Angeles, "Building Communities Through Faith," 267.
75. For example, the Taiwanese government's proposal to exclude migrant workers from the minimum wage policy was met with protests by Catholic labor activists. Tran, "Migrant Workers in Asia," 33.
76. See Kathleen Nadeau's story of how, at the height of Iraqi occupation of Kuwait, a group of forty Filipino men and women migrants banded together, each saying "He is my husband" or "She is my wife" to avoid the possibility of anyone being raped by Iraqi soldiers. Nadeau, "Out-migration from the Philippines With a Focus on the Middle East," 266.
77. Bonifacio and Angeles, "Building Communities Through Faith," 267.
78. Pope Francis, Message for World Day of Migrants and Refugees, August 5, 2013, https://w2.vatican.va/content/francesco/en/messages/migration/documents/papa-francesco_20130805_world-migrants-day.html, accessed September 15, 2016.
79. Robert Schreiter, "Spaces for Religion and Migrant Religious Identity," *Forum Mission* 5 (2009): 162–63.
80. Peter Cha's study of second-generation Korean Americans illustrates this difference. The reality, however, is that these second-generation Koreans also return to the ethnic churches of their parents once their own children reach school age precisely because ethnic-specific churches remain an important means of socialization into the heritage and ethnicity of their families. See Peter Cha, "Constructing New Intergenerational Ties, Cultures and Identities Among Korean Christian Americans," in Robert Priest and Alvaro Nieves, eds., *This Side of Heaven: Race, Ethnicity and Christian Faith* (New York: Oxford University Press, 2006): 259–74.
81. Tito Cruz and Rosanna Ella, "To Live Church More Authentically: Ministry with Asian and Pacific Catholics in the United States," *Pastoral Music* 27, no. 4 (April 2003): 19.

14

The Federation of Asian Bishops' Conferences and Pan-Asian Catholicism

EDMUND KEE-FOOK CHIA

Like a number of other regional bodies such as the Association of South East Asian Nations (ASEAN), the South Asian Association of Regional Cooperation (SAARC), the Christian Conference of Asia (CCA), the Asia Evangelical Alliance (AEA), and especially the non-aligned movement that gave rise to the notion of "Third World consciousness," the Federation of Asian Bishops' Conferences (FABC) was conceived at the same time that the disintegration of the colonial empire in Asia was taking place. Social and cultural enhancements, especially in the fields of communication, technology, and travel, as well as the threats and opportunities presented by extra-national interests, contributed in part to the need for transnational relationships and cooperation and the evolution of unified bodies that could speak on behalf of individual entities. The FABC has played such a role and can be regarded as the only body that can safely claim to speak for pan-Asian Catholicism, providing leadership to local churches in Asia as they try to negotiate their way through the variety of challenges posed by the increasingly globalized world. This chapter explores the significance of the FABC and the extent to which it is at once being shaped by the advances brought about by global forces as well as how it is shaping Asian Catholicism's need to deal with the onslaught of globalization.

More specifically, the current focus is on how the FABC has served as a forum for the evolution of pan-Asian theologies and pastoral strategies that have enabled members of local churches in Asia to be less reliant on colonial expressions of Christianity in favor of contextualized forms of Christian thinking and living. These new and contextualized forms of Christian expression take seriously the realities and impact of the religions, cultures, and especially the economic situations of the poor of Asia. They are the resources for theology that have propelled the FABC, in the words of Filipino Jesuit priest C. G. Arévalo (one of the key architects of the FABC), "to directly address the concrete situations in which they find themselves, concrete situations which question them and the Gospel, or challenge their real lives and real deeds.... If perhaps less dramatically than has been the case in Latin America, the Church in Asia has inserted itself rather resolutely into the history of its peoples, and has made its own 'turning to the Gospel' within history."[1]

The foundation of the FABC was, therefore, not merely a historical event; it was a theological one as well, and indeed a moment of grace. Its impact on pan-Asian Catholicism in general and local churches in particular over the last five decades has been invaluable and revolutionary. Before further exploring the contributions of the FABC, it is necessary to understand how the Christian faith was expressed prior to the advent of Asian Catholicism, as well as spell out from the outset the challenges that confront the Church in Asia.

COLONIAL CATHOLICISM IN ASIA

While Catholicism has been in Asia for at least the last five hundred years, it is only in the last fifty years that what has come to be known as Asian Catholicism truly existed. Previously, colonial Catholicism consisted of churches in Asia that could be said to be replicas of churches in the West, identified usually with their mother churches in Europe. There were European colonies of Dutch Catholicism in Indonesia, French Catholicism in Vietnam, British Catholicism in India, Spanish Catholicism in the Philippines, and so on. The situation was, of course, quite natural, as most of the initial missionaries to Asia came with Western European soldiers and merchants in the service of their compatriots as chaplains. The globalizing impulse continued from there, as over time the missionaries expanded their influence to the local communities, eventually recruiting them into the membership of the Church. The problem, however, is that even as the local peoples were evangelized and local Christian communities developed, the churches continued to be by and large European in ethos and character.

Publically, therefore, it comes as no surprise that local Christians in Asia were seen as having been "converted" to both Christianity and Western culture. Christianity in general has for many centuries been regarded as a foreign religion in Asia, a characterization that still persists today. In the Malay national language, for example, Christianity is sometimes known as *agama orang putih* (literally, white person's religion), just as the English language is often known as the white person's language. Aside from the stigma of being the religion of the colonial masters, there is also the issue of what Joseph Kitagawa calls the European Captivity, wherein Christian doctrines continued to be shaped predominantly by Greco-Roman thought patterns and Christian practices were presented in Western garb.[2] Some of Christianity's beliefs are as foreign to the Asian psyche as Baroque- or Gothic-styled church buildings are to the Asian landscape. The Church in Asia's colonial origins and heritage, its continued association with the West, and its dependence upon Western norms, finances, and authority are liabilities that confirm its foreignness. To make matters worse, the Church in some places secludes itself and forms little ghettos, making it in the main disengaged from the local populace. This adds to the perception that Christianity is by no means a religion of Asia.

Along with the image of foreignness is also the baggage of the internal division within Christianity. The Christian wars of Europe and the Catholic-Protestant conflicts have largely been transplanted to Asia through the churches. Where practicable, colonial administrations segregated Asian territories by denomination, so much so that Asians in general consider them as different religions. Evidence of this can be seen in the governments of Indonesia and China, which recognize both Catholicism and Protestantism as official but different religions. That the majority of Christians in the Philippines and Vietnam are Catholics and the majority in Indonesia are Protestants is testimony to the colonial legacy.[3] The Philippines was colonized by the Spaniards and Vietnam by the French (both predominantly Catholic countries), while Dutch Protestants colonized Indonesia. At the local level, the colonial practice was to encourage only one or two Church traditions to establish themselves in particular islands or cities or villages. Thus, where there was already a Presbyterian church in town, chances are that the Lutherans were not invited to establish a mission there. Or, if the Roman Catholics had a school in a village, in all probability the Methodists were asked to build elsewhere. This divide-and-rule policy by the imperial governments was the legacy that colonial Christianity left behind and which the new and upcoming Asian Church must address.

CHALLENGES CONFRONTING THE ASIAN CHURCH

Aside from the history of foreignness and the internal divisions that the Church in Asia had to deal with, there are also specific factors and challenges within the Asian context itself at the time of the birth of the Asian Church. To be sure, postcolonial Asia was not a bed of roses. The Asia that arose from the ashes of colonialism had not only been struggling with being weaned from its imperial authority but also needing to forge its own self-identity. The consequence of this was that many Asian countries saw the rise in the spirit of nationalism among their people, which at times was exaggerated and made manifest through anticolonial and even anti-Western activities. Corruption, authoritarian rule, militarization, and politicization of practically every facet of life have more or less hijacked the democratic system that many of these newly independent nations claim to subscribe to. Fragmentation of the nation-states, civil wars, and political oppression had been common occurrences in many parts of Asia in the last fifty years. It is easy to call to mind many events, such as the 1966–76 Cultural Revolution in China, the separation of East and West Pakistan in 1971, the annexation of East Timor by Indonesia in 1975, the Killing Fields of Pol Pot and the ultra-communist Khmer Rouge in Cambodia, the Vietnam and Korean Wars, martial law in the Philippines and the subsequent 1986 Peoples' Power Revolution, the Kwangju Uprising in South Korea in 1980, the military dictatorship in Myanmar, and the Tamil-Singhala civil war of Sri Lanka. In short, Asia has been anything but peaceful in the last few decades.

Asia is also, as recorded in the statement of the 1970 Asian Bishops' Meeting, a "continent of the teeming masses . . . [with] almost two-thirds of mankind. It is a face largely marked with poverty, with under-nourishment and ill health, scarred by war and suffering, troubled and restless. . . . A continent of the young. Nearly sixty percent of its people are below twenty-five years in age: the world of the youth of mankind."[4] These two points translate to the fact that Asia is a place where the "many" and the "young" have to compete for the scarcity of Asia's resources, much of which had already been plundered by the imperial powers and continues to be exploited by the neocolonialism of globalization. Moreover, according to Indian theologian Felix Wilfred, "the economic model being pursued in Asia continues to widen the gap between the poor and the affluent. Production, instead of being geared to fulfilling the basic needs of the majority, is dictated by the demands of the market. Multinationals and agri-business hold sway over the economy to the benefit of foreign investors and the local elite, with serious detriment to the survival of the poor."[5]

The existence of these many cultures and many religions is also a factor that the Asian Church has had to acknowledge: "There is, too, the face of the Asia that is the continent of ancient and diverse cultures, religions, histories and traditions, a region like Joseph's coat of many colors."[6] While other continents have arisen out of very diverse histories and cultures, Asia has been the cradle of practically all the world's major religions, each of which has its own history and culture. This might in part account for why the innate and relentless quest for the Divine continues to reside within the psyche of many people in Asia despite the onslaught of secularization that has been accentuated by globalizing forces. This spiritual quest has been made manifest over the millennia through a multiplicity of ways, resulting in the development of the many institutions of religions in Asia today.

This pluralism of religions, however, has often been abused for political and economic purposes, has been turned into sources of conflict and tension, and has pitted one community against another. Wilfred describes this situation succinctly: "In this volatile situation, what is remarkable is that religions, instead of being forces of unity, are spawning hatred, rivalry and divisions. Religious fundamentalism is springing up everywhere in Asia. Furthermore, politicians are instrumentalizing religion and religious symbols to their own ends."[7]

In the face of these complex and challenging contexts, the new Asian Church was born. It was going to be a church that is no more than a tiny minority of the populations of the different countries in Asia, much like the little flock, *pusillus grex,* that Luke describes in his gospel (Lk. 12:32). Except for the Philippines and East Timor (whose combined Christian population make up about two-thirds of all Christians in Asia) and Korea (with 25 percent of its population Christian), other countries in Asia have a Christian population that number no more than a few percent of their total populations. Christianity is, therefore, a minority religion in most countries across Asia, thus it comes with the complexes that accompany minority groups. For instance, the smallness of one's group can be so threatening that out-group members are often perceived as competitors, enemies, or even potential persecutors.

A church that suffers from the "minority complex syndrome" tends toward a maintenance mode. Its primary concern is with survival and most of its energies are directed toward activities that serve to maintain the group and the status quo. Church life has little to do with the society outside the church walls. It becomes an inward-looking church, concentrated on the development and growth of its own members, separated and divorced from the realities of the cultural milieu. Discipleship and Christian living is based on a spirituality of a personalized I-God relationship, often with little concern for one's neighbor or the injustices apparent in one's surroundings. There is also a preoccupation with how to increase the flock, since membership recruitment is necessary simply to preserve its existence. "Mission," therefore, refers to active evangelization with a view of converting others to Christianity and the church. Success in mission is measured in terms of the number of people who have come to embrace one's own religion and the numerical growth of one's little flock.

Such an attitude toward mission looks upon other religions or Christian denominations as competitors or targets. There is little interaction with them except for the purpose of evangelizing their members. The age-old adage *extra ecclesiam nulla salus* lends credence to these negative attitudes. If one's own Church is believed to be the only means of salvation, other religions are at best erroneous and even evil or demonic. The Christian's task is clearly spelled out in the mission mandate of the Bible: bring them to Christ and baptize them in the Church, lest they be banished into the fires of hell. The Christian missionaries' aim is to displace and replace other religions with the one true religion for all of humankind. These attitudes receive reinforcement from the Church's emphasis of its own uniqueness and the absoluteness of the message of Christ and of Christianity. These emphases provide the theological justification for the Church's noninvolvement with other religions and foster an attitude of superiority among Christians. Other religions are regarded as inferior and needing to be brought under the light of Christ. As a consequence, they should be allowed to go extinct.

Another characteristic of a minority religion is the fear of getting involved in actions on behalf of human rights and the cause of justice and peace. This is not so much because the Church does not believe in the virtues of justice and peace but because it is afraid of what such actions might entail. Oftentimes prophetic actions involve more than the alleviation of pain and suffering, to include speaking out against the societal structures that cause and perpetuate them. The process of challenging these structural evils may mean incurring the wrath of the powers that be, many of whom are usually associated with the government or ruling elite. It is obvious that any challenge to these powerful figures might mean serious retribution not only upon the church official who speaks out against the injustices but also upon the entire church itself. The reality of such threats often cows the Catholic Church to remain silent in the face of transgressions of human rights. At times the Church even chooses to side with the dominating elites and dictatorial regimes, especially if it can help preserve its own self-existence. The individual Christian prophet who proclaims the message of God's Kingdom of justice and peace often finds himself or herself alone, with little support from the institutional church. The following statement of the first Asian Bishops' Meeting of 1970 accurately captures the sentiments of the Church before the coming of the Asian Church:

> But we must acknowledge too, with regret, where we have been found wanting: where we have tended to foster only narrow and 'domestic' interests; where we could have shown more compassion and solicitude for the poor and have not been sufficiently vigorous in speaking out for justice and the defense of human rights; where we have not incarnated the Christian life and enfleshed the Church in ways and patterns of our respective cultures, and thus kept it an alien in our lands; where we have not sought understanding of, reconciliation and collaboration with our brothers of other Christian Churches and of other faiths.[8]

In response to these sentiments, according to Jesuit priest Vitalliano Gorospe, the editor of a summary report on the Asian Bishops' Meeting, the bishops decided that "if the Church is to be incarnate and relevant in the Asia of the seventies, it must become: 1) a Church that is truly Asian; 2) a Church of the poor; 3) a Church of the young; and 4) a 'new' Church more responsive to the national aspirations of Asians, alert to the voice of the masses, and appreciative of the hopes of the Asian youth, a Church, therefore, conscious of the visions of one Asian community."[9]

VATICAN II AND THE ADVENT OF ASIAN CATHOLICISM

It is within this context that Vatican II was so significant for the churches in Asia. The Johannine word *aggiornamento,* or updating, best captures its essence, both the council's process as well as its product. An emphasis on renewal, long overdue in the Church, shaped the way the council perceived the world outside of it. If prior to the council the perception was one of the Church against or above the world, Vatican II encouraged Catholics to view the Church as, in the words of *Gaudium et Spes,* working in the modern world, at once shaping it as well as being shaped by it. In that sense Vatican II was by no means a reform council. There was no explicit external crisis or urgent challenge to respond to, unlike Vatican I, which had to deal with the challenge of modernity or with the Council of Trent facing the Protestant Reformation.

Vatican II, instead, was summoned to enable the Church to catch up with the contemporary world; it was a renewal council. Sri Lankan theologian Aloysius Pieris posits that reform councils are represented by a "controlled and graduated process of change that keeps the institutional set-up of the Church intact," while the transformation resulting from renewal councils "irrupts from below and works its way up to the top volcanically."[10] This effectively means that for Vatican II to be brought to fruition, needed innovations and transformations must come from local churches at the peripheries. The practices and insights of those at the margins (i.e., Catholics in the Global South) will then flow back into the institutional center (in this case the Church in Rome, Europe, or the West in general). Thus, the Second Vatican Council set the stage for the Catholic Church in the rest of the world to lead the Church in the West in attending to the challenges of the twenty-first century in the increasingly globalized world. This shift in the locus of leadership from "the West to the rest" resonates well with Karl Rahner's thesis that the Second Vatican Council was just "the beginning of a tentative approach by the Church to the discovery and official recognition of itself as world-Church."[11]

The world Church focuses on areas outside of Europe and America; its face is seen most clearly in the non-Western nations of the Global South. The contributions of each of the continents in the Southern Hemisphere have been at once unique and revolutionary. The irruption from Latin America paved the way for the Church in addressing sociopolitical and economic issues in general and poverty and oppression in particular. It highlighted the need for the Church to be on the side of the poor and gave rise to what has come to be known as liberation theology. The culturally diverse tribal-based continent of Africa led the Church to engage with the challenges brought about by centuries of colonial cultural and anthropological domination. Its irruption is best captured in the varieties of theologies of inculturation. The Church's irruption in Asia, the cradle of the major religions of the world, is primarily in the area of interreligious relations and the development of theologies of dialogue and theologies of religions. It is the Asian Church that has been the key agent in the reception of as well as elaboration of the teachings of Vatican II on the Church's relationship with other religions. These teachings guide how Asian Catholics relate with the 90+ percent of the Asian population who adhere to religions other than Christianity. Pastorally it encouraged Asian Catholics to leave their church compounds in outreach to persons of other religions in dialogue and especially in collaboration for the common good of society. Theologically it enabled Asian Catholics to be liberated from the inherited doctrines that taught them that their neighbors, friends, and family members who belong to other religions will not be able to attain salvation.

Vatican II's document on the Church's relationship with religions other than Christianity (*Nostra aetate*) has, therefore, revolutionized much of how Asian Catholics view the Christian faith. But this document has to be read in concert with the documents on the Church (*Lumen Gentium*), its relationship with the modern world (*Gaudium et Spes*), its statement on religious freedom (*Dignitatis Humanae*), and its missionary activity (*Ad Gentes*). Together they invite Catholics to be less parochial and more focused on building the relationship of the Church *ad extra*. The Church's engagement with the world outside of Catholicism is now seen as critical for the practice of the Christian faith. The world has become a dialogue partner. The word "dialogue," in fact, was first introduced into the vocabulary of official Church statements only during the time of the Second Vatican Council and specifically in Pope Paul VI's 1964 encyclical *Ecclesiam Suam*, where he insists that "the Church must enter into dialogue with the world in which it lives."[12]

THE FEDERATION OF ASIAN BISHOPS' CONFERENCES

The Second Vatican Council is often regarded as the watershed moment when the Asian Church was conceived, for it was in Rome that many of the Asian bishops were meeting with one another for the first time. Prior to that, episcopal relationships were more vertical than horizontal. Asian bishops had developed greater friendships with their counterparts in Europe and Rome than they had with their brother bishops from neighboring Asian countries. The informal conversations of Asian bishops in the dining rooms and aulas during Vatican II planted the seed for establishing more organized relationships among themselves. The 1969 Synod of Bishops, which saw the attendance of more than a dozen bishops acting in their capacities as presidents of the Asian episcopal conferences, provided the venue for renewed discussions about an Asian-wide association. A year before, Sri Lankan theologian Tissa Balasuriya had published an article in the *Clergy Monthly* entitled "On the Need for an Asian Bishops' Conference."[13]

Paul VI's first visit to the Philippines in 1970 provided the occasion for the first official Asian Bishops' Meeting (ABM). It brought together some 180 bishops from seventeen Asian countries and regions and about thirty *periti* and a number of observers, including students. "What did the ABM do for the Church in Asia?" asks Vitaliano Gorospe. He responded by saying that it

> established among the Asian bishops a sense of dialogue, a spirit of "oneness," and a new "awareness." For the first time in the history of the Church in the East, the majority of

> Asian bishops began to talk to one another about common problems affecting their own regions. . . . Perhaps for the first time the bishops became aware of the real problems of their peoples, of the significant role that the Asian Church will have to play in the future of the Church, of the need for dialogue and cooperation among all concerned in building a Church that is truly Asian.[14]

Before concluding the meeting and in the presence of Pope Paul VI, the Asian bishops voted on and approved two statements that eventually were issued by the ABM. The first was a "Message of the Asian Bishops' Conference" and the second the "Resolutions of the Asian Bishops' Conference." Citing Yves Congar, C. G. Arévalo (who was present at that meeting and subsequently served as *peritus* to the FABC for many years), suggests that the ABM can be regarded as the beginning of the truly Asian Church: "And now the heirs have found their own voice; they can now speak for themselves. . . . It is now the time of the heirs."[15] Felix Wilfred, who also served for many years as executive secretary of the Theological Advisory Commission of the FABC, had this to say: "The meeting marked the beginning of a new consciousness of the many traditional links that united the various peoples of this part of the globe."[16] In the "Message of the Conference" the bishops acknowledged the following as part of their awakening to the new consciousness:

> We see the face of an Asia at long last coming to birth as a true community of peoples. For barriers which have so long isolated our nations from one another are falling one by one, and the desire grows among us to know each other and to find each other as Asian, sister-nations among whom relationships of friendship and trust, of collaboration, sharing and genuine solidarity may be firmly lastingly wrought."[17]

The second statement, the resolutions, released by the bishops at the end of the ABM began by loudly and clearly (using uppercase letters in the document) stating the following:

> THAT THE EPISCOPAL CONFERENCES HERE REPRESENTED ARE URGED TO AUTHORIZE AND SUPPORT A PERMANENT STRUCTURE FOR THE EFFECTIVE IMPLEMENTATION OF THE DECISIONS OF THIS MEETING; THIS PERMANENT STRUCTURE TO BE SUBSTANTIALLY DESCRIBED IN ANNEX "A" TO THIS DOCUMENT.[18]

Annex "A" went into detail to spell out the type of structure this was intended to be: how it was to be set up, who would govern it, when it would meet, where the central secretariat would be located, and what it was supposed to do. It emphasized that "the Central Secretariat is a service agency, with no juridical competence to issue directives to, or in any way to infringe on the authority and autonomy of, the Episcopal Conferences."[19] The resolutions concluded by noting that the first meeting of the Central Committee, comprising the presidents of all the national episcopal conferences, would take place within four months, that is, March 1971 in Hong Kong.

At that first meeting in Hong Kong, a follow-up committee led by Cardinal Stephen Kim of Korea was charged with the responsibility of drafting the plan and constitution for the establishment of a permanent structure for the bishops in Asia. A spanner was thrown into the works which almost resulted in the plan's stillbirth. Cardinal Kim shares this bit of information twenty-five years later: "Through Cardinal Edward Cassidy, then an archbishop and apostolic pronuncio in Taipei, we heard that some in the Roman Curia expressed critical or negative comments about establishing a permanent Asian bishops' organization."[20] The Asian bishops nevertheless persisted, worked through many ups and downs, and finally had their draft plan and constitution approved by twelve Asian episcopal conferences. This was brought to Rome before Pope Paul VI. "He liked the idea we presented," writes Cardinal Kim, "but was concerned it might develop into something like CELAM (the conference of Latin American bishops)."[21] One recalls here that the propositions of the 1968 Medellín Conference, which endorsed a fundamental option for the poor, had generated a lot of discomfort in the Vatican. CELAM had officially endorsed liberation theology, which represented the first irruption from the periphery following the renewal of Vatican II. Rome certainly did not wish to see yet another irruption, especially after the Asian Bishops' Meeting had more or less also endorsed the fundamental option for the poor. Filipino Bishop Julio Labayen commented later that the curial bishops had actually criticized the ABM statement as "a work of sociologists [rather] than [that of] Churchmen."[22] Anyway, in response to Pope Paul VI's concern, Cardinal Kim had this to say: "We assured him it would not become a structure with binding power. We promised him it would be a voluntary group, for fraternal solidarity, for the evangelization of Asia in pastoral areas, especially social justice and the advancement of human development and peace. Pope Paul VI approved the statutes of the Federation of Asian Bishops' Conferences on November 16, 1972."[23]

FABC PROGRAMS AND CONTRIBUTIONS

Beginning with the initial twelve national episcopal conferences, two others joined soon after FABC was officially constituted and many more, especially the conferences from Central Asia, joined after the 1998 Asian Synod. Today nineteen episcopal conferences are full members in the FABC, while another eight enjoy associate membership status, as they are countries with only a few bishops. The principal forum for the FABC bishops is the plenary assembly, which convenes once every three to five years, but between these plenaries the offices that service the FABC hold numerous programs and institutes. There are currently nine offices and each is responsible for a particular aspect of Church life: human development, evangelization, education, interreligious dialogue, laity, priestly ministry, consecrated life, social communication, and theological concerns. Programs run by these offices often carry the name Bishops' Institute for Social Action (BISA), Bishops' Institute for Interreligious Affairs (BIRA), Bishops' Institute for Missionary Apostolate (BIMA), or Bishops' Institute for Lay Apostolate (BILA). The nature, scope, thrust, and content of these bishops' institutes vary significantly and are generally organized in response to an acknowledged pastoral need. Initially meant for the formation of bishops, participants have now come to include priests, religious, and laity.

The Office of Theological Concerns (OTC), known earlier as the Theological Advisory Commission (TAC), enjoys special status. Unlike other offices that are constituted by four or five bishops and staffed by one or two executive secretaries, the OTC is represented by all the episcopal conferences. Each conference appoints its own theologian to serve on the OTC and they meet periodically to investigate particular issues of theology. Statements that issue from the OTC are usually lengthy, as they are the product of months or years of discussion, drafting, and revision. They therefore are privileged in the hierarchy of authority among FABC statements. All the statements coming out of the plenary assemblies and FABC offices are duly approved by the bishop-participants or bishops responsible for the respective offices. They can therefore be regarded as the voice of the bishops as well as the voice of the Asian Church, since most of the programs draw participation of bishops and priests and laity as well, and they usually come from all across Asia. It is primarily through the statements of the FABC plenary assemblies and FABC offices that the Asian bishops' orientations and positions are revealed and communicated to the rest of the world. They are the principal source by which one can discern the Asian bishops' thinking and hence the Asian Church's theology in general. Most of these official statements have been collated and published in the six-volume book *For All the Peoples of Asia*.

In view of the plurality of the FABC offices and the programs that they run, the FABC statements that have been issued are necessarily pluralistic as well. Like Vatican documents, a statement from the FABC office responsible for evangelization might differ significantly or even contradict another issued through the FABC office responsible for interreligious dialogue. This raises some questions: How then does one discern the theological orientations of the FABC? Is it possible to identify theological positions that are "typically" the FABC's and distinguish them from positions or statements that come from traditional classicist theology? Is there such a thing as an FABC theology in the first place? To address this dilemma, certain hermeneutical principles must be employed. The hermeneutical principles used in modern biblical scholarship, especially the criteria for establishing authentic sayings of Jesus, prove useful.[24] First, according to the principle of "multiple attestation," one can discern certain themes in the many FABC statements that seem to occur more frequently than they do in traditional theologies. Second, by the principle of "dissimilarity," themes that have few or no parallels in traditional theologies can be surmised as authentically or innovatively FABC/Asian material. Third, by the principle of "theological disharmony," themes that seem to differ radically from the declared objectives of a specific seminar or FABC office can be regarded as authentic FABC material.[25] Invoking these three principles, one can discern that themes such as "triple dialogue," "dialogue of life," "commitment to life," "harmony," "witness of life," "communion of communities," "pastoral cycle," and "new way of being Church" are creative insights that are probably specific to FABC or Asian theology.

FABC THEOLOGY AND METHODOLOGY

While the Asian Bishops' Meeting prepared the groundwork for the establishment of the FABC, the first plenary assembly, held in Taipei in April 1974, firmly rooted the theological and pastoral directions that the conferences and hence the pan-Asian Church was to take. Strategically adopting the theme of the September 1974 Synod of Bishops on evangelization, the theme of the first FABC plenary assembly was "Evangelization in Modern Day Asia." The final statement of FABC I served as a template for the statements of all future FABC plenary assemblies, as well as the institutes, consultations, and other documents that issued forth from the FABC over the last five decades. This final statement can be regarded as representing the theology and methodology of Asian Catholicism. Compared to Evangelii Nuntiandi, Pope Paul VI's post-synodal apostolic exhortation, one can note radical differences between the two statements.

Contextual Methodology

The final statement of FABC I begins with section one, "Introduction," which provides an overview of the challenges facing the Asian continent. Taking the lead from *Gaudium et Spes,* it seeks "to read the signs of the times."[26] This is a typically Asian approach to doing theology: it begins by scrutinizing the realities of the context (and has since come to be known as the contextual approach). Malaysian-American theologian Jonathan Tan offers a description of what this means: "From the various official documents of the FABC, one sees the development of a new way of doing theology with Asian resources in multireligious, multiethnic, multilingual and pluricultural Asia, which may be described as the contextualization of the salvific message of the Gospel in the diverse and pluralistic Asian *Sitz-im-Leben*."[27] The FABC Office of Theological Concerns expands on this in a document entitled "Methodology: Asian Christian Theology," wherein it asserts that "context or contextual realities are considered resources of theology (*loci theologici*) together with the Christian sources of Scripture and Tradition."[28]

This contextual starting point was later extended into a full-scale methodology for theological reflection and has now come to be known as the pastoral cycle. The seventh FABC Bishops' Institute for Social Action (BISA VII) spells this out as a four-stage process: it begins with 1) the experience of the peoples, discerned through exposure-immersion to the actual day-to-day lives and especially the challenges confronting Asians; which is then put through a 2) social analysis, employing tools from the social and behavioral sciences, as well as cultural and economic theories; which then needs to be integrated through a process of 3) reflection and contemplation in light of scripture and tradition as well as the values and teachings of the various Asian religions; and the result of which leads to 4) pastoral planning, where realizable policies and activities are implemented for the total human development and transformation of society in general.[29]

Proclaiming the Good News of Jesus Christ

Section two of the FABC I statement, entitled "The Proclamation of the Gospel," spells out the raison d'être of the Church's existence, which is the preaching of the Good News of Jesus Christ. Together with the universal Church, the Asian Church believes that it is "only in and through Christ and His Gospel, and by the outpouring of the Holy Spirit, that these quests [the challenges of the Asian situation] can come to realization." For the Asian Church, however, it is in Christ that "our peoples will finally find the full meaning we all seek, the liberation we strive after, the brotherhood and peace which is the desire of all our hearts."[30] Primacy, therefore, is given to the immediate needs of the peoples of Asia, of liberation, brotherhood, and peace. This constitutes the main reason why the proclamation of the Good News is necessary and urgent and not so much because the peoples of Asia are not Christian. Wilfred expresses this bluntly and succinctly: "Jesus is relevant to Asia, not because the bulk of the Asian masses are *non-Christians*, but because they are *poor*."[31]

These sentiments are explicitly articulated by some Asian episcopal conferences in their responses to the *lineamenta* prepared by curial officials in anticipation of the 1998 Asian Synod. The response of the Indian bishops included these sentiments: "At the very start we want to stress what Christ's mission means to us. Essentially it is nurturing life-unto-fullness and proclaiming this ever new life-in-Christ by words and deeds of loving service. . . . We are a community who do not seek to conquer but to serve."[32] The Japanese bishops observed that "in the context of evangelization in Asia, 'compassion with the suffering' has been identified time after time at the General Assemblies of the FABC as a most important element. [Hence,] in missionary work among those of other religions, what is more important than convincing words is the attitude of standing by the side of the weak and powerless and showing them compassion."[33] Along similar lines, the bishops of Thailand suggested that "Asian people are satisfied with their own religion, and feel that they are able to lead their personal and social life in a proper and peaceful way. . . . Evangelization must be a witness showing clearly that the teaching of Christ brings goodness and peace to the people, to a level they could not imagine."[34]

In other words, for the Asian bishops, evangelization in Asia should not take the form of aggressive proclamation of the Gospel or proselytism with a view of explicit conversion to Christ and baptism into the Church. Instead, it has to be through witness, good deeds, and service to life in order for the Good News to touch, seep into, and be thoroughly integrated into the lives of the peoples. This was later called by the Seventh FABC Plenary Assembly as "active integral evangelization."[35] It constitutes part of the overall thrust of the FABC, which is "to motivate the Churches in Asia towards 'a new way of being Church,' a Church that is committed to becoming 'a community of communities' [in union with the universal Church and in partnership with believers of other religions] and a credible sign of salvation and liberation."[36]

This new way of being church, therefore, has to be a "church of dialogue," which "means concretely a church in continuous, humble and loving dialogue with the living traditions, the cultures, the religions—in brief, with all the life-realities of the people in whose midst it has sunk its roots deeply and whose history and life it gladly makes its own."[37] The word dialogue features so often in FABC documents and discussions that Wilfred posits that "dialogue" can more or less summarize the entire orientation of the FABC.[38] A comparison between the statements of FABC I and Evangelii Nuntiandi reveals that the former, which is about five thousand words in length, has at least a dozen mentions of the word dialogue, while the latter makes only a single mention of it in its twenty-thousand-word length. Dialogue, therefore, is truly the new way of being Church in Asia. Dialogue is also how the Gospel is to be proclaimed, and dialoging is the method for doing theology in Asia. In short, dialogue is the life and mode of the Asian Church.

Dialogue with Local Cultures

The first of these dialogues is between the Church and the cultures of Asia. Accordingly, section 3 of the FABC I statement is entitled "The Local Church . . . Incarnate, Indigenous." This is how the section begins: "To preach the Gospel in Asia today we must make the message and life of Christ truly incarnate in the minds and lives of our peoples. The primary focus of our task of evangelization then, at this time in history, is the building up of a truly local church."[39] There are two separate but interrelated dimensions to this dialogue with Asian cultures: to incarnate the Gospel so as to make it indigenous to the peoples and to cultivate a local Church in view of shedding its foreign image. The former is aimed at enabling Christians to better appreciate the Good News while the latter is aimed at enabling Asians who are not Christians to better appreciate the Church as truly Asian. Both tasks can only be accomplished through an engagement of the Church with the local cultures.

The FABC Theological Advisory Commission (TAC) explored this engagement in depth and put forth a document entitled "Theses on the Local Church: A Theological Reflection in the Asian Context."[40] The document states that a realization had developed among the Asian bishops that the local churches are "no longer 'mere recipients' of a Western Christendom and/or Christianity in missionary expansion, no longer mere clones of the Church in Europe."[41] As such, "for the Churches in Asia the task of inculturation is as challenging as it is urgent against the background of long centuries of cultural estrangement that marked their histories of mission during the colonial period, and in the context of contemporary cultural awakening among various Asian peoples."[42] Aloysius Pieris points out that inculturation can never take place through a mere translation or adaptation of Christian symbol systems: "Inculturation is something that happens naturally. It can never be induced artificially. The Christian tends to appropriate the symbols and mores of the human grouping around it only to the degree that it immerses itself in their lives and struggles. That is to say, inculturation is the by-product of an *involvement* with a people rather than the conscious target of a program of action."[43]

In the context of Asia, inculturation is accomplished first through the Church's involvement with Asia's poor, with a view to facilitating their integral liberation. Second, because other religions have their own views of what liberation and salvation mean and because the majority of Asia's poor owe their allegiance to these other religions, the process of inculturation, which entails the Church's involvement with the poor, must also include dialogue with other religions. Inculturation, interreligious dialogue, and the process of integral liberation are mutually involving ministries, all of which are integral to the evangelizing mission of the Church in Asia.[44]

Dialogue with Asian Religions

This leads to a discussion of "In Dialogue with the Asian Religions," which is section 4 of the FABC I statement. It begins by stating that "in this dialogue we accept them [the other religions] as significant and positive elements in the economy of God's design of salvation."[45] (The bishops are ever conscious that religions of Asia have been the source and inspiration for generations of peoples and have helped in the spiritual development and growth of an entire continent for millennia. In light of this they ask, albeit rhetorically: "How then can we not give them [the other religions] reverence and honor? And how can we not acknowledge that God has drawn our peoples to Himself through them?"[46] Implicit in these statements are two dimensions that the Church in Asia must attend to: learning more about how other religions have nourished the lives of their believers and finding out how and where the Church fits within the rich mosaic of religious traditions in Asia.

The FABC Theological Advisory Commission had also done an in-depth study on this matter and, in its publication "Theses on Interreligious Dialogue" the commission suggests that it is on account of the Asian bishops' own personal experience with persons of other religions that they have a "positive appreciation of [the role of other religions] in the divine economy of salvation."[47] This experience in turn relies on the theological conviction that "God's plan of salvation for humanity is one and reaches out to all peoples." It is therefore not only inherent upon Christians to discern how God's saving activity is in operation and made manifest in other religions but, more importantly, to conscientiously discern where and how Christianity fits into God's universal plan of salvation. In other words, other religions do not revolve around Christianity but Christianity must find its place in the orbit of the world of many religions.

The Asian Church is convinced that interreligious dialogue is the mode of this Christian task and duty. Quoting Pope John Paul II, the TAC affirms that "by dialogue, we let God be present in our midst; for as we open ourselves in dialogue to one another, we also open ourselves to God."[48] It then goes on to assert that interreligious dialogue is "a demand of the Church of its very life as mission."[49] It is "a demand of our Christian faith in the Trinity, which is a mystery of communion in interpersonal dialogue. . . . Dialogue is a process of growing into the fullness of divine life. It is participation in the quest of all peoples for the full realization of the Truth."[50] Interreligious dialogue is therefore an activity between and among persons of different religions and is aimed at "journeying together in a communion of minds and hearts towards the Kingdom to which God calls all peoples."[51]

Dialogue with Asia's Poor

Journeying toward the Kingdom must always be done "in dialogue with the people, especially the poor," which is the theme addressed in section 5 of the FABC I statement. Here, again, there are two interrelated dimensions to this dialogue, namely, that the Church sides with the "multitudes of the poor" and speaks out against the "social, economic and political structures which have injustice built into them."[52] "The Kingdom of God," according to the statement of the Tenth FABC Bishops' Institute for Interreligious Affairs on the Theology of Dialogue, "confronts the forces of injustice, violence, and oppression. These forces combined form structures of sin, from which we need to be liberated. We uphold the preferential option for the poor, since they are victims of these structures. Hence, solidarity with the poor is a response to the Good News of God's Kingdom."[53]

Solidarity with the poor is especially crucial for the Church in Asia, not only in light of contemporary poverty and suffering of the people but also because it was the Christian West which committed much of the injustice of conquest, plunder, and domination upon the non-Christian East during the colonial era. The Asian Church, therefore, shares in the responsibility, together with the former colonial powers, for alleviating the current suffering of the poor. Moreover, Pieris reminds us of Jesus' teaching: "If you do this to the least of my brethren, you do it to me." While it is the disciples of Christ who proclaim the Kingdom of God, it is the poor and suffering, as vicars of Christ, who are its inheritors. In other words, Pieris asserts, there is "no salvation outside God's covenant with the poor." For it is through this solidarity with the poor in discipleship praxis by which the "Kingdom community" is given birth.[54] This was also referred to in the statement of FABC I, which insists that the dialogue with the poor

> has to take the shape of what has been called a 'dialogue of life.' It involves a genuine experience and understanding of this poverty, deprivation and oppression of so many of our peoples. It demands working, not for them merely (in a paternalistic sense), but *with* them, to learn from them (for we have much to learn from them!) their real needs and aspirations, as they are enabled to identify and articulate these, and to strive for their fulfillment, by transforming those structures and situations which keep them in that deprivation and powerlessness.[55]

PASTORAL IMPLICATIONS

The rest of the FABC I statement discusses practical means through which the proclamation of the Gospel through the triple dialogue with the cultures, the religions, and the poor of Asia can be implemented. It addresses issues of missionary formation, the mass media, the laity and religious, Churches under authoritarian regimes, ecumenism, and the youth of Asia, all of which were issues of concern in the early 1970s. In short, the proclamation of the Good News in Asia has to address the day-to-day concerns of the peoples, and all Catholics (not only priests) are called to share in the responsibility of evangelization in modern-day Asia. Since then, the FABC has been addressing many other issues of concern to society, which it advises are also the concerns of the Church as well.

The eleventh FABC plenary assembly, held in December 2016 in Colombo, Sri Lanka, for example, had as its theme the Catholic family in Asia. As is usually the case of FABC assemblies, the assembly was revisiting the theme of concern to the universal Church, as reflected in the Synod of Bishops (2015) held the previous year and the fruits of which took the form of Pope Francis's post-synodal apostolic exhortation on love in the family, Amoris laetitae (The Joy of Love). While the debate surrounding Amoris laetitae focused on the theological implications of divorced and remarried Catholics receiving Holy Communion and Church teachings on homosexual persons, the central question addressed by the FABC XI Assembly was "How can the Asian family be a domestic church of the poor that can credibly proclaim from within itself the mercy and compassion of God?"[56] Nothing whatsoever was said about divorced or remarried Catholics or gay marriage, as neither subject was the most urgent concern for the Asian Church. More critical and at times life-and-death issues dominated the discussions at the assembly.

To be sure, the Asian bishops were more focused on issues such as pervasive poverty, which forces members of families to break up because many have no choice but to take jobs as migrant workers or live as refugees. The bishops were also concerned about how Catholics practice their faith in Asia as minorities living in contexts where the rest of the population are committed adherents to a variety of ancient religions, and both the positive effects of intergenerational family kinship and the pastoral implications of interfaith marriages. Another issue of major concern to the Asian bishops was the pervasive religious and ethnic extremism that have been manifesting itself in the different forms of violence, resulting in families being driven away from their homes as well as threats to religious freedom and the basic peace and security of all the peoples of Asia in general. Other issues range from the scourge of human trafficking to the negative effects of economic globalization, including global warming and climate change all the way to the problems brought about by the digital revolution and throw-away culture.

As can be seen from the methodology employed and concerns addressed, the FABC's priority concerns are not with doctrine or systematic theology, but more with the pastoral implications of the theological reflections emanating from FABC plenary assemblies. Vietnamese American theologian Peter Phan expands on this with an example from the discussion about God: "A careful review of the FABC's official statements as well as of the various documents issued by the FABC's standing offices shows a significant fact, namely, that there has been little interest on the FABC's part in a purely philosophical or even theological discourse on God. . . . The FABC's overwhelming focus has been on God's activities in the world and God's relationship to us in history."[57] Hence, like Vatican II, which was a pastoral rather than a doctrinal council, FABC statements are also more pastoral than doctrinal orientations. There are certainly parallels between the FABC statements and Vatican II statements, as they express the same key ideas and themes of concern. In an official message to Catholics in Asia at the end of the Tenth FABC Plenary Assembly, which commemorated the fortieth anniversary of its foundation, the bishops remarked that "to this day the key ideas of the Council—the people of God, the Kingdom of God, integral evangelization, communion, co-responsibility, collegiality, participation, dialogue, liturgical renewal, engagement with the modern world—continue to serve as guiding principles for the renewal of the Church in Asia."[58]

RECEPTION AND IMPACT OF THE FABC

Looking back, there is no denying that the FABC and its statements have greatly influenced the thinking and praxis of Catholicism in Asia. Its teachings have successfully influenced the decisions of Church leaders at local levels and continue to provide inspiration for change and transformation, not only for the Church but for Asian society as well. FABC statements are so potent that C. G. Arévalo suggests that they have "become a *locus theologicus* in our time."[59] They are a source of inspiration for theologies that are at once pastorally relevant and contextually sensitive. Thanks to the exponential advances of the globalized world in the areas of technology and communication since the 1970s, the teachings of the FABC have been effectively disseminated to the various episcopal conferences around Asia so that we can safely say they have become truly pan-Asian teachings on how theological reflection is conducted and what constitutes "Asian theology."

The primary concern of the FABC is with whether the churches in Asia are living up to the Gospel message in the context of the realities of Asia. The Catholic Church's authority resides in its vision and message, not in its power and position. While it may lack the authority that typically comes with a position of power, it certainly does not lack the authority that comes on account of its message and vision.[60] Such authority inspires and engenders authentic support. It is authority that comes "from below"; it is not bestowed "from above." It is authority earned and respected, not because of its ecclesial status but because of the credibility of its directives. By itself the messages attract and so need no enforcing. In fact, episcopal member-conferences are constantly reminded that there is never any binding authority in the FABC statements. Nevertheless, most episcopal conferences throughout Asia have embraced the teachings and positions taken by the FABC. Reflecting on the twenty-five years of the FABC's existence, Archbishop Michael Rozario, the convener of the Sixth FABC Plenary Assembly (1995), testifies to this in his address: "Our Federation has been for us a very concrete and effective forum for sharing our Asian way of thinking about the implications of the Gospel of Jesus for all the peoples of Asia."[61] This was clearly and overtly articulated at the 1998 Synod of Bishops for Asia where, for the first time since the FABC's foundation, the Asian bishops were meeting together as a group in Rome to discuss the future of evangelization on the continent. Most of the statements they made before and during the synod reflected the orientation and teachings of the FABC. In fact, the bishops were not only guided by FABC teachings but were confident that there was much that the bishops in Rome and elsewhere in Europe could learn from them on what it means to be Church in Asia. Peter Phan had this to say:

> In front of the pope and the Roman Curia, with surprising boldness and candor, humbly but forcefully, the Asian bishops affirmed that the Churches of Asia not only learn from but also have something to teach the Church of Rome as well as the universal Church, precisely from their experiences as Churches not simply *in* but *of* Asia. What was being proposed is not a new doctrine but a new way of being Church.[62]

VISION VERSUS REALITY

While the FABC has made a lot of advances in introducing a new way of "being church" in Asia, it cannot be said that all the churches in Asia have actually embraced its teachings and vision at the parish and grassroots levels. In fact, one can observe that the FABC has been repeating the same teachings at practically every plenary assembly since its foundation, especially its insistence on the triple dialogue for churches in Asia. It appears that not much has changed since the 1970s in the dioceses and parishes across Asia. This problem was in fact expressed in the Tenth FABC Plenary Assembly. The final statement of FABC X conspicuously confesses the shortcomings of the churches in Asia:

> Yet while thanking the Lord for countless blessings, we are sadly aware that our decisions and actions do not always match our words and intentions. Renewal of values and mind-sets, of agents of evangelization and of church structures towards a new way of being Church has not been steady and consistent. The FABC vision and its key ideas, its programs and projects have not yet impacted grassroots to the extent that we had desired. We have a long way to go towards the vision of a new way of being Church. For this we humbly say to the Lord, mea culpa, mea maxima culpa (§16).[63]

Hence it appears that what has been passed on is primarily the vision of the bishops for what the Church in Asia should be. Unfortunately, much of that vision has not yet been translated into reality, especially at the parish level. Some see this as simply a problem in the implementation of FABC teachings; others point to differences in opinion among the bishops themselves in that not all of them endorse what the FABC has attempted. To be sure, both are equally valid reasons for the ineffectiveness of FABC teachings, with the lack of consensus within the FABC as a very real possibility. Just as there is debate over the hermeneutics of continuity versus discontinuity with regard to the teachings of the Second Vatican Council, a similar debate can be found within Asia with regard to the FABC's vision and directives. While some see the FABC as advancing a set of teachings that seem like a rupture from the classical and traditional teachings of the Church, others believe they are faithfully in continuity with a colonial approach. These differences in interpretation and approach remain and result in the reception of FABC teachings to be ambiguous at best.

But, just as we rejoice over the sixteen documents of the Second Vatican Council and the spirit of renewal it inspired, we must also rejoice that the Asian Church has a vision and blueprint for its own renewal. If the reality on the ground does not seem consistent with this vision it is also partly because authentically fulfilling the dictates of the new way of being the Catholic Church in Asia can be a true challenge. A truly contextualized, enculturated, and incarnated local church that opts for the triple dialogue necessarily means that the Church has to live in full Christian discipleship, perhaps to the point of experiencing a baptism on the cross. Not only does this look unappealing, it can be rather threatening as well. That is the meaning behind the message of the bishops at the end of the Tenth FABC Plenary Assembly in Xuan Loc, Vietnam: "We are not to fear. We have the Lord's assurance, 'Take heart, it is I; do not be afraid' (Matthew 14:27)."[64]

NOTES

1. C. G. Arévalo, "The Time of The Heirs," in Gaudencio Rosales and C. G. Arévalo, eds., *For All the Peoples of Asia: Federation of Asian Bishops' Conferences, Documents from 1970 to 1991*, vol. 1 (New York: Orbis, 1992), xviii.
2. See Joseph Mitsuo Kitagawa, *The Christian Tradition: Beyond Its European Captivity* (Philadelphia: Trinity International, 1992).
3. See Peter C. Phan, ed., *Christianities in Asia* (Malden, MA: Wiley-Blackwell, 2011).
4. FABC, "Asian Bishops' Meeting," arts. 5 and 6, in Rosales and Arévalo, *For All the Peoples of Asia*, vol. 1 (New York: Orbis, 1992), 4.

5. Felix Wilfred, "The Federation of Asian Bishops' Conferences (FABC): Orientations, Challenges and Impact," in Gaudencio Rosales and C. G. Arévalo, eds., *For All the Peoples of Asia: Federation of Asian Bishops' Conferences, Documents from 1970 to 1991*, vol. 1 (New York: Orbis, 1992), xxiii.
6. FABC, "Asian Bishops' Meeting," art. 7, 4.
7. Felix Wilfred, "(FABC): Orientations, Challenges and Impact," xxvii–xxviii.
8. FABC, "Asian Bishops' Meeting," art. 17, 5.
9. Vitalliano R. Gorospe, *The Four Faces of Asia: A Summary Report on the Asian Bishops' Meeting* (Quezon City, Philippines: Ateneo de Manila University Press, 1971), 5.
10. Aloysius Pieris, "The Roman Catholic Perception of Other Churches and Other Religions after the Vatican's Dominus Jesus," *East Asian Pastoral Review* 38, no. 3 (2001): 215.
11. Karl Rahner, "Basic Theological Interpretation of the Second Vatican Council," in Karl Rahner, ed., *Theological Investigations: Concern for the Church* 20 (New York: Crossroad, 1981), 78.
12. Pope Paul VI, *Ecclesiam Suam* (Rome: Libreria Editrice Vaticana, 1964), 65.
13. Tissa Balasuriya, "On the Need for an Asian Bishops' Conference," *Clergy Monthly* 22 (1968): 341–57.
14. Gorospe, *The Four Faces of Asia*, 4.
15. Arévalo, "The Time of the Heirs," xv.
16. Wilfred, "(FABC): Orientations, Challenges and Impact," xxiii.
17. FABC, "Asian Bishops' Meeting," art. 12, 4.
18. Gorospe, *The Four Faces of Asia*, 53.
19. Gorospe, 59.
20. Cardinal Kim Sou Hwan, "A Founding Father Reflects on FABC's Origin and Development," in *The Federation of Asian Bishops' Conferences: Orientations, Challenges and Impact, FABC Papers* no. 69 (Hong Kong: FABC, 1995), 17.
21. Kim, "A Founding Father Reflects," 18.
22. Bishop Julio Xavier Labayen, "Historical Background of the Office of Human Development and the BISAs," *FABC Papers* no. 6 (Hong Kong: FABC, 1977), 7.
23. Kim, "A Founding Father Reflects," 18.
24. Dermot Lane, *The Reality of Jesus: An Essay in Christology* (Mahwah, NJ: Paulist Press, 1975), 29.
25. For example, BIMA I, a bishops' institute specifically organized to promote the mission agenda, wherein mission is understood as the explicit proclamation of Jesus Christ in view of bringing others to conversion in Christ and baptism into the Church, had this to say: "*Religious dialogue* is not just a substitute for or a mere preliminary to the proclamation of Christ, but should be the ideal form of evangelization" (emphasis in original). See Rosales and Arévalo, *For All the Peoples of Asia*, vol. 1, art. 10, 94. Because the notion of religious dialogue (often regarded as a "compromise" to the mission of evangelization) is not in harmony with the primary aims of a mission institute but yet appears in the statement, it must be a peculiarly FABC agenda that cannot be done without.
26. FABC I, "Evangelization in Modern Day Asia," in Rosales and Arévalo, *For All the Peoples in Asia*, vol. 1, 5.
27. Jonathan Tan, "Theologizing at the Service of Life: The Contextual Theological Methodology of the Federation of Asian Bishops' Conferences (FABC)," *Gregorianum* 81, no. 3 (2000): 565.
28. FABC Office of Theological Concerns, "Methodology: Asian Christian Theology," in Franz-Josef Eilers, ed., *For All the Peoples of Asia: Federation of Asian Bishops' Conferences, Documents from 1997 to 2001*, vol. 3 (Quezon City, Philippines: Claretian, 2002), 356.
29. FABC Office of Human Development, "BISA VII: Final Reflections of the Seventh Bishops' Institute for Social Action," in Rosales and Arévalo, *For All the Peoples in Asia*, vol. 1, 231–32.
30. FABC I, "Evangelization in Modern Day Asia," 13.
31. Felix Wilfred, "Images of Jesus Christ in the Asian Pastoral Context: An Interpretation of Documents from the Federation of Asian Bishops' Conferences," *Concilium* 2 (1993): 52.

32. "India: Indian Church Response to the *Lineamenta* for the Synod," *Union of Catholic Asian News*, January 14, 1998. The full text of these responses was published by *UCAN*, see its website, http://www.ucanews.com/html/search-intro.html.
33. "Japan: Asian Realities Must Set Agenda for the Synod for Asia," *UCAN*, July 30, 1997.
34. "Thailand: Thai Church Stresses 'Witness' as Evangelizing Means," *UCAN*, August 19, 1997.
35. FABC VII, "A Renewed Church in Asia: A Mission of Love and Service," in Eilers, *For All the Peoples of Asia*, vol. 3, 3.
36. FABC VI, "Christian Discipleship in Asia Today: Service to Life," in Franz-Josef Eilers, ed., *For All the Peoples of Asia: Federation of Asian Bishops' Conferences, Documents from 1992 to 1996*, vol. 2, (Quezon City, Philippines: Claretian, 1997), 3.
37. FABC I, "Evangelization in Modern Day Asia," art. 12, 14.
38. Wilfred, "(FABC): Orientations, Challenges and Impact," xxiii.
39. FABC I, "Evangelization in Modern Day Asia," art. 9, 14.
40. Theological Advisory Commission of the FABC, "Theses on the Local Church: A Theological Reflection in the Asian Context" in *FABC Papers* no. 60 (Hong Kong: FABC, 1991).
41. Theological Advisory Commission, "Theses on the Local Church," art. 6, 3.
42. Theological Advisory Commission, "Theses on the Local Church," art. 5.01, 19.
43. Aloysius Pieris, *An Asian Theology of Liberation* (Quezon City, Philippines: Claretians, 1988), 38.
44. See Edmund Chia, "Wanted: Interreligious Dialogue," *Studies in Interreligious Dialogue* 12, no. 1 (2002): 101–10.
45. FABC I, "In Dialogue with the Asian Religions," art. 14, cited in *For All the Peoples of Asia: Federation of Asian Bishops' Conferences, Documents from 1970 to 1991*, vol. 1.
46. FABC I, "Evangelization in Modern Day Asia," art. 15, 14.
47. Theological Advisory Commission of the FABC, "Theses on Interreligious Dialogue: An Essay in Pastoral Theological Reflection," arts. 2.2, 2.3, in *FABC Papers* no. 48 (Hong Kong: FABC, 1987), 7.
48. Theological Advisory Commission, art. 1.4, 5.
49. Theological Advisory Commission, art. 2.5.
50. Theological Advisory Commission, thesis 3, 8.
51. Theological Advisory Commission, thesis 4, 10.
52. FABC I, "Evangelization in Modern Day Asia," art. 19, 15.
53. FABC Office of Ecumenical and Interreligious Affairs, "Tenth Bishops' Institute for Interreligious Affairs on the Theology of Dialogue," art. 8, in Rosales and Arévalo, *For All the Peoples of Asia*, vol. 1, 314.
54. Aloysius Pieris, *God's Reign for God's Poor: A Return to the Jesus Formula* (Kelaniya, Sri Lanka: Tulana Research Centre, 1999), 42, 60–61.
55. FABC I, "Evangelization in Modern Day Asia," 15.
56. FABC XI, "The Catholic Family in Asia: Domestic Church of the Poor on a Mission of Mercy," *FABC Papers* no. 151 (Hong Kong: FABC, 2017), 12.
57. Peter Phan, *Being Religious Interreligiously: Asian Perspectives on Interfaith Dialogue* (Maryknoll, NY: Orbis, 2004), 121.
58. Renewed Evangelizers for New Evangelization in Asia, "Message of X FABC Plenary Assembly," Xuan Loc, Vietnam, December 16, 2012), 2, http://www.fabc.org/index_10th_plenary.html.
59. Arévalo, "The Time of the Heirs," xxii.
60. FABC commentators suggest that perhaps it is because of this lack of authority that FABC statements seem more bold and progressive. Without the burden of binding authority, the bishops seem to be free to endorse theological positions that may be regarded as controversial. Perhaps this is how the Spirit works: freedom from authority allows for greater faithfulness to the Spirit's prompting and, hence, to gospel imperatives. See Thomas Fox, *Pentecost in Asia: A New Way of Being Church* (Maryknoll, NY: Orbis, 2002), 26.

61. Michael Rozario, "Words of Greetings: Reflections on Twenty-Five Years, Christian Discipleship in Asia Today: Service to Life," Summary Report of the Sixth Plenary Assembly of the Federation of Asian Bishops' Conferences, in *FABC Papers* no. 74 (Hong Kong: FABC, 1995), 8.
62. Peter C. Phan, "The Reception of Vatican II in Asia (1972–1998)," in Klaus Koschorke, ed., *Transcontinental Links in the History of Non-Western Christianity* (Wiesbaden, Germany: Harrassowitz Verlag, 2002), 256.
63. FABC X, "FABC at Forty Years: Responding to the Challenges of Asia, a New Evangelization," Plenary Assembly at Xuan Loc and Ho Chi Minh City, Vietnam, December 10–16, 2012, http://www.fabc.org/10th%20plenary%20assembly/Documents/FABC%20-%20X%20PA%20Final%20Document.pdf.
64. Renewed Evangelizers for New Evangelization in Asia, "Message of X FABC Plenary Assembly," 4.

15

Modern and Contemporary Catholic Theology in Asia: Main Trends and Developments

PETER C. PHAN

The aim of this chapter is rather straightforward, namely, to describe the main trends and developments of Catholic theology in Asia since the arrival of modernity in the continent and to limn its future trajectory. As José Casanova has argued, globalization, or to be more precise, the first or proto-globalization, should be distinguished from the earlier or archaic and the later or modern forms of globalization that reached Asia (and Latin America) through the Iberian colonial expansion, the post-Tridentine (early modern) Catholic revival, and Renaissance Christian humanism.[1] These three phases of the globalization process affected all aspects of the Catholic Church, including its organization, evangelizing mission, liturgical worship, popular devotions, art and architecture, music, monasticism, spirituality, social services, pastoral ministry, and daily life. This aspect of the globalized Church in Asia theology, this quest of faith for understanding—to use Saint Anselm's celebrated phrase, *fides quaerens intellectum*—has been developed since the sixteenth century until today.[2]

The current regions under consideration are limited to South Asia, Northeast Asia, and Southeast Asia, excluding North Asia, Central Asia, Australia, and New Zealand.[3] Furthermore, the discussion is restricted to Catholic theology, leaving aside Orthodox, Protestant, Evangelical, and Pentecostal theologies.[4] It considers Catholic theology in three parts, corresponding to the three stages of globalization in Asia, with each part preceded by an explanation of its distinctive theological method. Of course, not every Asian country has an extensive elaboration of Catholic theology. Among the countries that do have a robust Catholic theology, India, the Philippines, and Sri Lanka figure predominantly.[5]

There are different ways to present an overview of Asian Catholic theology, namely, chronologically, geographically, or thematically. This discussion will combine all three approaches by examining the main themes and trends of Asian theology as they have developed historically and in different countries. The key themes and trends of Asian theology are three: inculturation; integral human development with an emphasis on economic and sociopolitical justice; and interreligious dialogue. These three themes have been proposed by the Federation of the Asian Bishops' Conferences (FABC) as the threefold task of the Church's mission in Asia.[6]

THE GOSPEL IN ASIAN CULTURES: INCULTURATION

The Catholic Church was not the first Christian church to enter Asia. From the inscription engraved on the Xi'an Stele (or the Nestorian Stele monument), erected in 781 and discovered ca. 1623–25, it is certain that in AD 635 a group of "Nestorian" missionaries of the "Luminous religion" (Jingjiao), under the leadership of the monk Aluoben, came from Da Qin (Persia) and arrived in Chang'an, the capital of the Tang dynasty.[7] The inscription, composed by a priest whose Chinese name is Jingjing and Syriac name is Adam, and consisting of eighteen hundred Chinese characters, opens with an exposition of the beliefs of the Luminous Religion. This first part of the inscription is of the greatest interest for our study of Asian theology of inculturation. It represents the earliest Christian attempt at expressing the Christian faith in Chinese. Borrowing terms from Buddhism, Daoism, and Confucianism, it expounds the Christian teachings on God, creation, human nature, sin, incarnation, salvation, baptism, the Eucharist, and the Christian life.[8] Despite its unavoidable tentativeness and imperfections, this Church of the East's pioneering attempt at inculturation, which makes use of the Chinese language and Chinese religions to express the Christian faith, serves as a fruitful example for the Catholic theology of inculturation. "Nestorian" Christianity, which had virtually disappeared from China at the end of the Tang dynasty (618–907), reappeared in Khanbaliq (present-day Beijing), the later-Yuan capital, around the middle of the thirteenth century, only to disappear again after the fall of the Yuan dynasty in 1368.

The Catholic Church first entered Mongolia (not China proper) with two missions of Friars Minor, who arrived as papal legates at the pre-Yuan capital of Qaraqorum (today Helin) in present-day Mongolia between 1245 and 1253.[9] Notable among these friars were Giovanni dal Piano del Carpini, Willem van Rubroek, and Giovanni da Montecorvino, the latter of whom was consecrated the first archbishop of Khanbaliq and the patriarch of the Roman Catholic Church in the entire East in 1313. Despite their successes at conversion, especially among the non-Chinese Öngüt tribe, this first contingent of Catholics in China did not produce notable achievements in theological inculturation as the missionaries of the Church of the East had done. On the contrary, apologetics and controversy marked their attitude toward other religions, as demonstrated by van Rubroek's debate with Muslims and Buddhists in defense of Christian monotheism on May 30, 1254. The Franciscan missions soon suffered decline due to the internal divisions of the order and the dissipation of the papal interest in missions to Asia, as the hope of recovering the Holy Land through a Western-Mongol alliance evaporated with the general decline of the Mongol khanates.

Serious and extended efforts at enculturating Christianity into Chinese society and culture had to wait until the arrival, under the patronage of the Portuguese and Spanish Crowns, of missionary religious orders—Dominicans, Franciscans, Augustinians, Missions étrangères de Paris, Lazarists/Vincentians, and above all, Jesuits—during the late-Ming and mid-Qing dynasties. This period marks the first phase of the globalization of the Catholic Church in China. In accord with the accommodationist policy of Alessandro Valignano, the Jesuits initiated the process of adapting to Chinese culture by learning the local languages and adopting first the lifestyle of Buddhist monks and then that of the Confucian *literati*.[10]

Their evangelization method was "from the top down," hoping that the conversion of the emperor and the literati would bring about that of the people in China and Asia in general. They also tried to convert the Chinese by introducing European science and technology, including clocks, paintings, translation of mathematical writings, astronomy, calendar, mapmaking, and agriculture.[11]

In this inculturation enterprise, Matteo Ricci (1552–1610) stands out as a giant among the Jesuits, especially with his book *Tianzhu shiyi* (The true meaning of the Lord of heaven).[12] In this pathbreaking work, purporting to be a dialogue between a Western and a Chinese scholar and consisting of eight chapters divided into two parts, Ricci cites passages from the Confucian canon, especially the *Book of History* and the *Book of Poetry*, and argues that the Chinese *shangdi* (the high lord) is equivalent to the Christian God, implying thereby that Christianity is not completely a foreign religion imported from Europe. Furthermore, he shows that there is much in common between Confucianism and Christian ethics. On the other hand, Ricci attacks Daoism for superstitions and Buddhism for its teachings on reincarnation, karma, nonkilling, and vegetarianism and defends the Christian teachings on heaven and hell, the afterlife, the rewards for virtue, and the punishment for the evils of materialistic Neo-Confucianism.

Though Ricci is rightly celebrated for his openness to and adaptation of Chinese ideas and values, his eminence should not lead to the neglect of the important indigenizing work by other Jesuits such as Michele Ruggieri, Giulio Aleni, Nicholas Trigault, Philippe Couplet, and several Jesuit scientists, astronomers, and artists working at the court of the emperor, notably Ferdinand Verbiest, Johann Adam Schall von Bell, and the French "Mathématiciens du Roy." The latter's "figurism," especially as propounded by Joachim Bouvet and Joseph de Prémare, claims that the Chinese classics, in particular the *Book of Changes*, contain "examples" (*figurae*) of the Christian doctrines of God the Creator, the Trinity, and the expectation of a redeemer. Figurism can be considered one type of inculturation of Christianity into the Chinese culture.[13]

Furthermore, it must be noted that inculturation was done not only by foreign missionaries but also by the earliest Chinese converted literati—especially the three "pillars" of the Chinese Church, Xu Guangqi, Li Zhizao, and Yang Tingyun—who were actively engaged in the dialogue between the Christian faith and their Native culture. In general, during this phase of inculturation, these three pillars examined the similarities and differences between Confucianism and Christianity, regarding the beliefs in the one God (monotheism), the Trinity, creation, the incarnation, passion, and redemption of Jesus, sin and retribution, and moral ideas and practices.[14]

Tragically, the "Ricci way" and the Jesuit inculturation method were not observed in the so-called Chinese Rites Controversy. This controversy covers three issues, namely: the correct Chinese term for God, whether *tian* (heaven) or *shangdi* (the high lord); whether Christians were permitted to make financial contributions to community festivals in honor of non-Christian deities; and, most importantly, whether celebrations of the cult of Confucius, which the literati and state officials were required to perform every year, and the cult of ancestors, which was a sacred duty of all Chinese, were acceptable. The third issue turns on the question of whether these two rites can be regarded as not having religious significance but being only "civil and political acts" and therefore permissible for Christians. Ricci and his Jesuit confreres considered them to belong to the second category and therefore licit. Most members of the mendicant orders, and especially Bishop Charles Maigrot of the Missions Étrangères de Paris, condemned them as superstitious and denounced the Jesuits' practices to Rome. The controversy lasted almost three hundred years (1645–1941) and involved seven popes and two papal legates, the Holy Office and the Sacred Congregation of the Propagation of the Faith, two Chinese emperors and their courts, the kings of Portugal, Spain, and France, missionaries and their religious orders, Jansenists and the theology faculty of the Sorbonne, Leibnitz and Voltaire, and, of course, Chinese Christians.[15]

Following Pope Benedict XIV's final prohibition of Chinese rites in 1742 and the suppression of the Society of Jesus in 1773 and violence of the Taiping Heavenly Kingdom Rebellion (1850–64), the Chinese Catholic Church underwent a period of decline. The second phase of the globalization of Christianity in China, which occurred in the second half of the eighteenth and the nineteenth centuries, was vastly aided by the "golden age" of Protestant missions, the colonizing enterprise of Western powers (especially France and England, by means of the Unequal Treaties), the return of religious missionaries to China after the restoration of the Society of Jesus in 1814, and especially France's protectorate of the Chinese Catholic Church. As a result, the Church lost whatever inculturation achievements it had made.[16]

During the Republican era (1912–49), the Church briefly reprised the indigenization program by adopting Chiang Kai-shek's *Xinshengyunding* (new life movement), which promoted the four Confucian virtues of *li* (propriety), *yi* (uprightness), *lian* (integrity), and *chi* (modesty). This effort at inculturation through a dialogue with Confucianism was enthusiastically promoted by the apostolic nuncio, Celso Costantini, the Belgian missionary Vincent Lebbe (who vigorously promoted a Chinese episcopacy and became a Chinese citizen), authorities at Fujen University (established in Beijing in 1925), the scholar and jurist John Wu Ching Hsiung, and the Benedictine monk Lu Zhengxian. After its victory in 1949, the Communist Party forced the Chinese Catholic Church to adopt the Three-Self Patriotic Movement by founding in 1957 the Chinese Patriotic Catholic Association. In response, a Chinese Catholic theology of Christian identity and nationalism developed, led by the Jesuits Xu Gongze and Zhang Boda, but even today it lags far behind the Chinese Protestant theology (a "theology with Chinese characteristics") that was spearheaded by figures such as Zhao Zichen, Wu Leichuan, Wu Yaozong, and Ding Guangxun.[17]

Beyond China, inculturation went hand in hand among Catholic missions in other Asian countries as well, notably India, the Philippines, and Vietnam. As in China, Catholic Christianity was not the first to enter India. Saint Thomas the Apostle is alleged to have come from Syria to Malabar, Kerala, on the west coast of India, in AD 52, and his followers are known as St. Thomas/Mar Thoma/Malabar Christians. These earliest Indian Christians were settled north of Cranganore (Kodungallur) and were called the "northists." In 345, a group of some 400 Christian refugee families came from the (Nestorian) Church of the East in Persia under the leadership of Thomas of Cana; the group settled south of Cranganore and were called the "southists." Though the southists were socially more exclusive, choosing to avoid ritual pollution, both groups were well indigenized into their local cultures and claimed to be "Hindu in culture, Christian in faith, and Oriental in worship."[18]

The peaceful and vibrant life of Thomas Christians as a unified Christian community, which continued for about a millennium, was interrupted by the arrival of Vasco da Gama in Kerala in 1498, and soon followed, under the *padroado real* of Portugal, by Catholic religious missionaries such as Franciscans, Dominicans, Augustinians, Carmelites, Capuchins, Oratorians, and Theatines, and, above all, Jesuits, who by 1584 numbered 349. Among the latter, the most illustrious is Francis Xavier, who arrived in Goa, then the capital of the Estado da Índia, in 1542. The encounter between the Latin Church and Thomas Christians was at first amicable but soon turned hostile as *padroado* Catholics attempted to impose their Latin rites and authority on Thomas Christians, whom they accused of the Nestorian heresy. This heavy-handed Latinization reached its peak at the Synod of Diamper, held June 20–26, 1599, under the leadership of Alexis de Menezes, the archbishop of Goa. The synod's two hundred decrees represented in part a rejection of the centuries-long inculturation of St. Thomas Christians regarding theology, liturgy, and church administration. Moreover, culturally, Indian Christians on the west coast (at Mumbai/Bombay, Goa, and Mangalore), in contrast to those on the east coast in Tamil Nadu (at Chennai/Madras and Madurai), were forced to give up their old social customs, take up the last names of their Portuguese godfathers in baptism, and adopt the Portuguese way of life.

Such anti-inculturation practices were reversed a hundred years later by Italian Jesuit missionary Roberto de Nobili (1577–1656), who came to Goa in 1605, traveled to Cochin, and finally settled in Madurai, Tamil Nadu, in 1606. Realizing that only low-caste Paravars from the Pearl Fishery Coast had accepted the Christian faith, de Nobili wanted to convert the Brahmins. For this purpose, implementing Alessandro Valignano's accommodation method as his Jesuit confreres had done in China, de Nobili learned the local languages, including Sanskrit, Tamil, and Tegulu, and composed catechisms, apologetic works, and philosophic discourses in Tamil. He also adopted local Indian customs, such as living and eating like an Indian, becoming a vegetarian; shaving his head and keeping only a tiny tuft (the *kudumi*), a distinctive sign of the Brahmin caste; donning the saffron dress and wooden sandals of a *sanyasin*; and wearing the *tilak*, a mark on the brow, and the three-stringed thread across the chest, both also signs of the Brahmin caste. De Nobili also permitted his Brahmin converts to do the same. He did not require them to take Latin or Portuguese surnames but gave them Tamil ones instead.[19]

While de Nobili's inculturation method was welcome by the Brahmins of Madurai, some of whom converted, his Portuguese colleagues attacked it as overtolerant and obscuring of the distinctiveness of Christianity. Christopher de Sa, the archbishop of Goa, summoned de Nobili before the Inquisition of Goa, where he was defended by his Jesuit confreres. The dispute was submitted to Rome and the grand inquisitor of Portugal, and in 1623 Pope Gregory XV pronounced in favor of de Nobili. In response to criticisms that de Nobili's method neglected the mission to the poor and outcast, the Jesuits divided themselves into two groups: the *brahminsannyasis*, who would work with high-caste peoples, and the *pandaraswamis*, who worked among the lower castes.

Unfortunately, de Nobili's evangelization method came under attack again some fifty years after his death. In 1687, French Jesuits arrived in Pondicherry; together with their fellow Jesuits in Madurai, they carried out missions in Mysore and the Carnatic, using de

Nobili's method. In 1703, their missionary practices were denounced to the Congregation of the Propagation of the Faith. The ensuing dispute gave rise to what is called the Malabar Rites/Indian Rites Controversy, with "rites" referring not to cultic rituals (as in China) but to cultural and caste customs. Archbishop Charles Thomas Maillard de Tournon, who had been appointed *legatus a latere* by Pope Clement XI to resolve the Chinese Rites Controversy, stopped at Pondicherry on his way to China in 1703. After receiving reports from various missionaries, on June 23, 1704, de Tournon issued a decree, confirmed by the Holy Office the following year, condemning sixteen practices permitted by the Jesuits. De Tournon's decree was contested by the Jesuits several times; finally, in 1744, Pope Benedict XIV reaffirmed the decree and enjoined an oath on all missionaries to abide by de Tournon's sixteen prohibitions.

Despite this papal prohibition, the program of inculturation was picked up again by Brahmabandhab Upadhyay (1861–1907). A Catholic theologian, journalist, and freedom fighter, Brahmabandhab declared himself a "Hindu Catholic": "By birth, we are Hindu and shall remain Hindu till death. . . . We are Hindus so far as our physical and mental constitution is concerned, but in regard to our immortal souls, we are Catholic. We are Hindu Catholic."[20] By the early 1940s the Indian Rites Controversy, along with the Chinese Rites Controversy, was brought to an end, and these "rites" were permitted on the grounds that they are civil acts that do not possess religious meaning. Shortly afterward, the Second Vatican Council mandated a thorough program of inculturation in all aspects of Church life. The Federation of Asian Bishops' Conferences repeatedly urged that missions be practiced as a triple dialogue, that is, with Asian cultures (inculturation), with Asian people, especially the poor (liberation), and with Asian religions (interreligious dialogue).[21]

Before Vatican II there had already been attempts to adopt certain forms of Hindu asceticism into Christian monastic life. Notable names include Jules Monchanin (1895–1957), Henri Le Saux, widely known as Swami Abhishikananda (1910–73), Bede Griffith (1906–93), François Mahieu (1919–2002), Vandana Mataji (1921–2013), and Sara Grant (1922–2000). In the aftermath of the council an astonishingly large number of Indian theologians, using both their productivity and their originality, put the Indian Catholic Church on the map as one of the most important theological centers of the world. Some of the theologians engaged in the various aspects of inculturation were expatriates such as Joseph Neuner (1908–2009), Raimon Panikkar (1918–2010), Jacques Dupuis (1923–2004), Lucien Legrand (1926–), and George Gispert-Sauch (1930–2020). The majority, however, were Indian-born and include the notable Samuel Ryan (1920–2019), Sebastian Kappen (1924–93), George M. Soares-Prabhu (1929–95), Sebastian Karotemprel (1931–2014), Kurien Kunnumpuram (1931–2018), Albert Nambiaparambil (1931–2017), Doraiswamy S. Amalorpavadass (1932–90), Francis Xavier D'Sa (1936–), Michael Amaladoss (1936–), Sebastian Painadath (1942–), Julian Saldahna (1942–), Felix Wilfred (1948–), and Jose Kuttianimattathil (1955–). These theologians as a rule deal with inculturation in intimate connection with liberation and interreligious dialogue.

In connection with India it is important to mention Sri Lanka, "the pearl of the Indian ocean." The Catholic Church came to this small island in the wake of the arrival of the Portuguese in 1505, followed by the Dutch Reformed Church in 1658 and the Anglican Church in 1845. Given the religious diversity and the unjust social conditions of the country, Catholic theologians who flourished after Vatican II emphasized inculturation as part of liberation theology and interreligious dialogue, especially with Buddhism. Notable theologians include Peter A. Pillai (1904–64), Leo Nanayakkara (1917–82), Tissa Balasuriya (1924–2013), Paul Caspersz (1925–2017), Michael Rodrigo (1927–89), Aloysius Pieris (1934–), Antony Fernando (1932–2021), Nihal Abeyasignha (1939–), and Vimal Tirimanna (1955–).

Another country where inculturation has assumed a lion's share in theology is the majority-Catholic Philippines. Given its centuries-long history of subjugation by Spain and the United States and long-standing domination of the local clergy by foreign missionaries, mostly Spanish friars, within the Church the inculturation in early Filipino Catholic theology took two major forms: national independence and recovery of Native cultures and religious traditions. Leaving the first theme to the discussion of liberation theology later, inculturation entails the recovery of Filipino cultural values and folk religion for the development of Filipino theology. Major figures in this effort include Catalino Arévalo (1925–2023), Vitaliano Gorospe (†2002), Francisco F. Claver (1929–2010), Leonardo Mercado (1935–), Anscar Chupungco (1939–2013), Benigno Beltran (1946–), José M. de Mesa (1946-2021), and Agnes M. Brazal (1960–).

The last country to be considered under the rubric of inculturation in Catholic theology is Vietnam. Jesuit missionaries first arrived in Vietnam in 1615, initiating the first phase of the globalization of Christianity in Vietnam. Among the Jesuits who came in 1624, Alexandre de Rhodes stands out as one who did most to indigenize the Christian faith into the Vietnamese culture during this first period of globalization. Beside his travelogues, his histories of Christian missions in Vietnam, his Vietnamese-Portuguese-Latin dictionary, and his grammar of the Vietnamese language, de Rhodes is best known for his *Cathechismus pro ijs, qui volunt suscipere baptismum in octo dies divisus* (Catechism for those who want to receive baptism divided into eight days). Published in 1651, the book presents the Latin and Vietnamese texts side by side, the latter in the Romanized script invented by the Jesuits. The *Cathechismus* represents the first attempt at inculturating the Christian doctrines and worship into Vietnamese cultures and religions.[22]

During the second phase of globalization, that is, in the eighteenth and nineteenth centuries, the Vietnamese Catholic Church suffered severe persecutions and thus had no means and opportunities to develop a Native theology. In the third phase of globalization, the twentieth century, the main concern of the Church was, like the Filipino Catholic Church, to defend itself against accusations of lack of patriotism, mostly by the Communists, and to argue for a Vietnamese-Catholic identity. The victory of the Communist North over South Vietnam in 1975 severely hampered the development of a robust Vietnamese theology. Currently, thanks to the government's religious tolerance (albeit limited) and the work of Vietnamese theologians in the diaspora, steps have been taken to elaborate a Vietnamese theology and way of living the Christian faith.

SALVATION AS INTEGRAL LIBERATION

Liberation theology developed within the Catholic Church in Asia mainly as a response to the challenges of Vatican II, especially its pastoral constitution *Gaudium et Spes*, a collaboration with Latin American theology through organizations such as the Ecumenical Association of Third-World Theologians (EATWOT, established in 1976), and as a result of the exploration of effective ways to live the Church's social doctrine in the turbulent sociopolitical and economic conditions of many Asian countries in the decades of 1970–80, especially in India, Sri Lanka, Korea, the Philippines, and Vietnam.

Whereas the open or official Chinese Catholic Church, which was largely controlled by the Communist Party (as distinct from the underground or unregistered Church), was unable to respond intellectually and practically to the seismic political and social convulsions in China in the twentieth century, the Church in other countries took an active stance against dictatorship and acted in solidarity with the oppressed and the poor, and in the process elaborating extensive theologies of liberation. One concern, powerfully expressed by Aloysius Pieris, one of Asia's foremost liberation theologians, was that the earlier trends of inculturation, not least in India, ran the risk of promoting an elitist and escapist form of Christianity.[23] As a result of this criticism, most trends and movements of Asian Catholic theology today contain a strong liberationist element. The FABC has repeatedly insisted on liberation as a constitutive dimension of the Church's mission.[24] Over the years, it has expanded its understanding of "the poor" to include not only the economically poor but also people in rural and urban areas, migrants, physically and sexually abused persons, victims of war and sex trafficking, the landless, women living in patriarchal societies, domestic workers, children forced into child labor, the Dalits, the Tribals, those harmed by environmental degradation, and victims of neocapitalist consumerist globalization.[25]

In India, two sociopolitical, economic, and religious liberationist movements have given rise to Dalit theology and Tribal theology.[26] Though they originated outside the Catholic Church as a protest against the caste system and economic exploitation, they have been vigorously supported by Indian Catholic theologians. Prominent among these are Sebastian Karotemprel, Michael Amaladoss, Francis Gonsalves, and especially Felix Wilfred.

In Korea the Catholic Church, which began with the baptism of Yi Sung Hun in 1784, since its beginnings suffered ferocious persecutions by the Joseon dynasty (1392–1897), especially in 1801, 1839, and 1866–71. During the Japanese occupation of the country (1910–45), though the Korean Catholic Church did not participate in the independence movement led by the Protestant churches (known as Sam-Il, or literally Three-One or March First), its sense of social and political responsibility grew noticeably after the defeat of Japan and its occupation of Korea in 1945. The most prominent contributor to this social consciousness is Daniel Chi Hak Soon (1921–93), bishop of Wonju diocese, who took an active part in movements for democracy, anti-corruption, and human rights, especially prior to the establishment of the Fourth Republic of Korea (1972–81) following the approval of the Yunshin Constitution. For these activities the bishop was sentenced by the Park Chung Hee administration to fifteen years' imprisonment and his civil rights were suspended for another fifteen years.

The Church was deeply involved in the struggle against the dictatorship of Park Chung Hee (president 1961–79). Cardinal Stephen Kim Su Hwan (1925–2009, the archbishop of Seoul from 1968 until retirement in 1998) was a universally respected leader of Korea's tumultuous transition from dictatorship toward democracy. In the 1970s, while *minjung* theology was developed by Protestant theologians such as Suh Nam Dong, Ahn Byung Mu, Hyun Young Hak, Suh Kwang Sun, and Kim Yong Bock, Catholic theologians were more focused on inculturating the Christian faith into Korean cultures by means of Korean church history, Korean cultural and spiritual values, and art. Of great importance is the work of Min Anselm Kyong Suk (1940–2020), though he spent his academic life in the United States. One notable figure is the lay Catholic poet Kim Chi Ha (1941–), who was a vocal critic of social injustice, political corruption, and military violence. One event that would set the church-reform agenda for the Korean Catholic Church is the 1984 Pastoral Congress, held to commemorate the bicentennial of Catholic Christianity in Korea. A current political issue hotly debated among Korean Christians is national reconciliation, that is, the reunification of North Korea and South Korea, and the removal of nuclear arms from the Korean Peninsula, two projects that the Korean Catholic Church strongly supports.

Liberation theology is also highly influential in the Philippines, where the struggle for national independence has given rise to a nationalist clergy and Filipino theology. The execution in 1872 of three priests, José Burgos, Mariano Gómez, and Jacinto Zamora, collectively known as the Gomburza, by Spanish colonial authorities fueled the debate on national identity and Filipino Christianity. José Rizal (1861–96), arguably the greatest hero of Filipino national independence, was deeply affected by the death of his friend Burgos, and himself was executed by Spanish colonial authorities in 1896 on the charge of insurrection. Rizal is the icon of Filipino liberation theology. The eventual founding of the Iglesia Filipina Independiente by Isabelo de los Reyes and Gregorio Aglipay in 1902 was essentially an assertion of Filipino nationalism and liberation from the Spanish friars.

After the US colonization of the Philippines ended in 1946, the Catholic Church became deeply engaged in social activities, especially through Catholic Action and the leadership of Jesuits Joseph A. Mulry (1889–1945), Walter Hogan (fl. 1950), and Horacio de la Costa (1916–77). Bishop Julio Javier Labayen (1927–2016) was very active in the work for social justice and human rights. At the same time, a vigorous liberation theology was formulated by Carlos Abesamis (1934–2018), Pedro V. Salgado (1937–), Louie G. Hechanova (1940–), and Edicio de la Torre (1943–).[27] The dictatorship of President Ferdinand Marcos sparked the People Power Revolution, also known as the EDSA Revolution, in 1986, which was openly supported by Cardinal Jaime Sin, the archbishop of Manila, and the Catholic Bishops' Conference of the Philippines. This event highlighted the effective role of nonviolence and spirituality in the work for justice and peace.

In Vietnam, the struggle for national independence from France and the rise of Communism under Ho Chi Minh in the 1950s presented the Vietnamese Catholic Church with issues of national identity and the role of the Church in national reconstruction. Lê Hữu Từ, bishop of Phát Diệm (1897–1967), though a fierce opponent of the Communist Party, was an ardent supporter of the cause of anticolonialism and national independence, and together with Phạm Ngọc Chi, bishop of Bùi Chu (1909–88), succeeded in keeping their two dioceses as autonomous zones free from both French and Communist control. On the other hand, the condemnation of "atheistic communism" by the Vatican prevented Vietnamese Catholics from collaborating with Hồ Chí Minh to end French colonial rule after Ho turned to communism to achieve his nationalist agenda. The exodus of some 600,000 Catholics and 918 priests from the north to the south in 1954 exacerbated the conflict between the Vietnamese Catholic Church and the Communist Party.

While Church life in North Vietnam was stifled, in South Vietnam it was vibrant, thanks largely to the reforms of Vatican II and the opportunities for the clergy to be trained abroad, especially at Roman universities. Unfortunately, no significant Indigenous theology was produced between 1955 and 1975, except for the first scholarly translation of the Bible into Vietnamese. During the presidency of Ngô Đình Diệm (1901–63) and Nguyễn Văn Thiệu (1923–2001), both Catholics, and the Vietnam War, several priests were involved in denouncing the war, corruption, and violation of human rights, and actively worked for justice and peace, notably Vương Đình Bích (1928–2015), Trần Thiện Cẩm (1933–2014), Trương Bá Cần (1930–2009), Nguyễn Ngọc Lan (1930–2007), and Phan Khắc Từ (1941–). Some of these priests founded journals and periodicals to promote their social and political liberationist agenda, such as *Chính Nghĩa* (Just cause) and *Đối Diện* (Face to face) and, after 1975, *Công Giáo và Dân Tộc* (Catholicism and people). It was in this struggle for justice and peace that a rudiment of Vietnamese liberation theology was formulated.

One last aspect of Asian liberation theology is feminist theology. Inspired by feminist thought on gender and sexuality, especially among French and American thinkers, and rooted in the Bible as a whole and in particular the teachings and examples of Jesus, Asian Catholic women have voiced sharp criticism of the patriarchal and androcentric system within the family, society, and the Church and have demanded equal treatment and full participation in various ecclesial ministries.[28] In general, feminist theology is more developed in Asian Protestant churches, but significant Catholic voices are emerging.[29] In India, there are Vandana Mattaji (1921–2013) and Stella Baltazar (1952–), and in Hong Kong, Angela Wong Wai-ching (1959–). In Korea, a numerous cohort of female theologians, writing on gender issues, the silencing of women's voices, the lack of participatory democracy in the Church, and ecofeminism, includes Han Soon Hee, Choi Hae Young, Kim Sung Hae, Kang Young Ok, Kim Jeoung Ha, Leo Kim, Silvia Chung, Cecelia Han, Yang Hee Ok, Miriam Kim Hyun Ok, and Cheon Se Hyung;[30] in the Philippines is an even larger group of female theologians, including Virginia Fabella, Mary John Mananzan, Agnes Brazal, and more than a dozen others.[31]

DIALOGUE WITH OTHER RELIGIONS

The third and highly controversial trend in Asian Catholic theology is interreligious dialogue.[32] As a minority religion in most countries, except in the Philippines and East Timor, the Catholic Church in Asia has recently regarded interreligious dialogue as one of the three constitutive dimensions of its mission, and this has been repeatedly affirmed by the FABC.[33] This dialogue with believers of other religions takes four forms, namely, sharing a common life (dialogue of life), collaboration for the common good (dialogue of action), theological discussion (dialogue of theological exchange), and sharing religious experience (dialogue of religious experience).[34]

From the doctrinal point of view, interreligious dialogue is the most threatening of the three dialogues, as it calls for a rethinking of all major Catholic doctrines in the context of religious pluralism. Chief among these doctrinal questions relates to Christology: In what sense can Jesus be said to be the unique and universal savior? But no less challenging are questions such as: Who is God, especially in light of nontheistic (not atheistic) religious traditions such as Buddhism, Jainism, and Daoism, and polytheistic religions like Hinduism? Are there ways of expressing the Trinity using non-Christian categories? Is there divine revelation outside Christianity and the Bible, for example, in the Vedas? How is the Church's evangelizing mission to be understood and carried out? Can non-Christians be saved and, if they can, what salvific role does religion play in God's plan of salvation? How should salvation itself be understood, beyond redemption from sin and sharing in the Divine Nature? Is there the possibility, even desirability of multiple religious belonging? These and many other questions have been taken up by several Asian theologians and some of their proposals have been looked upon suspiciously and even condemned by the Congregation for the Doctrine of the Faith, especially under the pontificates of Popes John Paul II and Benedict XVI.

Among those who have dealt with these questions, pride of place must be given to Indian theologians, especially Raimon Panikkar, Samuel Ryan, John Chethimattam, Michael Amaladoss, Sebastian Painadath, Felix Wilfred, Jose Kuttianimattathil, and Dominic Veliath, in addition to the inherently interreligious monasticism of the expatriate monks and nuns mentioned earlier. Sri Lankan Aloysius Pieris must be counted as one of the most influential theologians of interreligious dialogue. In China, Hong Kong, and Taiwan, the dialogue is mainly with Confucianism and Daoism and, to a lesser extent, Buddhism. Catholic theologians notable for their work on interreligious dialogue include Benoît Vernander and Thierry Meynard in China; and John Tong, Vincent Shen, Joseph Wong (who has been living in the U.S.), Edward Chau, Maria Goretti Lau, Kwong Lay-kuen, Judith Xu Chan, Ho Chuk-ping, and Lok Shung-fai in Hong Kong.[35] In Taiwan are Tien Liang, Ch'eng Shih-kuang, Stanislaus Lo Kwang, Aloysius Chang Ch'un-shen, Mark Fang Chih-jung, Yves Raguin, and Luis Gutheinz;[36] in Japan are Heinrich Dumoulin, Hugo Enomiya-Lassalle, Joseph John Spae, Johannes Kadowaki Kakichi, Inoue Yoji, Jan Van Bragt, James W. Heisig, Ruben Habito, and several younger theologians.[37] Korea has Park Il Young, Kim Ung Tai, and Sim Jong Hyeok;[38] Indonesia has Robert Hardawiryana, Franz Magnis-Suseno, Johannes Baptista Banawiratma, and recently deceased John Prior;[39] and in the Philippines, where the dialogue is chiefly with Islam, are James Kroeger and Sebastiano D'Ambra of the Silsilah Foundation in Zamboanga, which was established to foster relations between Christians and Muslims.

There is, of course, no consensus among these many theologians on the issues involved in interreligious dialogue, nor is such a consensus possible or even desirable. However, one common thread runs through their work: the conviction that Asia is the birthplace of religious pluralism and that Christianity must find "a new way of being church," a favorite expression of the FABC. In the context of religious pluralism, a Christian theology appropriate for Asia cannot be elaborated except interreligiously.

CONCLUSION

As the three massive bibliographical volumes *Asian Christian Theologies* eloquently testify, Christian theology in Asia is both ancient and vibrant. Asian Catholic theology began with the coming of missionaries to India and then to East Asia in the sixteenth century, the time of the first globalization of Christianity in Asia. Its primary genres were apologetics and catechism, though a serious attempt was made to show that the Christian faith, albeit superior to other religions, is compatible with them. During the eighteenth and nineteenth centuries, the second period of Catholic globalization, the Catholic Church suffered an eclipse in most Asian countries, mainly because of persecutions and wars and because no significant Indigenous theology was produced. In the third phase of Catholic globalization in the twentieth century a veritable explosion of theologies burst forth in almost all Asian countries, with India and the Jesuits at the forefront. (Protestant theology, which is not under consideration here, has often outstripped Catholic theology.) Many factors contributed to this theological efflorescence, including religious freedom, decolonization, national independence, the establishment of local hierarchies, Vatican II, and the founding of the FABC.

Recent developments of Asian Catholic theology can be conveniently described under the form of the triple encounters of inculturation, liberation, and interreligious dialogue. In the foreseeable future these three dialogues will continue to serve as the foci of Asian Catholic theology. To gain a more influential voice and a coherent structure, an attempt should be made at creating what may be called a "pan-Asian theology," something that was done by the FABC and its many offices but which has lost steam in recent years. Perhaps the celebration of the fiftieth anniversary of the FABC in 2022 will spark a new era of Asian Catholic theology.

NOTES

1. See José Casanova's chapter in this volume. Here I show how the coming of missionaries in Vietnam in the seventeenth century represents the first phase of globalization in that country.
2. The best bibliography of Asian theology is the three-volume, 2,131-page work by John C. England et al., eds., *Asian Christian Theologies: A Research Guide to Authors, Movements, Sources, Vol. 1: Asia Region, South Asia, Austral Asia*; *Vol. 2: Southeast Asia*; *Vol. 3: Northeast Asia* (Maryknoll, NY: Orbis, 2002).
3. For an introduction to Christianity in Asia, see Felix Wilfred, ed., *The Oxford Handbook of Christianity in Asia* (Oxford: Oxford University Press, 2014); Peter C. Phan, ed., *Christianities in Asia* (Oxford: Wiley-Blackwell, 2011); and Peter C. Phan, *Asian Christianities: History, Theology, Practice* (Maryknoll, NY: Orbis, 2018).
4. Orthodox theology is limited to the churches that self-identify with the Saint Thomas tradition in India, mainly the two branches of the Orthodox Syrian Church, the Chaldean Church of the East, the Mar Thoma Church, the Syro-Malabar Catholic Church, and the Syro-Malankara Catholic Church. In tandem with the Western colonial enterprise, Protestant missions flourished in Asia, beginning with William Carey in India and Robert Morrison in China, and eventually led to a development of theology that reached its culmination at the World Missionary Conference at Edinburgh, Scotland, in 1910. See Brian Stanley, *The World Missionary Conference, Edinburgh 1910* (Grand Rapids, MI: Eerdmans, 2009); and David A. Kerr and Kenneth R. Ross, eds., *Edinburgh 2010: Mission Then and Now* (Pasadena, CA: William Carey International University Press, 2009). On evangelical theology in Asia, see Timoteo D. Gener and Stephen T. Pardu, eds., *Asian Christian Theology: Evangelical Perspectives* (Manila, Philippines: Asia Theological Association, 2019); and David H. Lumsdaine, ed., *Evangelical Christianity and Democracy in Asia*

(Oxford: Oxford University Press, 2009). On Pentecostal theology in Asia, see Allan Anderson and Edmond Tong, eds., *Asian and Pentecostal: The Charismatic Face of Christianity in Asia* (Oxford: Regnum Books International, 2005); and Denise A. Austin, Jacqueline Grey, and Paul W. Lewis, eds., *Asia Pacific Pentecostalism* (Leiden: Brill, 2019).

5. Asian countries that have developed extensive and influential Protestant theologies are India, Japan, Korea, mainland China, Hong Kong, and Taiwan. Some of these countries have developed distinctly Indigenous theologies, such as Dalit theology, Tribal theology, Minjung theology, three-self theology, Sino-Christian theology, and homeland theology. These are, however, beyond the scope of this discussion.
6. The FABC was founded in 1970 on the occasion of Pope Paul VI's visit to Manila, Philippines. Its statutes, approved by the Holy See *ad experimentum* in 1972, were amended several times and approved again each time by the Holy See. For the documents of the FABC and its various institutes, see Gaudencio Rosales and C. G. Arévalo, eds., *For All the Peoples of Asia: Federation of Asian Bishops' Conferences, Documents from 1970 to 1991*, vol. 1 (New York: Orbis, 1992); Franz-Josef Eilers, ed., *For All the Peoples of Asia: Federation of Asian Bishops' Conferences, Documents from 1992 to 1996*, vol. 2 (Quezon City, Philippines: Claretian, 1997); Franz-Josef Eilers, ed., *For All the Peoples of Asia: Federation of Asian Bishops' Conferences, Documents from 1997 to 2002*, vol. 3 (Quezon City, Philippines: Claretian, 2002); Franz-Josef Eilers, ed., *For All the Peoples of Asia: Federation of Asian Bishops' Conferences, Documents from 2002 to 2006*, vol. 4 (Quezon City, Philippines: Claretian, 2006); and Vimal Tirimanna, ed., *For All the Peoples of Asia: Federation of Asian Bishops' Conferences, Documents from 2007–2012*, vol. 5 (Quezon City, Philippines: Claretian, 2014) (all hereafter cited by volume number). The FABC Documentation Centre, located in Bangkok, regularly publishes "papers" that do not necessarily represent the teachings of the FABC but are best viewed as theological ideas and opinions of individual Asian Catholics. For a presentation of the teachings of the FABC, see Jonathan Y. Tan, *The Federation of Asian Bishops' Conferences (FABC): Bearing Witness to the Gospel and the Reign of God in Asia* (Minneapolis: Fortress, 2021).
7. For a survey of this Xi'an Stele and the missionary activities of Aluoben and his companions, see Nicolas Standaert, ed., *Handbook of Christianity in China, Vol. 1, 635–1800* (Leiden: Brill, 2001), 1–42. This volume and the second volume, R. G. Tiedemann, ed., *Handbook of Christianity in China, Vol. 2, 1800–present* (Leiden: Brill, 2010), are indispensable and best tools for the study of Christianity in China.
8. In addition to the Xi'an Stele, several Chinese Christian documents, part of the "Dunhuang Documents," give important information on the early history of the Church of the East in China. For helpful histories of Christianity in China, see Jean-Pierre Charbonnier, *Christians in China: A.D. 600 to 2000*, M. N. L. Couve de Murville, trans. (San Francisco: Ignatius, 2007); and Daniel H. Bays, *A New History of Christianity in China* (Oxford: Wiley-Blackwell, 2012).
9. For a brief survey of Nestorian and Catholic Christianity under the Yuan dynasty (1279–1368), see Standaert, *Handbook of Christianity in China*, 43–108.
10. On Alessandro Valignano (1539–1606) and his policy of accommodation, see Artur K. Wardega, ed., *Portrait of a Jesuit: Alessandro Valignano* (Macau: Macau Ricci Institute, 2013).
11. On the contributions of the early Jesuits to globalization, see Luke Clossey, *Salvation and Globalization in the Early Jesuit Missions* (Cambridge: Cambridge University Press, 2008); and Thomas Banchoff and José Casanova, eds., *The Jesuits and Globalization: Historical Legacies and Contemporary Challenges* (Washington, DC: Georgetown University Press, 2016).
12. See Matteo Ricci, *The True Meaning of the Lord of Heaven*, trans. Douglas and Peter Hu Kuo-chen (Saint Louis, MO: The Institute of Jesuit Sources, 1985); and Matteo Ricci, *Le sens réel de "Seigneur du ciel,"* Thierry Meynard, trans. (Paris: Les Belles Lettres, 2013). For a highly accessible overview of the work of Ricci, see R. Po-chi Hsia, *Matteo Ricci and the Catholic Mission to China, 1583–1610: A Short History with Documents* (Indianapolis: Hackett, 2016). For a brief history of

Jesuit missions in China, see Benoît Vernander, *Les Jésuites et la Chine: De Matteo Ricci à nos jours* (Brussels: Éditions Lessius, 2012).

13. On figurism, see Standaert, *Handbook of Christianity in China*, 668–74.
14. For a discussion of how these beliefs were debated by both missionaries and Chinese Christians, see Standaert, *Handbook of Christianity in China*, 632–67. On Joseph de Prémare, see David E. Mungello, *The Silencing of Jesuit Figurist Joseph de Prémare in Eighteenth-Century China* (Lanham, MD: Lexington, 2019).
15. See George Minamiki, *The Chinese Rites Controversy: From Its Beginning to Modern Times* (Chicago: Loyola University Press, 1985); Ray R. Noll, ed., *100 Roman Documents Concerning the Chinese Rites Controversy (1645–1941)* (San Francisco: Ricci Insititue, 1992); and David E. Mungello, ed., *The Chinese Rites Controversy: Its History and Meaning* (London: Routledge, 1994).
16. On France's religious protectorate of the Chinese Catholic Church and its deleterious impact, see Ernest P. Young, *Ecclesiastical Colony: China's Catholic Church and the French Religious Protectorate* (Oxford: Oxford University Press, 2013).
17. See Chloë Starr, *Chinese Theology: Text and Context* (New Haven, CT: Yale University Press, 2016); and Alexander Chow, *Chinese Public Theology: Generational Shifts and Confucian Imagination in Chinese Christianity* (Oxford: Oxford University Press, 2018).
18. On Christianity in India, see Robert Eric Frykenberg, *Christianity in India: From Beginnings to the Present* (Oxford: Oxford University Press, 2008); and Leonardo Fernando and G. Gispert-Sauch, *Christianity in India: Two Thousand Years of Faith* (London: Penguin, 2004).
19. On de Nobili and his missionary method, see Roberto de Nobili, *Preaching Wisdom to the Wise: Three Treatises by Roberto de Nobili*, Anand Amaladass and Francis X. Clooney, trans. and intro. (St. Louis, MO: Institute of Jesuit Sources, 2000).
20. Brahmabandab Upadhyay, "Are We Hindus?," quoted in Julius Lipner, *Brahmabandab Upadhyay: The Life and Thought of a Revolutionary* (Dehli: Oxford University Press, 1999), 209. See also Sebastian Painadath and Jacon Parapally, eds., *A Hindu Catholic: Brahmabandab Upadhya's Significance for Indian Christian Theology* (Bangalore: Asia Trading, 2008).
21. See, for instance, *For All the Peoples of Asia*, vol. 1 (1992), 13–16, 34–35, 58, 276–77; vol. 2 (1997), 2–3; vol. 3 (2002), 120–22; vol. 4 (2006), 31–37; vol. 5 (2014), 44–45.
22. See Peter C. Phan, *Mission and Catechesis: Alexandre de Rhodes & Inculturation in Seventeenth-Century Vietnam* (Maryknoll, NY: Orbis, 1998); and Peter C. Phan, *In Our Own Tongues: Perspectives from Asia on Mission and Inculturation* (Maryknoll, NY: Orbis, 2004).
23. See Pieris's *An Asian Theology of Liberation* (Maryknoll, NY: Orbis, 1988). Pieris is also a leading proponent of Buddhist-Christian dialogue. See his *Love Meets Wisdom: A Christian Experience of Buddhism* (Maryknoll, NY: Orbis, 188) and *Fire and Water: Basic Issues in Asian Buddhism and Christianity* (Maryknoll, NY: Orbis, 1996).
24. See *For All the Peoples of Asia*, 1:15–16; 4:33, 3–5; 3:1–3; 4: 5–18; 5:58–65.
25. For an expansive list of victims of violence in Asia, see *For All the Peoples of Asia*, 2:13–15.
26. Among the many works on Dalit theology, see Sathianathan Clarke, Deenabandhu Manchala, and Philip Vinod Peacock, eds., *Dalit Theology in the Twenty-First Century: Discordant Voices, Discerning Pathways* (Oxford: Oxford University Press, 2010). On Tribal theology, see K. Thanzauwa, *Theology of Community: Tribal Theology in the Making* (Guwahati: Labanya, 1997). To be noted are the Dalit Resource Centre in Arasaradi, Madurai; the Tribal Study Center in Jorhat, Assam; the Jeevan Vikas Maitri in Asha Deep, Chattisgarth; and the Don Bosco Centre for Indigenous Cultures in Shillong.
27. Filipino liberation theology is often referred to as "theology of struggle." See Eleazar S. Fernandez, *Toward a Theology of Struggle* (Maryknoll, NY: Orbis, 1994).
28. For the works of Asian Catholic women in general, see the three bibliographical volumes *Asian Christian Theologies*, under the sections "Women Doing Theology."

29. One important journal for Asian feminist theology is *In God's Image,* a half-yearly journal published since 2010.
30. There is the Korean Catholic Women's Community for a New World, founded in 1993, to promote the role of women in the Church and society.
31. There is the Institute of Women's Studies at St. Scholastica's College in Manila, founded in 1988, whose goal, as implied by its name, is to investigate the issues concerning women through formal and informal courses and seminars.
32. See Peter C. Phan, *Being Religious Interreligiously: Asian Perspectives on Interreligious Dialogue* (Maryknoll, NY: Orbis, 2004).
33. See *For All the Peoples of Asia,* 1:14–15, 35, 278; 2: 2–3; 3:3, 4; 5:44–45, 51.
34. See Pontifical Council for Interreligious Dialogue and Congregation for the Evangelization of Peoples, *Dialogue and Proclamation: Reflections and Orientations on Interreligious Dialogue and the Proclamation of the Gospel of Jesus Christ* (self-published, 1991), no. 42.
35. The Catholic Church in Hong Kong has the Holy Spirit Study Centre, a research institute with a focus on China, and three journals with strong focus on interreligious dialogue: *Tripod,* since 1981; *Theology Annual,* since 1986; and *Spirit,* since 1989.
36. Fujen University and Fu Jen Faculty of Theology of Saint Robert Bellarmino are important centers for the dialogue between Christianity and the Chinese religions.
37. The Catholic Church in Japan has two prominent centers for interreligious dialogue: Sophia University in Tokyo and Nanzan Institute for Religion and Culture in Nagoya.
38. The Catholic Church in Korea has Sogang University, which provides opportunities for dialogue with Indigenous religions, especially Shamanism.
39. The Catholic Church in Indonesia has Universitas Sanata Dharma to foster interreligious dialogue, mainly with Islam.

About the Contributors

JOSÉ CASANOVA is a senior fellow at the Berkley Center for Religion, Peace, and World Affairs and an emeritus professor of sociology and theology and religious studies at Georgetown University. He holds a master's degree in theology from the University of Innsbruck and a PhD in sociology from the New School for Social Research, where he served as a professor of sociology. His book *Public Religions in the Modern World* (University of Chicago Press, 1994) is considered a modern classic and has been translated into many languages. He is also the author of *Global Religious and Secular Dynamics* (Brill, 2019) and collections of essays in German, Spanish, and Ukrainian, as well as the coeditor, with Thomas Banchoff, of *The Jesuits and Globalization* (Georgetown University Press, 2016) and, with Jocelyne Cesari, of *Islam, Gender, and Democracy in Comparative Perspective* (Oxford University Press, 2017). In 2021, Casanova delivered the CIUS Bohdan Bociurkiw Memorial Lecture, titled "The Three Kyivan Churches of Ukraine and the Three Romes," which was published in *East/West: Journal of Ukrainian Studies* (2022).

EDMUND KEE-FOOK CHIA is originally from Malaysia. He served from 1996 to 2004 as executive secretary of interreligious dialogue for the Federation of Asian Bishops' Conferences. He then joined Catholic Theological Union in Chicago, where he taught for seven years, and since 2011 has been on the faculty of the Australian Catholic University in Melbourne. He is the author of *Asian Christianity and Theology* (Routledge, 2021) and *World Christianity Encounters World Religions* (Liturgical Press, 2018), and the editor of *Confucianism and Christianity* (Routledge, 2021) and *Interfaith Dialogue: Global Perspectives* (Palgrave Macmillan, 2016).

GEMMA TULUD CRUZ holds a PhD in theology from Radboud Universiteit Nijmegen in The Netherlands. She taught undergraduate theology and Catholic studies for several years in the United States before moving to Australia. She was a senior lecturer in theology at the Melbourne campus of Australian Catholic University, where she taught postgraduate classes and is currently an honorary fellow. She is the author of numerous publications, including *Christianity Across Borders: Theology and Contemporary Issues in Global Migration* (Routledge, 2021), and editor of *Catholicism in Migration and Diaspora: Cross-Border Filipino Perspectives* (Routledge, 2023). Cruz is currently involved in scholarly projects on women migration and social justice, Filipino Christianity, and Filipino theology of migration.

ROBERT DIXON was the foundation director of the Australian Catholic Bishops Conference Pastoral Research Office (now the National Centre for Pastoral Research) from 1996 to 2016. He is an honorary research fellow at the University of Divinity and a former honorary professor at Australian Catholic University. He is the author or coauthor of many publications and reports about the demography of the Australian Catholic population and aspects of Catholic belief and practice. His recent publications include "Post-Secularity and Australian Catholics" in *Faith and the Political in the Post-Secular Age*, edited by Anthony Maher (Coventry, 2018); "Australian Catholicism and Globalisation" in *Weaving Theology in Oceania: Culture, Context and Practice*, edited by Beatrice Green and Keiti Ann Kanongata'a (Cambridge Scholars, 2020); and, with coauthors Ruth Webber and Stephen Reid, "Contemporary Approaches to Religious Vocations in Australia" in *Australasian Catholic Record* (July 2021). Dixon holds a PhD in sociology from Monash University as well as degrees in science, theology, and education.

KEVIN M. DOAK holds the Nippon Foundation Endowed Chair in Japanese Studies at Georgetown University, where he is professor in the Department of East Asian Languages and Cultures and affiliate faculty member in the Department of Theology and Religious Studies. He has published widely on Japan and Catholicism, including in *Nova et Vetera, First Things, New Oxford Review*, and others. His recent major publications include *Xavier's Legacies: Catholicism in Modern Japanese Culture* (University of British Columbia Press, 2011) and a study of Japan's leading Catholic jurist, *Tanaka Kōtarō and World Law* (Palgrave Macmillan, 2019). He has also translated *Miracles* (Wiseblood, 2021), a work by Japan's leading Catholic novelist, Sono Ayako, which follows her investigation into the miracles attributed to St. Maximilian Kolbe. Doak's current research is a study and translation of Japan's most important Catholic theologian, Yoshimitsu Yoshihiko.

JOSÉ MARIO C. FRANCISCO, SJ, is a Filipino Jesuit priest and professor at Loyola School of Theology at Ateneo de Manila University. Since his completion of postgraduate studies in the Philippines and at the Graduate Theological Union (Berkeley, California) in 1986, his research has focused on cultural and theological studies in Philippine and Asian contexts. He has lectured at Pontifical Gregorian University (Rome), at the Jesuit School of Theology in Berkeley, and at Boston College as the Thomas I. Gasson Professor. His publications include critical editions of Philippine texts as well as essays in international journals and anthologies and *Between Celebration and Critique: Snapshots from 500 Years of Philippine Christianity* (Ateneo de Manila University Press, 2021). Francisco serves on the editorial boards of the *International Journal of Asian Christianity* and *Asia Pacific Mission Studies*. He has held leadership positions at the East Asian Pastoral Institute and at the Loyola School of Theology and remains a board member in different religious and civil society institutions.

PHILIP GIBBS, SVD, is a Divine Word missionary priest, serving in Papua New Guinea since 1973. He was born in New Zealand and studied sociology and history at Canterbury University, Christchurch, then anthropology at Sydney University. He studied for a master's degree in theology at Catholic Theological Union (Chicago) and later earned a PhD in sacred theology from Pontifical Gregorian University (Rome). He has served in various capacities: as a parish priest, as a researcher into social concerns, and as a lecturer and visiting lecturer at the East Asian Pastoral Institute and other locales in Oceania. In 2018, Gibbs was awarded the Most Excellent Order of the British Empire (OBE) for his service to the Church and the people of Enga in Papua New Guinea. Currently, he is professor of social research and president of Divine Word University in Papua New Guinea.

DENIS WOO-SEON KIM, SJ, is a Jesuit priest and professor in the Department of Sociology at Sogang University, Korea. He has published numerous articles on the intersections between religion and globalization in East Asia, examining issues such as the Church's public role, compressed modernization, and international migration. His recent articles have appeared in the *Korean Journal of Sociology*, *Theological Perspective*, *Journal of Ethnic and Migration Studies*, and others.

RICHARD MADSEN is Distinguished Research Professor and director of the UC-Fudan Center for Research on Contemporary China at the University of California, San Diego. He is the author of eighteen books on moral order and religion in the United States and China. His books include *Democracy's Dharma: Religious Renaissance and Political Development in Taiwan* (University of California Press, 2007) and, most recently, he coedited, with Becky Yang Hsu, *The Chinese Pursuit of Happiness: Anxieties, Hopes, and Moral Tensions in Everyday Life* (University of California Press, 2019).

CHANDRA MALLAMPALLI is the Fletcher Jones Foundation Chair of the Social Sciences and a professor of South Asian history at Westmont College. In 2021–22 he was Yang Visiting Scholar of World Christianity at Harvard Divinity School. He is the author of books and articles that explore the religious, cultural, and legal history of colonial India. Among them are *Christians and Public Life in Colonial South India* (RoutledgeCurzon, 2004); *Race, Religion and Law in Colonial India* (Cambridge University Press, 2011); and *A Muslim Conspiracy in British India?* (Cambridge University Press, 2017). His book *South Asia's Christians: Between Hindu and Muslim* (Oxford University Press, 2023) describes the long history of interactions that Christians have maintained with Hindus and Muslims of the Indian subcontinent.

MARY JOHN MANANZAN, OSB, is a missionary Benedictine sister. She obtained her PhD in philosophy, with a major in linguistic philosophy, at Pontifical Gregorian University in Rome and a degree in missiology at the Wilhelmsuniversitaet in Münster, Germany. Her academic work includes charting new paths for the academy and being with the masses, especially women. As a feminist activist she has given birth to many women-centered programs, among them the Institute of Women's Studies, the Women Ecology and Wholeness Farm, and the Women Crisis Center. For eighteen years she was the national chairperson of GABRIELA, a broad alliance of women's organizations. She served two terms as president of the College of St. Scholastica in Duluth, Minnesota. She just finished her second term as prioress of the Missionary Benedictine Sisters of the Manila Priory. She was a member of the administrative council of the Communio Internationalis Benedictinarum (CIB). She was awarded the Dorothy Cadbury Fellowship in 1994 in Birmingham and in 1995 at the Henry Luce Fellowship at Union Theological Seminary in New York.

EVELYN MONTEIRO belongs to the Congregation of the Sisters of the Cross of Chavanod. She holds a PhD in systematic theology from the Centre Sèvres of the Facultés jésuites in Paris. She was a faculty professor of systematic theology at Jnana-Deepa, the Pontifical Institute of Philosophy and Religion in Pune, India, for many years and continues as visiting professor at Jnana-Deepa and other theological faculties. She is the cofounder of Ecclesia of Women in Asia (EWA), a forum of Catholic women theologians in Asia. She has authored *Church and Culture: Communion in Pluralism* (Indian Society for Promoting Christian Knowledge, 2004), has edited several books, and has published several articles in national and international theological journals. Monteiro's research and publications focus on ecclesiology, particularly in situating the conciliar and postconciliar understanding of the Church in the pluralistic religious and sociocultural contexts of Asia and India, and contextual and liberation theologies.

PETER C. PHAN holds three PhDs and four honorary PhDs. He has authored and edited some forty books and published more than three hundred essays. He currently holds the Ignacio Ellacuría, SJ, Chair of Catholic Social Thought at Georgetown University. He is completing a book on the theology of migration and editing the *Handbook to Asian Christian Theology* (Oxford University Press, forthcoming). He is the first non-Anglo to be elected president of the Catholic Theological Society of America and of the American Theological Society. In 2010, he was awarded the John Courtney Murray Award, the highest honor given by the Catholic Theological Society of America for outstanding achievements in theology.

JOHN MANSFORD PRIOR, a native of the United Kingdom, was a member of the Society of the Divine Word who lived in Indonesia since 1973. He obtained his PhD in intercultural theology from Birmingham University (1987) and lectured at St. Paul's Institute of Philosophy in Ledalero, Indonesia. Prior was involved with the Evangelization and Interreligious Offices of the Federation of Asian Bishops' Conferences since 1990. He was active in the International Association for Mission Studies since 1996 and coordinator of its Biblical Studies in Mission Study Group since 2004. Prior served on the board of the International Association of Catholic Missiologists and was the author of 170 articles and book chapters, the editor or coeditor of over forty volumes, and the author of seven books, including *Berdiri di Ambang Batas: Pergumulan seputar Iman dan Budaya* (Standing at the threshold of boundaries: Wrestling with faith and culture) (Ledalero, 2007); and *Menjebol Jeruji Prasangka: Membaca Alkitab dengan Jiwa* (Breaking through barriers of prejudice: Reading the Bible with soul) (Ledalero, 2010). He passed suddenly in June 2022.

Index

Information in tables and figures is indicated by *t* and *f*, respectively.

www.ingramcontent.com/pod-product-compliance
Lightning Source LLC
LaVergne TN
LVHW082001060826
844660LV00005B/271

* 9 7 8 1 6 4 7 1 2 3 7 8 9 *